Seamless Object-Oriented
Software Architecture

D. COLEMAN, P. ARNOLD, S. BODOFF,
C. DOLLIN, H. GILCHRIST, F. HAYES
AND P. JEREMAES
Object-Oriented Development: The Fusion Method

S. COOK AND J. DANIELS
Designing Object Systems

B. HENDERSON-SELLERS
A Book of Object-Oriented Knowledge

B. HENDERSON-SELLERS AND J. EDWARDS
Book Two Object-Oriented Knowledge: The Working Object

K. LANO AND H. HAUGHTON (eds)
Object-Oriented Specification Case Studies

H. KILOV AND J. ROSS
Information Modelling: An Object-Oriented Approach

J. LINDSKOV KNUDSEN, M. LÖFGREN,
O. LEHRMANN MADSEN AND B. MAGNUSSON (eds)
Object-Oriented Environments: The Mjølner Approach

M. LORENZ
Object-Oriented Software Development: A Practical Guide

D. MANDRIOLI AND B. MEYER (eds)
Advances in Object-Oriented Software Engineering

B. MEYER
Eiffel: The Language

B. MEYER
An Object-Oriented Environment: Principles and Applications

B. MEYER
Reusable Software: The Base Object-Oriented Component Libraries

B. MEYER AND J.-M. NERSON (eds)
Object-Oriented Applications

P. J. ROBINSON
Hierarchical Object-Oriented Design

R. SWITZER
Eiffel: An Introduction

K. WALDÉN AND J.-M. NERSON
*Seamless Object-Oriented Software Architecture:
Analysis and Design of Reliable Systems*

Seamless Object-Oriented Software Architecture

Analysis and Design of Reliable Systems

Kim Waldén

Enea Data, Stockholm

Jean-Marc Nerson

SOL, Paris

Prentice Hall

New York   London   Toronto   Sydney   Tokyo   Singapore

First published 1995 by
Prentice Hall International (UK) Ltd
Campus 400, Maylands Avenue
Hemel Hempstead
Hertfordshire, HP2 7EZ

A division of
Simon & Schuster International Group

This book was typeset in Times Roman on a Sun SPARCstation
10/41 using Groff 1.07 from the Free Software Foundation
and the BONUS preprocessor and macro package
developed by Kim Waldén.

Printed and bound in Great Britain by Bookcraft (Bath) Ltd.

Library of Congress Cataloging-in-Publication Data

Waldén, Kim.
    Seamless object-oriented software architecture : analysis and
design of reliable systems / Kim Waldén, Jean-Marc Nerson.
        p.   cm.—(Prentice Hall object-oriented series)
    Includes bibliographical references and index.
    ISBN 0-13-031303-3
    1. Object-oriented programming (Computer science)   2. System
analysis.   3. System design.   I. Nerson, Jean-Marc.   II. Title.
III. Series.
QA76.64.W35   1995
005.1'2—dc20
                                                            94–30456
                                                            CIP

British Library Cataloguing in Publication Data

A catalogue record for this book is available from
the British Library

ISBN: 0-13-031303-3

---

2   3   4   5   99 98 97 96 95

Contents

Series editor's preface

A rumor has been spreading for some time among people that follow progress in object-oriented analysis and design: "Wait for BON!" Those not in the know would ask what in the world BON could be. Indeed, the publicity around the Business Object Notation has been modest—an article in the *Communications of the ACM*, presentations at a workshop or two, public seminars in Europe and North America, tutorials at TOOLS and other conferences—but it was enough to attract the attention of many O-O enthusiasts who were dissatisfied with the limitations of first-generation analysis methods. In the meantime, BON was being taught to many practitioners, applied in numerous industrial projects, and repeatedly polished as a result.

As this book finally reaches publication it is certain to cause a major advance in the field of object-oriented methods. Its most remarkable feature is the thoroughness with which it applies object-oriented principles, unencumbered by leftovers from earlier methods. Going O-O all the way is not a matter of dogmatism, but the secret for obtaining the real benefits of the method, following in particular from two principles developed at length in the book: *seamless development*, the removal of artificial gaps and mismatches between successive software development activities; and *reversibility*, the recognition that at any step of the development process, including implementation and maintenance, it must be possible to update the results of earlier phases such as analysis and design, and still maintain full consistency between the analysis, design, implementation and maintenance views. By ensuring seamlessness and reversibility it is possible to obtain a continuous software development process, essential to the quality of the resulting products.

This book is also one of a select few in the OOAD literature that pays serious attention to the question of software reliability, by using some elements of formal reasoning, in particular assertions, as a way to specify semantic properties of a system at the earliest possible stage.

Following the presentation of the model and method in parts I, II, and III, a large section of the book (part IV) is devoted to a set of in-depth case studies and to exercises, drawn for the most part from projects in which the authors acted as consultants. This abundant practical material will help readers apply the ideas of BON to their own application areas.

From now on, no one will be able to claim knowledge of object-oriented analysis and design who has not read Kim Waldén and Jean-Marc Nerson.

Bertrand Meyer

Preface

In the past few years, object-oriented techniques have finally made the passage from the programming-in-the-small island to the mainland of programming-in-the-large. Accompanying this transition has been a change in the role and perception of software methods: in addition to their well-established use in the earliest stages of a project—requirements analysis and system specification—they are increasingly viewed as providing the intellectual support needed across the entire software construction process, through design and implementation to maintenance and reengineering. The object-oriented approach is best suited to achieve this *seamlessness* of the software development process, without which it would not be possible to meet the quality and productivity challenges that confront the software industry.

This book shows how a consistent set of object-oriented abstractions can be applied throughout the process, based on three major ideas: seamlessness, reversibility, and contracting.

Seamlessness, as in the first word of the title, follows from the observation that the similarities between the tasks to be carried out at the various steps of a project far outweigh their inevitable differences, making it possible to obtain a continuous process that facilitates communication between the various actors involved, ensures a direct mapping between a problem and its software solution, and results in a high level of quality for the final product.

Reversibility means that the seamless procedure must work in both directions: if one modifies a system that has already reached the implementation phase—a frequent case in practice—it must be possible to reflect the modification back to the higher levels of design, specification, and analysis. Without such reversibility the products of these earlier stages would soon become obsolete, raising disturbing questions about their very role in the software process. Since current object-oriented methods are still dominated by hybrid approaches—that is to say, encumber the application of object-oriented principles with techniques drawn from non-object-oriented analysis methods and with constructs drawn from non-object-oriented languages—reversibility has so far been almost absent from the concerns of the object-oriented literature.

The contract model was introduced to a wider audience as early as 1988 by Bertrand Meyer in his magnificent introductory book *Object-Oriented Software Construction* (OOSC), which quickly became, and still is, the standard reference on basic object-oriented concepts. In a sense, the present book is a continuation of OOSC, carrying some of its software engineering ideas to their logical conclusion in the area of analysis and design. The result is a method called BON (Business Object Notation) which contains a set of concepts and corresponding notations to support object-oriented modeling centered around the three principles of seamlessness, reversibility, and software contracting.

In the rapidly growing field of object-oriented software development, many subfields have now accumulated enough experience and techniques to warrant books of their own. When presenting our ideas, we therefore had to make a choice: either to cover most of the interesting areas and remain shallow, or to limit the scope and leave room for more substance. We chose the latter, and BON concentrates on the basic application-independent ideas of general analysis and design of software systems.

We have also refrained from including yet another explanation of the basic object-oriented concepts. There are two main reasons for this. First, the concepts may be simple enough to define, but understanding their implications in a deeper sense takes much longer. Therefore, a short overview will not be enough for those who do not already understand the concepts, while a more substantial discussion will add significant volume and be utterly boring to experienced readers. Second, in the general spirit of this book, we believe good texts should be reused rather than rewritten each time they are needed.

So we will assume that the meaning of classes, instances (objects), polymorphism, dynamic binding, etc., is already familiar to the reader. If not, we recommend the OOSC book cited above (a significantly revised second edition is to appear during 1994). As a small compensation for a basic overview, we have included a reasonably extensive glossary of terms with brief explanations of the most important BON concepts and many of the familiar object-oriented terms. It can be used by the novice as a starting point for further reading, and by the knowledgeable reader to find out more precisely what flavor we have chosen for widely used terms whose meaning is not fixed in the object-oriented literature.

BON was initiated in 1989 by Jean-Marc Nerson, then chief developer of the ISE Eiffel 2.2 environment, who presented early ideas in a tutorial at the second TOOLS conference held in Paris in 1990. The ideas were picked up at Enea Data in Sweden by Kim Waldén, then technically responsible for the company's Eiffel distribution in Scandinavia, who started to teach courses on BON in Sweden shortly after. This was the beginning of a collaboration which gradually led to a joint development of the notation and method. The BON technique was applied in several industrial developments, and Jean-Marc published three articles in 1991–92. However, we soon realized that more substantial documentation on the subject would be necessary to make the method available to a wider audience, and in 1993 we made the bold decision to jointly publish a book on BON (bold, because the only time available for this work was evenings and weekends).

As is often the case with visions whose fulfillment requires far more resources than are available, it is best not to understand the full extent of the work beforehand—then you can just go ahead and do it anyway, which is what happened with this book although at the expense of our friends and families. However, we found that writing about something you believe in wholeheartedly has the mysterious capacity of extending the number of daily hours well beyond the standard 24 (in itself a possible subject of another book). If we succeed in communicating to our readers just a small fraction of the joy involved in writing this book, the effort will have been worthwhile.

Scope of the book

The book is intended for software professionals as well as for students at the graduate and undergraduate levels. We believe it can be read by anyone who has acquired a general understanding of the problems of software engineering, and who has some inclination for abstract thinking.

The knowledgeable software engineer used to dealing with practical solutions may discover that it is not all that easy to keep analysis and design models free from premature implementation decisions. On the other hand, to achieve a deep understanding of the technology, it is probably even more important for the high-level analyst to occasionally take an object-oriented design (not necessarily large) all the way through implementation. Never to do this is somewhat like trying to become a mountaineer without ever climbing: there is little replacement for watching polymorphism and dynamic binding in live action.

Book structure

The book consists of an introduction, three main parts, and five appendices. The main parts treat in order: the concepts and notations of BON; the BON process for producing analysis and design models; and a practical part with three case studies and exercises.

The introduction (chapters 1–2) discusses the general principles which have guided the development of BON and positions the method relative to other approaches.

The model part (chapters 3–5) explains the static and dynamic models of BON and the corresponding notation. Untyped modeling charts are used for the very early phases, and these are later refined into fully typed descriptions with semantic specifications added. This part is the core of the book around which everything else is built, so it should be read carefully. (Sections 3.11–3.13 on the BON assertion language may be skipped on first reading by those less interested in formal specification.)

The method part (chapters 6–8) describes how work is carried out with BON. It starts with a discussion of a number of general modeling issues (chapter 6). This serves as background for a detailed description of the BON process tasks, presented in chapter 7. These tasks concentrate on what should be produced (the deliverables). Finally, chapter 8 discusses the standard modeling activities needed to produce the desired results, and is focused on how to attack the various subproblems.

The practical part (chapters 9–12) then presents three case studies and a number of exercises (collected in chapter 12). The three case studies model in turn: a conference management system; the control system of a video recorder; and a mapping between a relational database and an object model.

The concluding five appendices contain in order: a complete grammar for the BON textual language; a number of examples in the form of textual versions for several of the graphical diagrams presented earlier in the book; a quick reference to the BON notation; a list of references to other analysis and design approaches; and a glossary of terms.

Acknowledgments

BON started as an attempt to extend the concepts of the Eiffel language into the realm of analysis and design, so indirectly we owe our greatest debt to its designer Bertrand Meyer. His systematic effort to introduce the powerful idea of software contracting to the systems development industry, and make it part of everyday software engineering, has served as our main source of inspiration. We also thank him for valuable comments and discussions on draft versions of the book, and for his general moral support.

We gratefully acknowledge the reviewers of Prentice Hall for their insightful critique and supportive attitude, and Brian Henderson-Sellers for taking the time to read a full draft and provide helpful comments. We thank Hans Marmolin for sharing his views on user-centered design and for letting us present his reference model in chapter 6.

We thank the members of the European consortium "Business Class", derived from the ESPRIT II Research and Development Program, which partly sponsored early work on BON through the development of a Design Workbench under the project leadership of Jean-Pierre Sarkis.

We would also like to thank the staff at Enea Object Technology, many of whom have served as guinea pigs when new ideas were tried out. Special thanks go to Per Grape, who followed the text closely as it developed, read a number of successive book drafts, and contributed several improvements to the overall method and notation. Nils Undén, Björn Strihagen, and Michael Öberg read full drafts and helped weed out early mistakes. Magnus Lövkvist raised several issues during the application of BON in a commercial project, which lead to improvements of the text, and Roland Persson provided interesting views from his experience with Smalltalk applications. Daniel Rodríguez, Björn Strihagen, Lennart Gustafsson, Jan Erik Ekelöf, Niklas Odenteg, Mike Henry, and Michael Öberg used BON in several contexts and provided valuable feedback. We thank them all for their contributions.

We are grateful to Anders Johansson from Cap Programator for helpful comments on successive drafts, and for his strong support of the BON approach. Thanks also to Roy Clarke from LM Ericsson Data and Keith Gunn from SHL Systemhouse for their detailed comments on the English language and for detecting errors in some of the examples through careful reading. Special thanks to Michael Öberg and Juha Juslin, present and former managers of Enea Object Technology, for their positive attitude regarding the production of this book.

The initial impulse on object-oriented analysis and design leading to the basic ideas that later became BON was given by David J. Hopkins. The BON acronym was first coined by Christine Mingins, and later reinterpreted as "Business Object Notation". In all, the BON method and notation has been influenced and recast by more than four years of continuous industrial practice and experience.

Finally, we express our gratitude to all friends and family members for bearing with us during a full year of almost total anti-social behavior.

Stockholm and Paris   K. W.
August 1994   J.-M. N.

Trademark notice

All trade names, service names, trademarks, or registered trademarks
mentioned in this book are property of their respective owners.

Authors' addresses

Kim Waldén, Enea Data AB
Box 232, S-183 23 Täby, Sweden
Electronic mail: kim@enea.se

Jean-Marc Nerson, Société des Outils du Logiciel,
104 rue Castagnary, 75015 Paris, France
Electronic mail: marc@eiffel.fr

Part I
Introduction

1 Object-oriented software development

1.1 INTRODUCTION

What is the potential of the object-oriented paradigm? How much improvement of the software development process can we reasonably expect from using this technology, which 25 years after its initial invention finally seems to be conquering the software industry?

Fred Brooks, in his well-known article "No Silver Bullet: Essence and Accidents in Software Engineering" [Brooks 1987], divides the difficulties of building software into *essence* and *accidents*. The essence of a piece of software is a construct of interlocking concepts: data sets, relationships among data items, algorithms, and function invocations. This construct is the general architecture of the software—that part of its logical structure which is independent of any particular machine representation, but still detailed enough to allow unambiguous translation to executable code. The accidents, by contrast, are everything else—all the gory details and contortions necessary for representing the essence in a given computing environment.

Brooks believes the hard part of building software is the specification, design, and testing of the essential conceptual constructs, as opposed to representing them and testing the fidelity of the representations (the accidental part). If this is true, he concludes, building software will always be hard. Languages and tools, no matter how powerful, can only take us that far when the real problem is to decide what exactly we want to express.

At first sight, Brook's conclusion may seem to invalidate all claims that object-oriented abstraction has the potential to increase software productivity by a significant factor. In fact, if object-oriented techniques are mainly taught and used to build new systems from scratch, as often seems to be the case in industry today, only marginal productivity improvements can probably be expected. If, on the other hand, the emphasis is shifted from individual systems to the

3

production and use of tailorable software components, a profound change becomes possible.

Benefits of a reusability approach

There are two reasons for optimism. First, the cost of software can still be reduced by an order of magnitude by removing most of the accidental difficulties from industrial software engineering—maybe not for a single system version, but surely over a product's life cycle. Methods and implementation languages are not enough, however, to achieve this cost reduction, no matter how conceptually powerful and highly automated. We also need access to a large base of reusable components which encapsulate the basic concepts that are being reinvented over and over in today's industrial software projects.

Second, reusable abstractions are not limited to hiding accidental difficulties, but can also be used to attack the essence of software design. The complexity involved in solving a problem depends not only on the problem, but just as much on the primitive concepts available for reasoning about the problem. So if we can increase the expressive power and understandability of these primitives in various problem areas, the complexity of corresponding abstract designs can also be reduced.

As a side effect, investing in reuse brings another crucial advantage. Software components that are used and reused many times in many different contexts stand the chance of acquiring much higher quality through successive improvement than is ever economically feasible for components that are just used within a single project. This enables new abstractions to gradually evolve until they become conceptually strong enough to become part of the system developer's standard vocabulary. This may, in turn, lead to the discovery of new useful abstractions at yet higher levels that would otherwise not have been found owing to the initial effort required.

Initial difficulties

There has been significant effort invested over the past two decades to build and use repositories of software components for industrial systems development. Although certain application areas have seen some successes, achieving a high degree of reuse in the general case has turned out to be much more difficult in practice than first expected. Much of the failure has been attributed to organizational shortcomings, such as lack of clear responsibility roles (reuse managers), no consistent management policy, lack of automated tools support, and conflicts with short-term project budgets. Other problems are commercial in nature, such as how to protect reusable designs enough to make the effort invested worthwhile for the originators. These problems do not go away just because we switch technology, and must still be solved.

But the key to it all is object-oriented abstraction—the only technique flexible enough for building the general components needed. Since reuse efforts have mainly relied on traditional techniques, it is no surprise that they have largely failed. As long as we lack the basic means to produce the right components, formal organization and automated browsing tools can do little to help. On the other hand, object-orientation does not automatically solve all problems, and many object-oriented projects have also reported difficulties attaining their reuse goals.

This, however, must not be taken as a sign that large-scale reuse is unattainable in practice, or that the object-oriented approach does not work. On the contrary, there are a number of reasons why these initial difficulties are only to be expected. First, most industrial object-oriented projects are still using hybrid languages or hybrid methods, or both. The resulting mix of partly contradictory concepts creates confusion and delays the mental shift necessary to take full advantage of the new approach. The requirement of backward compatibility for hybrid languages also makes it impossible to support cleanly all of the central object-oriented concepts, which in turn makes the construction of high-quality component libraries difficult.

Second, even if the technical means are a prerequisite and must come first, the organizational aspects are also crucial. Many projects have failed because of inadequate training, lack of management support or reuse coordination. These are problems that must be addressed in parallel, particularly for large organizations.

Third, the size and quality of commercially available class libraries is highly variable, and even the best object-oriented environments only cover a small part of what one would wish for. Since good abstractions need to be developed incrementally with many alternative approaches tried, it will naturally take some time before we can expect anything close to a complete encapsulation of the most commonly reinvented software components.

The road to reuse of knowledge

If we compare the current trend towards object-oriented languages with the transition to high-level languages in the 1970s and early 1980s, the situation, although it has many similarities, is also quite different. The control structures of languages like Pascal and C embody abstractions that the assembly programmers were already using mentally (often occurring as comments in some pseudo-Algol notation), so the big payoffs were immediate. When the tedious and error-prone translations of these constructs into sequences of machine instructions were no longer needed, work could proceed as before, only much faster.

In some important areas, the same is true when moving from what can be considered a traditional language today (such as Pascal or C above) to a good object-oriented environment. The ability to use off-the-shelf components representing the basic data structures so fundamental for almost any computing algorithm (lists, hash tables, queues, stacks), without the need to know anything about their implementation, is a direct parallel. Another such area is graphical interfaces. But object-oriented abstraction means much more, since it can also be used to create new concepts in almost every conceivable area. This means its greatest potential (in the long run) lies not in representing the concepts with which we are already familiar, but rather in serving as a vehicle for inventing new ones.

This is the main reason why object-oriented technology is a technology of investment more than of short-term profit (even if the latter is by no means precluded). The really big payoffs will come from reuse at more domain-specific levels. It is possible to capture whole application types in so-called frameworks, and only tailor the small portions that need to be different from one situation to another. Successful frameworks are hardly ever conceived as such from the beginning. Rather they evolve by gradual adaptation of a group of components solving a particular problem into also solving other, similar problems that occur in practice. The usefulness of the resulting structures is thus empirically proven, which guarantees low cost/benefit ratios.

So we must not despair if things appear to go slowly—after all, we are reaching for the stars. The future potential is enormous, and even though extensive training and organizational support is necessary and not free, we need not go very far down the road to reuse before our investment starts to show returns. And from there, things will only get better.

In this book, we will present a view of object-oriented analysis and design derived from the basic premise that extensive software reuse is indeed essential, and that it can be attained in practice provided we take advantage of the object-oriented concepts in a way that is compatible with this goal. This view emphasizes certain aspects of object-oriented technology which we think have not been sufficiently addressed.

What exactly, then, are the object-oriented qualities that have the capacity to turn software reuse into standard practice and finally give the term software engineering its intended meaning? In addition to the extreme flexibility provided by the class concept—allowing us to build open components that can be combined and tailored through inheritance—three crucial aspects of object-orientation already mentioned in the preface, seamlessness, reversibility, and software contracting, deserve much more attention than they have had so far in the literature on analysis and design. We will take a look at them in order.

1.2 SEAMLESSNESS

The object-oriented approach is the only method known to date that has the potential to turn analysis, design, and implementation of general software systems into a truly seamless process. A smooth transition from user requirements over analysis and design into running systems has been the goal of software engineering for over 20 years, but traditional methods (although often claiming to have the solution) have generally failed in practice. This is not surprising, since the designers of concepts and notations for such methods are forced to choose between Scylla and Charybdis. Either you provide an easy translation to some traditional programming language, which forces the notation to become just another procedural language (often introducing more complexity than it solves), or you invent a completely different high-level notation and keep the barrier between specification and code.

What makes object-orientation so attractive is that the same abstraction mechanism (the class) can be used in all development phases. The basic concepts needed to model objects representing such external notions as hospitals, airplanes, and wide area networks are not essentially different from what is needed for objects representing quadruple precision floating point numbers, street addresses, or process dispatchers. The semantic interpretation of the abstractions encapsulated by the classes may vary, but the general problem remains the same: to specify class consistency, relations with other classes, and behavior through applicable operations.

Being able to keep the same paradigm from initial feasibility study all the way through production and maintenance of a working system brings enormous advantages. Communication between project members with different roles is greatly improved when the basic concepts are the same for everybody. Education is facilitated and the artificial barriers between specifiers and implementors vanish, making room for a holistic view of the system life cycle. Seamlessness also facilitates requirements traceability. Since the classes introduced in the analysis phase will still be present in the final system, tracing the propagation of initial requirements through design and implementation becomes much easier.

1.3 REVERSIBILITY

True seamlessness means more than just easy transition from specification to implementation. Far too many object-oriented methods rely on the unspoken assumption that the analysis and design notation will only be used in the early development phases, and then translated once into program code—object oriented or not. But at some point (in fact, very soon) the initial system will be modified to meet new requirements. Ideally, this would mean changing first the topmost descriptions, and then successively propagating all changes downwards until the code is reached. However, this is not the way it works in practice for most systems.

Since high-level specification can only represent a crude sketch of a system, lots of details and problems ignored at that point will have to be taken care of before the specifications can be made executable. This means that a whole new world of abstractions in terms of implementation language concepts will be created, and the main interest and creative effort will gradually shift to this environment. Successive refinements and corrections will tend to be applied directly to the program code, since only there do we have enough expressive power to resolve all obscurities and detailed decisions that could not be addressed by the specifications. And some of these details will nearly always turn out to have a significant impact on the system structure. (If the program code could be automatically generated from the specifications, the latter would simply become our new programming language and we would not need to talk about the lower levels at all.)

However, if abstract system description is to keep its value beyond the first translation into program code, changes to the code must be reflected back into the specifications at regular intervals. Here is where all traditional methods break down. If the conceptual primitives used by the specification and implementation languages, respectively, cannot be directly mapped to each other (which is always the case in non-object-oriented approaches) this will lead to a creeping divergence between specification and implementation. It simply becomes too expensive to keep the two worlds consistent as the system evolves, since this would mean repeated non-trivial translations between more or less incompatible conceptual structures.

In fact, even if you try hard to keep all specifications up to date, there is no way of knowing if they really are (because of the conceptual mismatch) so people will usually not trust them anyway. After all, only the executable specifications, that is the program code, ever get to talk to the hardware which carries out the system actions. It is the complete program code that decides whether the airplane will take off and land safely, not the blueprints drawn by the analyst/designer. A correct system can run without problems even if its specification is wrong, but not the reverse. Therefore, when we need to choose in practice which description to favor, the choice is easy.

The value of the specifications is therefore directly related to the ease by which they can be seamlessly translated to and from program code. Those claiming that only the very high-level requirements and analysis models matter, without giving any hint as to how the mapping to and from the executable code can be done, do not seem to have fully understood what it means to manage the multi-billion dollar investment represented by today's software. It is probably not a coincidence that the high-level modeling concepts of object-oriented technology were discovered by people who were struggling to master the complexity of programming.

Unlike any other approach, the object-oriented method is inherently reversible. Since the classes of analysis and design can be made part of the final system, any changes to the implementation affecting the structure and interface of these classes then become immediately visible, but only if we refrain from including elements from other fields, such as entity–relationship diagrams, state transition diagrams, or data flow diagrams as standard parts of our approach. Mixing paradigms breaks the reversibility and introduces new complexity, which will in most cases outweigh the expected benefits.

This does not mean that such techniques can never be used in object-oriented systems. Some applications may benefit from an occasional entity–relationship diagram, and modeling certain abstractions using state transition diagrams can be extremely powerful, but basing a *general* method on them misses the point. Instead, we should take advantage of the special qualities of object-orientation: its simplicity, coherence, and extreme generality. It provides the same support for abstraction at all levels without forcing them to be viewed in any particular way. This makes the approach unique among development methods, and its basic concepts have proved sufficient to specify and implement most of the software we need, almost regardless of application area.

1.4 SOFTWARE CONTRACTING

Software designed for reuse needs to be of extra high quality, since its potential to increase productivity also brings the risk of causing much more harm than before. Writing most of the software from scratch in traditional style at least has the advantage of limiting the effects of mistakes to the particular system being developed. However, if an inadequate software component is used in thousands of applications, the accumulated damage can be very high indeed. To a certain extent this is countered by the extensive testing a heavily reused piece of software is subjected to, but testing can only reveal a small percentage of potential errors and whenever the usage pattern changes, previously concealed problems are likely to manifest themselves.

The whole idea of the object-oriented approach is to design software to mirror the high-level concepts in various application domains by building successively more powerful components in layers of abstractions, each standing on the shoulders of the previous ones. We know of no better way to master complexity, but it also means that the resulting structure becomes totally dependent on the correct functioning of its constituent parts; if some of the central abstractions fail, the whole building may fall apart. It is therefore even more important than before to find ways to guarantee software correctness.

Fortunately, in recent years a very promising method has been proposed to bring elements from the research fields of abstract data types and formal specification into standard use in software engineering. This is the theory of *software contracting* [Meyer 1992c]. The idea is to use *assertions* to define the semantics of each class. The prerequisites and resulting behavior of each operation are specified through *pre-* and *postconditions*, and the overall class consistency through the *class invariant*. These semantic specifications then form the basis for a *contract* between each class, the *supplier*, and all classes using its operations, the *clients*. A software system is viewed as a network of cooperating clients and suppliers whose exchange of requests and services are precisely defined through decentralized contracts.

Based on the contracts, a consistent error handling mechanism is possible. If the assertions are monitored at run-time, contract violations can be made to cause system exceptions. Decentralized handlers may then be defined and implemented as part of a general exception management facility to take care of error recovery.

Software contracting represents a significant step towards the routine production of correct software and should be included in any object-oriented analysis and design method aimed at building reliable, high-quality professional products.

2   The BON approach

2.1 INTRODUCTION

The method described in this book is called BON, which stands for "Business Object Notation". It presents a set of concepts for modeling object-oriented software, a supporting notation in two versions—one graphical and one textual— and a set of rules and guidelines to be used in producing the models. BON focuses on the fundamental elements of analysis and design, and the method is meant to be integrated with and adapted to the various development frameworks and standards that may apply in different organizations.

BON supports general software development with no special application types in mind, and is particularly aimed at products with high demands on quality and reliability. The concepts and notations are designed to encourage a reusability approach by emphasizing the points raised in the previous chapter: seamlessness, reversibility, and software contracting. Contrary to the somewhat resigned attitude found also in many object-oriented camps about the attainability of massive reuse, we claim that this is indeed the major goal of the technique.

BON does not introduce any fundamentally new concepts; the basic object-oriented ideas combined with elements from software specification are sufficient as primitives. Rather it is the detailed definition and arrangement of the concepts expressed by a scalable notation that can make a qualitative difference. (To a certain extent, BON is defined by what it does *not* include, since seamlessness and simplicity are the guiding stars.)

The reader may of course wonder whether this goal could not have been achieved without introducing a new notation when so many have already been published. Could we not just adapt one of the more widely used existing notations to fulfill our purpose? Unfortunately not. Although the concepts used in many proposed methods may seem to be more or less the same (classes, operations, relations), there are subtle differences below the surface that prevent a one-to-one mapping between them. Since a notation is just a way of presenting the underlying concepts in a comprehensive and readable form, reuse does not work in this case.

The field of object-oriented analysis and design is still young and immature, and it is only natural that many competing approaches and accompanying notations will continue to emerge until it is time for a general shake-out. Even though this may create some confusion for potential users, it is really in their best interest. Standardizing too early is extremely harmful, since it narrows the modeling perspective and stands in the way of real understanding. (We are pleased to see that this view is shared by many well-known specialists in the field through a recent open letter "Premature Methods Standardization Considered Harmful" [Mellor 1993].)

2.2 WHAT IS NOT IN BON

Many existing methods for analysis and design, probably the majority, include either data modeling using some variant of the entity–relationship approach (ER modeling [Chen 1976]) or finite state machines (FSM modeling), or both, as a significant part of their high-level system description. The idea is to combine the strengths of these techniques (which are well understood and have been in use for a long time in traditional environments) with those of the object-oriented concepts, in order to benefit from both worlds.

However, such approaches seriously impede the seamlessness and reversibility advocated in the previous chapter. In our view, this disadvantage far outweighs any benefits gained. With FSM modeling, the impedance mismatch is obvious since there is no easy mapping between the state transition graphs and an eventual implementation (unless we actually model every object as a state machine, thereby giving up all abstractional power of the class concept). With ER modeling, the situation is a bit more complicated.

Why not ER modeling?

Proponents of analysis-level ER modeling claim that binary associations are more general than references between classes, since in the latter case explicit design choices have been made that are still kept open in the former. This is of course true, since a particular association between two classes can be represented in many ways. However, the alternatives kept open by restricting all class dependencies to binary associations are usually not the interesting ones.

In fact, in order to arrive at a good system model we cannot keep everything open, because this would effectively prevent us from understanding the problem. So the question is not whether design decisions should be made, but rather which ones to make.

ER modeling is of course no exception to this. On the contrary, just as many arbitrary or questionable decisions must be taken in order to arrive at an ER model, as with a pure object-oriented model. In the latter case, we must choose which concepts to model as classes and which ones should become operations on the classes. With ER modeling, we must instead choose which concepts to represent as entities, which ones will become attributes of the entities, and which ones will become associations between them. This is by no means easier or less susceptible to change than choosing classes and operations.

For example, an attribute in ER modeling is viewed as a "property" of an entity, and is represented by a value. But what is a property? Consider the entity EMPLOYEE and the concept of being the most popular person in a service department. Clearly, being most popular is a personal property, but modeling it as an attribute of EMPLOYEE may be quite wrong from the system's point of view. The employee abstraction may not know about its condition, and the only way this knowledge will manifest itself may instead be as a combination of attributes of other entities, perhaps STATISTICS and CUSTOMER_POLL.

So we have a problem here: either an attribute is thought of as corresponding directly to a data value stored in the entity, in which case it is too low level, or else it is just a vague "property", which is too high level, since it does not tell us enough about the system. The object-oriented middle way is a class operation returning a value, which may be of any type. This avoids premature decisions about where various values will be stored, but still tells enough about the system behavior to allow for seamless transition into implementation.

Another trouble spot is what level of "normalization" to choose for the attributes and relations between entities. A binary association between two entities A and B is generally not supposed to tell anything about *how* A and B are connected (other than through semantic labels, such as "works for" and the reverse role "employs"). By this reasoning, the transitive law must also apply: if B is in turn associated to C through the association "has child", then A is associated to C through "works for parent of", and C to A through "is child to employer of" (see figure 2.1). Since ER models are usually connected graphs, applying the law recursively yields a diagram where every entity has a binary association to every other entity.

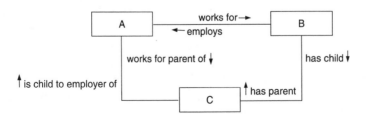

Figure 2.1   ER modeling: transitive law

Therefore, only the relations considered most important are included in the graph, while the rest remain implicit. Some authors recommend separating an orthogonal base of independent attributes and relations, and mark the others as derived if they are shown at all. However, it is far from evident which ones to choose as the orthogonal base, and it is also not clear what "derived" means.

For example, consider the entities depicted in figure 2.2. We may pick the two associations between MOTHER–SON and MOTHER–DAUGHTER as the orthogonal base. The brother–sister association between SON–DAUGHTER then becomes derived, since for any pair of SON and DAUGHTER we can infer whether they are siblings or not. But we could also have chosen any other two as the orthogonal base (assuming brother–sister means full siblings, sharing both parents).

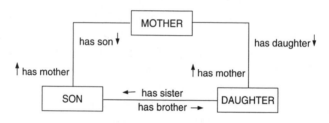

Figure 2.2   ER modeling: derived relations

Moreover, properties of derivability are often global in nature. From the viewpoint of the SON, the mother and sister roles may be equally important, and the fact that one happens to be derivable from the other should not always be emphasized. On the contrary, it may later turn out that the mother role in the system can also be fulfilled by the entity STEPMOTHER, and then the derivability will no longer hold.

For the same reason, the difference between derived attributes and base attributes is not always clear either. To determine derivability one must often make premature assumptions about the underlying information content. These problems disappear with a pure object-oriented approach, since we are then concentrating on system behavior rather than on what information needs to be stored. Since this behavior is what is needed to fulfill system functionality, placing the emphasis there results in much more resilience to future change.

The bottom line is that we give up the seamlessness inherent in an object-oriented approach if we mix in ER modeling at the analysis and design levels, but we do not get much in return. In practice, real systems often have several hundred potential entities and relations between them. The resulting complete ER diagram becomes huge and is essentially a flat structure.

To achieve some locality, large diagrams are often split up into smaller overlapping parts, where each part contains some group of entities together with a subset of mutual relations. This is made possible by the more or less arbitrary omission of associations. The technique resembles the splitting of program flowcharts in older days, but instead of leaving lots of dangling arrows with references to other diagrams, the borderline relations are simply suppressed. However, this does not change the inherent flatness of the structure, and rather than the "zooming" capability so important for understanding a large system, we are stuck with a form of "panning".

The emphasis on associations as a modeling concept separated from object behavior favors a global system view. It breaks encapsulation and concentrates more on short-term detail than on local concepts that may have the potential to survive longer. ER modeling as part of an analysis and design approach will not help us find classes which represent interesting concepts with the potential of being used in other contexts, except solving part of the current problem. The seamlessness and reversibility inherent in object-oriented development can therefore not be fully exploited, which in turn works against reuse. Furthermore, we do not need this type of separate association, since the object-oriented primitives can be used directly to model any concepts we want.

For these reasons, BON has been designed to follow a different track. Rather than trying to include concepts from traditional data modeling or the so-called structured techniques with all their accompanying drawbacks, a more fruitful alliance is sought: the combination of object-oriented flexibility with the clarity and expressive power of strong typing and formal contracts between classes.

2.3 OTHER METHODS

Somewhere between 20 and 50 object-oriented methods have been published to date (depending on which ones are viewed as separate approaches) and the number is still growing. Therefore, any kind of short summary will necessarily become oversimplified and unfair to some. Moreover, most of the methods are continuously evolving and so it is very difficult to know whether you are really criticizing the latest version or just something that is already considered obsolete by the authors.

The reader will therefore not find the usual overview of analysis and design methods in this book, but is instead referred to the many summaries and comparisons already available, as for example in [Graham 1994, Wilkie 1993]. A list of publications on other approaches can be found in appendix D.

BON concentrates on the seamless, reversible specification of software, using the contract model. The basic difference compared to most other methods thus becomes obvious in the light of the previous discussion. The majority of the methods listed in appendix D are hybrid methods based on ER modeling and/or FSM modeling. Some are oversimplified and not expressive enough, while others are trying to include too much and therefore lack the simplicity necessary to be an effective help in the search for reusable abstractions.

A few methods are purely object oriented, and as such approaches with which we sympathize. However, none of them employ strong typing, which makes it practically impossible to deal with software contracting, other than through natural language.

We will not go into any detail regarding the strong and weak points of other proposed methods, since this is not the purpose of this book. An extensive bibliography on object-oriented literature in general can be found in [Booch 1994].

2.4 THE BON POSITION

Because of its flexibility, it is not difficult to find mappings into other domains which would seem to indicate that object-oriented modeling is really equivalent to finite state machine modeling, or data modeling with operations added, or process modeling with signal passing, or even functional abstraction. However, these mappings are not very useful (they are applicable in much the same sense as any procedural program is equivalent to a Turing machine). To achieve full benefit from the technology one needs to concentrate on the aspects which are most important.

Object-oriented encapsulation is an extremely general approach. It can be used to capture abstractions of such clarity that they act as live teachers to anyone reading the specifications. On the other hand, inappropriate encapsulation can create a mess of incomprehensible complexity. The class concept takes no stand about what is represented; it is up to the designer to fill the corresponding type with meaning. In many other disciplines this attitude of generality would be considered too tolerant, but in software production it is exactly the quality we seek.

Since software is developed to meet just about any conceivable need, the concepts used to mold it must be tailorable in any desired direction. As soon as we think we know what is best in all situations and start imposing one detailed model for all needs, we are doomed to fail for applications that need a different view of the world. Our imagination is inherently limited, and the blacksmith's child tends to see the world as a collection of tilt hammers and iron bars. Engineers brought up in environments where system size is measured in thousands of modules are often convinced that any development needs at least ten layers of standardized structure descriptions before detailed design can even begin, while garage floor developers may regard anything beyond a big whiteboard and a good language environment as mere bureaucratic obstacles.

Only the basic concepts for expressing object-oriented abstractions are general enough to reconcile these extremes; the rest has to do with tailoring and should not be included in a general method. Strong typing and the software contract model, on the other hand, fit like a glove on this flexible instrument and can provide the support for correctness and reliability needed by the software industry without impairing its generality.

With the previous discussion as background, we are now ready to present the basic principles underlying the design of the BON notation.

2.5 CHARACTERISTICS OF THE NOTATION

Generality

The notation is not restricted to any specific application domains, nor does it try to cover every special need that may arise for certain applications or for certain programming languages used. Instead, BON concentrates on what is essential for object-oriented development in general, and tries to define a consistent notation to support the corresponding concepts. The user is then free to complement the notation with whatever more might be needed for a particular project.

Seamlessness

BON regards the seamless approach as the only possible road to extensive future reuse. Formalisms from other fields, which are often adapted and used as part of proposed object-oriented analysis and design methods, such as state transition diagrams, process diagrams, Petri nets, entity–relationship diagrams, data flow charts, etc., are therefore not addressed in BON. In case one should want to use some of them as extra support in some projects or application domains, there are enough existing notations to select from. In particular, we recommend the statecharts of David Harel as complementary notation for state transition diagrams, which can be very helpful for some applications [Harel 1988].

Reversibility

To promote reuse and achieve true seamlessness, the core elements of a notation for analysis and design should represent concepts that are directly mappable not only to, but also from, an executable object-oriented language.

Besides making it possible to maintain long-term consistency between specification and implementation, reversibility is also important for the reuse of analysis and design elements. We cannot expect the current set of proposed notations for analysis and design to be standardized in the near future. As advocated earlier, this is not even desirable, since we first need more experience from their use in real projects. Therefore, broad reuse of high-level specification elements will have to rely on something more stable. A small extension of a widely available standardized object-oriented language can fill the need for a common reusable and exchangeable representation, whose graphical view may vary. At present, Eiffel [Meyer 1992a] seems a good candidate as the reference language for such a notation.

The great advantage with this approach is that the notation can be guaranteed to map easily to a set of concepts proved to be implementable in practice, and with adequate efficiency for industrial software products. The notation should also be applicable to already existing networks of classes and then used as a high-level documentation aid. The ability to generate high-level views on collections of classes developed without notational support would mean a tremendous advantage when trying to understand large, external class libraries.

Scalability

The system examples found in textbooks on analysis and design are nearly always small, which is natural since important points need to be illustrated without being obscured by too much irrelevant detail. However, we must make sure that the notation will scale up, and still be useful for large systems. A diagram for a toy example might look nice and clean using almost any notation, but facing real-life systems is quite another story.

The first thing to note is that whenever system size reaches more than 20–30 classes, we need something more than the class concept to describe its structure: a facility to group classes into higher-level units. We will use the term *clustering* for such a facility, and a group of classes chosen according to some criterion will be called a *cluster*. The reason clusters are normally not included among the basic concepts of object-oriented languages is that classes are reusable abstractions that may be grouped differently at different times and in different contexts. The cluster therefore represents a much looser structuring than the class, and the exact configuration of classes is more flexibly handled by system descriptions outside the programming language proper.

In fact, during implementation we usually need at least two ways of clustering the classes in a system. First, we need to tell the compiler environment where to look for classes that are being referenced by other classes. This is often done through specification of a number of class directories, and a search order. Different class versions can then be substituted by simple modification of the search list. Second, we need a different clustering to be used in analysis and design diagrams (usually with more layers for the high-level classes) whose purpose it is to make the system more understandable to human readers.

The second thing to note when scaling up is that flat partitioning is not enough to get comprehensive views of large systems. We need views at different levels of detail and the ability to "zoom" between them. The BON notation uses nested clustering and element compression to achieve this. Element compression means representing a set of graphical or textual elements with a simpler element, its *compressed form*. A typical example is the use of *icons* in window-based graphical user interfaces. Elements containing compressed forms may in turn be compressed, yielding a powerful method to create views at different levels.

Since the level of compression can be independently selected for each structural element (recursively), the user may freely choose the amount of detail shown for each part of a system. New interesting aspects can be shown in comprehensive form while still keeping the overall structure for easy reference. This is what is meant by *scalability*, a major goal in the design of BON.

A few simple changes in the compression levels may lead to a dramatically different architectural diagram, making the approach particularly well suited for automatic tool support. Although often used in advanced systems for structured document manipulation (see for example [Meyer 1988b]), this powerful idea does not seem to have been exploited in other analysis and design methods.

Typed interface descriptions

A class interface consists of the syntax and semantics of its operations. The syntactic part of an operation, often called its *signature*, consists of its name, the number and types of its arguments (if any) and the type of its return value (if any). There are two basic policies with regard to types—static typing and dynamic typing.

Static typing means that the user must specify the types of all operation signatures (along with the types of all local variables used) in the class text. This policy is employed by most object-oriented languages which are targeted at industrial software production, for example C++ [Stroustrup 1992] and Eiffel [Meyer 1992a], and permits type checking at compile time, as well as generation of efficient code.

Dynamic typing means that only the names of operations and arguments are specified in the class text, while the actual object types are decided at run-time. This policy is employed by languages where extreme flexibility is deemed more important than safety and efficiency, notably Smalltalk [Goldberg 1983].

What many analysis and design approaches fail to recognize is that static typing not only permits early type checking and implementation efficiency—it is also an essential aid for system specification. Assigning types to entities is really classification, which increases the information content of a set of interface descriptions considerably. (A *type* in this context refers either to a basic type like an integer, a real number, a boolean value, or to a class.)

Instead of having to rely on a combination of uncertain naming conventions and general comments to guess what types of object will be bound to what names at run-time, the reader can see the types directly. The precise properties of each type can then be found by simply inspecting the corresponding class or basic type, so readers are automatically provided with a *data dictionary*.

As a simple example we may take a class attribute that will refer to a sorted list of airplanes (where the order relation could be based on the number of seats for passenger planes and the load capacity for freighters). In Smalltalk the untyped attribute name would typically be something like:

>   *fleetOfSortedAircraft*

which may be compared with the corresponding typed Eiffel declaration:

>   *fleet*: *SORTED_LIST* [*AIRCRAFT*]

The amount of precise information conveyed by the two forms is very different. (In fact, the Smalltalk community is beginning to recognize the lack of static typing as a problem, and extensions to add typing to the language have been proposed [Bracha 1993, Wirfs-Brock 1991].)

BON adopts a fully typed notation for class interfaces, but also provides a very high-level untyped view to be used in communication with non-technical people.

Support for software contracting

The theory of *software contracting* [Meyer 1992c] is an important advance in the quest for correctness and robustness in professional software products. As was pointed out in the previous chapter, these qualities become even more important for reusable components, whose behavior will affect many applications. Since software contracting means adding specification elements to classes, it is ideally suited as part of a method for object-oriented analysis and design.

Despite this, the contracting idea is at best briefly mentioned in books and articles on the subject, but seldom emphasized the way it deserves. One reason may be that few other methods employ a typed notation for specifying class interfaces, and without typed interface descriptions of each class, it is difficult to express software contracts formally. So besides its general classification power, typing also plays an important role in software contracts.

Another crucial point is that seamlessness requires an object-oriented system and its specification to be based on the same conceptual view of the world. This important principle needs elaboration.

The specification elements or *assertions* used in software contracts (pre- and postconditions and class invariants) are statements about the *state* of the system before and after applying certain operations. Since an object-oriented system should be defined exclusively by the external behavior of its objects, the system state is only available indirectly through public operations, called *queries*, which are applicable to the objects.

Including lower-level details, like state variables, in external specifications would break the encapsulation. Therefore, the primitive elements in assertions are object queries and basic constants, which may be combined by operators to form logical expressions. The semantics of each query used in an assertion is in turn specified by the class of the object on which the query is applied. So an object-oriented system specification is a set of classes, some or all of whose operations are defined in terms of the specification of other classes in the set (recursively).

Most of the objects queried in assertions will also be part of system execution, and thus the corresponding classes part of the implementation. This is fairly obvious, since there would not be much point in specifying the behavior of the objects in a system by mostly reasoning about the behavior of an entirely different set of objects. Some classes may have been introduced strictly for specification purposes, such as predicate logic support or advanced set operations, but these may still be implemented to enable assertion checking at run-time.

Classes will be added in later phases for two main reasons: incomplete initial specification and choice of implementation. But the conclusion is that an object-oriented system and its specification should share the same base of class abstractions. The idea is that in a well-designed system, most of the classes and operations needed in specifications to capture the necessary state information are already available as part of the system. The rest can be added as new application classes, new operations on existing application classes, or as general specification support classes.

The result is a system which contains its own decentralized specification as an integral part. The class operations are partly defined by successively referring to already specified operations whose semantics are known, thus making them fit to use as extensions of the specification language. Care must of course be taken to avoid circular specification and the classes need to be checked and tested in suitable order to give a well-defined result, but these are issues that must be addressed by any method.

The great advantage of the approach is that when specification and implementation share the same set of abstractions, system changes will automatically be applied to both at the same time. Instead of having to witness theory and reality gradually drift apart as a system evolves over time, software managers can now watch the two act as one organic unit turning in concert to meet the changing requirements of a competitive market.

The specification language of BON uses first-order predicate logic to combine state functions. This is not enough to fully specify a system, but it takes us a significant step forward. The recursive contracting model represents a powerful view of software development that can help produce systems of much greater clarity and correctness.

Simplicity

Perhaps the most important of all general principles for conceptual models, as well as for notations, is simplicity. The deep results of the natural sciences seem to indicate that nature is inherently simple—that complexity is only introduced by our lack of understanding. The essence is well captured by the French writer and aviator Antoine de Saint-Exupéry:

> It seems that the sole purpose of the work of engineers, designers, and calculators in drawing offices and research institutes is to polish and smooth out, lighten this seam, balance that wing until it is no longer noticed, until it is no longer a wing attached to a fuselage, but a form fully unfolded, finally freed from the ore, a sort of mysteriously joined whole, and of the same quality as that of a poem. It seems that perfection is reached, not when there is nothing more to add, but when there is no longer anything to remove.   [Terre des hommes, 1937]

Of course there is still a long way to go before object-oriented analysis and design reaches the maturity of airplane construction, but the above may serve as a main source of inspiration.

The BON notation strives for simplicity and tries to minimize the number of concepts. For example, there are only two basic relations between classes: the inheritance relation and the client relation. To obtain multiple views of a system, we also need relations between classes and clusters and between clusters and clusters. However, instead of introducing new concepts we use the *compression* mechanism discussed earlier to generalize the class relations, and give them well-defined semantics when clusters are involved.

The classes of a system need to be grouped according to various criteria in order to make their structural and functional properties visible. Although the nature of these groups may be very different—subsystems, classes with related functionality, heirs of a common ancestor, individual parts of a whole—BON uses only one concept to cover them all: the cluster. Also, there is only one type of inheritance; differences in purpose and semantics are instead taken care of by contracting elements.

Space economy

The abstract concepts underlying the elements of a graphical notation are certainly much more important than the particular symbols used. Discussing details of geometric shapes becomes meaningless unless you know exactly what you want to illustrate. However, this does not mean that the notation is unimportant. On the contrary, if it were, we could just forget about fancy graphics requiring special equipment and software and use only plain text. The reason we still insist on a graphical presentation is the possibility of communicating views of the underlying model much faster and more accurately to a human user.

A graphical notation is a language, and like any language it can give rise to endless discussions about individual elements—should we use single or double arrows, ellipses or rectangles, dashed or continuous borderlines?—whose merits are very much related to personal taste, cultural context, and plain habit. (Again, this does not mean that such elements are unimportant or basically equivalent, only that it is difficult to achieve consensus about them.) However, there is one aspect of any notation designed to give a global overview of a potentially large and complex structure which is important regardless of the details, and that is *economy of space*.

The amount of information that can be conveyed by an overview of some part of a system—a cluster, a group of clusters, a group of related classes—is very much dependent on what can be made to fit on one page (where a page is a terminal screen, a paper sheet, or whatever can be inspected in one glance). Breaking up an integral context into several pieces that must be viewed separately is extremely detrimental to the global picture. Since systems often require that quite a few classes be shown simultaneously for the user to get comprehensive views of the system structure and the relations between its parts, it becomes very important to avoid wasting space.

The BON notation pays attention to this problem by providing compressed forms for all space-consuming graphical layouts. For example, it is too restrictive (as in many other notations) to have a full class interface with operations and attributes as the only way to show a class. In BON, the compressed form of a class is simply its name enclosed in an ellipse (possibly annotated by small graphical markers). Similarly, BON provides the iconization of clusters and compression of relationships between classes belonging to different clusters into relationships between clusters.

It is often possible to pack a considerable amount of information in one high-level view of a system (or part if it), and still keep the view on one page. The key is interactive tailoring by successive compression and expansion of various parts of a diagram until the user's intent is optimally conveyed.

Basis for intelligent case tools

Well-designed object-oriented systems tend to be small compared to traditionally developed systems with equivalent functionality. This is because common patterns of behavior are reused in layers of abstraction rather than repeated over and over with small variations; flat code is thus transformed into system structure. However, the advantages gained are not completely free—there is a price to pay for the increased flexibility and reduction of overall complexity. The compact object-oriented code is by necessity more intricately structured in order to achieve more functionality per line of text. Particularly, extensive use of inheritance tends to fragment the class text. It is often very hard to grasp the full abstraction represented by classes which have maybe 10–20 ancestors along multiple lines of heritage if the only means is inspecting the bodies of the classes involved.

Obviously, we need automatic tool support. For example, as client to a class we are not necessarily interested in its position in a classification structure. Therefore, we need a tool that can present the full set of operations of any class, whether these operations were inherited or not. One of the great advantages with the increased semantic content in a typed object-oriented notation with software contracts is that it provides the foundation for much more intelligent object-oriented case tools than is possible in untyped environments.

2.6 STATIC AND DYNAMIC MODELS

There are many ways to describe a software system, but all descriptions can be characterized as being either *static* or *dynamic*. Static descriptions document the structure of a system: what the components are and how these components are related to each other. They do not take time into consideration, but are either time independent or represent snapshots at certain points in time.

Static descriptions are of two kinds: they either tell you something about the structure of the system software (that is, how the program modules are organized in the eventual implementation), or they tell you something about the structure of the interacting components that come into play when the system is executed. Both are of course necessary for maintainability of the software being developed, but the good news is that with a pure object-oriented language the same static description can be used to capture both aspects. Since a class describes the behavior of a certain type of object—and nothing else—using the class as the basic program module makes the static structure of the class text in the software system map directly to the structure of the objects at execution time.

Dynamic descriptions, by contrast, document how the system will behave over time. In an object-oriented context, this means describing how objects interact at execution time; how they invoke operations on each other (passing messages in Smalltalk terminology) and how the information content of the system changes, as reflected by the values of the class attributes (state variables) in the system.

These two types of description are very different, and confusion can easily arise unless they are kept apart. An object-oriented system is best viewed as a structured collection of classes, each being a (possibly partial) implementation of an abstract data type. The classes constitute the blueprints specifying the behavior of each object (class instance) created during a system session. At system execution time, on the other hand, only communicating objects will exist, while the classes are left on the engineer's desk. Each object will behave as prescribed by its class (serving as its genetic code), but just like a biological creature it has no access to what is actually governing its pattern of behavior.

The analysis and design of an object-oriented system using the BON method will result in static and dynamic descriptions of the system being developed. The static descriptions form the *static model* of the system. This model contains formal descriptions of class interfaces, their grouping into clusters as well as client and inheritance relations between them, showing the system structure. The dynamic descriptions, on the other hand, make up the system's *dynamic model*. This model specifies system *events*, what object types are responsible for the *creation* of other objects, and system execution *scenarios* representing selected types of system usage with diagrams showing object message passing.

Part II (chapters 3–5) will describe these views in detail, the graphical notation used, as well as the underlying concepts. Part III (chapters 6–8) will then be devoted to the BON method, containing rules and guidelines to be used in producing the models.

Part II
The model

3 The static model—classes and clusters

3.1 INTRODUCTION

The static model shows the classes making up the system, their interfaces, how they are related to each other, and how they are grouped in clusters. It concentrates on the *what* part and downplays the *how*. It also fits well when object-oriented formal specification techniques are used in the early development stages (for an overview, see [Lano 1994]).

There are two parts to the static model. The first part is a collection of very high-level untyped modeling charts, which can be used early in the analysis process to enhance communication with domain experts and end-users, and as partial documentation aimed at non-technical people. The charts work much like a set of structured memos to help sort out the initial disorder and overwhelming amount of requirement details (often contradictory) so common in early modeling. They were inspired by the index cards used in the CRC method at Tektronix [Beck 1989].

The second part is a structured description containing fully typed class interfaces and formal specification of software contracts. This is the main part of the static model in BON, and its notation has been developed with graphical manipulation tools in mind. Classes are grouped into clusters, and clusters may in turn contain both classes and other clusters.

There are two variants of the BON notation: graphical BON and textual BON. The graphical form is intended for use with automatic tool support as well as for sketches on paper and whiteboards. It contains a mixture of drawing elements and text elements, but the text elements are considered graphical as well, since their location in a two-dimensional figure may be used to convey information.

The textual form is intended for communicating BON descriptions between various automatic processing tools and for maintaining evolving architectures by simple file editing in environments that lack dedicated BON case tools. It also has a formal grammar defined, which may be used as a compact description of the whole set of BON's notational concepts, as well as to clarify possible ambiguities that may occur in the natural language descriptions.

There is a one-to-one structural mapping between the graphical and textual form of a BON description, but the textual language does not (for obvious reasons of simplicity) contain any description of spatial layout. It is thus possible to generate many different diagrams from the same textual description (all topologically equivalent). The much more complex problem of choosing a good presentation layout is left to the designers of BON case tools.

Since graphical BON is the most readable and compact form, it will be the preferred notation in this book. The corresponding textual forms will only be mentioned occasionally in the general description of the BON method. The complete formal grammar of textual BON and examples of its usage are collected in appendices A and B.

This chapter will describe the basic elements of the static model: the classes and clusters. We will start with the untyped modeling charts and then proceed to typed class interface descriptions. We will see that textual descriptions can be made much more concise using graphical representations of the specification elements. The formal specification language of BON, based on first-order predicate logic, will be described.

Finally, we look at the scalability of the BON graphical notation through compression and expansion: how classes may be compressed into headers, how clusters may be iconized, and so forth. The next chapter will then be devoted to the static relations between classes and clusters.

3.2 BON MODELING CHARTS

Very early in the process, informal charts may be used to communicate basic ideas to non-technical people like end-users, customers, and domain experts. These charts may also later serve as very high-level documentation for the system, and be stored with the more formal descriptions by a case tool. There are three types of modeling chart in the static model:

- system chart

- cluster chart

- class chart

The layout of the charts has been chosen so as to give a feeling of physical cards. Much of the advantages reported from the use of CRC index cards [Beck 1989] stems from the social communication they give rise to when analysts and people from the customer side work together to make a first model of the problem, and actually pass the cards around in order to fill in the information needed.

The modeling charts can be used in a similar way if they are printed in fixed format as templates on paper and then filled in manually during modeling sessions. The analyst can later transfer the information to a case tool, which will store it as complementary documentation. The case tool may also translate the information in the class charts into a form that can be used as the beginning of the more formal class interface specification.

System charts

The system chart (exactly one per system) contains a brief description of each top-level cluster in the system. In BON, a system consists of one or more clusters, each of which contains a number of classes and/or subclusters. By convention, BON does not allow classes at the topmost level, so each class belongs to exactly one (immediately) enclosing cluster. An example of a system chart for a car rental system is shown in figure 3.1.

The header of a modeling chart is separated from its body by a double line with the top two rows in standard format. The first row has the chart type to the left (SYSTEM in this case) followed by the name of the system/cluster/class described and a chart sequence identification. Sequencing is needed, since all

SYSTEM	CAR_RENTAL_SYSTEM	Part: 1/1

PURPOSE
    System keeping track of vehicles and rental agreements in a car rental company.
	INDEXING
	    author: Jean-Marc Nerson
	    keywords: vehicle, rental	

Cluster	Description
CONTRACT_ELEMENTS	Concepts that have to do with rental agreements such as contracts, clients, means of payment, rentals.
RENTAL_PROPERTIES	Properties of individual rentals such as vehicle, rate, extra options, insurance policy, certified drivers.
VEHICLE_PROPERTIES	Properties of rentable vehicles such as availability, location, models.
OPTIONS	Selectable rental options.
OPTION_TYPE	Types of options available such as two-door versus four-door models, automatic versus manual transmission, sunroof and hifi stereo equipment.
SUPPORT	General support classes for handling of time and date, executable commands and data structures.

Figure 3.1 System chart for a car rental system

the entries might not fit on a single chart. The second row has a comment clause to the left describing the purpose of the chart, and an indexing clause to the right. The indexing clause contains a number of index entries, and each index entry consists of a keyword with a list of words attached. The number of entries and what keywords to use is decided per project. The purpose is to record interesting properties of systems, classes, and clusters, and to facilitate browsing.

Note that the indexing clause in figure 3.1 has two keywords: **author** and **keywords**. The name of the second keyword suggests, of course, that by the conventions used for recording indexing information in the organization where this car rental system is developed, *vehicle* and *rental* will be considered keywords. However, this last interpretation occurs inside the target system and has nothing to do with the general syntactic keyword construct of BON charts. From BON's perspective *vehicle* and *rental* are just words attached to the keyword **keywords**.

The above illustrates an important point in all types of abstract modeling—the risk of confusing language with metalanguage. The distinction may be obvious in this example, but there are much more subtle cases where our cultural background makes it all too easy to automatically assign meaning to words and symbols also in contexts where we are not supposed to.

Cluster charts

A cluster chart contains a brief description of each class and subcluster in the cluster. Subcluster names are enclosed in parentheses to separate them from class names. The recommended procedure is to list all classes first, and then the subclusters, if any. This is because subclusters often group local services that are used by the topmost classes in a cluster. A subcluster may, for example, contain all specialized descendant classes of a given class.

Clusters may be nested to any depth. Two cluster charts are shown in figure 3.2, where the first cluster contains a subcluster described by the second chart. Cluster chart headers are similar to system chart headers, but the name now refers to the cluster instead. The indexing clause contains an entry with keyword **cluster**, listing the nearest enclosing cluster of the class.

Class charts

The class charts model individual classes. Classes are viewed as black boxes, and the information in the class charts is the result of answering the following questions:

- What information can other classes ask from this class? This translates into *queries* applicable to the class.

CLUSTER	*ORGANIZATION*	**Part:** 1/1

PURPOSE
Handles all major events occurring during the organization and completion of a conference.

INDEXING
    author: Kim Waldén, Jean-Marc Nerson
    keywords: organization, staff

Class/(Cluster)	Description
CONFERENCE	The root class of the conference system.
PROGRAM	Information about the final conference program and its preparation.
TIMETABLE	Repository of scheduled events.
(COMMITTEES)	The committees engaged in the conference organization to take care of the technical and administrative parts.

CLUSTER	*COMMITTEES*	**Part:** 1/1

PURPOSE
Groups all general and special types of committees.

INDEXING
    cluster: *ORGANIZATION*
    author: Kim Waldén, Jean-Marc Nerson
    keywords: committee, scientific board, steering board

Class/(Cluster)	Description
COMMITTEE	General committee abstraction.
STEERING_COMMITTEE	Committee in charge of practical arrangements.
PROGRAM_COMMITTEE	Committee in charge of selecting technical contributions.

Figure 3.2 Cluster chart

- What services can other classes ask this class to provide? This translates to *commands* applicable to the class.

- What rules must be obeyed by the class and its clients? This translates into *constraints* on the class.

In this book, when we talk about something (like operations or constraints above) being applicable to a class, we really mean applicable to the objects whose behavior is described by the class. Since classes in BON are strictly viewed as description, not as objects, there should be no risk of confusion.

An example of two class charts is given in figure 3.3. The class chart header is similar to those of the system and cluster charts. The comment entry (explicitly labeled "type of object") contains a short description of the purpose of

CLASS	CITIZEN		Part: 1/1
TYPE OF OBJECT Person born or living in a country	**INDEXING** **cluster:** *CIVIL_STATUS* **created:** 1993-03-15 jmn **revised:** 1993-05-12 kw		
Queries	Name, Sex, Age, Single, Spouse, Children, Parents, Impediment to marriage		
Commands	Marry. Divorce.		
Constraints	Each citizen has two parents. At most one spouse allowed. May not marry children or parents or person of same sex. Spouse's spouse must be this person. All children, if any, must have this person among their parents.		

CLASS	NOBLEPERSON		Part: 1/1
TYPE OF OBJECT Person of noble rank	**INDEXING** **cluster:** *CIVIL_STATUS* **created:** 1993-03-15 jmn **revised:** 1993-05-12 kw, 1993-12-10 kw		
Inherits from	*CITIZEN*		
Queries	Assets, Butler		
Constraints	Enough property for independence. Can only marry other noble person. Wedding celebrated with style. Married nobility share their assets and must have a butler.		

Figure 3.3 Class charts: types of citizen

the class. Keywords for version control have been added to the indexing clause, since classes represent the evolving basic components of a system (keeping track of changes to clusters is usually not very interesting). After the chart header a number of dynamic entries follow, specified only when non-empty:

- Inherits from
  – lists classes that are direct ancestors to this class.
- Queries
  – lists applicable queries (value return; may not change system state).
- Commands
  – lists applicable commands (no value return; may change system state).

- Constraints
  - lists consistency requirement of the class and its operations as well as general business rules and other information that may affect the design and implementation of the class.

The constraints may later be translated into formal assertions on the class (pre- and postconditions and class invariants), but also serve as a kind of formatted memo for the class. Some constraints at the early analysis level may record information that will never become formal assertions, but rather serve as a guide for future design decisions (see the Conference case study for some examples). This is the reason we have chosen the name *constraints* for this field in the BON class charts, rather than the more precise *assertions*.

This completes the description of the static untyped modeling charts in BON, and we may proceed to the notation used for more exact specification. But before we do, we will say a few words to clarify how the operations of a class relate to the system state.

3.3 SYSTEM STATE INFORMATION

So far, we have deliberately refrained from discussing state variables (*class attributes* in this book), since the internal state of an object is not part of its interface. In some languages, notably Eiffel [Meyer 1992a], attributes may be exported as read-only variables. However, this is just a convenient trick to simplify language syntax and should not affect the way we think about the visible operations of a class. Conceptually, an exported attribute should be viewed as a function returning the value of some hidden state information that just happens to have the same name.

The only visible part of an abstract data type is its operations with pre- and postconditions and the class invariant. Whether it stores necessary history information as internal variables or just magically remembers the past is none of the client's business as long as the data type behaves according to its software contract.

In this book, we will use the term *class feature* or just *feature* to cover both the operational aspects and the state aspects of class operations. In many applications—particularly when persistent objects are involved—the designer often has an early idea about which features should be implemented as state variables, but there is no reason to make future change harder by letting the design depend on these ideas. Often the decision whether to store a value as a data attribute or instead compute it each time it is needed is only a question of space/time tradeoff which should be postponed as long as possible. Therefore, the BON notation does not include symbols for state variables.

3.4 TYPED CLASS INTERFACES

Using modeling charts may be a good way to start analysis, particularly when non-technical people are involved, but the analyst/designer will soon need something more expressive. This leads us to the main part of the BON notation: the structured static diagrams with typing and software contracts.

Class interfaces will be described first; then we will go through the BON assertion language in more detail. At the end of this chapter class clustering will be discussed. The static relations are postponed until the next chapter.

A class interface consists of a number of sections, some of which may be empty. The sections are:

- Class header

- Indexing clause

- Inheritance clause

- Class features

- Class invariant

Compression of interface sections

Class interfaces may be described either textually or graphically. Each graphical descriptive element in BON has two representations: one *expanded* form and one *compressed* form. With the exception of the class header, each section in a graphical class interface (empty or not) may be compressed, which means it will be hidden.

The whole class interface may also be compressed; it is then represented by its header enclosed in an ellipse. We will see more of this at the end of the chapter, when clustering and scaling is discussed.

Graphical representation

The graphical form of a class interface with all sections expanded is shown in figure 3.4. The full interface may look a bit crowded, but in practice only a few sections will be displayed at a time (we are assuming automated case tool support here). The indexing section, for example, is usually hidden unless explicitly requested. Note also that the restricted sections of a class interface (as explained below) only come in during detailed design; the early phases should always concentrate on public features.

We will now look at each interface section in turn, and show its specification in both textual and graphical BON.

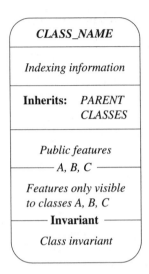

Figure 3.4   Class interface: expanded sections

3.5 CLASS HEADER

The class header consists of the class name, which may be annotated to highlight certain key properties of the class. The complete set of header annotations is shown in figure 3.5.

3.6 INDEXING CLAUSE

The indexing clause contains general information about a class to be used for browsing and configuration management purposes. It consists of a list of index entries, and each index entry is a keyword followed by a list of words. The semantic interpretation of keywords and the conventions to be used in creating indexing information are decided per project. The indexing clause may for example contain references to arbitrary text, graphics, and perhaps sound, and be used as the starting point for an advanced multi-media class library documentation system. A simple indexing clause is shown in figure 3.6.

What keywords to use for the classification of items via indexing clauses depends strongly on the environment in which they are used. It is probably best to start out with very terse information and gradually let each new keyword justify its inclusion as an index entry when experience shows that it is really useful. It is important that both users and providers of indexing clauses perceive the contents as relevant information, not as yet another administrative burden.

CLASS HEADER ANNOTATIONS		
Graphical form	**Textual form**	**Explanation**
 *NAME*	**reused class** *NAME*	Class is reused from a library of existing components.
 ● *NAME*	**persistent class** *NAME*	Class instances are potentially persistent.
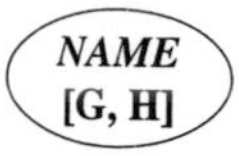 *NAME* [G, H]	**class** *NAME* [*G, H*]	Class is parameterized.
 * *NAME*	**deferred class** *NAME*	Class will not be fully implemented: it has no instances and is only used for classification and interface definition purposes.
 + *NAME*	**effective class** *NAME*	Class is implementing the interface of a deferred class, or reimplementing the interface of an ancestor.
 ▲ *NAME*	**interfaced class** *NAME*	Class is interfaced with the outside world: some class operation encapsulates external communication (function calls, data, etc.).
 *NAME*	**root class** *NAME*	Class is a root class: its instances may be created as separate processes.

Figure 3.5 Complete set of class header annotations

synonyms: car, transportation means
application_domains: car rental, car lease
author: John W. Smith
version: 1.1
revision_date: March 30, 1992
spec_refs: srs.1.3.3, srs.3.4.7
keywords: rental, agency, car, vehicle, automobile

Figure 3.6 Indexing clause for a *VEHICLE* class

3.7 INHERITANCE CLAUSE

The inheritance clause lists all parents of the class, if any. It corresponds to the "Inherits from" entry in the class modeling chart.

3.8 CLASS FEATURES

The features of a class are grouped into feature clauses, which may have different degrees of visibility:

A. Public features, visible to any client class.

B. Restricted features, available only to a certain group of other classes. Such features are often implementation oriented and therefore only exported to classes whose implementations are allowed to depend on them.

   Since different features may have different restrictions, there can be any number of restricted feature clauses, each listing the set of classes permitted to use them. Listing the single name *NONE* yields a private feature clause, not visible to any other class.

   Restricted sections are rarely used at the analysis level, but may come into play when BON is used for detailed design and the implementation language is known.

Feature names

Within each feature clause, the feature names are listed with optional markers showing their implementation status, as illustrated by figure 3.7.

FEATURE NAMES		
Graphical form	**Textual form**	**Explanation**
name *	**deferred** *name*	Non-implemented feature
name $^+$	**effective** *name*	Implemented feature
name $^{++}$	**redefined** *name*	Reimplemented feature

Figure 3.7 Feature implementation status

A feature may be marked as:

- *deferred*, which means the feature will not be implemented in this class, but in some descendant class. This implies that the class is also deferred, that is cannot have instances of its own, and is used exclusively through inheritance.

- *effective*, which means the feature will be implemented in this class. Usually this signifies that a deferred feature was inherited and given an implementation, but the marker may also be used just to emphasize that the feature will have an implementation.

- *redefined*, which means an effective feature is inherited from another class, and the implementation changed.

Feature signatures

Class features are fully typed in BON. This means that the *signature* (number and type of possible arguments and return value) is specified for each feature. Figure 3.8 shows the symbols used.

FEATURE SIGNATURES (partial table)		
Graphical form	**Textual form**	**Explanation**
name: *TYPE* → *arg*: *TYPE*	*name*: *TYPE* –> *arg*: *TYPE*	Result type Input argument

Figure 3.8   Typed signatures

If a feature returns a value, its name is followed by the corresponding type separated by a colon. (The table is partial, since it is also possible to express variants of client relations, namely aggregations and shared results. These additional signatures will be explained in the next chapter.) As an example, the signature of a feature returning the seat number for a given passenger is shown below:

> *seat_assignment*: *NUMERIC*
> → *passenger*: *PERSON*

Feature renaming

After the feature name with its possible return type declaration, there may follow a rename clause which makes it possible to specify occasional feature renamings that may occur when a class inherits from another class. The clause consists of a pair of curly braces enclosing the name of the class from which the renamed feature was inherited (not always obvious with multiple inheritance) and the old feature name separated by a dot. The rename clause looks the same in both graphical and textual form. An example is shown below, where the feature *co_pilot* is inherited from class *VEHICLE* under the name *co_driver* and then renamed.

class *AIRCRAFT* **inherit** ...

co_pilot⁺⁺: PILOT { ^VEHICLE.co_driver }

The feature was also redefined as indicated by the ⁺⁺ symbol into returning the type *PILOT* instead of *DRIVER*. However, the original return type is not shown in the rename clause. Since redefinitions may affect the full signature of a feature (including the types of input arguments), we must look at the interface of class *AIRCRAFT* to find out more details. The caret of the rename clause suggests that the names refer to entities "above this class".

The next few lines of the feature specification may contain an optional header comment (each line preceded by a double dash) giving a terse description of the purpose of the feature. Then the input arguments follow, if any, each preceded by a small arrow.

Assertions

Finally, after the possible arguments, an optional *precondition* and an optional *postcondition* follow in turn. The notation used for assertions is shown in figure 3.9.

ASSERTIONS	
Graphical form	**Textual form**
[?] *routine preconditions*	**require** *routine preconditions*
[!] *routine postconditions*	**ensure** *routine postconditions*
[written in invariant section] *class invariant*	**invariant** *class invariant*

Figure 3.9   Software contracting clauses

The precondition states a predicate that must be true when the feature is called by a client. It is the *client's* responsibility to ensure that the precondition is indeed fulfilled before calling a supplier.

The postcondition states a predicate that must be true when the feature has been executed and the supplier object returns control to the client. Given that the precondition is true on feature entry, it is the *supplier's* responsibility to ensure that the postcondition is true before returning control to the client.

The laws of software contracting [Meyer 1992c] restrict the semantics of descendant classes so as not to violate the abstraction carefully crafted by the ancestors. For example, it may be good practice for a *RECTANGLE* class to redefine the implementation of an *area* feature inherited from a general class *POLYGON* to obtain better efficiency, but it would be a disaster if the redefined feature suddenly started to return the circumference instead. The laws of contracting reduce this risk by stipulating the following:

1. The class invariants of all ancestors must also be obeyed by all children.

2. Inherited preconditions may only be *weakened*. This means a new implementation may never restrict the circumstances under which a client call is valid beyond what has been specified by the ancestor. It may, however, relax the rules and also accept calls that would have been rejected by the ancestor.

3. Inherited postconditions may only be *strengthened*. This means a new implementation must fulfill what the ancestors have undertaken to do, but may deliver more.

Contrary to some other environments, notably Smalltalk, the concepts of *subtype* and *subclass* are viewed as identical in BON. Therefore, specification of types is directly transferred to specification of the corresponding classes, which is why the semantically strong contracting laws make sense. Coupled with these laws BON assumes what is known as the *covariant rule* for inherited features, which says that signatures of redefined features may only be of the same corresponding types as before, or *descendant types*.[1]

Example

We will use the two classes described by the class charts in figure 3.3 as an example, and give the corresponding formal specifications in both textual and graphical form. The textual description is shown in figure 3.10 and figure 3.11, and the graphical equivalent in figure 3.12.

The deferred class *CITIZEN* models a citizen in a country. The first three features are queries returning the name, sex, and age of the current citizen object, each of type *VALUE*, while the fourth feature returns a possible spouse of type *CITIZEN*. The next features are also queries, *children* and *parents*, both returning *SET* [*CITIZEN*] since there can be more than one of each attached relative.

---

[1] Some object-oriented notations and languages have instead adopted the *contravariant rule*, stating that signatures may only be redefined into ancestor types. This can lead to a simpler mathematical model of the type system, but is in our experience much too restrictive for practical use in large developments.

```
deferred class CITIZEN
feature
    name, sex, age: VALUE
    spouse: CITIZEN                          -- Husband or wife
    children, parents: SET [CITIZEN]         -- Close relatives, if any
    single: BOOLEAN                          -- Is this citizen single?
        ensure
            Result <-> spouse = Void
        end
    deferred marry                           -- Celebrate the wedding.
        -> sweetheart: CITIZEN
        require
            sweetheart /= Void and can_marry (sweetheart)
        ensure
            spouse = sweetheart
        end
    can_marry: BOOLEAN                        -- No legal hindrance?
        -> other: CITIZEN
        require
            other /= Void
        ensure
            Result -> (single and other.single
            and other not member_of children
            and other not member_of parents
            and sex /= other.sex)
        end
    divorce                                  -- Admit mistake.
        require
            not single
        ensure
            single and (old spouse).single
        end
invariant
    single or spouse.spouse = Current;
    parents.count = 2;
    for_all c member_of children it_holds
        (exists p member_of c.parents it_holds p = Current)
end -- class CITIZEN
```

Figure 3.10 Formal specification using textual BON

Then a query follows whose *BOOLEAN* result tells whether the current citizen is single or not. The semantics of the feature is specified through a postcondition. The condition states that the return value of *single* will be true if and only if *spouse* returns *Void* (no spouse object attached to current citizen). *Result* is a predefined variable carrying the return value of a query. The symbols ↔ and ∅ stand for *equivalence* and *void reference* respectively (see figure 3.13).

The next public feature is *marry*, a deferred command (shown by an asterisk in figure 3.12) that returns no value, but instead alters the object state. It requires

```
effective class NOBLEPERSON
inherit
    CITIZEN
feature
    assets: NUMERIC                          -- The bare necessities of life
    butler: CITIZEN                          -- Irons the morning paper
    redefined spouse: NOBLEPERSON            -- Lord or Lady
    effective marry                          -- Celebrate with style.
        -> fiancee: NOBLEPERSON
        ensure
            butler /= Void;
            assets <= old assets + fiancee.assets − $50,000
        end
end -- class NOBLEPERSON
```

Figure 3.11 Formal specification (continued)

an input argument (marked by an arrow) also of type *CITIZEN*. The formal argument is named *sweetheart*, so that it can be referenced in the semantic specification of the feature.

The precondition states that *marry* may only be invoked if there is a sweetheart available, and there is no impediment to marriage between the two parties. The postcondition asserts that unless legal reasons forbid, execution of the command *marry* will indeed attach *sweetheart* as the *spouse* of the current *CITIZEN* object.

Legal hindrance is defined by the next query, *can_marry*, which rules out bigamy and incest and allows only heterosexual unions. It may only be called on a non-void citizen. BON assertion expressions use the common syntax $o.f(a, b)$ to mean invocation of feature f on object o with input arguments a and b.

The feature *divorce*, which comes next, is also a command. It requires the citizen to be non-single, so there will be somebody to divorce. The postcondition then ensures that after the divorce, both parties will indeed be single again.

To express this, we use the special symbol **old**, which refers to the value an expression would have returned, had it been evaluated *just before* calling the feature. The parentheses are used to alter operator precedence, so the feature *single* is applied to the old spouse object, but with the current system state (after execution of *divorce*). Writing **old** *spouse.single* would mean applying *single* to the old spouse object with the old system state (before execution of *divorce*), which would return **false** since the citizens were then still married.

We save the invariant for the next section, and turn to the second interface— that of the class *NOBLEPERSON*. The class is effective (header marked with plus symbol in the graphical form) and the inheritance clause shows it is a child

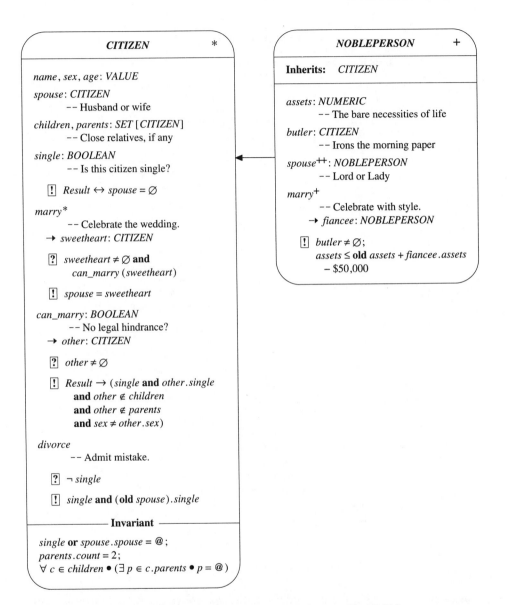

Figure 3.12   Equivalent specification using graphical BON

of *CITIZEN*. (In figure 3.12, this may also be seen from the single arrow which, as we shall see in the next chapter, represents the inheritance relation.)

The first two features of *NOBLEPERSON* represent necessary extensions: an *assets* feature of type *NUMERIC* (absolutely essential, considering the ridiculous prices charged for good hunting grounds these days), and the obligatory

ASSERTION ELEMENTS		
Graphical BON	**Textual BON**	**Explanation**
Δ *name* **old** *expr*	**delta** *name* **old** *expr*	Attribute changed Old return value
Result @ ∅	*Result* *Current* *Void*	Current query result Current object Void reference
+ − * / ^ // \\	+ − * / ^ // \\	Basic numeric operators Power operator Integer division Modulo
= ≠ < ≤ > ≥	= /= < <= > >=	Equal Not equal Less than Less than or equal Greater than Greater than or equal
→ ↔ ¬ **and** **or** **xor**	-> <-> **not** **and** **or** **xor**	Implies (semi-strict) Equivalent to Not And (semi-strict) Or (semi-strict) Exclusive or
∃ ∀ | • ∈ ∉ : *type* { } ..	**exists** **for_all** **such_that** **it_holds** **member_of** **not member_of** : *type* { } ..	There exists For all Such that It holds Is in set Is not in set Is of type Enumerated set Closed range

Figure 3.13 Elements of assertions

manservant. The third feature redefines the *spouse* query so it will now return *NOBLEPERSON*, thus satisfying both tradition and the covariant rule. Finally, the *marry* command is defined to reflect what is expected from a high-class wedding. The signature is again changed, and the postcondition extended to ensure that noble couples who link their destinies will not lack domestic support, and that each party will have access to the accumulated fortune minus the amount that must be spent to ensure a wedding with style.

Evaluation order

Logical conjunction (**and**), disjunction (**or**), and implication (**implies**) have so-called semi-strict interpretation in BON assertions. This means that the corresponding binary expressions are assumed to be evaluated left to right, so that if the left operand is true (in the case of **or**) or false (in the case of **and** or **implies**) the result will be directly inferred without evaluating the right operand.

This makes the precondition of *marry* above meaningful also when *sweetheart* is not attached to any object. With the standard interpretation of the logical connectives, the precondition would not be fully specified since the expression *can_marry* (*sweetheart*) is not defined for void arguments.

Therefore, some care must be taken when BON assertions are translated to implementation languages. For example, in Eiffel **and then** and **or else** have to be used, while in C++ the corresponding operators already have semi-strict semantics. A language-specific case tool could allow individual expressions to be marked as strict (in case they can be evaluated in any order), to allow for optimized assertion checking.

3.9 CLASS INVARIANT

Before explaining the details of the invariant example, we would like to reassure those readers who are likely to break out in a rash when exposed to anything reminiscent of mathematical formulas: there is nothing in the BON method that forces you to write formal specifications. The symbols in figure 3.13 are only there to help you when you want to specify something exactly, and avoid the risk of misunderstandings always present in natural language.

If you do want precise specifications, all usable notations tend to look a bit scary at first, but once gotten used to they can provide enormous help and really put the user in control. A very interesting example showing how difficult it can be to express even very small everyday problems in natural language with enough precision to allow correct and unambiguous implementation can be found in [Meyer 1985]. However, during early analysis, the need for lengthy formal statements is mostly quite limited.

With this in mind, we proceed with our social example. The class invariant clause of class *CITIZEN*, which expresses consistency constraints for the whole class as an abstraction, contains three statements. They must always be true both before a visible feature is called by a client and after feature execution, just before returning to the client.

The first invariant statement says that if you are a citizen, you must be either single or else married to somebody who is also married to you (the @ symbol in figure 3.12 stands for *current object*, cf. figure 3.13). The second statement simply says a citizen has always exactly two parents (not necessarily alive, but that does not alter the fact). The *SET* class is typically a reused library class with well-known semantics and a feature *count* returning the current number of elements.

The third statement is a trifle more complicated. It uses the familiar quantification symbols from predicate logic, "for all" and "there exists" (see figure 3.13), to assert that if you are a citizen with children, each one of them must have you as one of their parents.

The interpretation is as follows. For each child c which is a member of the list of children of this citizen, the statement inside parentheses holds. This statement, in turn, says that there is a parent p among the members of the list of parents to c, such that p is the current object (this citizen).

3.10 GRAPHICAL AND TEXTUAL SPECIFICATION

The graphical class interfaces are not to be viewed as yet another set of modeling charts to be filled in slightly differently. While the untyped charts are mainly used in the very early phases in communication with people from the problem domain (where a certain amount of manual handling can often be an advantage), the graphical forms clearly need case tool support. Some people, being more used to plain text specifications as in figures 3.10 and 3.11, might find the symbols used in figure 3.12 somewhat confusing at first.

However, the symbols are really just abbreviations of their textual counterparts, and the result is a much more compact specification. The graphical specification elements have been designed to be simple also to draw by hand for whiteboard engineering sessions and when no case tool is available. When used for sketching, the rounded boxes are probably not drawn and the different sections written as indented blocks delimited by the class name and textual labels like **inherit** and **invariant**.

Once a reader has become familiar with the graphical elements, this form can be read much faster. Care has been taken to only introduce graphical symbols where they really serve a good purpose, and to keep them as simple as possible.

The use of ? and ! for pre- and postconditions, respectively, may require some explanation. Obviously, when new symbols are introduced it will never be possible to please everyone, since the associations they trigger depend too much on general background and personal taste. However, the most important point is that they are simple and unambiguous enough to feel natural after some time of usage.

One may object that the interrogative/imperative meaning of the two symbols could just as well have been used to specify whether a feature is a query or a command. This may be true, but since types of results and arguments are specified using the familiar colon separator which can hardly be misunderstood, the reader will quickly learn that the framed symbols signal assertions and not feature signatures. What is then important in the long run, is that it should not be possible to confuse the assertion symbols with each other.[2]

The graphical assertion symbols should be read as follows. Before an operation is executed it is checked against the software contract:

$\boxed{?}$ *cond* $\quad --$"Does the client fulfill his part of the deal?"

$\boxed{!}$ *cond* $\quad --$"If so, the following condition is guaranteed!"

With this interpretation in mind, there should be no risk of confusion. (Using the interrogation metaphor is reminiscent of Hoare's CSP language [Hoare 1978], where the same characters signify input and output.)[3]

This concludes the general description of how to write formal class interface specifications in BON. Before we proceed to discuss system scalability, we will spend the next sections on a more detailed description of the language used for specifying software contracts. Readers who find the semantic specification aspects of modeling boring may proceed directly to section 3.14.

3.11 THE BON ASSERTION LANGUAGE

Assertions in BON are statements about properties of objects. Externally, such properties show up as system behavior, but viewed from the inside of an object, properties of other objects can only manifest themselves through return values from queries to the objects. Since an assertion must have a truth value, only queries that return objects of type *BOOLEAN* may be used directly as assertions.

However, non-boolean query results are still useful in two ways: as targets of new queries, or as input arguments to queries on other objects. As long as the last query returns a *BOOLEAN*, any type of object may be part of such query expressions. This enables system properties to be captured indirectly by the successive combination of query results from individual objects.

---

[2] This was a problem with older versions of the BON notation, and readers who have seen earlier examples [Nerson 1991, Nerson 1992b, Nerson 1992a] may note quite a few improvements and general simplifications of the graphical class interfaces in this book.

[3] The main source of inspiration, however, was some correspondence between the French novelist Victor Hugo and his publisher, said to be the shortest in history. Hugo, who was away, wrote a letter inquiring about how his latest book *Les Misérables* had been received by the public. When the publisher opened the envelope, he found a single question mark written across the page. Since the book had been a great success, the reply was equally economic—a single exclamation point.

A number of specification elements are available for use in pre- and postconditions and class invariants to express semantic properties of class behavior. We will now return to figure 3.13 where the complete list is found, and look at each group of related elements in order.

State changes

The first group in this table contains two special symbols that can only occur in postconditions of command features. The **delta** symbol indicates that execution of the command may lead to a state change affecting the feature *name*. This means that the next time *name* is invoked, it may return another value than it would, had it been called just before the current command was executed.

Name is thus assumed to be a function returning a value representing an interesting state for the object that has the feature. Whether it actually corresponds to a state variable or not is left to implementation, so the modified state may very well be indirect through changes to several concealed state variables.

The **old** symbol refers to the value of *expr* just before calling the command (**old** captures the whole system state as it was when the call was made). Using **old** makes it possible to specify how the values returned by functions may change as a result of executing a command. Most often **old** is used to quantify changes in abstract attributes. For example, *count* = **old** *count* + 1 expresses that *count* was increased by one.

Basic object expressions

The second group contains symbols referring to the *current result* to be returned by a query, the *current object*, and the special value for *void reference*. The last two are central concepts of the object-oriented execution model. Any assertion starts by querying the current object, or one or more possible input argument objects in the case of pre- and postconditions. We also frequently need to express whether an object is attached to a reference or not. The *Result* symbol is needed to express postconditions in queries.

Since an unqualified query implicitly refers to the current object, no special symbol is needed for such a call, but it is needed to supply the current object as input argument to a query on some other object.

Constant values of basic types, such as 17, 3.14, **false**, 'C', and "Fahrenheit 451", are also directly available. Each value represents an immutable object accessible by a function whose name is precisely the value itself (expressed by the notation above). So even if a constant occurs in several places, it is always attached to the same object; there are no copies of basic values. (We may think of the basic value functions as inherited from a top-level class *ANY*.)

We have chosen *INTEGER, REAL, BOOLEAN, CHARACTER,* and *STRING* as default basic value types. This set may be changed depending on implementation language, and BON value types need not be represented as such. For efficiency, the most basic string type is nearly always implemented as a reference type, and defined by a special system class.

Numeric expressions

Objects of numeric type may be combined by the usual numeric operators, which are in the third table segment. These (as well as the relational and boolean operators in the following segments) are prefix and infix operators for ease of expression, but using them is really no different from any query invocation. For example,

a + 5 * b

should be thought of as

a.plus (5.times (b))

Adopting this view makes the object-oriented model extremely simple, since almost everything can be expressed as feature invocation in the end. (The implications of this are discussed further in the chapter on dynamic modeling.)

Relational expressions

The fourth table segment contains the standard relational operators. The results of two queries may be combined using the = or ≠ operator to express that the corresponding objects are, or are not, identical.[4] If the return types of the queries have a common ancestor defining an order relation, the results may also be combined using the <, ≤, >, ≥ operators.

Basic boolean expressions

In the second last table segment, we find the standard logical operators for building boolean expressions. As we have explained earlier, implication is semi-strict, meaning that the implied part (the consequent) in $P \rightarrow Q$ will only be evaluated if P (the antecedent) is true. If P is false, the result of the implication is considered false regardless of Q. This is important for dealing with partial functions.

---

[4] Since objects may have reference type or value type, the precise semantics of the equality and non-equality operators is allowed to depend on the target language.

We have chosen the symbols $\rightarrow$ and $\leftrightarrow$ for logical implication and equivalence, respectively, rather than $\Rightarrow$ and $\Leftrightarrow$. There are two main reasons for this. First, in order to use only standard characters for portability, textual BON requires multi-character operators. Combining => and <=> with the relational operators <=, >=, =, /= in the same boolean expressions makes the result very hard to read. Choosing single arrows avoids this confusion.

Second, in formal logic, the single arrow forms are more commonly used as boolean connectives when building a single proposition, while the double arrows are used when proving theorems from chains of propositions.

This leaves the last table segment containing the basic elements of first-order predicate logic used in BON to reason about sets of objects.

3.12 THE BON PREDICATE LOGIC

Basic boolean expressions are easy to translate into efficient code, so assertions built from them can be made optionally executable for testing purposes. Contract violations may then trigger exception handlers, which may be used for precise error reporting and recovery. However, the semantics that can be conveyed with only basic boolean expressions is limited.

For lower-level implementation details, it goes a surprisingly long way and may raise the level of correctness and understandability of a system significantly. Replacing so-called defensive programming by clearly defined responsibilities and a large number of executable assertions is perhaps the most generally efficient way available today for reducing the cost of test and error repair. We will discuss this issue in more detail in section 8.6.

But for analysis and design we need to go a step further. Whether it will ever be possible to find a purely formal method to be applied by the average software engineer to mainstream systems development projects remains to be seen. Instead, we are trying to find a reasonable balance between simplicity and power of expression. This is no easy task, since success depends very much on what turns out to be useful in practice.

The possibility to use queries on other objects is crucial, since this is what enables the recursive specification necessary for large systems. It also permits dynamic extension of the specification language to support various application areas. Classes (often generic) expressing fundamental semantic properties about a problem domain then act as new specification elements.

The basic specification notation may of course also be extended, and more experience from use in real systems will guide the future direction of the BON assertion language. So far, we have taken a conservative approach and only added the predicate logic extensions described in this section. However, predicate logic can be used to form boolean expressions involving properties of object groups ranging over sets, which is significantly more than is possible with only propositional logic.

Set operations

The sets used in assertions are usually standard library container classes, such as *SET*, *SEQUENCE*, *TABLE*, and *STACK*. We assume they all contain a boolean query returning whether a given object is an element in the set or not. This operation and its inverse are defined by the infix symbols ∈ and ∉ (pronounced "is in" and "is not in") as seen in figure 3.13. (Although a client is only allowed to remove the top element from a *STACK* container, the query *elem* ∈ *my_stack* is still supposed to return **true** if *elem* is one of the hidden elements.)

Besides querying objects to obtain references to sets, there is also a way to construct new sets by direct enumeration of elements enclosed in braces. The ".." operator may be used to specify intervals for the two basic types *INTEGER* and *CHARACTER*. For example,

$i \in \{2, 5, 8..13\}$
$char \in \{'a'..'z'\}$
$primary\_color \in \{"red", "green", "blue"\}$
$nephew \in \{huey, dewey, louie\}$

assert that the object referenced by *i* is one of the integers 2, 5, 8, 9, 10, 11, 12, 13; that *char* refers to a lower case character; that *primary_color* is attached to one of the string constants "red", "green", or "blue"; and that *nephew* refers to one of the objects *huey*, *dewey*, or *louie*.

Quantifiers

Using quantifiers and groups of variables, each ranging over a set of objects, we may express properties that must hold for the object groups referred to by the variables. There are two types of quantified statements: universal and existential.

- *Universal* quantification asserts that *every* combination of the quantified variables satisfying the conditions of a range expression will also satisfy a given proposition.

- *Existential* quantification asserts that *at least one* combination of the quantified variables satisfying the conditions of a range expression will also satisfy a given proposition.

The initial quantifier ∀ or ∃ (pronounced "for all" and "there exists") tells which type of quantification we are dealing with. A general quantified statement has the following abstract syntax (extracted from the grammar in appendix A):

> Quantification ≢ Quantifier Range_expression [Restriction] Proposition

The quantifier is followed by a range expression which selects an initial set of objects (or set of object groups, if there is more than one formal variable present). Next an optional restriction follows, which may be used to select a subset of the initial set, and finally comes the proposition. If the quantifier is ∀, the quantification states that the proposition is true for all elements of the resulting set. If the quantifier is ∃, it means instead that the proposition is true for at least one of the elements.

Quantified variables

There are two types of specification elements that can be used in a range expression: member ranges and type ranges. A type range states that each variable in a list of formal variables must be of a given type, while a member range states that the variables must all belong to a given set of objects. Below are some examples:

> ∀ v: VEHICLE   [Restriction] Proposition
> ∀ c ∈ children   [Restriction] Proposition
> ∃ x, y: REAL   [Restriction] Proposition

The first ranges over all objects of type *VEHICLE*, the second over all children in a set, and the third over all pairs of type *REAL*. The expression *children* (a query on the current object) is assumed to return a container type whose semantics defines the ∈ operator for the corresponding data structure.

Notice that the elements of the set denoted by a range expression are a combination of one object for each of the variables specified. Thus, if the formal variables are *v1*, *v2*, *v3* ranging over the corresponding sets *R1*, *R2*, *R3*, the proposition will apply to tuples in the cartesian product set *R1* × *R2* × *R3*.

Several range specifications may be combined in a range expression separated by a semicolon, and the two types above may be combined. For example,

> ∃ c ∈ children; b ∈ baby_sitters [Restriction] Proposition
> ∀ b: BOSS; o ∈ clerks   [Restriction] Proposition

talks about the existence of a combination of one child and one baby sitter, and all combinations of one *BOSS* object and one object from the set *clerks*.

Finally, if the range part is omitted for a variable list, this is interpreted as an abbreviation for type *ANY*. Thus, the first two and the last two of the following assertions are equivalent:

$\forall\, x, y$ [Restriction] Proposition
$\forall\, x, y\colon ANY$ [Restriction] Proposition
$\forall\, a, r\colon REAL$ [Restriction] Proposition
$\forall\, a; r\colon REAL$ [Restriction] Proposition
$\forall\, a\colon ANY; r\colon REAL$ [Restriction] Proposition

Propositions

The proposition clause consists of the symbol • (pronounced "it holds") followed by a boolean expression. It provides the condition that must be true for all of the selected elements, or for at least one, depending on the quantifier.

In the invariant of a class representing a table of *ELEM* objects which are inserted and retrieved by a key value of type *KEY*, the following are possible (equivalent) assertions:

$$\forall\, e \in @ \;\bullet\; (\exists\, k\colon KEY \bullet item\,(k) = e)$$
$$\forall\, e\colon ELEM \;\bullet\; e \in @ \;\rightarrow\; (\exists\, k\colon KEY \bullet item\,(k) = e)$$

They both state that each element in the table must have a key associated with it. (The @ symbol signifying current object is used here to refer to the set represented by the container class itself.)

The alert reader will have noted that the $\in$ symbol has been used in two slightly different ways. In the propositional part, $\in$ simply means the infix form of the "is in" query that must be defined for any container type participating in BON assertions. Since the query returns a boolean result, it may be used like any other boolean expression to build successively more complex propositions.

However, the notational elements of the primary range selection (just after the quantifiers $\forall$ and $\exists$) are not boolean expressions. Therefore, in this context the symbol $\in$ has a different meaning and is instead pronounced "in" (the corresponding type range symbol ":" is pronounced "of type"). This simplifies a large number of standard assertions considerably. Instead of being forced to write

$$\forall\, p\colon T \;\bullet\; p \in S \rightarrow P$$

where the declaration of T is superfluous (since it is already implicit in the type of p) we may simply write

$$\forall\, p \in S \;\bullet\; P$$

By analogy with the above, we also allow the range symbol ":" to be used as a boolean operator in the propositional part (then pronounced "is of type") to express whether an object is of a given type or not. Thus $a\colon T$ will return **true** if the (dynamic) type of a is T and **false** if not.

This makes it possible to specify different things about objects returned by queries depending on the dynamic type of the result, which is often necessary when reasoning about polymorphic structures. For example, if the class *NIGHT_CLUB* keeps its guest record as a *SET* [*PERSON*], but has different admission rules for objects of type *MAN* and *WOMAN*, this can be captured by the class invariant:

$$\forall \; g \in guests \; \bullet$$
$$g : FEMALE \; \rightarrow \; g.age \geq 20;$$
$$g : MALE \; \rightarrow \; g.age \geq 25$$

Following the general object-oriented rule to search for dynamic binding, we could instead have introduced a deferred feature *is_old_enough_for_night_clubs* in a common ancestor class *PERSON*, and let *MAN* and *WOMAN* provide their own versions. Then the simpler invariant

$$\forall \; g \in guests \; \bullet \; g.is\_old\_enough\_for\_night\_clubs$$

would suffice. However, this is generally not a good idea when the distributed concept (as in this case, night club age limit) has nothing to do with the basic abstractions, but instead reflects specific client usage, that is a possible *supplier role*.

Range restriction

The optional restriction clause consists of the symbol | (pronounced "such that") followed by a boolean expression. It reduces the initial set of object tuples by a subselection according to a boolean condition on the formal variables. Strictly, the restriction clause is not necessary, since each assertion

Quantifier Primary_range | C • P

can be rewritten as

Quantifier Primary_range • C → P

However, we still think it is important to add a restriction construct, because it simplifies many assertions and encourages a more natural way of thinking about the propositions. Consider the assertions in figure 3.14. All six are logically equivalent statements, but the syntactic groupings express quite different lines of thought, which has a profound effect on human readability.

In the context of animals being transported together, the first two assertions are statements about lions, the next two about hungry lions, and the last two about lion–zebra combinations. Depending on where the focus of interest lies, we may prefer one of these views to the others.

Alternative views on joint transportation

$\forall\, a, b \in animal\_transport$ •
  $a: LION \rightarrow ((a.hungry$ **and** $b: ZEBRA) \rightarrow a.eats\,(b))$
 $\forall\, a, b \in animal\_transport\;\mid\; a: LION$ •
  $(a.hungry$ **and** $b: ZEBRA) \rightarrow a.eats\,(b)$

$\forall\, a, b \in animal\_transport$ •
  $(a: LION$ **and** $a.hungry) \rightarrow (b: ZEBRA \rightarrow a.eats\,(b))$
 $\forall\, a, b \in animal\_transport\;\mid\; a: LION$ **and** $a.hungry$ •
  $b: ZEBRA \rightarrow a.eats\,(b)$

$\forall\, a, b \in animal\_transport$ •
  $(a: LION$ **and** $b: ZEBRA) \rightarrow (a.hungry \rightarrow a.eats\,(b))$
 $\forall\, a, b \in animal\_transport\;\mid\; a: LION$ **and** $b: ZEBRA$ •
  $a.hungry \rightarrow a.eats\,(b)$

Figure 3.14 Equivalent assertions

In each of the three cases above, the form using a restriction clause is more readable. There are two main reasons for this. First, it requires less parentheses and avoids nested implications, which are always hard to understand. Second, as soon as the restriction clause has been read, the proposition can be interpreted in the new local context. This permits us to deal with one thing at a time as opposed to unrestricted assertions, which must be understood as a whole.

3.13 ASSERTIONS AND PARTIAL FUNCTIONS

In the specification examples so far, we have implicitly assumed that all queries used in logical expressions always return well-defined values. However, this is not automatically the case, since we often need queries that are partial functions to return interesting system states. Such queries return meaningful values only when the corresponding preconditions are true.

Therefore, we must ensure that no precondition violation can occur when queries are evaluated as part of an assertion. (We are not talking about imperative execution here, only the logical evaluation of query expressions needed to establish the meaning of an assertion.) Any precondition violation would yield an undefined query result, making the assertion lose its truth value for the corresponding object values.

For example, one might find the following assertion natural for expressing the existence of at least one pair of matching elements with the same integer index in two arrays A and B:

$$\exists\, i\colon INTEGER \;\bullet\; A.item\,(i) = B.item\,(i)$$

However, since the quantification is only bound to integers in general, the assertion has no meaning for indexes that fall outside the range of either A or B. So we have to use a more restricted quantification ensuring that the values we talk about are within the range of both data structures:

$$\exists\, i\colon INTEGER \;\mid\; A.has\_index\,(i)\; \textbf{and}\; B.has\_index\,(i)\;\bullet$$
$$A.item\,(i) = B.item\,(i)$$

The reason why implication is defined as semi-strict in BON is the possibility to use the operator as a kind of "if-statement" in a proposition. For example,

$$\forall\, p\colon PERSON \;\bullet\; p \neq Void \rightarrow p.name \neq Void$$

states that whenever a *PERSON* object is attached to p, that person must have a name. With the usual definition of $P \rightarrow Q$, the above assertion would not be well defined. For similar reasons (as already explained in 3.8), the connectives **and** and **or** are also semi-strict in BON, permitting assertions like:

$p \neq Void$ **and** $p.name \neq Void$
$p = Void$ **or** $p.name \neq Void$

There are a number of possible approaches for dealing with non-denoting terms that may appear as a result of partial function evaluation [Farmer 1990, Parnas 1993], but they all introduce other complexities that have to be dealt with instead. A discussion of these falls beyond the scope of this book. For an introduction to the logic of programming and the semantics of programming languages see [Hehner 1984, Meyer 1990a].

Although including the restrictions needed to guard against precondition violations generally leads to longer assertions than what is possible with some of the alternative semantic models, this is less of a problem in an object-oriented environment.

First, more high-level features will generally be available to express the restrictions more compactly. In a traditional language environment, the second last assertion (transcribed into object notation) would more likely look like:

$$\exists\, i\colon INTEGER \;\mid\; A.min \leq i\; \textbf{and}\; i \leq A.max\; \textbf{and}\; B.min \leq i\; \textbf{and}\; i \leq B.max\;\bullet$$
$$A.item\,(i) = B.item\,(i)$$

Second, a formal notation no matter how cleverly designed can only be used in practice to specify a small subset of all interesting system properties. The real leverage will come from successively extending the specification language with elements in the form of queries to problem domain classes. Only the object-oriented extensibility provides enough flexibility to express exactly what we want; formal languages with comparable expressive power will be too complex for routine use in the software industry.

3.14 SCALABLE SYSTEM DESCRIPTION

We now have a means of specifying the basic components in our system—the classes—which captures both the syntax and semantics of the services they provide. The rest of this chapter shows how the class components can be grouped recursively into higher-level structures using clustering.

The possibility to compress and expand the graphical descriptive elements of BON addresses the scaling and partitioning problems discussed earlier, which always arise when large system architectures are modeled graphically. By selecting a mixture of compressed and expanded forms, many different views can be obtained at various levels of detail.

Levels of description

There are three basic levels of static description in BON:

- system level

- cluster level

- class level

The system level shows a set of clusters. The cluster level shows a set of classes and possibly other clusters. Finally, the class level shows class interfaces with their operations and contracts. The system and cluster levels may each comprise several levels of nesting. For example, a large system may first be partitioned into a number of subsystems (which will be clusters) and each subsystem may again have subsystems (more clusters). As long as we only show clusters we are still at the system level. When class headers start to appear we are at the cluster level, and this continues until we show class interfaces. At that point we have reached the class level.

Nothing prevents us from mixing the levels of detail in a view by showing, say, a cluster with only a few class headers expanded into class interfaces. In that case, the description is said to be at the lowest level contained in the view.

3.15 CLASS HEADERS

Building a static diagram often begins with the identification of a number of classes and some relations between them, so class headers play an important role in BON.

Graphical representation

A class header is represented graphically by an ellipse. The class name is an alphanumeric string with possible underscores, whose first character is alphabetic. The name, with possible annotations, is centered inside the ellipse (upper case, bold italic font recommended).

The class header annotations translate to top annotations and bottom annotations. Top annotations appear above the class name and bottom annotations below the name inside the ellipse. The complete set of header annotations was shown in figure 3.5. Figure 3.15 contains a set of annotated class headers illustrating various uses and combinations of the class header annotations (or just *header annotations* for short).

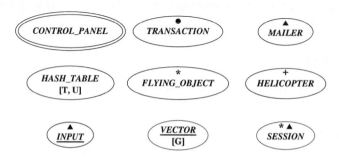

Figure 3.15   Examples of annotated class headers

Compression of classes

A class header is the compressed form of a class interface.

3.16 CLUSTERS

A cluster represents a group of related classes (and possibly other clusters) according to a selected point of view. Classes may be grouped differently depending on the particular characteristics one wants to highlight. Possible criteria are:

- subsystem functionality
- user categories
- application-domain-dependent factors
- reuse versus new development
- hardware or software platforms

- license restrictions versus public domain
- abstraction level
- cohesion grouping or factorization

A class could for example be at the same time a user interface class, a reused class, and a class supporting the X window platform. Such a class would then qualify for membership in at least three different clusters. However, to avoid ambiguity and confusion we need to lay down some rules for clustering.

System views

By a *system view* we mean a partitioning of the classes of a system into a set of clusters, such that each class belongs to exactly one cluster. This does not mean we have to use only one type of classification criteria for the clustering; some clusters may represent subsystems, others general functionality, and still others just groups of classes with the same ancestor. But for each individual class, one of the possible groupings must be selected.

There may be several system views defined for a given system, but in practice only one is used during analysis and design. Since the cluster structure will evolve gradually as system development progresses, it usually becomes too complicated to support several views simultaneously. However, if (as should always be our goal) part of the classes developed in a software project are later refined and merged with a general class library, their classification will probably be quite different in that context.

Nested clusters

Besides classes, clusters may also contain other clusters. This makes it possible to collect clusters which are only used locally, and group them with their client classes. It also gives a facility for nesting subsystems of a large system to any desired depth. In fact, very large systems will often have several layers of clusters representing subsystems before any classes appear.

The cluster nesting is part of the system view. This means that not only different partitioning of the same set of classes, but also different nesting of the same set of clusters, will lead to different views. As modeling proceeds, patterns are often detected that will cause the developers to restructure sets of existing classes in order to better understand their roles.

Notice that the system (defined by a set of classes and its root class) and the system view (defined by grouping the classes into possibly nested clusters) are independent concepts. Changing the clustering does not affect the system, only how we view it, while changing a class leads to a new system but does not affect the clustering structure.

Graphical representation

A cluster is drawn as a box with rounded corners representing the cluster body with the name in a separate rounded box (the cluster tag). The tag is positioned just outside the cluster body touching its borderline. Cluster names follow the class name convention: alphanumeric strings with possible underscores, starting with an alphabetic character. Underlining the name signifies a reused cluster, in analogy with the class header notation. The name is centered inside the tag, and upper case roman font is recommended to make the label differ from class names. A cluster tag may appear anywhere along the cluster borderline to facilitate the presentation of complicated diagrams. An example of a data structure cluster with two other clusters nested inside (one reused and one newly developed) is shown in figure 3.16.

The line style of clusters must be different from the one chosen for classes. The recommended practice is to use continuous borderlines for class interfaces and class headers and dashed borderlines for cluster bodies and cluster tags. BON was designed with case tool support in mind, and recommendations like the one above are mainly directed to implementors of software generating BON graphical diagrams. When used on paper or whiteboard, the fact that it is much easier to draw continuous lines by hand may take precedence.

Layered clustering—not hierarchical development

Since every class belongs to exactly one cluster in a system view, the resulting cluster structure is a hierarchy. However, this does not mean that BON favors top-down hierarchical development in any way. On the contrary, such an approach to object-oriented analysis and design suffers from many of the worst disadvantages of the traditional methods. It forces the developer to make premature decisions with far-reaching consequences very early in the project, when problem understanding is still vague and many of the central abstractions have not yet crystallized.

Instead, the overwhelming initial complexity may be gradually reduced by successively modeling parts of the system that we do understand (and there are nearly always such parts). When good abstractions have been found for these areas, what is left will be somewhat easier to grasp thus allowing for new patterns to be recognized and abstracted. Of course, we should not postpone the hard parts, since this may give a false sense of rapid progress and later lead to very unpleasant surprises. The general idea is to divide and conquer. We will still discover errors at times and have to redo things, but the effects will usually be more local and less catastrophic.

When more and more of the abstractions (classes) are in place, we may gradually *discover* that some of them are only used in certain subparts of the

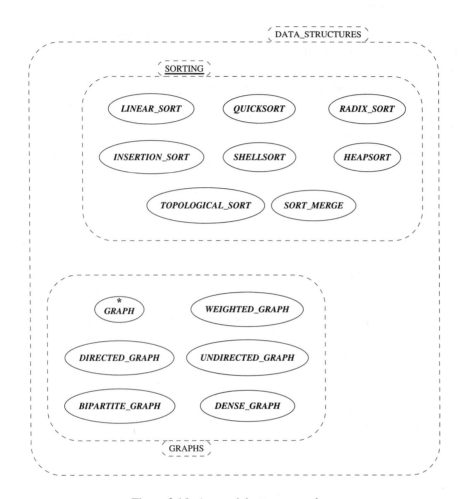

Figure 3.16   A nested data structure cluster

system and reflect this by nested clustering. However, the potential reusability of the classes of inner clusters is not affected by such a hierarchy. If we later find more global use for them, we simply move the corresponding clusters out of their local clusters. The cluster structure just serves to document how the classes are *used* in this system, not how they could be reused in other systems.

Local naming

Clusters may correspond to different conceptual domains, so it is quite natural that two classes in different clusters could have the same name but model entirely different concepts.

For example, in an administrative system for a vocational school the class *BOARD* could appear in the *SCHOOL_ADMINISTRATION* cluster and in the *MATERIALS* cluster used in the carpentry classes. There is really no reason to prohibit such name clashes during analysis and design, since they are easily resolved by the context in which they appear.

Similarly, clusters which are nested inside different clusters may also be permitted to have the same name. When the design is eventually turned into implementation, the name clashes must be resolved through renaming or qualification schemes in the object-oriented languages used, but this is merely a syntactic problem.

To maintain a clear typographical difference between type names and role names (type usage), we will consistently use upper case for class names and lower case for class features in this book. A set of recommended naming rules are discussed in section 8.4.

Compression of clusters

A cluster is compressed into its tag attached to an empty, iconized body. When a cluster icon is expanded (or *opened*), its constituent parts first become visible in compressed form, thus showing class headers and cluster icons (see figure 3.17). The inner parts may then be opened recursively, until we reach the class interfaces.

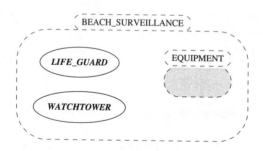

Figure 3.17 An iconized cluster

4 Static relations

This chapter describes the relations between classes and clusters in the static model. Only two kinds of static relations are needed in object-oriented systems, *inheritance* relations and *client* relations. By combining them in various ways and letting the resulting network of classes be guided by well-defined software contracts, almost any type of semantic modeling needed can be achieved. Moreover, we will see how the system scalability can be further refined by extending the compression/expansion facilities to also include relations.

4.1 INHERITANCE RELATIONS

A class may inherit from one class (single inheritance), from several classes (multiple inheritance), or several times from the same class (repeated inheritance). Inheritance is simply defined as the inclusion in a class, called the *child,* of operations and contract elements defined in other classes, its *parents.* A class that is either parent or grandparent (recursively) of a class is called an *ancestor* of the class. Similarly, a class that is either child or grandchild (recursively) of a class is called a *descendant* of the class.

Inheritance may translate differently depending on the object-oriented language used, so the definition is kept very general in BON. A special form of complementary documentation called semantic links may be attached to inheritance relations to show the designer's intent in each case. These are described in a later section.

Graphical representation

An inheritance relation is represented by a single arrow pointing from the child to its parent, called an *inheritance link.* Inheritance links may be broken to avoid crossing other elements, but the recommended practice for case tools is to only use horizontal and vertical directions. A set of inheritance links representing several children of the same class (or several parents of the same class) may be joined to simplify a diagram. In the case of direct repeated inheritance, instead of drawing *n* inheritance links, one may use one link with a marker attached (small lozenge) containing the count.

The diagrams in figure 4.1 illustrate different types of graphical inheritance representation. From left to right and top to bottom it shows: single inheritance using horizontal and vertical links, direct repeated inheritance, multiple inheritance combined with indirect repeated inheritance, and single inheritance with joined links. (Direct repeated inheritance makes sense if the multiply inherited features are separated through renaming.)

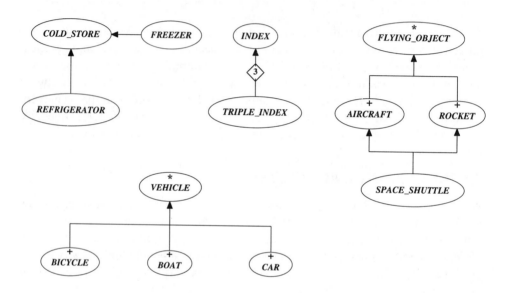

Figure 4.1   Different type of inheritance

Inheritance involving clusters

The inheritance relation can be generalized to apply also to clusters:

1. If *all* elements (classes or clusters) in a cluster *X* inherit (directly or indirectly) from an element *A* outside of *X*, then the cluster *X* is said to inherit from *A*. All direct inheritance links from elements in *X* to *A* can then be compressed into one inheritance link from *X* to *A*.

2. If an element *A* outside a cluster *Y* inherits (directly or indirectly) from *all* elements in *Y*, then *A* is said to inherit from *Y*. All direct inheritance links from *A* to elements in *Y* can then be compressed into one link from *A* to *Y*.

3. An inheritance link between two elements can be compressed into being hidden (not shown in a diagram).

Rules 1 and 2 state that in order for a cluster to be child or parent of another element, *all* elements inside the cluster must have a corresponding relation to this element. (We shall see later that the corresponding rules for client relations only require that *some* enclosed element is involved in the relation. This is not the only possible convention, but it is the one we have found most useful in practice. We will give some more justification for it in the discussion on client relations.) Rule 3 makes further simplification possible by presenting less information.

Notice that we used the word *element* instead of *class* in rules 1 and 2 above to allow for recursive compression. This is essential already for large inheritance structures, but will become even more important for client relations. In fact, recursive compression is the central key to achieving system scalability. Three examples are shown in figure 4.2.

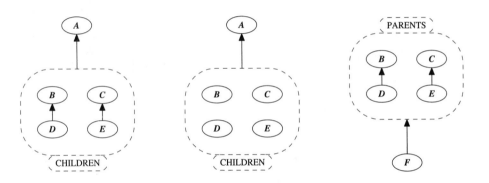

Figure 4.2 Compressed inheritance relations

The leftmost diagram shows a cluster after application of rule 1. We can infer that the classes *B*, *C*, *D*, and *E* all inherit either directly or indirectly from class *A*, but we cannot strictly tell which inheritance is direct. For example, although *B* appears to be a top-level class in the cluster (implying direct inheritance from *A*), it need not be. It could be a child of *E* with the inheritance link hidden through application of rule 3. However, in practice the developer knows enough about the system structure to rule out such esoteric possibilities, and then diagrams containing a large number of inheritance links can often be greatly simplified without losing information (see 5.17).

The reason rules 1 and 2 only talk about replacement of direct inheritance links is that we often want to keep local inheritance visible also after applying one of these compressions, since it conveys additional information. To hide more, we just continue the compression process by applying rule 3 a number of times, as illustrated by the middle diagram in figure 4.2. The rightmost diagram, at last, shows an application of rule 2.

We do not need to define inheritance between two clusters separately. When such a relation exists, it can be obtained by repeated application of rules 1 and 2 as shown in figure 4.3. From the initial view (upper left), we may either apply rule 1 twice to get the upper right diagram, or apply rule 2 three times to get the lower left diagram.

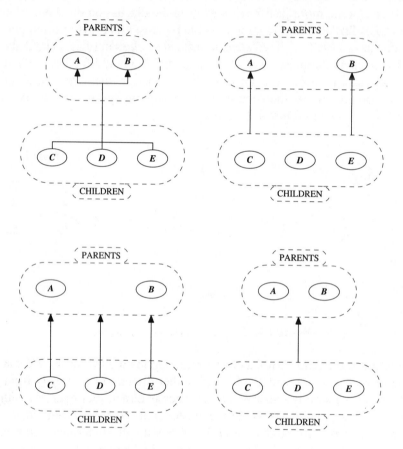

Figure 4.3 Recursive compression

If we choose the first alternative, applying rule 2 once more yields the final result (lower right). Conversely, if we choose the second alternative, applying rule 1 will yield the same result. In practice, a cluster inheriting from a class occurs often, a class inheriting from a cluster is less common, and a cluster inheriting from a cluster is rare.

Compression of inheritance relations

Case tools may employ different strategies for the compression of inheritance relations, as long as they comply with rules 1–3 above. For example, it may be advantageous to hide all inheritance relations to certain groups of classes in order to emphasize some overall aspect of the system. Typical candidates for exclusion are general support classes, but also application classes considered less important in the context studied.

4.2 CLIENT RELATIONS

A client/supplier relationship, or *client relation* for short, between a client class *A* and a supplier class *B* means that *A* uses services supplied by *B*. This leads to a *class dependency* between *A* and *B*, which means that if the *specification* of *B* is changed, *A* may have to be changed too (its specification or implementation or both). However, it also leads to a potential *object dependency* between instances of *A* and *B* (or of descendants of *A* and *B*) when the system is executed. We will return to the distinction between class and object dependencies in section 4.3.

Static relations between classes

It has become popular (and sometimes profitable) in recent years to compile superficial articles and industry reports comparing various methods for object-oriented analysis and design, which result in checkboxes with answers to the questions: "Does notation X support concept Y?" The underlying assumption seems to be that whenever a concept can be identified that may have an influence on system behavior, being able to express that concept in an analysis and design notation increases the power of the method. The BON approach disagrees with this attitude.

Analysis and design is all about abstraction. We want to get away from details that we do not necessarily need to keep track of, and leave them to underlying structuring mechanisms and automatic support. This is why we group objects into classes and classes into inheritance networks. In BON, contrary to many other methods, there is no direct notation for expressing static dependencies between objects—only between classes.

The reason is again reversibility. An object-oriented system is specified as a structured collection of classes with precisely defined interfaces. It is through the classes—and only through them—that object behavior is defined. Therefore, if we make dependencies between individual objects (class instances) part of our high-level static notation, there are two possibilities. Either the object structure can be inferred from the class structure and vice versa (which means the notation is not needed in the first place) or there is no simple mapping, in which case we break the seamlessness of the approach. When we need to emphasize structural details about individual class instances, this is instead done through assertions in the corresponding class interfaces.

Associations and aggregations

There are three types of client relation: association, shared association, and aggregation. Each relation represents the supplier being used by the client to fulfill a certain *role*. There can be several relations from one client to the same supplier class, whose instances are then used to play multiple roles.

An *association* between a client class and a supplier class means that (at system execution time) some instances of the client class may be attached to one or more instances of the supplier class. A particular instance of the supplier class may take part in many such attachments, thus permitting supplier objects to be shared by different clients.

A *shared association* between a client class and a supplier class is a special case meaning that whenever an instance of the client class is attached to an instance of the supplier class, it will always be to the *same* supplier instance (or one in a fixed set). This permits specific instances to be shared by all client objects of a certain type. BON includes notation to express this type of relationship, as we will see later.

An *aggregation* relation between a client class and a supplier class means that each client instance may be attached to one or more supplier instances which represent "integral parts" of the client instance. The parts may in turn have client relations to other classes, which may be aggregations (subparts) or associations.

Aggregation (whole vs. parts) is an important semantic concept, useful when thinking about the properties of objects in a system—which is why it has a special notation in BON—but not so easy to define exactly. For example, some operations applied to the whole will naturally propagate to its parts. Moving a house will automatically move all the rooms inside. On the other hand, painting a house does not in general mean that each room gets painted. Selling a house may seem to imply that everything inside goes with it, but it is fully possible to sell an apartment building without selling any of the owner apartments contained in it.

Sometimes the internal parts of an object can only be accessed by the object itself and therefore cannot be shared by any other client. In other cases, it may be more practical for the enclosing class to export some of the parts as public operations. Deleting an object usually means that all its aggregated parts will also be deleted, but even in this case there are other possible strategies.

The conclusion is that the modeler must be allowed some freedom in using the aggregation concept, and that its exact semantics will probably vary from one context to another also within the same system. Therefore, we cannot prescribe any particular implementation of aggregation relations compared to ordinary associations. That will depend on the objects involved, the language environment, as well as general efficiency considerations.

However, we can state one absolute rule for aggregations: a particular object can be an integral part of at most *one* other object. For example, an engine can only be part of one vehicle (at a time) but may be referenced by other parties, such as the manufacturer, the owner's service garage, and the vehicle registration authorities.

All types of client relations may be labeled with the names (in the client class) of the features giving rise to the relation. These names should mirror the corresponding role played by the supplier.

Graphical representation

A client relation is represented by a double line extending from the client to the supplier. We call this line a *client link*. Client links may be broken to avoid crossing other elements, but just as for inheritance relations the standard rule is to only use horizontal and vertical directions. (Again, these are recommendations for case tool construction; on whiteboard and paper we do not impose any such restriction.) Association links end with an arrowhead pointing to the supplier, as illustrated by figure 4.4.

Figure 4.4 Association relations

Aggregation links end with an open brace, as in figure 4.5. A client link can be labeled with one or several names, corresponding to class features in the client which cause the relation. In the case of multiple labels, the link represents multiple relations of the same type, one for each name.

The reader may wonder why the particular directions for class relations were chosen in BON. Well, there are also valid arguments for using the reverse conventions. For example, inheritance links pointing from parent to child could indicate feature propagation or extension of functionality, and links from supplier to client could suggest provision of service. However, signaling

Figure 4.5 Aggregation relations

dependency is usually more important: a child depends on its parents and needs to know about them, but not the reverse. Similarly, a client depends on its suppliers and needs to know about them, but not the reverse. In fact, a major point in object-oriented development is that classes should not know beforehand to what extent they will be used as suppliers or parents during their lifetimes.

Bidirectional links

A set of client association links in each direction between two classes may be combined into one double link with an arrowhead at each end, as in figure 4.6.

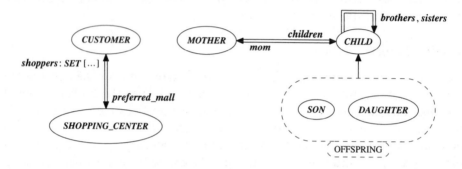

Figure 4.6   Bidirectional association links

In the case of labeled bidirectional links, we need a convention to show which relation each label refers to. The rule is simply to put each label closer to the supplier side. In figure 4.6 *preferred_mall* thus refers to a feature in class *CUSTOMER* of type *SHOPPING_CENTER*, while *shoppers* refers to a feature in *SHOPPING_CENTER* of type *SET* [*CUSTOMER*]. The latter is an example of the use of generic classes in client relation labels, and will be explained later. (Note that only bidirectional links require labels to be put closer to the supplier side in order to remove ambiguity. For the vast majority of links, which are unidirectional, labels may be put anywhere along the link.)

Bidirectional aggregation links might seem like a contradiction in terms: two objects cannot both be part of each other. However, we must recall that client relations are between classes, and it is not impossible for a class *A* to have an integral part of type *B* and class *B* to have an integral part of type *A*, provided that different class *instances* are involved. In fact, such recursive structures often occur in practice. Figure 4.7 shows three examples: the first is the famous Russian doll, and the second illustrates a common type of document, where each section consists of an introduction followed by the main text. The third example in figure 4.7 shows a bidirectional client link where one end is aggregation and

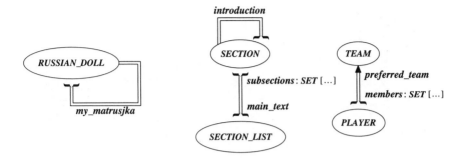

Figure 4.7 Bidirectional aggregation links

the other association. A team has members, but some members may secretly dream of playing in another team.

Multidirectional links

To simplify diagrams with many relations, we allow client links to be joined as shown in figure 4.8. The five airplane parts in the figure could also have been collected in a subcluster with the parts relations compressed into a cluster relation. This is the recommended style when there are many parts.

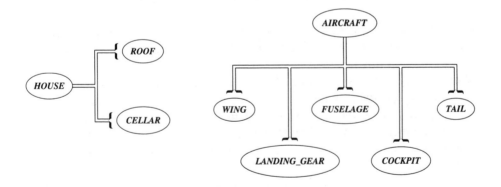

Figure 4.8 Grouped client links

When several clients share the same supplier (figure 4.9), placing a label near a client means that it only corresponds to a relation from that client, while near a supplier means that all the clients are related to the supplier through this name.

Finally, we may also have several clients *and* several suppliers. Then the semantics is as follows: each client has a relationship to each supplier of the type indicated (arrowhead or brace). Figure 4.10 shows four network nodes sharing a

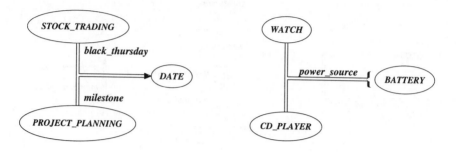

Figure 4.9 Avoiding ambiguities by label placement

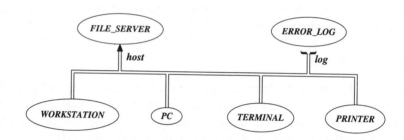

Figure 4.10 Multiple clients and suppliers

file server, each node keeping a private error log. When there are several suppliers, labels are only permitted to be put close to a supplier, since close to a client would be ambiguous.

Joining only suppliers without any clients is not permitted for more than two classes, since a network where all ends of the double lines have an arrow or a brace attached looks too confusing: any interpretation would be *ad hoc*, and difficult to remember. A number of bidirectional links (described in the previous section) can be used instead. Joining only clients without any suppliers obviously does not make sense.

Links involving generic suppliers

Generic classes are special in that they do not correspond to one type each, but to a potential group of types. Each new combination of actual parameters given to a generic class will derive a new type. (This is sometimes called *type instantiation*, but we use the alternative term *type derivation* in this book to avoid confusion with the term *class instantiation*, which means creating objects as instances of classes.)

One characteristic of genericity is that it is generally not possible to conclude the client dependencies of a generic class by simply inspecting its interface (and possibly private features), as can be done with non-generic classes in a typed environment. The information needed is distributed among the clients, and the dependencies are therefore deduced by the supporting compiler environment. This calls for some special conventions with respect to the graphical notation.

Before embarking on a description of these conventions, we make it clear that the BON notation does not support all possible uses of genericity. First, recursive propagation of formal parameters from one generic class to another can lead to very complex situations, where full understanding requires inspection of the interfaces proper (and perhaps also the code). Second, a very detailed graphical notation would require the target language to be fixed.

However, there are a few typical cases where the use of genericity can be very helpful already during analysis and early design—most of them involving very general data structures—so we want to provide some notational support but still keep things simple. There are two main situations in which generic derivation arises: through a generic supplier class or through a generic parent class. We look first at generic suppliers.

Assume that a geometric figure has a list of points outlining its border. This can be expressed using the notation described so far, as shown in figure 4.11.

Figure 4.11 Indirect client dependency through generic derivation

To highlight that the client relation to class *POINT* (labeled *item*) corresponds to a generic derivation (that is, a declaration of type *item*: *T* inside class *LIST*, rather than *item*: *POINT*), we use the formal generic parameter as a label marker. The marker is in a different font (bold, non-italic in this case) to show that it is not a type but a formal name. The name or parenthesized list of names of the client features whose signatures contain the generic derivation may precede the marker, separated by a colon.

This is shown in figure 4.12, where we have also added a center point to the figure. The label now shows that the type of the feature *item* in class *LIST* is the

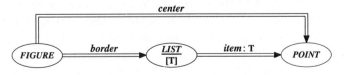

Figure 4.12 Generic label marker

formal parameter *T* generically derived as *POINT* to form the client dependency expressed by this link.

Compacted generic links

However, the generic classes involved in analysis and design are often extensively reused library classes, representing high-level data structures. In such cases, it is generally much more informative to emphasize the indirect relationship between the client class and the data structure elements. Knowing that a figure consists of points is normally more important than knowing if the points are kept as a set or as a sequence. The structural properties can then instead be put as additional information on the client/supplier links, thus playing the role of semantic labels often found in entity–relationship diagrams.

To achieve this, we allow client relations arising from generic derivation to be *compacted*. This means that links to the corresponding generic class are suppressed, and the generic class name appears instead as part of a label on a link connecting the client and the supplier corresponding to a derived generic parameter.

The label of such a compacted link contains the name of the generic class followed by its actual type parameters in square brackets, where the parameter corresponding to the supplier has been replaced by an ellipsis. The name or parenthesized list of names of the corresponding client features may precede the generic class name, separated by a colon. Using this form simplifies the previous diagram (figure 4.13).

Figure 4.13 Compacted generic relation

When several client classes use the same generic supplier or there is more than one generic parameter, the benefits of the compacted forms become even more apparent. In figure 4.14, the upper part shows the full client dependencies resulting from two derivations each of the generic classes *LIST* and *TABLE*, while the corresponding compacted forms are in the lower part.

The *TABLE* class is an example of a very general class with more than one generic parameter, used to store various elements for later retrieval through a specified key of some type. Only classes that inherit from class *KEY* may be used at the second generic parameter position in a *TABLE* derivation (shown by the → *KEY* suffix), which guarantees the existence of an operation for constructing a unique key code.

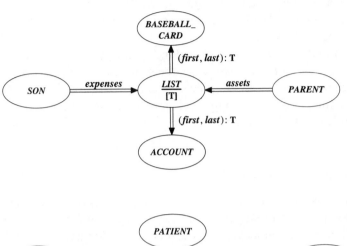

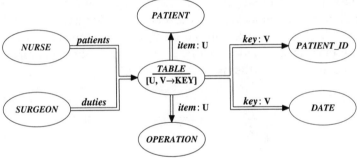

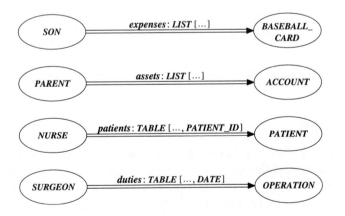

Figure 4.14   Multiple generic derivation

We see that besides being much simpler to read, the compacted relations also remove the ambiguity regarding who is really related to what list or table elements. Even if labels like *expenses* and *patients* give hints as to what they refer to, we cannot be sure.

In contrast to the semantic labels used in ER modeling, whose meaning suffers from the vagueness of natural language, the semantics of the generic classes used in client relation labels can be precisely specified through formal assertions. Carefully defining a set of high-level generic classes may thus serve as an extension of the BON notation to tailor it to the needs of different application areas.

Links involving generic parents

Besides the direct derivation of a generic supplier class, there is also the case when a class inherits from a generic parent, and thus creates a client dependency to the derived type parameters. This can be expressed as in figure 4.15, where we again use a generic marker in the label, this time preceded by an arrow to indicate the inheritance relation involved. The corresponding compacted form is shown in the lower part of the figure.

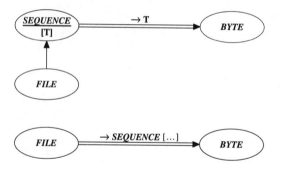

Figure 4.15   Generic client relation through inheritance

Role multiplicity

There can be many client relations between the same two classes *A* and *B*. So far, we have expressed this by attaching several labels to the same graphical link from *A* to *B*. In some cases (though not very often), one might want to emphasize the number of links rather than the names. As an alternative to labeling, it is therefore possible to use a marker (small lozenge, similar to the one used for direct repeated inheritance) containing the number of links. Multiplicity markers may also be attached to bidirectional client relations. The lozenge is then split in two parts to indicate the direction corresponding to each number. This is shown in figure 4.16, which expresses the following:

- Arriving aliens hold *two* attachments to landing document.

- An apartment contains *three* attachments to room.

- A house has one architect and each architect has three house attachments.

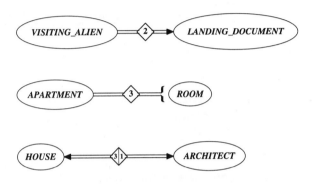

Figure 4.16 Multiplicity markers

Before proceeding, we want to make it completely clear that the above numerical markers are *not* there to express multiplicity in the traditional data modeling sense. There is a fundamental difference here: multiplicity notation in data modeling is about the number of class *instances* (often called *object instances* in traditional contexts), while BON's multiplicity markers refer to the number of different *roles* under which a certain class is used by another class (note the word *attachment* in the list above explaining figure 4.16).

Since one normally gets a much clearer picture by naming the roles instead of just counting them, multiplicity markers are used very sparingly with BON. Usually, the previous diagram would be something along the lines of figure 4.17.

However, the multiplicity included in most other object-oriented analysis and design notations simply mirrors the instance multiplicity from data modeling. The reasons for emphasizing this information are historical: the multiplicity affects the way database records are designed in traditional environments.

But with an object-oriented approach this is no longer a problem, since it handles instance multiplicity as a duck takes to water. The designer whose object-oriented systems must be extensively restructured because we must now handle two objects of a certain class instead of just one should not be trusted with industrial projects. Therefore, in our opinion, a constraint on the number of instances of a certain class (of the type *many-to-one, one-to-one,* etc.) is

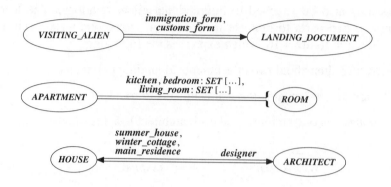

Figure 4.17   Naming, rather than enumerating, roles

irrelevant information at the system level, and should instead be placed where it belongs: in the class interface specifications as part of the software contract.

Instance multiplicity

Whether we use multiplicity markers or labels in BON, they only express *potential* associations and aggregations. For example, in figure 4.16 an instance of class *VISITING_ALIEN* may (at different times during system execution) be associated with zero, one, or two instances of class *LANDING_DOCUMENT*. What the diagram really means is that class *VISITING_ALIEN* contains exactly two *entities* of type *LANDING_DOCUMENT*, but how and when these entities will be bound to objects of the corresponding type is decided dynamically.

Perhaps surprisingly, this also applies to aggregations. The *APARTMENT* objects of figure 4.17 are probably thought of as containing their *ROOM* objects directly when created, but this is not a general property of abstractions modeling part-of relations. Clearly, an electronic document may be regarded as consisting of its pages, sections, and paragraphs at any point in time, even if this structure is allowed to change dynamically. The Russian doll in figure 4.7 may also be considered an aggregation. Each doll has another smaller doll as a potential subpart, but at some point we must find an empty doll. The same holds for any recursive parts explosion: at least some of the classes used in the modeling must describe objects that sometimes have subparts and sometimes not.

This shows that aggregation cannot be identified with what is known as value types or expanded types in object-oriented languages, that is types whose objects are fully expanded already when system execution starts. Such types are useful for performance reasons (or in some cases, like heavy numerical processing, even necessary), but they are issues of implementation, not of high-level modeling.

Instance sharing

So, in accordance with the above reasoning, the notation for multiplicity only addresses the number of entities introduced in the client class. Contrary to dynamic instance multiplicity, these entities are important, because they mirror a conscious choice of *roles* assigned to classes in various contexts, which will eventually be reflected in the implementation to be debugged and maintained. More detailed constraints on individual instances may be specified in the contracts of the corresponding classes.

There is, however, one special aspect of instance association which merits special treatment, and that is *object sharing*. Very often groups of related objects share a common supplier, which provides a certain service to the group. Standard examples are window objects in a graphical user interface system all sharing the same mouse object, or a set of diskless workstations sharing a common file server.

By placing a special *sharing* marker (small circle) on a client link, the BON user may specify that when a certain entity in a class is attached to an instance of the supplier class, it will always be to *the same instance*. Figure 4.18 shows a *HOCKEY_PLAYER* class whose instances all share the same instance of the class *PUCK*. (Allowing each player to instantiate a private puck might lead to some interesting surrealistic matches, but there would clearly be a consensus problem regarding the final result.)

Figure 4.18 Necessary sharing of one instance

All instances of a client class may also share a *fixed number* of supplier instances. This may occur in two ways. First, there may be several shared static relations from one class to another. All instances of class *STUDENT* may, for example, share one instance of class *ROOM* through a static link labeled *kitchen*, and at the same time share another *ROOM* instance labeled *bath_room*.

Second, instead of being attached to the exact same instance, each static link may be attached to any of a fixed number of instances. The *STUDENT* instances may, for example, have access to one of three instances of class *TENNIS_TRAINER* through a static link labeled *current_trainer*, but be attached to at most one at a time. This is expressed by replacing the number 1 inside the shared circle symbol by the corresponding number (in this case 3).

Several examples are shown in figure 4.19. In the left part of the figure, the three diagrams express that all *PC* objects have two static links, each sharing an

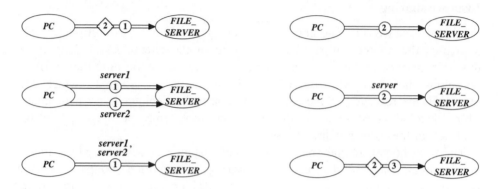

Figure 4.19   Different ways to express sharing

instance of class *FILE_SERVER*. (These two instances could actually be the same, but are probably not.) The links are unnamed in the upper diagram, and named in the other two. The lower diagram is exactly equivalent to the middle one, only more readable and compact.

Turning to the right part of the figure, the upper diagram shows a *PC* class whose instances may be alternatively attached to one of two *FILE_SERVER* objects. The middle diagram is exactly the same, only the link has now been labeled. The lower diagram, at last, shows that each *PC* object has two shared static relations to class *FILE_SERVER*, where each link may be attached to one of three specific *FILE_SERVER* objects.

Finally, figure 4.20 shows how local sharing within several related groups can be factored using inheritance. If a parent class contains a shared client relation to

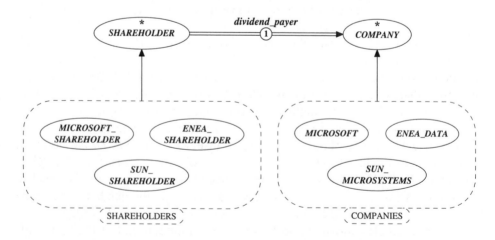

Figure 4.20   Sharing through inheritance

a supplier class, but the corresponding feature is deferred, this means that sharing will be effected by descendant classes. In figure 4.20, the shareholder classes corresponding to each company will make the deferred feature *dividend_payer* effective by defining an implementation for it, which ensures that all instances of this class (and possible descendant classes) will share the same supplier object (in this case, an instance of the proper company).

If, by contrast, the *dividend_payer* feature had been declared effective already in class *SHARE_HOLDER*, all instances of all the companies would have shared the same supplier object, which is not what was wanted in this case. Once a feature representing a shared relation has been effected, it cannot be redefined by a descendant class since this would violate the global sharing.

Client relations involving clusters

Just like the inheritance relation, the client relation may be generalized to apply also to clusters. Figure 4.21 shows an example. The *ORGANIZATION* cluster of a conference system is a client of the *CONFERENCE_DATA* cluster, which in

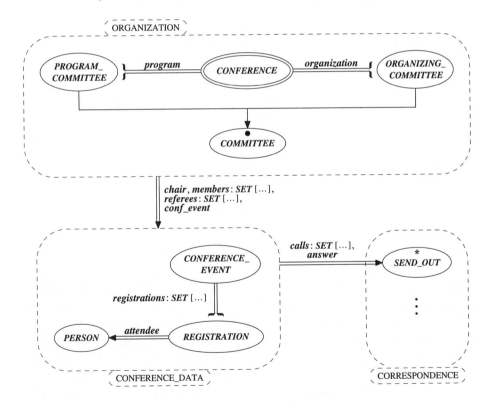

Figure 4.21 Client relations involving clusters

turn is a client of the class *SEND_OUT* in a third cluster. The labels refer to features of classes in the client cluster that are clients of some class in the supplier cluster, but we cannot tell which ones from the diagram. However, the names often provide enough guidance for the analyst/designer who has worked extensively with the model to know more or less which classes are involved. If more information is needed, the client links may be expanded to present instead a view like the diagram in figure 4.22.

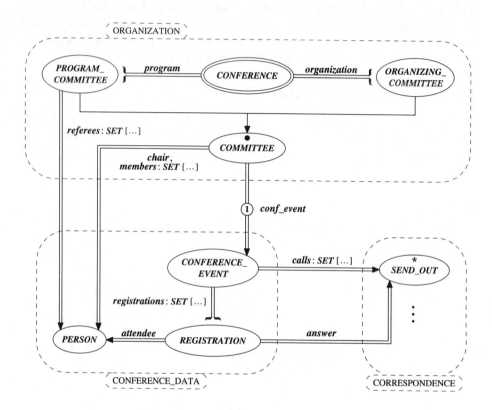

Figure 4.22 Expanded client relations between clusters

Here, the individual class relations between clusters have become visible at the expense of a more complicated diagram. This is a typical example of scaling in BON, which is so fundamentally important for large systems. If we want more detail, we expand down to the individual class interfaces; to get more overview, we compress into clusters at higher levels. The labels may of course be hidden if we are only interested in the general structure of a system.

As was pointed out earlier, the semantics of client relations involving clusters is different from the corresponding semantics of inheritance relations. While an inheritance relation having a cluster at either end carries over to relations with *all* classes in the cluster, client relations only refer to *at least one* class in each cluster.

This might seem a bit strange at first sight, but is really quite straightforward. The general semantics of inheritance is that of "all or nothing"—either you are my son and then you have all my genes, or you are not my son at all. A child class cannot select the operations to inherit from its parent; it receives everything. (It *can*, however, modify the behavior of chosen operations, which we may think of as computational *mutation*, but contrary to biological mutation only modifications that are in accord with the software contract collectively laid down by the ancestors are accepted.)

By contrast, the general semantics of being a client is that of "free choice". A client can request any service provided by a supplier class, but is not obliged to use everything. So if we think of the classes of a cluster as somewhat analogous to the operations of a class, the conventions used for cluster relations are easy to remember. The rules for generalizing client relations to involve clusters may be put more precisely:

1. If *one or more* elements (classes or clusters) in a cluster X are clients of an element A outside of X, then the cluster X is said to be a client of A. All the corresponding client links can then be compressed into one client link from X to A.

2. If an element A outside a cluster Y is a client of *one or more* elements in Y, then A is said to be a client of Y. All the client links can then be compressed into one link from A to Y.

3. A client link between two elements can be compressed into being hidden (not shown in a diagram).

All three cases occur frequently in practice, and have to do with the scaling level chosen. Notice again the use of *element* instead of *class* in the above definition to allow for recursive compression. As was shown earlier for inheritance relations (figure 4.3), client relations between classes in two different clusters may be successively compressed into client relations between the two clusters. For large systems, many levels of cluster compression is common practice.

Compression of client relations

Case tools may employ different strategies for compression of client relations, as long as they comply with rules 1–3 above. For example, it may be advantageous to be able to hide all client relations to certain groups of classes in order to emphasize some overall aspect of the system. Typical candidates for exclusion are general support classes, but also application classes considered less important in the context studied.

Compression of labels

The labels of a client link between two classes are compressed as follows:

- *Unidirectional links*. If there is more than one label attached to the link, the labels are compressed into the first label with a marker (ellipsis) indicating that not all labels are shown. If there is only one label (marked or not) it is compressed by being hidden.

- *Bidirectional links*. The unidirectional rules apply separately to the label groups of each direction. Recall that labels on bidirectional links must be placed closer to the supplier.

- *Multidirectional links*. The unidirectional rules apply separately to the label groups closest to the same client or to the same supplier. Recall that if there are multiple suppliers, then labels can only be put close to one or more of the suppliers, which means the names correspond to features in all the clients.

4.3 CLASS VS. OBJECT DEPENDENCIES

There is a fundamental difference between dependencies among the elements of a system (the objects) and among their *descriptive* elements (the classes). The full collection of objects at run-time is potentially a set of gargantuan proportions, and would be totally unmanageable if the elements always had to be dealt with individually. Fortunately, object-oriented development reduces this set by orders of magnitude by grouping objects with similar behavior into classes. The collective dependency of objects of type A on objects of type B may then be captured through one dependency link from class A to class B.

However, even with this reduction the resulting number of dependencies may become quite large. The good news is that another of the object-oriented key features—inheritance with dynamic binding—can carry the reduction one step further (one example being the factored sharing of figure 4.20). We will clarify the principle with yet another example. The classes in figure 4.23 represent some different vehicle types and a set of potential owners. Since any owner can own any vehicle, there are nine class dependencies to keep track of. These have been compressed into one cluster dependency for convenience. (Recall that a client relation between clusters X and Y means that *at least* one class in X is a client of *at least* one class in Y; here all classes in X happen to be clients of all classes in Y, which is somewhat unusual.)

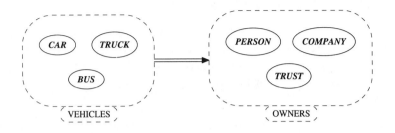

Figure 4.23 Multiple class dependencies

If, instead, we let the vehicles and owners inherit from common ancestors encapsulating the interaction as depicted in figure 4.24, the scene changes radically. The nine class dependencies have now been reduced to just one.

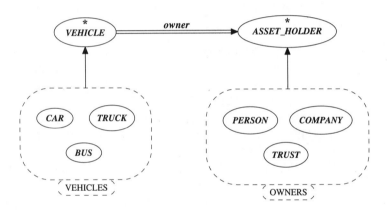

Figure 4.24 Factored class dependencies

The object dependencies have not changed—*CAR* objects are still clients of *COMPANY* objects and so forth (and the deferred ancestors are never instantiated)—but the big win is that the vehicle classes and the owner classes have become totally independent of each other. Changes to one class do not affect the correctness of the others, whereas in the first case changing, adding, or deleting an owner class would potentially require modification of all vehicle classes.

The bottom line is this: if we can only control our class definitions to make sure all objects will behave correctly at execution time, we can forget about the complexity of object dependencies—they will take care of themselves. That is why we must concentrate on classes and downplay individual objects.

4.4 INDIRECT CLIENT DEPENDENCIES

A client relation between a client class *A* and a supplier class *B* means *A* is dependent on services supplied by *B*. The services of *B* may be used for specification, as part of the public interface of *A*, or behind the scenes in the implementation of *A*. A client link from *A* to *B* may correspond to one or more of the following cases:

1. A public feature in *A* returns a value of type *B* (or a type derived from *B*, if *B* is generic).

2. An input argument of a public feature in *A* is of type *B*.

3. An actual parameter in a generic type derivation specified in *A* as part of the public interface is of type *B*.

4. The implementation of *A* uses an entity of type *B*. This includes the signatures of private features, as well as state variables and local variables used inside features.

In BON, as we have seen, dependencies arising from public query return values and generic derivation (cases 1 and 3 above) may be captured directly in client labels. Regarding public input arguments and implementation (cases 2 and 4 above), these can be captured by unlabeled client links. Extending the labeling syntax to also cover these cases would confuse the notation and does not seem worthwhile. When more precise information is needed, we can turn to the formal class interfaces and/or the source code.

It is a general principle in BON to strive for direct correspondence between the information expressed by client links in static diagrams and the formal interfaces of the classes involved. Therefore, the colon separating query names from their return type in class interfaces can be adorned to show the type of relation (association, shared association, or aggregation). Since the two last types of client relation have been explained at length in this chapter, we may now present the full feature signature table (figure 4.25), for which a partial version was earlier given in chapter 3.

FEATURE SIGNATURES (full table)		
Graphical form	**Textual form**	**Explanation**
name: *TYPE*	*name*: *TYPE*	Result type
name:{ *TYPE*	*name*:{ *TYPE*	Aggregation result type
name:(n) *TYPE*	*name*:(n) *TYPE*	Shared result type (n objects)
→ *arg*: *TYPE*	–> *arg*: *TYPE*	Input argument

Figure 4.25   Typed signatures revisited

4.5 SEMANTIC LINKS

A semantic link is an annotation associated with an inheritance or client relation between two classes that details the designer's intent when defining the relationship. Examples of semantic links are listed in figure 4.26, but the list is extensible. The semantic links are stored as comments with the corresponding relations.

Inheritance			Client/Supplier		
[DESCENDANT]	*is a*	[PARENT]	[CLIENT]	*requests*	[SUPPLIER]
[DESCENDANT]	*behaves like*	[PARENT]	[CLIENT]	*uses*	[SUPPLIER]
[DESCENDANT]	*implements*	[PARENT]	[CLIENT]	*needs*	[SUPPLIER]
[DESCENDANT]	*combines*	[PARENT]	[CLIENT]	*has a*	[SUPPLIER]
[PARENT]	*defers to*	[DESCENDANT]	[CLIENT]	*consists of*	[SUPPLIER]
[PARENT]	*factors out*	[DESCENDANT]	[SUPPLIER]	*provides*	[CLIENT]

Figure 4.26 Typical examples of semantic links

5 The dynamic model

5.1 INTRODUCTION

The static model of a system shows the high-level classes grouped into clusters and the relationships between them (client and inheritance). It also shows the class operations, their signatures and semantic specification through pre- and postconditions, as well as the overall consistency rules for the corresponding objects expressed as class invariants. These are the class contracts so fundamentally important for reliable systems. Getting them right is a big step towards mastering the task of systems development.

However, even if the semantics of the class operations is clearly specified (which is certainly not the case for most systems today), a crucial detail still remains: their implementation. Procedural functions do not magically disappear just because we structure our systems as collections of classes. On the contrary, we probably get many more of them than with traditional approaches, but with two main differences. First, the operations are not global to the system but local to the context in which they serve their purpose: the respective classes. Second, they are normally much smaller and easier to understand, since the abstractions they use as elements can be made to mirror the problem domain that much better.

But easy does not mean trivial. There is no such thing as an automatic generator of class operations from a semantic description of a class (unless of course the description is a full program in which case nothing has been gained). That is why we still need programming languages to describe the procedural steps of our class operations in enough detail to be executable by a machine.

Analysis and design does not include implementation, but it does include ensuring that implementation is indeed possible at reasonable cost and with adequate performance of the resulting product. Therefore, we need at least a vague idea already at the early development stages of how the operations of our high-level classes can fulfill their specifications by calling other operations (in the same or in other classes). To help capture and communicate this idea is the purpose of the BON dynamic model.

Object-oriented execution

One of the really nice things about object-oriented abstraction is that there are very few basic concepts to keep track of. This has led to an extremely simple execution model. A full execution of a system is simply the invocation of *one* operation on a so-called root object. When this operation terminates, system execution is over. The root object is instantiated automatically from the root class by the system environment when the corresponding process is started.

A class operation performs a set of actions in sequence. There are only two possibilities for each action: either terminate the operation by returning to the caller, or invoke another operation. Since the decision whether to return or make a new call—and if so, what other operation to call—may depend on the system state, we also need a few basic control primitives. In fact, we only need two: multiple choice and iteration, both based on a boolean condition.

Except for these control primitives, everything in an object-oriented execution can be boiled down to operation invocation.[5] This includes basic arithmetic and logic, which traditionally uses operand/operator expressions that do not resemble feature calls. However, this is just a syntactic convention. For example, the expression

$$n + 5 < k * 2$$

can be rephrased as

$$n.plus\,(5).less\_than\,(k.times\,(2))$$

without changing any semantics. Some object-oriented languages support prefix and infix forms of class operations, making it possible to write calls like the expression above in the familiar algebraic style.

What the above shows is that not only the object-oriented *specification* model, but also the corresponding *implementation* model have an inherent coherence, simplicity and beauty that are truly remarkable. This is crucial for our approach, where the goal is to achieve true seamlessness not by reflecting low-level details of code in the analysis and design, but by bringing high-level abstraction all the way down to the executable instructions. When the artificial barriers between the noble art of specification and the dirty (but unfortunately necessary) workmanship of implementation have been torn down, and we realize that there is no conceptual difference between the two, then we can hope for some real progress in software productivity.

---

[5] Well, almost; for completeness we do need a few more very basic primitives, like state variable assignment and test for object equality.

What should be captured by a dynamic model?

The previous section showed that feature calls, or *message passing* between objects, are what constitute a system execution. Consequently, this is what should be expressed in a dynamic model as a complementary view to the static model. Using a notation based on other concepts again loses reversibility and breaks the seamlessness of the approach.

Nevertheless, we have yet seen very little useful notation for documenting object communication in books on analysis and design. Mostly, they dwell for a page or two on an oversimplified scenario of perhaps four or five objects whose interactions are illustrated by the equivalent of an event trace diagram (a diagram with objects on one axis and time on the other). Realizing that the expressive power of such diagrams is much too weak for real-life systems, they then quickly move on to methods outside the object-oriented world, mostly state transition diagramming and/or data flow analysis.

In our view, functional modeling with data flow analysis should not be used at all in an object-oriented method, since the impedance mismatch and model confusion it introduces far outweigh any benefits gained. It can always be replaced by better ways of arriving at good abstractions.

State transition diagramming, on the other hand, is a powerful technique that is sometimes very useful also in object-oriented contexts. When large amounts of discrete events need to be handled by an object, *finite state machines* (FSMs) may be used to systematically take care of all possible combinations that can occur, and to give each required action its natural place in a general structure. A simple introduction to FSMs can be found in [Allworth 1990].

But it is important to understand that this technique is not a panacea. To recommend that each class should model its internal behavior using state machines is, in our view, totally inappropriate. It is like proposing that all mathematical functions should be described by enumerating their return values for each input value. This is fully possible on computers using a fixed storage size to represent their numbers, but it is hard to conceive of a more simple-minded approach, the side effects being increased complexity, waste of space, and total lack of reusability.

On the contrary, the goal to strive for is always higher-level abstractions that can be naturally described with much fewer parameters—where we do not need to use what is known as the British Museum method of explicit enumeration. Only for the unfortunate cases, where no nice continuous abstractions can be found for the behavior, do we call upon the state machine brigade to come in and sort out the disorder and transform the unstructured spaghetti logic into controllable and structured spaghetti logic (all global dependencies still there, but now sorted and tagged).

A typical such case, where state modeling can be of great help, is the design of user interfaces, where many alternative actions can be chosen by the user in various contexts and the system has no way of predicting what the next choice will be. When state diagramming is needed, there are many well-proven notations to choose from, so BON does not invent its own variant. Instead, we recommend David Harel's statechart formalism [Harel 1988], which has the ability to structure large diagrams through nesting.

The conclusion is that although state diagramming may be useful in special cases, the dynamic model of a *general* object-oriented method should instead concentrate on describing behavior through simple message passing between objects in the system. However, a more expressive notation than event trace diagrams is needed.

The BON dynamic notation uses sequence labels to capture time, which frees the second spatial dimension of a diagram to show the interaction between a larger number of objects than is possible with event trace diagrams. Moreover, it contains an object grouping facility that can capture more general scenarios and also illustrate dynamic binding. Potential message passing between selected objects is shown using a third kind of relationship, the *message relation*.

Besides object communication, the dynamic model contains three additional BON modeling charts. These are: the *event chart*, which records incoming and outgoing system events; the *scenario chart*, containing descriptions of selected object communication scenarios; and the *object creation chart*, showing what classes create new instances of what other classes. The informal charts and the dynamic notation for expressing object interaction will be described in detail in the rest of this chapter.

5.2 DYNAMIC CHARTS

System events

A system may be viewed as a "black box" whose behavior is defined by the response it gives to various stimuli. A stimulus that can change the course of action of a system and make it react is called a *system event*. System events are of two kinds. An *external* event is triggered by something in the external world over which the system has no control. Examples of *incoming* external events are user terminal input, calls from other systems, arrival of data from sensory devices, and hardware clock interrupts.

An *internal* event, on the other hand, is triggered by the system itself as part of its reaction to one or more external events. Some of the internal events are *outgoing,* which means that they send stimuli to the outside world triggering an (outgoing) external event, mostly as a response to external input.

For example, a user at a workstation may click on a menu to print a certain report. The receipt of the mouse click is then an external event, which may lead to a whole series of internal events triggering various parts of the system to search databases, compile information, and send the result to a printer. At least one of these internal events (not necessarily the last one) will be an outgoing internal event representing the system response, perhaps directed to a network spooler.

Event charts

The object interactions which make up the execution of a system are ultimately caused by external events. Therefore, it is often a good idea to compile a list of external events that may trigger object communication representing principal types of system behavior. The event list is then used as a guide for choosing the scenarios to include in a dynamic model of the system. However, only a small subset of all possible external events is interesting and representative enough to be listed.

For example, to register a new subscriber for a monthly comic magazine, an operator may first click on a principal subscription menu, then choose the entry for the complete Carl Barks Library in color, then enter the name and address of the subscriber along with the subscription period, and finally click on the button "accept subscription". In this series of operator actions, each mouse click will constitute an external system event (in fact, usually two: one when the mouse button is depressed and one when it is released). Depending on the supporting system (widget handling, mouse tracking, etc.) each character keystroke may or may not be an individual event, and each of these events may lead to a large number of operations being applied to many objects.

But the only event in the above sequence likely to be included in a high-level system dynamic model is the receipt of "accept subscription". This event corresponds to the commit statement of a transaction, and is probably a significant part of the system behavior. The other events have to do with how the necessary subscription data is actually collected and transmitted, and since this can be implemented in many different ways, the details will in most cases not be decided until later. Unless a novel interface model is part of the system design, the menu selections will just follow the standard practice of some basic general GUI library, and thus not be included in the dynamic model.

The idea is to capture a small number of external events each triggering a principal type of system behavior, so that a representative set of scenarios can be chosen. These scenarios will then sketch how the necessary actions can be carried out by communicating objects (which are instances of the classes in the static model) to achieve the desired behavior. Figure 5.1 shows a BON *event chart* for a conference system, collecting some interesting incoming external events. For each external event, the event chart lists the types of object that may become involved as part of the system response.

EVENTS	CONFERENCE_SUPPORT	Part: 1/2
COMMENT Selected external events triggering representative types of behavior.	**INDEXING** **created:** 1993-02-15 kw **revised:** 1993-04-07 kw	
External (incoming)	**Involved object types**	
Request to register a submitted paper	*CONFERENCE, PROGRAM_COMMITTEE, PAPER*	
Request to accept a paper	*CONFERENCE, PROGRAM_COMMITTEE, PAPER, STATUS*	
Request to assign a paper to a session	*CONFERENCE, PROGRAM_COMMITTEE, PROGRAM, PAPER, PAPER_SESSION*	
Selection of a session chairperson	*CONFERENCE, PROGRAM_COMMITTEE, PROGRAM, PAPER_SESSION, PERSON*	
Request to register an attendee	*CONFERENCE, ORGANIZING_COMMITTEE, REGISTRATION, PERSON*	
Request to print conference attendee list	*CONFERENCE, ORGANIZING_COMMITTEE, REGISTRATION, PERSON, ATTENDEE_LIST*	

Figure 5.1 Event chart: incoming external events

Analogously, the event chart gives the same information for a list of important internal outgoing events as shown in figure 5.2. Since all outgoing events are indirectly triggered by incoming events, the outgoing events listed all have one or more corresponding incoming external events.

For example, the outgoing event "call for papers is sent" was probably triggered by an incoming event "request to send call for papers" resulting from user keyboard input. Or else the calls may be sent automatically at some preset date, but then the system clock interrupt may be considered as the incoming external triggering event. Similarly, each incoming external event usually has a corresponding outgoing event. A request to register a conference participant will almost certainly yield some kind of confirmation being sent back to the user—at least indirectly by issuing a standard system prompt as opposed to an error message—indicating that the registration was successful.

In either case, both the incoming and the outgoing events will point to the same scenario, so there is normally no need to list both related events in the

EVENTS	CONFERENCE_SUPPORT	Part: 2/2
COMMENT Selected internal events triggering system responses leaving the system.	**INDEXING** **created:** 1993-02-15 kw **revised:** 1993-04-03 kw	

Internal (outgoing)	Involved object types
Call for papers is sent	*CONFERENCE, ORGANIZING_COMMITTEE, PERSON, MAILING*
Invitations are sent	*CONFERENCE, ORGANIZING_COMMITTEE, PERSON, MAILING*
A paper is sent to referees	*CONFERENCE, ORGANIZING_COMMITTEE, PAPER, STATUS, REVIEW, PERSON*
An invoice is sent	*CONFERENCE, ORGANIZING_COMMITTEE, REGISTRATION, PERSON, INVOICE, INVOICE_FORM*
Warning issued for exceeding tutorial session capacity	*CONFERENCE, REGISTRATION, TUTORIAL*
An author notification is sent	*CONFERENCE, PROGRAM_COMMITTEE, PERSON, PRINT_OUT*, LETTER_FORM*

Figure 5.2   Event chart: outgoing internal events

event chart. Outgoing events like "warning issued for exceeding conference capacity" are different, since these are triggered when the system state reaches certain values. Such triggering states are of course also the indirect result of incoming events, like trying to register one more attendee, but it is not always easy to know exactly which ones, so we normally record this group of outgoing events separately.

System scenarios

A *system scenario* is a description of a possible partial system execution. It can be viewed as a sequence of events initiated by one or more triggering events (internal or external) and showing the resulting events in order of occurrence. Some of the events in a scenario will usually be external, but not always. Particularly during design there may be many interesting, purely internal scenarios that are worth capturing as part of the high-level system description.

Anyway, the great majority of events in most scenarios will be internal events; that is, generated by the system itself. As we recall from the beginning of this chapter, object-oriented system execution is really nothing but message passing between objects, so all events except the incoming external ones are caused by operations being applied to objects. Some of these operations change the system state (the commands), and some of them do not (the queries).

When describing the internal events of our scenarios, we basically have two choices:

1. View the system as a finite state machine and let the events correspond to transitions between certain interesting system states.

2. View the system as a set of communicating objects, and let the events correspond to message passing between them.

Most books on analysis and design containing any kind of elaborate notation for dynamic modeling seem to take the first approach, and then use some kind of state diagramming technique. However, this approach immediately runs into trouble, because there is no natural mapping from the state diagrams to the static model of the system classes.

BON instead takes the second approach, viewing internal events as operations applied to objects. Then every message passed from one object to another can be directly related to the corresponding classes and operations specified in the static model. So rather than representing different worlds with no logical connection between them other than the poor developer's brain, as is the case with state machine approaches, the static and dynamic models can now reinforce each other and lead to a better understanding of the system under construction.

We will see in section 5.3 what dynamic diagrams with message passing may look like.

Scenario charts

Using the system event chart as a starting point, we may select a set of interesting system scenarios to illustrate important aspects of the overall system behavior. A short description of each scenario (for which a dynamic diagram may later be produced) is then collected in the system's *scenario chart*. An example is figure 5.3. Each entry has two short descriptions: the first is just a few words which can also be used as a scenario name for quick reference, and the second a few sentences explaining the scenario a little more.

Object creation charts

Investigating the creation of new objects may serve as a link between the static and dynamic models. Some classes in a static diagram may be marked as deferred, which means they contain operations that will never be implemented in the class itself, but only in descendant classes. Such classes will never be instantiated, so objects of the corresponding type cannot occur in the dynamic

SCENARIOS	CONFERENCE_SUPPORT	Part: 1/1
COMMENT Set of representative scenarios to show important types of system behavior.	**INDEXING** **created:** 1993-02-16 kw	

Send out calls and invitations:
Using mailing lists and records of previous conference attendees and speakers, prepare and send out calls for papers and invitations to attend the conference.

Create sessions and chairs:
Partition the conference into sessions of suitable length; allocate session rooms and select a chairperson for each session.

Register paper and start review process:
A paper is registered and three referees are selected; the paper is sent to each referee, and the paper status is recorded.

Accept paper and notify authors:
A submitted paper is selected and an acceptance date is entered; a notification letter is created and sent to the authors.

Assign paper to session:
A session suitable for the paper is selected and the paper is entered in the list of presentations for that session.

Register attendee:
An attendee is registered with his/her address and selected tutorials are recorded.

Print conference attendee list:
All registrations are scanned and a list with attendee names, addresses and affiliations is produced and sent to a printer.

Print badge:
An attendee is selected, and the corresponding badge is printed in appropriate format.

Figure 5.3 Scenario chart for a conference system

model. All other classes, however, must potentially have objects created at some point during system execution, otherwise they are superfluous and should be removed (unless, of course, we are developing libraries of reusable classes).

Thinking through how objects are created may thus help find possible fossil classes, but it also helps the developer form an impression of how some of the operations in the dynamic diagrams may be realized. The idea is to produce an *object creation chart*, where for each class that may create other objects, the types of these objects are listed. (Only high-level analysis classes are considered here; keeping track of created lower-level objects is not the intention.) An example for the conference system is shown in figure 5.4.

The class *PRESENTATION* in the creation chart is a deferred class with the classes *PAPER* and *TUTORIAL* as descendants. Note that deferred classes may occur in the left column of object creation charts, because a deferred class may contain operations that create other objects. Regardless of whether these

CREATION	CONFERENCE_SUPPORT	Part: 1/1
COMMENT List of classes creating objects in the system.	**INDEXING** **created:** 1993-02-18 kw	

Class	Creates instances of
CONFERENCE	PROGRAM_COMMITTEE, TECHNICAL_COMMITTEE, ORGANIZATION_COMMITTEE, TIME_TABLE
PROGRAM_COMMITTEE	PROGRAM, PAPER, PAPER_SESSION, PERSON
TECHNICAL_COMMITTEE	TUTORIAL, TUTORIAL_SESSION, PERSON
ORGANIZATION_COMMITTEE	MAILING, ADDRESS_LABEL, STICKY_FORM, REGISTRATION, PERSON, INVOICE, INVOICE_FORM, ATTENDEE_LIST, LIST_FORM, POSTER_SIGN, POSTER_FORM, EVALUATION_SHEET, EVALUATION_FORM, STATISTICS
PRESENTATION*	STATUS, PERSON
PAPER	REVIEW, ACCEPTANCE_LETTER, REJECTION_LETTER, LETTER_FORM, AUTHOR_GUIDELINES
TUTORIAL	ACCEPTANCE_LETTER, REJECTION_LETTER, LETTER_FORM
REGISTRATION	CONFIRMATION_LETTER, LETTER_FORM, BADGE, BADGE_FORM

Figure 5.4   Object creation chart

operations will actually be implemented by the deferred class or by its children, if we know their invocation may lead to the creation of objects of certain types, this information should not have to be duplicated in all descendant classes. By listing the classes *STATUS* and *PERSON* in the entry for *PRESENTATION*, we can avoid repetition for the child classes *PAPER* and *TUTORIAL*, and may instead focus on the differences.

It is usually best to exclude frequently reused library classes, such as *SET*, *TABLE*, and *DATE*, from the creation chart, since it is rarely interesting to follow the creation of such objects in detail.

5.3 DYNAMIC DIAGRAMS

Objects

We are now ready to describe the BON dynamic notation used in system scenarios. A dynamic diagram consists of a set of communicating objects passing messages to each other. An object is represented by its type, that is its class name, and an optional object qualifier.

Graphical representation

Objects are represented graphically by rectangles to make them stand out from the class ellipses. An effort is made in BON to make the dynamic and static diagrams look different enough to preclude any confusion between them. There is a deep semantic difference between a class and its instances that is sometimes very obvious, but may at times be quite subtle, depending on the discussion context and the general backgrounds of the people trying to communicate.

Mixing statements about classes with statements about class instances in the same context is akin to mixing language and metalanguage in the same phrases; it can easily lead to severe misunderstandings. Static and dynamic descriptions should therefore be kept strictly apart and not be allowed to share the same diagrams.

The name of the corresponding class is centered inside the rectangle in upper case (bold italic font recommended). A single rectangle in a diagram always refers to an individual object, so two single rectangles with the same name will refer to two individual objects of the same type. A qualifying identifier may be written below the class name, enclosed in parentheses (lower case recommended), to distinguish several objects of the same type occurring at different positions in a dynamic diagram.

An object rectangle may be double, in which case it refers to a set of objects of the corresponding type. Passing a message to a double object rectangle means calling some object in the set. Three single objects and one set of objects are shown in figure 5.5.

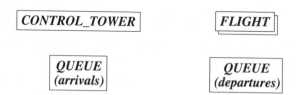

Figure 5.5 Objects are identified by class name, context, and optional id

Additional object qualifiers should only be used when really needed, since having a lot of them may easily clutter a diagram and lead to more confusion than help. Even if there is more than one object of a certain type in a diagram, individual identification is not always interesting, or else the spatial context may be enough to tell which object is which.

Message relations

In this book, we switch freely between the message passing metaphor and the feature call metaphor (objects invoking operations on each other) depending on what view is most convenient for the particular issue being discussed. We may thus at times talk about sending a message to an object, calling a class feature, or invoking an operation on an object, but this will always mean the same thing.

For the relationship between a calling object and the callee, we use the term message passing relation or *message relation* for short.

Graphical representation

A message sent from one object to another is represented graphically by a dashed arrow extending from the calling object to the receiving object. The message arrows (or *message links*) may be labeled with sequence numbers. These numbers serve a double purpose. First, they represent *time* in the scenario, that is the order in which calls are made. Second, they correspond to entries in a *scenario box* where the role of each call may be described using free text.

In this way dynamic diagrams can be kept clean and easy to read, while the natural language text in the scenario boxes provides the freedom to express special semantic details at greater length when needed. The scenario box has a header containing a scenario name, which is the corresponding short entry of the scenario chart. An example is shown in figure 5.6.

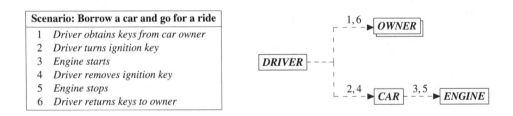

Figure 5.6 A BON dynamic diagram

A message relation is always *potential;* that is, we cannot tell from the diagram whether the call will actually occur in a specific execution. For example, if the car battery is flat, turning the ignition key may not lead to any message being sent from the *CAR* object to the *ENGINE* object. Also, obtaining keys from a car owner (label 1 in figure 5.6) may involve asking several owners or the same owner several times before someone is persuaded to lend their car.

For reasons of simplicity and abstraction, we exclude all forms of conditional control (such as multiple choice and iteration) from the BON dynamic notation, and instead let it be implicit in the message relations. For the same reasons, we also exclude any data flow indications. Some messages will implicitly cause return values to be passed in the reverse direction, but this is not shown in the diagrams. In case we need to express more, separate dynamic notations may be used as a complement. The path expressions for high-level descriptions of patterns of interaction between object groups described in [Adams 1994] may be a candidate.

Bidirectional links

A set of message relations in each direction between two objects (or sets of objects) may be expressed by a double link with an arrowhead at each end, like in figure 5.7.

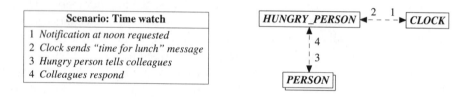

Figure 5.7   Bidirectional message links

As in the static notation, this is just a compacted form of individual relations, and we employ the same convention to show which direction each sequence label corresponds to. A label is always put closer to the *supplier* object, that is the object being called (the *receiver*). In figure 5.7, label 1 therefore represents a call from the hungry person to the clock, and label 2 refers to the clock responding. Similarly, message 3 refers to the hungry person summoning the lunch team members, while message 4 represents their answers.

Multidirectional links

To simplify diagrams with many relations, we allow message links to be joined, as shown in figure 5.8. A joined message link must have at least one calling

Figure 5.8   Concurrency: send to many

object and one receiving object attached, and it represents potential calls from all the callers to all the receivers. Placing a label close to a caller means that it refers to messages from this caller to all receivers in the diagram.

Joining multiple calls from the same caller, as in figure 5.8, is also a way of grouping concurrent messages: we may not be interested in whether the right or the left leg takes the first step, as long as it leads to a useful walk. (The notation may mean true concurrency, or simply that we do not care.)

Similarly, placing a label close to a receiver refers to messages from all callers in the diagram to this object (or set of objects). This is illustrated by figure 5.9, where a pilot needs to receive clear signals from various sources both inside and outside the airplane before taking off, but where no particular order is required.

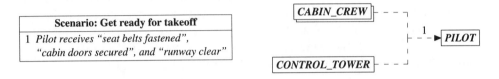

Figure 5.9 Concurrency: receive from several

In figure 5.10, labels 1 and 2 represent messages from one parent to both children, while labels 3 and 4 represent messages from both parents to one of the children.

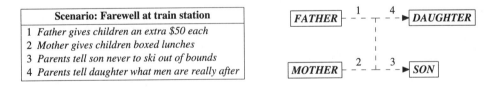

Figure 5.10 Concurrency: multiple send to many

Object grouping

We have seen that the simple labeling and joining conventions of the dynamic diagrams introduced so far already give us the possibility to express many different types of object communication. But we may take a significant step further, which is particularly important for scenarios containing a larger set of interacting objects. This step is the ability to send messages between groups of objects.

An *object group* is a set of objects treated as a unit in some message passing context. An object group may contain single objects (corresponding to single rectangles), sets of objects (corresponding to double rectangles), and also other object groups. A message link to an object group is simply the compression of one or several message links to one or several of the elements in the group. Similarly, a message link from an object group is the compression of one or several message links from one or several of the group elements.

Graphical representation

Object groups are drawn as boxes with rounded corners representing the group body with an optional group label in a separate rounded box. The group label (if present) is positioned just outside the group body touching its borderline. BON recommends letting dynamic group labels start with a capital letter with the rest in lower case, to make them stand out from static cluster labels. A group label may appear anywhere along the group borderline to facilitate the presentation of complicated diagrams. Some examples are shown in figure 5.11.

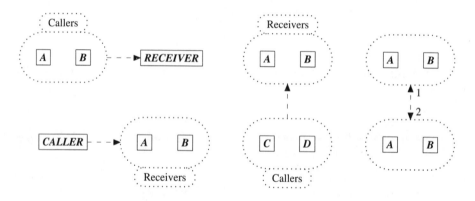

Figure 5.11 Compressed message relations

The line style must be different from the one chosen for objects, and preferably also from classes and clusters. The recommended practice is to use continuous borderlines for objects, and to use dotted borderlines for object groups and group labels.

Compression of objects and groups

An object group is compressed into its group label attached to an empty, iconized body (see figure 5.12). Unlabeled object groups cannot be compressed. When a group icon is expanded (or *opened*), its constituent parts first become

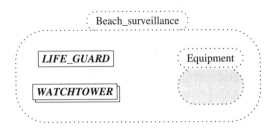

Figure 5.12   An iconized object group

visible in compressed form, thus showing objects and other group icons. The inner parts may then be opened recursively, until the objects are reached.

Messages involving object groups

Message relations between callers and receivers may be compressed as follows:

1. If *one or more* elements (objects, sets of objects, or groups) in a group send messages to an element outside the group, all the message links involved can be compressed into one message link from the group to the outside element.

2. If *one or more* elements (objects, sets of objects, or groups) in a group receive messages from an element outside the group, all the message links involved can be compressed into one message link from the outside element to the group.

3. A message link between two elements can be compressed into being hidden (not shown in a diagram).

Compression of message relations

When object groups are being compressed or expanded in a dynamic diagram, the labels and corresponding entries in the scenario boxes may have to be renumbered to reflect the overall message sequencing. Case tools may employ different strategies as long as they comply with rules 1–3 above.

Recursive messages

It is often important to express recursive message passing in a dynamic diagram. Figure 5.13 shows three different cases. The first case represents a specific object calling itself, and is therefore drawn using a single rectangle. The second case shows a set of objects of a certain type calling objects in the same set.

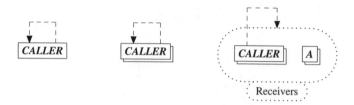

Figure 5.13 Recursive messages

Whether individual objects actually call themselves is not specified. Finally, the third case uses grouping to express recursive calls to a group of objects which may include the caller itself.

Active and passive objects

The objects in the dynamic model correspond exactly to the classes in the static model, but the structures of static and dynamic diagrams describing the behavior of a set of objects are often very different. The client relations in the static diagrams are of course closely related to the message relations in the dynamic diagrams; each call to an object is applied to an entity associated with the object, and it is precisely these entities that indirectly define the static client relations. Whether the object association is an address pointer produced by a compiler and loader in a tightly integrated system running as a single task, or a symbolic object identification used by a series of object brokers or traders to communicate calls in a distributed system, is irrelevant to the discussion.

Regardless of the calling mechanism used, static diagrams show the access structure to the services needed, while dynamic diagrams show control. The difference is illustrated in the next two figures. Figure 5.14 shows an agent dealing with real estate who has access to a repository of sales leads, each listing a prospective buyer and the buyer's address.

Figure 5.14 Static diagram: estate sales data

The static diagram is a typically layered information structure. By contrast, a corresponding dynamic diagram is shown in figure 5.15, where the scenario is to produce a list of addresses of possible buyers. We see that the structure here is completely different. Instead of showing layers of information, the dynamic

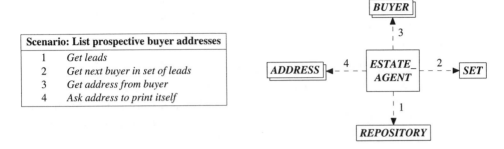

Scenario: List prospective buyer addresses	
1	*Get leads*
2	*Get next buyer in set of leads*
3	*Get address from buyer*
4	*Ask address to print itself*

Figure 5.15 Dynamic diagram: active and passive objects

diagram shows the estate agent as the only caller in the scenario, while all other objects simply act as data containers.

An object sending a message is said to be *active,* while the receiving objects are *passive.* Being active or passive is a *role;* to carry out its task when called as a passive object, the called object may have to call other objects and thus become active. Many objects, perhaps most, will thus act in both capacities at different times. However, it is often interesting in a dynamic context to separate the objects playing the active parts from the passive ones, since the former are the ones causing things to happen. In BON dynamic diagrams, this is immediately visible through the occurrence and direction of the message relations.

When building a dynamic scenario with the aid of a corresponding static diagram, it is then very important to realize that an indirect call chain to print the address of the next buyer in the structure shown in figure 5.14, which can be written:

>   *info.leads.item.addr.print*

does *not* mean that *ESTATE_AGENT* calls *REPOSITORY*, which calls *SET*, which then calls *BUYER*, which in turn calls its *ADDRESS* object. Instead, *ESTATE_AGENT* calls *REPOSITORY* to get a reference to a *SET* of leads. Using the reference, *ESTATE_AGENT* then makes a second call to the *SET* object to get the next *BUYER* object, then a third call to *BUYER* getting its *ADDRESS* object, and then a last call to this *ADDRESS* asking it to print itself.

This is what is really expressed by the call above. Nested calls of this type are only allowed for syntactic convenience, and are semantically equivalent to:

>   *info*: *REPOSITORY*
>   *s*: *SET* [*BUYER*]
>   *b*: *BUYER*
>   *a*: *ADDRESS*

$s := info.leads$
$b := s.item$
$a := b.addr$
$a.print$

If we use local variables for implementation as above, the corresponding static structure becomes the one in figure 5.16. However, we normally do not want this reflected in our high-level static diagrams, since it only makes them more difficult to read. Therefore, an essential property of a case tool is to permit the hiding of client dependencies resulting from local variables or private features.

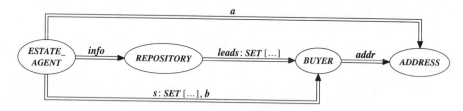

Figure 5.16 Modified static diagram

A more complex example: moving graphical objects

To give the reader a general idea of the potential strength of the BON dynamic notation, we will spend the rest of this chapter on two examples where the object interaction is a little more complex.

The first example will show how the notation can be used to express dynamic binding. Assume we want to model a simple graphical editor with grouping. A static diagram for the editor is shown in figure 5.17. It can handle three types of graphical object: pixel map objects for arbitrary images, graphical text objects with variable font and point size, and geometric objects consisting of a set of defining points and a shape. All the geometric figures inherit from the deferred class *FIGURE*, which is associated with a set of graphical points.

Selected objects may be grouped and treated as a unit, for example when moved, rotated, or resized. To be of any use, groups may also contain other groups besides primitive objects. This is conveniently expressed in figure 5.17 by letting all graphical objects (including the *FIGURE* objects) inherit from a second deferred class *DISPLAY_OBJECT*, and then letting the *GROUP* class have an aggregation relation to a set of *DISPLAY_OBJECT*.

Since a *DISPLAY_OBJECT* can be either a primitive graphical object or a group, we get the required recursion for free through dynamic binding. Combining generic derivation with inheritance in this fashion is a very common

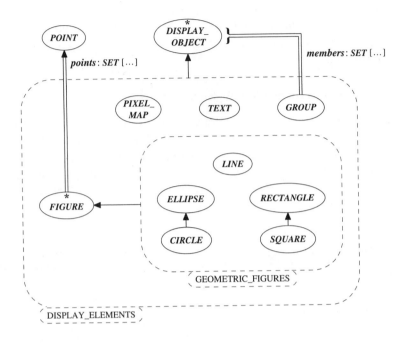

Figure 5.17 Graphical objects with grouping (static diagram)

and powerful method to handle complex structures with object-oriented modeling. We also note that by using clustering and compression of inheritance links it is possible to express quite entangled classification structures with very few arrows. Without the compression possibility, this diagram would be at least an order of magnitude more difficult to read.

Now let us try to illustrate a dynamic scenario where a group object is being moved. A group created by the editor is shown in figure 5.18.

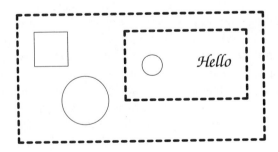

Figure 5.18 Graphical editor example: a grouped object with nesting

The group contains a nested group and two geometric objects: a square and a circle. The inner group contains one smaller circle and a graphical text object. The thick, dashed boxes just illustrate the grouping, and are not part of the graphical figures.

The need for two-dimensional object diagrams

The typical way to show object communication found in other approaches, such as OMT [Rumbaugh 1991], the Booch method [Booch 1994], and OOSE [Jacobson 1992], is through one-dimensional sequencing diagrams called *event trace diagrams* or *interaction diagrams*. Figure 5.19 shows a diagram of this type for our small example, without the graphical points that are part of the geometric figures.

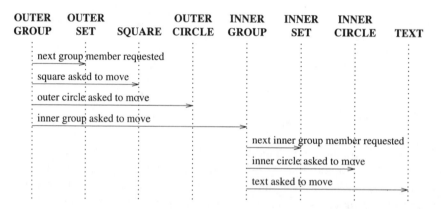

Figure 5.19   Move example group: event trace diagram

The eight objects involved (excluding the points)—two groups, two set objects containing group elements, and four primitive figures—just about hit the limit for what can be expressed with reasonable readability in one-dimensional diagrams. Including the points would clutter the figure. Considering the simplicity of the example, it is clear that diagrams of the type represented by figure 5.19 are too weak for dynamic modeling. This may be compared with figure 5.20 which uses the two-dimensional BON notation.

Freeing the time axis has made the actual communication diagram smaller, while moving the temporal explanations to a separate place. The spatial positioning of objects in two dimensions permits them to be locally grouped. We have therefore been able to drop the qualifying identifiers for the *SET* and *CIRCLE* objects, since the geometric contexts give enough information.

Scenario 1: Move example group
1 *Next outer group member requested*
2 *Square asked to move*
3 *Outer circle asked to move*
4 *Inner group asked to move*
5 *Next inner group member requested*
6 *Inner circle asked to move*
7 *Text asked to move*

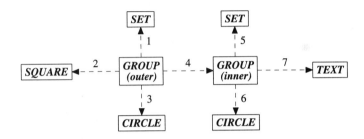

Figure 5.20 Move example group: two-dimensional BON diagram

The increased space available now permits us to go one step further to illustrate the movement of geometric objects in more detail. We assume that such an object is moved by moving, in turn, its defining points (a circle may be defined by two points: its origin and one point on the circumference). Figure 5.21 shows the resulting diagram. It now contains 11 single objects and 3 object sets without looking too crowded, while the corresponding event trace diagram would no longer be readable.

General scenarios need object grouping

What is immediately striking, however, is that the scenario feels very special; instead of showing individual move examples, one would want to capture the general scenario of moving any group. To do this, we must employ the grouping facility. A first attempt is illustrated in the upper diagram of figure 5.22.

Collecting the geometric figures in one group and the non-geometric ones in another,[6] makes it possible to illustrate the various cases of dynamic binding that may occur. Call 1 of scenario 3 gets the next group member. Applying the

---

[6] We assume it is clear from the context when the word *group* refers to an object group in the dynamic notation, and when it denotes a group in the editor example.

Scenario 2: Move example group
1 *Next outer group member requested*
2 *Square asked to move*
3 *Next square point requested*
4 *Point asked to move*
5 *Outer circle asked to move*
6 *Next outer circle point requested*
7 *Point asked to move*

Scenario 2: (continued)
8 *Inner group asked to move*
9 *Next inner group member requested*
10 *Inner circle asked to move*
11 *Next inner circle point requested*
12 *Point asked to move*
13 *Text asked to move*

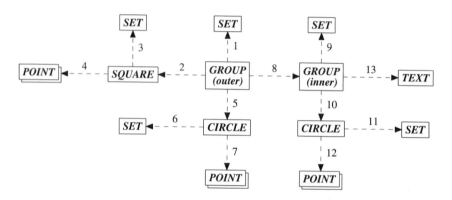

Figure 5.21   Move example group: extended to include points

move operation on this member then has to be split into calls 2–6, since different things happen depending on the type of member. In fact, only one of call 2, call 3, or calls 4–6 will occur for a given member.

The diagram may be further improved as shown in scenario 4 (lower part of figure 5.22) by nesting the groups that hold the polymorphic objects. We then get a diagram which illustrates the dynamic binding of the move operation very directly. If we compare scenario 4 with the static description in figure 5.17, we see that the similarity is striking.

The deferred classes *DISPLAY_OBJECT* and *FIGURE*, which are never instantiated, are replaced in the dynamic diagram by two object groups (outer and inner). Moreover, the inheritance relations between the pairs *CIRCLE–ELLIPSE* and *SQUARE–RECTANGLE*, respectively, are not shown in the dynamic diagram. It would have been possible to use one more layer of nested groups to include them, but when geometric shapes are manipulated, circles and ellipses are usually not perceived as related objects, and the same holds for squares vs. rectangles. Therefore, the scenario looks more natural without this last grouping.

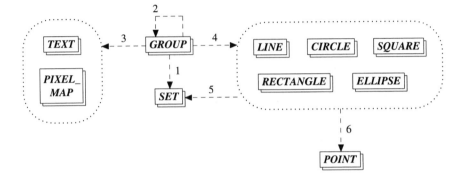

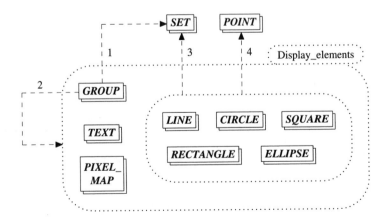

Figure 5.22 Polymorphism: needs object grouping

A different use of object grouping

Finally, we show a second example where grouping is useful, but where the objects called are not necessarily related through common inheritance. Figure 5.23 contains a typical scenario that can be divided into sequential subtasks with some shared data between them.

It shows the general interactions needed to deal with an insurance company as a result of a car accident without personal injury. Getting the car fixed may be divided into three phases. First, various reports are filled out to document what really happened and establish damages for which the insurance holder may be

Scenario 5: Settlement of claims for damages resulting from car accident
1–3   *Owner obtains necessary statements and certificates from involved parties, fills in damage report, and sends it to insurance company.*
4–7   *Insurance adjuster evaluates damage claims and sends settlement statement back to owner.*
8–9   *Owner agrees on car rental and repair details based on settlement.*

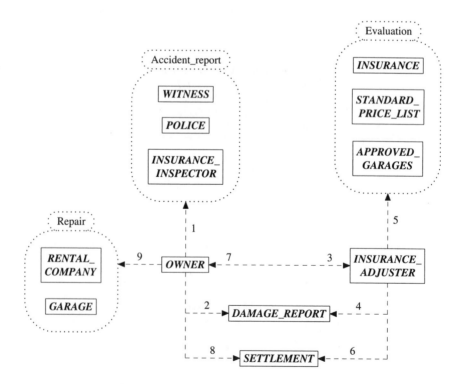

Figure 5.23   Grouping into sequential subtasks

entitled to compensation. These reports are based on statements from people being involved or witnessing the accident, and may need formal certification by an insurance inspector and perhaps the police. This is captured by message links from the *OWNER* object to the object group labeled "Accident_report", to the *DAMAGE_REPORT* object, and to the insurance company, representing formal submission of the claims.

Second, an adjuster at the insurance company makes an evaluation of the claims based on the accident report and the general terms of the applicable insurances. A maximum cost is often specified based on agreed standards on acceptable repair charges for various types of damage, and sometimes the insurance company will only accept certain trusted garages to do the job. The message link from *INSURANCE_ADJUSTER* to the "Evaluation" object group illustrates this. The result of the evaluation is a formal settlement statement from the insurance company, approving or disapproving parts or all of the owner's claims (message links to *SETTLEMENT* and back to *OWNER*).

Based on the outcome of this, the owner may then carry out the third phase of the scenario, which is to negotiate with a suitable garage and perhaps also rent a car to replace the one under repair (message link to "Repair" group).

This example is very different from the graphical editor for two reasons. First, the messages sent to the objects in the groups may represent operations that are totally unrelated and therefore do not mirror any inheritance structure in the system. Second, the object groups may not correspond to any kind of grouping in the static model of the system, but simply represent a convenient way of viewing a somewhat complicated scenario to make it easier to understand.

There are many such cases in practice, where a system—perhaps consisting of a number of loosely connected heterogeneous components as is becoming more and more common in distributed environments—is used in a way that creates abstractions that were never part of the system model. In fact, an important characteristic of really useful systems is often that they provide a certain number of basic facilities that the user can combine in different ways to create usage patterns that the system designers could never anticipate (and should not try to).

Use cases

So system usage can give rise to abstractions of its own that may be worth modeling, but we must also issue a word of warning in this context. Systematic elaboration of *use cases*, as advocated in OOSE [Jacobson 1992], is often a good way to gain more insight into what is really needed in a system. But using them as the basis for system decomposition risks ending up with a product whose structure reflects system usage more than long-term concepts. We will return to this issue in chapter 6.

For these reasons, the dynamic diagrams in BON are normally not as stable as the static model, and will frequently change as we gain more insight into the problem. In fact, some dynamic diagrams will just serve as temporary help to evolve the static model, and will be thrown away at later stages. Others may survive longer and fill a role as complementary system documentation.

Part III
The method

6 Issues of a general method

6.1 INTRODUCTION

Developing high-quality professional software requires great intellectual skills and long experience. It is a creative process that can never be replaced by the rigid procedures of an ultimate "methodology". Unless we are working in a very narrow application area, the possible variations in system views make the task of finding a good model too close to general human problem solving, which just does not lend itself to any useful formalization.

Despite the fact that everybody in the trade knows this (except perhaps for some bubble and arrow specialists who have never really been forced to implement their own diagrams), there is a remarkable gullibility in many parts of the software community. Somewhat like instant cures for baldness, almost any kind of simplistic *ad hoc* procedure seems to sell if it only promises to turn general systems development into an orderly, controllable procedure. A tailored variation of the generic approach in figure 6.1 is then often used.

The universal method M   (apply recursively when required)
1. This is the important beginning step, where we solve the first part of the problem.
2. Welcome to the middle of the method: in this step we solve the second part.
3. Now all that remains is solving the last part, and we will soon be done.

Figure 6.1   The archetype of many software "methodologies"

So the manager's secret dream of totally manageable (and easily exchangeable) employees for software development is still far off, and the reader should not expect any miracles from the BON method either in this respect. Its goal is to provide the developer with a strong set of basic concepts and corresponding notation to be used as a framework for creative thinking, complemented by a set of guidelines and recommended procedures that may help in the search for good models. BON can never substitute for talent, but it can hope to serve as an inspiration for developing one's personal skills.

The reader may also have noted that we use the term *method* for these guidelines and procedures, rather than the more popular buzzword "methodology". This is for two reasons. First, using a longer name does not add any substance to a method, and second, according to available dictionaries the latter form simply does not have the intended meaning:

method, n.
  1. a way of proceeding or doing something esp. a systematic or regular one.
  2. orderliness of thought, action, etc.
  3. (*often pl.*) the techniques or arrangement of work for a particular field or subject.

methodology, n.
  1. the system of methods and principles used in a particular discipline.
  2. the branch of philosophy concerned with the science of method and procedure.

(*Collins English Dictionary*, 3rd edn, 1992)

Since BON is presenting a view of its own rather than trying to unify what everybody else in the field is doing, we will discuss a method in this book and not worry too much about methodology. The BON method will introduce a recommended analysis and design *process* consisting of nine major tasks to be carried out. Each task uses a set of *input sources* and produces a set of well-defined *deliverables* (either new or updated) as part of the end result.

To complete the tasks, a developer will be involved in a number of standard *activities* (also nine as it happens), some of them more related to analysis (problem domain) and some more related to design (solution space). These activities may occur in varying degrees during several of the tasks, and are therefore considered orthogonal to the process.

This chapter will discuss some issues that are considered important in the BON method for analysis and design. The next chapter will then describe the nine major tasks of the BON process: what should be performed and which deliverables to produce. Finally, chapter 8 will discuss the typical analysis and design activities that will occur as part of carrying out the individual tasks of the process.

6.2 SIMULATING AN IDEAL PROCESS

Anyone who has been involved in intellectually taxing activities—trying to understand and solve a complex problem—knows that the process of arriving at a good solution is far from regular. On the contrary, the most common impression during the course of the effort is often a sense of total disorder and utter confusion. This is also true for cases where the final result eventually turns out to be very simple and elegant, and the greatest sense of confusion is often experienced shortly before the crucial perspective is discovered.

So the bad news is that a rational modeling process, where each step follows logically from the previous ones and everything is done in the most economic order, does not exist. Complex problem solving just does not work that way. But the good news is that we can fake it. We can try to follow an established procedure as closely as possible, and when we finally have our solution (achieved as usual through numerous departures from the ideal process), we can produce the documentation that would have resulted if we had followed the ideal process [Parnas 1986].

This gives us a number of advantages:

- The process will guide us, even if we do not always follow it. When we are overwhelmed by the complexity of a task, it can give us a good idea about how to proceed.

- We will come closer to rational modeling if we try to follow a reasonable procedure instead of just working *ad hoc*.

- It becomes much easier to measure progress. We can compare what has been produced to what the ideal process calls for, and identify areas where we are behind (or ahead).

Such an ideal process is part of BON and will be presented in the next chapter, but first we will discuss some general modeling issues.

6.3 ENTERPRISE MODELING

Object-oriented analysis may be used as the top-level instrument for the design and implementation of software, but its modeling capabilities extend far beyond that. Any type of scenario consisting of a number of *actors* exhibiting certain *behaviors* is potentially a candidate for object-oriented modeling, regardless of whether computers will be involved at some point or not.

For example, human communication and mutual understanding within an organization may be greatly enhanced by creating unified models of company-wide concepts and tasks and their interactions. This type of analysis, often called *enterprise modeling*, may very well turn out to be one of the major areas of application for object-oriented techniques in the future. In large organizations, one can hardly overestimate the importance of a common view of the terms and concepts used as a basis for making decisions in various areas of responsibility.

Object-oriented techniques have a great potential for enterprise modeling, which needs both the abstractional power to model very diverse organizational entities, and the simplicity to be understandable to a large number of people with various roles and backgrounds. The metaphor of describing reality as a set of communicating objects that can be asked to behave in certain ways through a set of applicable operations seems to be very appealing to many people outside the computer industry. This is of course no coincidence, since it resembles the way we normally classify things around us and make decisions by picturing alternative future scenarios in our minds.

One may argue that enterprise modeling needs more than the basic object-oriented concepts to be expressive enough. This may very well be true for complicated cases, but the additional needs are probably quite different for different types of organization.

6.4 WHAT IS ANALYSIS AND WHAT IS DESIGN?

If we interpret the words analysis and design according to their normal use in most disciplines, the question in the section title becomes trivial. Analysis means taking things apart for examination, while design is to work out the structure or form of something. Both activities are of course needed in *all* phases of software development, although different parts and structures may be involved at different times.

In recent years, however, the terms have gradually started to acquire an alternative meaning in the object-oriented world. The approximate consensus in many current books and articles seems to be the following:

- Object-oriented analysis means creating an object-oriented model from the external requirements (a model of the problem).

- Object-oriented design means refining the analysis model into a high-level object-oriented model of a solution.

In our opinion, more appropriate terms should be found for the activities above, since the words analysis and design are much too general and useful to be robbed of their original meaning. The ambiguity introduced creates even greater confusion in a field that is difficult enough as it is. However, until something better catches on, we accept the new interpretation as *de facto* usage.

In this book, we will therefore use analysis and design in both the new and the traditional sense. Analysis classes and design classes will refer to abstractions at different levels in our system (problem vs. solution). Both categories will of course emerge through analysis of various prerequisite conditions. On the other hand, the reader should not be surprised to find hybrid statements like "designing an analysis model". The intended meaning of each term should be clear from the context.

Recursive analysis and design

If we go back to normal language usage, analysis means investigating the details of something, while design means building a new structure. Whenever we decide the form of something, we are designing—no matter if we are building a model for the real-time distribution of X-ray pictures in a wide area network of hospitals or figuring out the best organization for storing prime numbers. And every design needs analysis in order to be carried out properly.

Object-oriented technology yields a very flexible recursive model here. First, the initial requirements are analyzed and an initial model is designed. The class structure and public interfaces of this model then become a new set of requirements for the next level of abstraction. The dual application of analysis/design is then repeated the number of times needed to reach the desired level. This usually means executable code at some point, but not necessarily.

Since class interfaces only specify how the corresponding objects should behave—not what internal mechanism may be used to achieve this behavior— the recursive model is not just theoretically pleasing, but highly realistic and usable in practice. The idea that any software development should be divided into exactly three parts (analysis, design, and implementation) is in fact arbitrary.

Multiple language metaphor

Since we are never interested in data *per se* in a system (only in various manifestations of it) we should employ the philosophy of the abstract data type. All data is viewed only indirectly through the behavior of certain black box objects which can return values or change information. Whether the objects supplying information actually store the values or just cheat by asking other objects behind the scenes, the clients do not want to know about.

The collective interface of a set of classes specialized to solve a certain general task is actually a language tailored to applications in the corresponding area. Therefore, designing an object-oriented model of a certain problem domain behavior can be viewed as designing a language in which it is easy to express that type of behavior. (This perspective was presented already in 1969 by Edsger Dijkstra in his seminal monograph "Notes on Structured Programming" [Dijkstra 1972]. There, program development is viewed as the successive design of languages for a series of abstract machines.)

Once the language is there, it is a simple matter to specify the high-level behavior and also modify it later, provided we stick to the area which the language was meant for. Instead of twisting our high-level concepts to fit an obsolete standard language whose limitations we cannot do anything about (the reality of most programmers for the last 30 years), we can simply change the rules and invent new specialized languages as needed.

What remains is then to implement the operations of the new language. We therefore create a second language consisting of classes with operations that are particularly good at expressing the behavior needed by the operations of the first language, so they can be easily implemented. This is repeated until the innermost language can be understood and translated into executable code by some compiler (or we stop earlier if no execution is desired). Of course, we take care not to invent languages which are close to existing ones, and all the general principles for constructing good class libraries apply [Johnson 1988, Meyer 1994a].

Note that when we talk about multiple languages in the object-oriented sense, we are referring to semantic content. The syntax of the languages remains uniform at all levels (feature calls on objects), and seamlessness can thus be preserved in spite of the great diversity.

So a system model consists of many layers of abstraction, each viewed as a specialized language. Some of the layers may be hierarchically nested, while others extend orthogonally across the system. Therefore, no natural borderline between design and implementation exists; what is considered design will just have to be decided from one case to another. And what is more—in spite of many authors giving the opposite impression—there is no clear dividing line between the analysis and design models either.

What is problem and what is solution?

The world has no *a priori* structure. A bird flying across a forest looking for a good place to build a nest will certainly classify the trees very differently from the lumberjack who is at the same time clearing his way below the foliage in search of material for his employer's new line of ship fittings. And if we could talk to the neurons firing off the classification patterns in the lumberjack's brain, they would probably consider the whole concept of tree arbitrary and useless. So anyone who thinks reality is just there for the analyst to discover is in for a surprise.

To understand a problem, we need to impose a structure on its parts—but a good structure is defined by what we want to achieve. If our task is to computerize some manual work in an organization, we can often start from a set of concepts and views more or less shared by the people involved. We may have to study the area for a long time to detect these views, and when we do, it only means we have a better understanding of the problem and how things are carried out today. It does not necessarily mean we should keep the views (not even their core elements) when transferring to the electronic world. Sometimes traditional concepts carry over very naturally; sometimes the new opportunities inherent in automatic processing may change the picture completely.

So we need to create an analysis model whose abstractions make it easy to understand the desired system behavior, but are still flexible enough to allow many different realizations. This may result in classes representing tangible objects, but may just as often result in classes that are abstractions of what users consider independent concepts of the enterprise or of more general concepts the users have not even thought about. In fact, physical objects in the problem domain, which many books recommend as a starting point, are often too special to be suitable as classes at the highest level in the resulting analysis model (see for example the case study modeling a video recorder). We should often look for something beyond the common view held by actors in the problem domain, since our classification needs are not necessarily the same as theirs.

6.5 REUSE

Reusability should always be our goal, and the aim with shifting to object-oriented development is that the amount of reuse should increase dramatically compared with traditional approaches.

Levels of reuse

This increased reuse comes from several levels of abstraction. We can distinguish at least three such levels:

- The *basic level* whose components are expected to be needed by almost any application, regardless of type.

- The *domain level* covering typical needs in a certain application area.

- The *corporate level* containing reusable components tailored to the specific needs of the enterprise.

At the basic level, expected to be part of any good object-oriented language environment, there are the fundamental data structures of lists, sets, stacks, arrays, hash tables, and trees that constitute the archetypical "wheel" of software engineering since they are constantly reinvented day and night, at high cost, by programmers all over the world using traditional languages.

The basic implementation algorithms are known to any literate programmer, yet have enough variation to prevent effective reuse in all but the object-oriented approaches. Large, coherent, and extensively used data structure libraries exist in Smalltalk and Eiffel, while the hybrid character of C++ and its *ad hoc* memory management makes the creation and combination of such libraries much harder.

Another prominent component at the basic level is support for standardized graphical interface elements. Only very special applications can still afford to repeat the enormous effort invested in GUI toolkits like X/Motif or Microsoft Windows, yet most users expect graphical interfaces in modern systems. Higher-level object-oriented models can be built on top of standard toolkits, and provide developers with the means of creating very sophisticated user interfaces at very low cost through easy reuse. The class libraries should then support distinctive user metaphors like the MVC model for Smalltalk [Krasner 1988], InterViews for C++ [Linton 1989], Nextstep's Workspace for Objective-C, or EiffelBuild and EiffelVision for Eiffel [Meyer 1994b].

At the domain level, we should expect in the future to be able to buy or acquire reusable components for most of the familiar problems connected with a certain application type rather than developing these ourselves. However, the offerings so far are quite limited, so we may have to wait some time before this becomes reality. In the meantime, many such components will have to be developed and maintained as part of the corporate-level class library. Good libraries at this level may become the most valuable assets a corporation may have in the future, since they represent accumulated knowledge that can be capitalized. This is perhaps especially important in the software business, whose turnover rate is extremely high.

Reuse policy

Besides trying to locate already existing reusable components, it is also important to take an active decision regarding the future reusability of the software under development. Even if the sign of a good object-oriented developer is in fact a Pavlovian reflex of almost physical nausea whenever a familiar pattern must be repeated, there is always a short-term cost associated with building reusable software. This cost may very well be regained already through increased clarity and reuse within the scope of the project, but not always.

At the *basic* reuse level, reusability should always be our first concern, since it normally pays off immediately. Developing a well-structured set of classes for building error messages, manipulating general strings, handling command line arguments, etc., does not cost very much in a good object-oriented environment (in case they are not already available). Repeating *ad hoc* solutions over and over, on the other hand, will not only cost more in the long term, but also hinder the fundamental shift of attitude so extremely important for the next generation of programmers: that it is possible to take control instead of just being controlled by the course of events (see the last section of this chapter).

When a developer builds a reusable component that encapsulates a recurring problem pattern, this is not only an act of reducing future workloads—it also represents a significant personal investment. By constructing components, developers gain insight into parts of problem domains that will improve their future ability to construct good models at all levels. It leads to greater job satisfaction, since everybody wants to be on top of things instead of just being used by the circumstances. The increased enthusiasm will wear off on others through discussions at whiteboards and over coffee, and will gradually lead to a substantial increase in the so-called human capital currently being recognized by the economic sciences as the real asset of modern society.

So, we should in fact go for reusability even when it appears to cost a little more in terms of time and salary, since in the long term it will not. However, there is a limit to everything and it is particularly important that if we invest in reusable components, the anticipated reuse should also happen in practice.

Since future reuse of more specialized elements at the *corporate* or *domain* levels depends on many factors, these must be actively addressed before determining how much should be invested here. If the company's product strategy changes, reusable components supporting what was produced yesterday may quickly be rendered useless. High-quality libraries that remain aesthetic monuments in a software database make no one happy, least of all the originators.

Just as for any other project activities we must make a *cost/benefit* analysis to decide where we should put our money and effort, and when. For the application of this economic principle in a software engineering context, see for example [Boehm 1981].

Planned vs. accidental reuse

There is a debate going on in some object-oriented circles about whether reuse should be "planned" or "accidental". The more orthodox school seems to advocate that we should only allow reuse of software initially built to be reusable. We find this line of argument very strange.

First, if all reuse were planned beforehand there would not be any point in calling it "reuse", since it would just be plain usage. We do not say "Today I reused my word processor," because the word processor was built to be executed any number of times compiling various documents. A class library is no different; if it was built as a general toolbox open to anyone, when we say we are "reusing" a class from this library, we really mean "using".

Second, the fact that the word reuse has a flavor of unplannedness about it is no coincidence, but an important strategic point. The reason to move from traditional to object-oriented techniques is not only to get more flexibility for building families of abstractions from scratch, but also to get out of the straitjacket of deciding too much too soon (cf. the *open–closed* principle in [Meyer 1988a]).

In fact, the rapid changes in technology and software requirements guarantee that we will only know (or even suspect) for a minority of cases what will be needed in the future. Therefore, restricting reuse to what can be successfully planned would not leave us much better off than with the old techniques.

The decision whether to reuse a piece of existing software should only be based on how well it can solve the current problem. Anything else is beside the point, and we would much rather reuse a good-quality class built without a thought of ever being used outside its context, than employ a planned "reusable" component of poor quality.

It is true that developing highly reusable software is not easy, and effective reuse does not happen by itself just because we now have classes instead of subroutines. Careless reuse of small heterogeneous pieces here and there may of course risk losing consistency and miss global patterns. But this is no different from the general problem with any evolving system. When successive additions tend to degrade the initial system integrity we must restructure and generalize, no matter if the added pieces were new or reused.

In practice, so-called accidental reuse will therefore mostly require some modification to the set of classes in order to make them more general, more robust, and better documented, but this is just a logical consequence of the incremental nature of object-oriented development.

Sometimes we know that we are going to need a whole set of related abstractions, and then we may plan early for a large library of reusable components. In most cases, however, we simply cannot see this until the system has evolved for some time. In the meantime, we are much better off with "accidental reuse" than with no reuse at all.

Reuse manager

Reuse of other people's products requires trust. If we do not have strong reasons to believe that the quality and understandability of a reusable class is indeed high enough, we will prefer to create a new class to gain full control. This is particularly true in good object-oriented environments where the development of new abstractions requires so much less effort. The "not invented here" syndrome may sometimes play a part, but not nearly as often as many people seem to think.

In fact, it is our experience that good developers who are accustomed to routinely creating reusable abstractions are also very eager to reuse existing work, as long as they can trust the quality. The standards of a reusable library must be therefore be high, so that people can always rely on the components and do not need to think twice about using them (provided the functionality fits). Since the cost of reuse also depends very much on the difficulty of identifying suitable candidates, easy access to well-indexed class libraries through efficient class browsers and good general documentation becomes extremely important as the number of components grows large.

For both these reasons, if we want to promote a corporate database of reusable components, particularly in large organizations where the people involved do not all know each other, somebody *must* be assigned the responsibility of keeping this database in good shape. The classes must be consistent and adhere to certain company standards, so it becomes easy to judge whether a particular component is suitable or not.

We call such a responsible person a *reuse manager*, and the role should be assigned to somebody with high skills in three areas: abstract modeling, the technology and problem domain embodied by the reusable components, and human communication. Some even claim that without assigning a suitable person to this role and setting aside a budget for it, reuse on a broad scale within an organization will just never happen [Goldberg 1991].

Besides administrating the professional components, an important task of the reuse manager is to take care of potentially reusable software. Very often good ideas arising in projects are only carried to a point sufficient to cover the needs of the current development, as time and budget will not permit the investment needed to create a product usable in more general contexts. The work done may nevertheless be quite substantial, and it is then important to pave the way for future capitalization of the effort.

Therefore, a high-quality *component library* is not enough—there should also be a less demanding formal collection of software artifacts, which may be called a *reuse repository*. Project software with the potential of becoming fully fledged reusable components, or simply representing general designs that may be of interest to other projects, should be submitted to the reuse manager for inclusion in the reuse repository.

The repository must be consistently organized and documented well enough for users to assess the potentials of its elements. However, the quality of the individual contributions must be allowed to vary much more than in the corresponding component library.

6.6 USER CENTERED DESIGN

As computer-based tools are becoming part of the everyday life of a rapidly increasing number of professionals, the concept of *system usability* is considered more and more important. It has even been given an ISO definition [ISO 1990]:

A concept comprising the effectiveness, efficiency and satisfaction with which specified users can achieve specified goals in a particular environment.

In this section, we will briefly discuss a reference model for an approach called user centered design presented by Hans Marmolin in [Marmolin 1993], aiming to apply the results from the research on human–computer interaction to the design of software.

Roles of users and computers

Since the 1960s there has been a gradual paradigm shift in the sciences of both psychology and computing. The majority of researchers now view computers as vehicles for enhancing the human intellect rather than ultimately replacing it. (Some AI researchers still advocate, like Douglas Hofstadter [Hofstadter 1980], that it may, at least theoretically, be possible to describe the human mind by algorithms. However, the theoretical physicist Roger Penrose recently presented a very intriguing and convincing reasoning to the contrary [Penrose 1989].)

Since users normally know best how to solve their own professional problems, a system should not try to lay out a rigid work plan in advance. Rather it should provide basic facilities to be combined freely by users, thus taking advantage of the unique capabilities of humans to analyze complex situations, recognize patterns, follow many threads simultaneously, and adapt quickly to new requirements from the environment.

A reference model for user centered design

The model for human–machine interaction chosen in [Marmolin 1993] views user behavior as a goal-oriented process, and human–machine interaction as a stepwise transformation from goal to primitive actions through a number of levels describing different aspects of the interaction. These levels are of course in reality tightly interlaced, and must be chosen somewhat arbitrarily (up to 12 different levels have been suggested by other researchers). Marmolin uses only three, thus keeping the model simple:

- *The pragmatic level.* A description in goal-oriented terms of the tasks a user should be able to solve assisted by the system (the user requirements).

- *The conceptual level.* A description in system-related terms of functions, objects, and processes that can be used to achieve the goals.

- *The interface level.* A description of how to deal with system functions and objects and of the words and symbols that must be used to activate them. This includes the physical operations needed, and the physical presentation of information by the system.

The user achieves a goal by successively laying out a strategy for approaching it stepwise through a series of actions which can be solved by the system. The more knowledge the user has about the system properties on all its conceptual levels, the easier it becomes to translate a goal into an effective set of physical operations applied to the user interface.

For example, the user goal to clean up a text file directory (pragmatic level) must be translated into a series of subgoals like creating safety backups, removing old files, reorganizing and renaming (still pragmatic level). Each subgoal must then be translated into functions applicable to system objects, like removing a file by submitting its corresponding representation to a garbage bin (conceptual level). Finally, these conceptual actions must be translated into syntactically correct system actions, like depressing a mouse key on the file icon and dragging it to the garbage bin icon (interface level).

During the course of the action, both goals and strategy are often modified based on information about what has happened so far. For example, looking at the set of file icons in the directory as it gradually becomes more readable may reveal that a changed file structure (perhaps a merge with some other directory) would in fact be preferable. Relevant system feedback to stop unnecessary work or unwanted effects is therefore extremely important for usability.[7]

In terms of this model, the purpose of user centered design can be defined as finding ways to decrease the cognitive distance between the successive levels. By designing the conceptual level to map naturally to the goals represented by the user requirements, finding relevant system functions for a task is facilitated; by reflecting the system concepts in the user interface, choosing the right keystrokes or mouse clicks to invoke a chosen function becomes obvious.

The model represents, of course, a highly simplified view of reality, disregarding the strong dependencies between the levels. Nevertheless, it can give new insights into the problem of designing usable systems. We will look some more at the aspects of interaction represented by each level.

---

[7] We certainly do not speak for the kind of feedback that used to be standard practice in many early traditional environments ("Welcome to the File Copier XYZ, Copyright QED: 0001 files copied"). Rather, we favor the UNIX principle to shut up when things proceed according to plan, and only report anomalies or obvious dangers of unintended results. Routine verbosity always hides relevant information.

The pragmatic aspect

The tasks at the pragmatic level are directly related to the user's representation of the problem domain, which usually contains much more than what is in the system. So the basic concepts at this level are domain specific and system independent, but the system concepts chosen must facilitate the transformation of goals and tasks at the pragmatic level into a series of system actions.

The most characteristic property of such a transformation is that it is *not* a sequential process guided by a well-defined plan. The order and application of tasks vary; several tasks are often in process simultaneously, even if they cannot be done in parallel. The human limitations in memory capacity and precision usually prevent any effective long-term planning. The strategies tend to be fuzzy, variable, and flexible depending on continuous reassessments of the situation. Humans seem to solve problems by going back and forth between various tasks in a seemingly "random walk" towards a goal [Cypher 1986].

The conceptual aspect

The domain-level tasks must be expressed by the user in terms of functions and objects supplied by the system [Moran 1983]. Computer systems are regarded by users as complex models of reality, which they are constantly trying to understand by relating new experiences with the system to previous ones. The user gradually builds a model of the system, and only the functions in accord with this model are ever used. The user's perception of a system is incomplete and partly wrong, based on analogies and seldom corrected, since it is often possible to find reasonable (but erroneous) explanations for the system behavior in various situations [Carroll 1982].

Efficient interaction requires that the model offered by the system (on which its design is based) closely matches the user's mental model of the system. The fact that users often perceive word processors in close analogy with their mental model of a typewriter has been studied, showing how the matching parts were easily mastered while the differences gave rise to many errors and slow typing [Douglas 1983].

An important aspect of this level has to do with the user's choice of system functions to fulfill a certain task. A user does not always choose the best way of solving a problem, but rather one which minimizes the subjective cost of usage. This cost is based on the effectiveness of the functions, their perceived complexity, how well they are understood, and the effort required to learn how to use them. These factors are valued differently by different users.

So-called naive users tend to favor simple functions, even if they are not very effective and may require unnecessary repetitions. They value minimal study and often overrate the difficulty of learning new and more efficient functions.

They prefer to use well-known procedures, while experienced users tend to learn more functions, valuing usability more than extreme simplicity. Usually, only a small fraction of the functions offered by an environment is used routinely. It was found that among the 400 commands generally available on UNIX systems in the beginning of the 1980s, the 20 most frequently used covered 70% of all usage [Kraut 1983].

The interface aspect

Having decided what system functions to use for a given domain-level task, the next step a user has to perform is to invoke the selected functions by transforming them into a series of physical operations (keying commands, selecting from menus, dragging and dropping, pressing buttons, etc.). This may be considered the syntactic part of the total translation from subgoal to action. The user's perception of the system is often strongly guided by the interface, since the continuous process of using it tends to play a far more important role than formal education ("if everything else fails—read the manual").

This routine of "learning by doing" often leads to naive models and rigid system usage: what is known to have worked before is repeated even when the user suspects it is not the right way. It is important to recognize this practice, and that users will learn by making mistakes. Therefore, care must be taken regarding system responses to strange or unexpected user behavior.

Another thing to note is that learning is often unevenly distributed over the system functions, so the average degree of user knowledge may not be all that relevant. Occasional users may know some functions well, while experienced professional users often are occasional users of some functions.

Finally, three different cognitive states of a user may be distinguished when working with the interface model of a system: a verbal, a spatial, and a controlling state. The verbal state corresponds to command dialogs, the spatial to direct manipulation dialogs (drawing, pointing, dragging), and the controlling state to multiple choice dialogs (menus, buttons, function keys).

For example, when editing a document in a multi-media environment the user switches between various forms of interaction. Sometimes the text content is changed, sometimes the document layout is manipulated, and sometimes predefined document processing functions are invoked. Choosing an interface that forces a cognitive state that does not match the current interaction form closely (such as going through a menu hierarchy to move a figure) often leads to time delays and increased error frequency because of the extra mental transformations required. Particularly when a user is trying to solve a difficult problem that requires deep concentration, cognitive state changes forced by the computing tools can be very taxing.

User metaphors

A significant characteristic of a good system is that it presents a clear abstract model of what is going on during execution. Instead of just offering chunks of vaguely related functions and letting the user group them to create enough structure to figure out what to do, the system should actively support the mental picture of a virtual world populated with certain actors that behave according to clearly understandable rules. This applies regardless of whether the user is human or another program (since somewhere behind a client call there lurks a programmer with the same basic needs to understand how to use the system properly). We call this mental picture a *user metaphor*.

A metaphor can often be chosen to mimic analogous physical environments that are part of the cultural heritage of most users and therefore natural to use and easy to remember [Lakoff 1980]. For example, if a system for handling documents supports the metaphor of a set of ordered racks with drawers, where each drawer contains a number of folders with individual documents in it, it does not take many seconds for a user to transpose the familiar layout of an office into that of the screen.

Some of these metaphors may be quite elaborate and thus very expressive, but since they are so well known, people do not perceive them as intricate. We therefore get a full-blown communication language between the user and a complex system for free, and we get immediate acceptance also from users who would not touch anything that had the slightest air of complexity about it.

Graphical user interfaces have done much to popularize this idea, since in this case the metaphor is so obvious that it can hardly escape anybody. When the graphical interface paradigm—mostly developed at Xerox PARC in the 1970s [Kay 1977]—was first presented to the people on a broad scale through the introduction of the Macintosh computer in 1984, so-called naive computer users could do the most amazing things right from the start, without even needing a manual. This was a true revolution made possible by hardware advances, but also by the necessary mental shift of software developers.

The important thing to remember about user metaphors, though, is that they must be part of the *user's* general knowledge. Therefore, it is not enough to talk to other developers (no matter how experienced) to find out what mappings to use. Interviews with several potential users, preferably in their normal workplaces, can reveal what mental pictures most of them share regarding their work, and what metaphors will therefore be likely to succeed in practice [Lovgren 1994].

The fact that direct manipulation of graphical icons through dragging and dropping using mouse buttons is often very appealing to inexperienced computer users does not automatically mean that it is the best way to communicate for a more sophisticated user. However, mouse clicks just represent command syntax; if we prefer a good textual language, this may be offered as an alternative without affecting the underlying metaphor.

Modeling of interaction levels

Marmolin has gone a step further and devised a user centered design method based on the reference model described above. In his method, the three interaction levels are mapped into three corresponding representations of the system: a requirements model, a design model, and an interface model [Marmolin 1993].

Such a general partitioning of the analysis model is not done in BON, because its usefulness depends very much on the kind of application we are developing. Maintaining a requirements model separate from the analysis model tends to break the seamlessness of the approach. It may still be worthwhile for large systems that are planned to be implemented in several different versions, or have special demands for requirements tracing, but for most systems one model will be enough.

As we will advocate in a following section, it is not clear where an interface model stops and a corresponding conceptual model starts, and the importance of the interface part will vary greatly from one system to another. However, the interaction levels and metaphor concept described in this section should be part of the developer's mindset and actively guide the analysis and design process.

6.7 ROLES OF ANALYSIS OBJECTS

If our goal is flexible systems that are likely to evolve gracefully over time to meet new requirements, we should not put all our emphasis on *de facto* objects in the problem domain (physical things, organizations, items handled, common domain terms, etc.).

Finding such objects is often a great help when trying to understand the problem, and some of them will serve as initial candidates to become classes. However, many of them are only manifestations of more general underlying patterns, which are what we should try and capture instead. Also, moving to a computerized solution usually opens up entirely new possibilities, which may call for a modified (or radically changed) set of basic concepts.

Anyway, no matter what model we come up with, the degree of potential reuse of the abstractions is always variable. Some classes will represent stable abstractions, such as general information structures, basic interaction facilities, and concepts fundamental to the enterprise or application domain. Others will reflect specialized, volatile behavior, acting more like temporary glue between comparatively stable components. The classes in a system will therefore play different roles, which has lead some practitioners to look for a fixed role separation that can form a basis for a general analysis method.

For example, OOSE [Jacobson 1992] recommends using three different types of analysis classes (called entity objects, interface objects, and control objects) depending on which one of three orthogonal system aspects (information, presentation, or behavior) is considered most prominent for the corresponding abstraction.

Entity objects are meant to represent more stable abstractions containing longer-term information needed by the system, control objects encapsulate the more volatile system behavior, while interface objects take care of external communication. Grouping the analysis classes into these three categories leads, in their view, to systems that are more adaptable to requirement changes.

Although a role separation is certainly useful in any system's analysis model (BON uses clustering for this) and will most probably lead to more flexible designs if done correctly, imposing one standard initial classification on the analysis abstractions in every system is too restrictive. Any predefined set of classification criteria will be arbitrary, and therefore counterproductive in cases where these criteria are less relevant.

As we will argue below, the external interface of a system usually consists of several layers, and what exact parts of it are to be considered the stable "essence" of the interface is by no means obvious. Therefore, assigning the interface responsibility to a specific set of classes at an early stage usually means taking premature design decisions which instead lead to *less* flexibility.

Moreover, what is important for achieving robust architectures is not to search for "behavior" versus "information"; it is to look for abstractions which are as *stable* as possible. This has to do with the respective generality (in the application context) of the encapsulated behavior, not with whether it needs to store information or not.

Object oriented abstraction supports free classification, and it must remain free if we are to take full advantage of its potential. Instead, the professional software engineer must be familiar with many different architectures, their strengths and weaknesses, and be able to choose one that best fits the conditions of a given project.

6.8 MODELING A SYSTEM INTERFACE

Systems as objects

At the highest level, a system can be viewed as a black box exhibiting certain well-defined behaviors in response to various incoming stimuli. So if we can identify the main types of incoming stimuli and specify the actions that should be taken by the system for each of them, we could in principle always view a system as one object whose operations correspond to the various responses to incoming stimuli from the external world.

In practice, however, the complete interface between a system and its environment is much too large and contains too many different types of communication to be modeled by just one class. Even if the number of top-level services available to the users of a system (where a user could also be another system or hardware device—not just a human operator) may be small, many auxiliary functions are usually needed. Primary commands will often trigger series of information exchanges between system and user to pass data through screen forms or graphical widgets, read from secondary storage files, handle external interrupts, or follow the conventions of various communication protocols.

The full system interface is therefore mostly distributed over many classes, some dealing with input from the keyboard and pointing devices, others communicating with the underlying file system or some database handler, yet others exchanging information with external processes. Although control is always initiated from some top-level objects in the system (ultimately one per system process—the root objects), the actual detailed communication with the external world is delegated to more specialized objects.

Front and back ends of systems

There are two main aspects of a system interface: passive and active. The *passive* system interface is the part that can be requested to perform some action on behalf of an external user.[8] This is the front end of the system. The *active* system interface, on the other hand, is the part that asks for services from the external world (files, databases, other systems), usually as part of servicing some incoming request. This is the system's back end.

These two types of interface play very different roles and cannot be seen as just encapsulations of the incoming and outgoing events respectively. An outgoing event could be either an active request (issued by the system) for an external service, or a passive response to an external request (issued by a system user). Analogously, an incoming event may be either an external request from a system user, or a response from an external system to a previous request from the system. Some external systems may play both roles: sometimes responding to requests from the system, sometimes issuing requests to it.

---

[8] Unless clearly stated in the context, a system *user* always refers to any external actor (human or machine) requesting services from the system.

Most of the active external system interface is elaborated during design, since it has more to do with *how* a service is to be fulfilled than *what* is to be done. However, sometimes well-defined external systems are important prerequisites that are really part of the system requirements, and then some of the back end may have to be modeled already during analysis. Here, we will concentrate on the passive interface, that is the collective services available to system users.

Several levels of interface

So what is it that really constitutes the interface to the system services? Superficially it can be viewed as the union of all the parts of the various objects handling external information interchange, since this is where the actual interaction between the system and its environment takes place. However, this view is usually too simplistic, because interfacing a system does not just mean passing some data back and forth, but rather communicating with an underlying metaphor.

Pinpointing exactly where this communication takes place is generally not easy and sometimes not even possible when many classes in several layers collectively model the metaphor. If the American ambassador in Moscow communicates with the Russian president through an interpreter, does that mean the interface object is the president or the interpreter? Well, it depends on what is considered important in the situation.

For example, assume we have a library metaphor offering the mental picture of a set of books to a certain type of system user. The internal system model actually handling the books may view them differently—as sortable objects, as copyrighted material, as stock items of certain size and weight, as assets with certain values—but the users view them as books.

The next question is how they should be presented to the user—as text lines on an alphanumeric terminal, as icons on a graphical display, as audio recordings for visually handicapped users? Given a graphical representation, how should it be detailed—books standing up or lying down, variable size or just one standard, possible to manipulate graphically or just simple icons? Given a detailed view, which look and feel should we pick—Macintosh style manipulation, X/Motif, Windows?

Some of the detailed views are usually not addressed during analysis, but sometimes they are part of the requirements and must be taken into account. As has been argued before, there is no objective level of abstraction for analysis, since what is special in one context may be quite general in another. What we should always strive for is a set of abstractions that will be as resilient as possible with respect to future requirement changes, but the nature of those changes is completely dependent on what we are developing.

No special analysis interface classes

What the previous section tries to show is that there is (in general) no fundamental "system interface" that can always be isolated and modeled as special classes. Rather, the communication between user and system passes through many layers of abstraction which gradually shift the focus of interest from sequences of basic mechanical data into the higher-level concepts actually symbolized by the data.

The codes of individual keys on a keyboard and the button clicks and corresponding coordinates of pointing devices are translated step by step over higher-level concepts such as graphical menus, buttons, and icons into objects collecting information that are beginning to mirror the objects of the chosen metaphor. Where the actual interface lies (which can supposedly change and therefore should be replaceable) varies radically from one system to another. In fact, we can usually expect changes at many levels—the one closest to the external world need not be the most volatile—so the classes collectively making up the interface should be treated just like any other set of evolving abstractions. The same general principles apply for finding common patterns and to separate different concerns.

The most natural interface to a domain object is captured by the abstract operations that a user would want to apply to it, and those operations should (in general) be viewed as operations on the domain object itself, not as operations on some artificial interface object. Typical domain objects in our last example might be books and bookshelves. Suppose we want to allow a move operation on books so they can be transferred by the user from one shelf to another. Modeling a separate book interface object containing a version of this operation would in most cases not make sense at all, but only increase complexity and decrease understandability.

On the contrary, the interface aspect when moving the book is a minor one that should not be allowed to influence the analysis model at all, but be postponed to later design. What is important here is the user's mental picture of moving an abstract book between abstract shelves that is so easy to comprehend because of its similarity to the physical reality in most cultures. This metaphor is what will make the system understandable and accepted; the details involved when telling the machine to do it can usually wait.

Of course the traditional GUI aspects are by no means unimportant for users, but they belong to another domain more or less independent of our application. So when we say that the details can wait, we assume that there will be adequate packages to choose from during design. Considering the amount of effort invested in major graphical interface packages, redoing such designs is not affordable for normal applications anyway.

Again, this is not to say that interface objects are never interesting. On the contrary, if the handling of many graphical views of the same underlying concept is deemed important or other changes can be anticipated that would be much easier to meet if the interface is modeled separately, interface objects can be very useful. Since external interface modeling can be done in many different ways, the normal procedure is to adopt a model supported by the development environment chosen for implementation.

However, without special knowledge of the system to be modeled, there is no *a priori* reason to favor a separate external interface abstraction before any other good way of structuring the system. Designing robust software is always a tradeoff between possible directions of future flexibility. Since a limited amount of effort is available for each development, rigidly favoring just a few of these directions will only decrease the chances of finding the abstractions that really pay off for a particular system.

6.9 SYSTEM USAGE

There are two aspects of any systems development: short-term requirements and long-term investment. Both are important for systems development.

The short-term requirements are often the direct reason to start a project, and fulfilling them is necessary to finance the development. These requirements are mostly expressed in terms of how this particular system is going to be used. The long-term investment has to do with how the system should be structured both internally and externally to be correct and reliable, easy to use, and easy to adapt to future requirement changes. Part of this investment has to do with finding components that can be reused not only in modified versions of this system, but also in other systems.

A good analysis and design method should concentrate on the investment aspect, since this will yield the greatest payoff in the long run. However, a prerequisite is of course that the short-term conditions be met. Therefore system usage is always an important factor in all developments.

A scenario in BON describes a characteristic type of system usage whose details may vary, like registering an attendee in a conference system, or preprogramming a recording on a VCR unit. Systematically going through scenarios is a good way of finding new classes and of checking the completeness of the evolving static structure of abstractions. However, always using scenarios as the top-level abstractions from which the system architecture is successively derived, as advocated in OOSE [Jacobson 1992] (where scenarios are called *use cases*), is going too far.

The goal is to find stable abstractions that lead to robust systems, but these abstractions may be found using different approaches. In some applications, certain usage patterns may be very stable (sometimes even regulated by formal business rules or standards), and then it may be quite helpful to model these patterns as separate classes in the system. A case in point is the telephone business, where a phone call has survived many different technologies and been executed by the user in more or less the same fashion since the beginning of the century. Under such circumstances the use cases "come for free", and we may benefit directly from the information they contain.

But when the requirements (as is usually the case) are vague and incomplete, it may simply not be cost-effective to spend a large part of the project budget on the systematic elaboration of many volatile use cases. Since use cases are only a means to an end, understanding what underlying problem the user is trying to solve is often more important. And the best way to reach this understanding is not always by concentrating early on individual use cases (describing how the user is going to work), but rather spending the initial effort on important concepts that will affect this work.

Once a clear understanding of the problem is reached and the right concepts established, a radically different set of use cases may instead fall out as a result of this understanding, perhaps fairly late in the process. Always basing the initial modeling on use cases suffers from many of the same disadvantages as the more traditional approaches of functional decomposition and data flow analysis; unless the use cases are very stable, much of the initial effort may later prove to be wasted.

One may of course argue that once a good system model has been found (by whatever means), the use cases should have become much more stable, and modeling them as abstractions in their own right would then simplify requirements tracing and make minor changes to individual use cases comparatively easy to do in future releases of the system.

However, this is not necessarily so. Since the set of use cases only represents one possible way of communicating with an underlying abstract model, allowing this particular usage to affect the system structure in any deep sense may instead make it more difficult to maintain a clear model and detect in what directions the usage could change to become more effective. Everything has a cost attached, and the important thing is to develop a nose for where the efforts should be concentrated to yield the best return in a given situation. Sometimes use cases are a major help when structuring a system, sometimes they are less important.

Of course, use cases may never be ignored altogether. Before modeling starts the analyst has always formed at least a rough idea about the collective set of use cases, detailed enough to allow an initial small set of classes to be selected. Depending on available user metaphors and other problem domain knowledge, the modeling of these classes may continue up to a point where further elaboration becomes difficult. It is then often useful to group use cases and go through them in detail to obtain more information about how to proceed.

However, this is not just a question of assigning operations to already identified classes. On the contrary, the needed system behavior successively revealed by the use cases should instead make the analyst go back to the drawing board and check for new classes (abstractions) that will help create a more understandable and reusable system. Recall that there is no *a priori* problem domain reality; how you choose to view it depends entirely on what you want to do with it. Therefore, the initial class structure will be far from fixed.

This switching between investigation of use cases and refinement of the evolving class structure may be iterated several times. For each iteration, only the operations which are very basic to the nature of the abstractions found should be assigned; the bulk of the operations come later when the class structure has reached some stability. Often many use cases are studied in parallel to detect common patterns of needed behavior as early as possible, but the focus of interest should always be on the underlying static model.

Class operations may sometimes fall out naturally from system usage, but more often use cases will instead hint at some interesting underlying pattern, perhaps leading to a modified system architecture. Whether this pattern is detected or not depends on the analyst's abstraction skills—not on any simple translation scheme.

6.10 A PARADIGM SHIFT

We conclude this chapter on method issues by drawing attention to a fundamental principle applicable to all software development, which lies at the heart of the BON approach. The next two chapters will then develop the BON method and the standard activities involved in performing its recommended tasks.

Object-oriented modeling and implementation with software contracts is very much a question of changed attitudes. Instead of making an attempt at a solution and then testing the result to see whether you succeeded, you should learn to trust your thoughts and structure your results enough to *know* that you are right before testing begins. You should be willing to bet your last dollar that your solution is (at least in principle) correct.

This is of course not fully possible or feasible in all cases, but the paradigm shift behind it is absolutely crucial. Once you discover that you can be in control instead of just being controlled by circumstances, your life changes radically and there is no return. The new peace of mind and intellectual liberation is just too great to ever let you fall back into the sloppy cut-and-try behavior practiced by programmers who do not know there is an alternative. The importance of this insight is very well expressed by Harlan Mills in [Mills 1975].

7　The BON process

With the discussion in the previous chapter as background, we now turn to the rules and guidelines recommended in BON. This chapter will present a general method for analysis and design, viewed as an idealized process with nine tasks. The next chapter will concentrate on the standard activities that arise as part of completing the tasks. Before embarking on a description of each process task in BON, we will take a look at the standardized BON deliverables.

7.1 THE BON DELIVERABLES

The goal of the BON process is to gradually build the products or *deliverables* shown in figure 7.1. The relative weights of these deliverables are far from equal. Clearly, the leading roles are played by the static architecture diagrams and the class interfaces. These represent the most precise specification of the structure and behavior of the system that will exist prior to implementation, and the idea is that in a suitable object-oriented language environment they should seamlessly be evolved into a set of executable classes. The thrust of the BON method is aimed at producing this static, declarative model.

Some of the object scenario diagrams may also be important, since they can give the developer a good idea of how to implement major public operations in the classes related to the problem domain. However, to a large extent the role of the dynamic scenarios is to help discover classes and suitable structures in the static model, and also serve as a check that what has been modeled is indeed capable of realizing important aspects of the system behavior.

The static charts are used during early analysis, and for communication with non-technical people and domain experts. Their relative importance varies greatly depending on the problem area, how well the task is understood, and the backgrounds of the people involved with problem analysis and others who need to understand early system descriptions. Depending on the circumstances, these charts may or may not be kept as part of the final system documentation. If kept, they should be automatically updated to reflect the evolving system.

System chart
Definition of system and list of associated clusters. Only one system chart per project; subsystems are described through corresponding cluster charts.

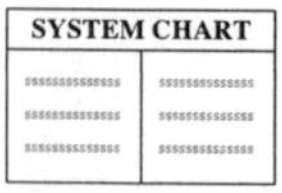

Cluster charts
Definition of clusters and lists of associated classes and subclusters, if any. A cluster may represent a full subsystem or just a group of classes.

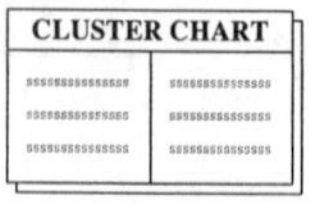

Class charts
Definition of analysis classes in terms of *commands, queries,* and *constraints,* understandable by domain experts and non-technical people.

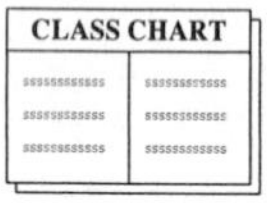

Class dictionary
Alphabetically sorted list of all classes in the system, showing the cluster of each class and a short description. Should be generated automatically from the class charts/interfaces.

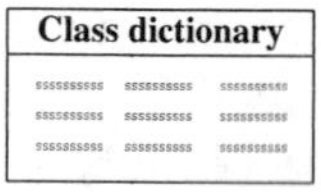

◊ **Static architecture**
Set of diagrams representing possibly nested clusters, class headers, and their relationships. Bird's eye view of the system (zoomable).

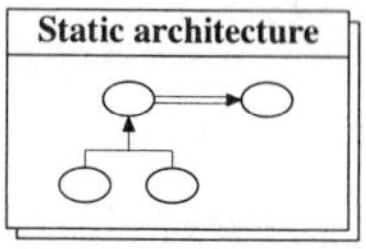

◊ **Class interfaces**
Typed definitions of classes with feature signatures and formal contracts. Detailed view of the system.

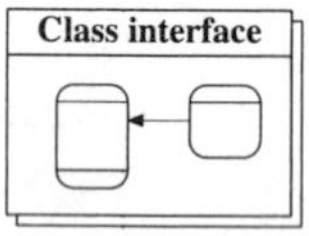

Creation charts
List of classes in charge of creating instances of other classes. Usually only one per system, but may be repeated for subsystems if desirable.

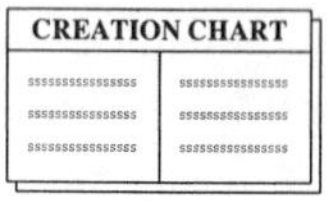

Event charts
Set of incoming external events (stimuli) triggering interesting system behavior and set of outgoing external events forming interesting system responses. May be repeated for subsystems.

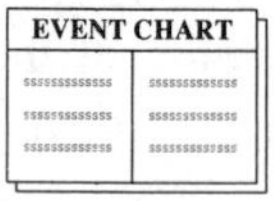

◊ **Scenario charts**
List of object scenarios used to illustrate interesting and representative system behavior. Subsystems may contain local scenario charts.

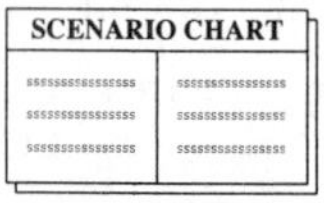

◊ **Object scenarios**
Dynamic diagrams showing relevant object communication for some or all of the scenarios in the scenario chart.

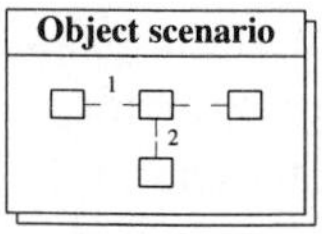

Figure 7.1 BON deliverables: ◊ indicates the most important ones

However, during system design the typed descriptions will dominate. In many cases where the problem is well known and the technical level of the people involved is high, one may prefer to skip the class charts altogether and go directly for typed descriptions. This may be done either with full graphical support through a case tool supporting BON, or by using a mixture of the graphical and textual BON notations (with any personal simplifications or additions that fit the situation). Regardless of case tools, the latter is common during whiteboard sessions among engineers.

The dynamic model may also be of interest during early design. In large systems, there may be many internal events that will lead to interesting non-trivial behavior, so the BON user is free to extend the event and scenario charts to also reflect corresponding internal scenarios that may benefit from a dynamic description. In such cases, local event charts, scenario charts, and object scenarios may be needed for some of the major subsystems.

Reversibility

The BON deliverables are not independent of each other. On the contrary, there are close mappings between several of them, which is precisely the idea of seamless, reversible software engineering. Depending on the situation (type of system, its size, the people involved), the analysis information gathered by the developers and the design decisions taken may enter the system model through different deliverables. The modeling information captured may then be propagated to other deliverables either manually or automatically, or through a combination of both. An overview of all BON deliverables and their interdependencies is given in figure 7.2.

Two complementary types of mapping are shown in the figure: those that require non-trivial human decisions (single arrows), and those that can be automated, at least in part (double arrows). The idea is that a developer should be free to work with the type of deliverable that best fits the situation, and then use mapping rules and automated support to generate or update other related deliverables. For example, one project team may choose to initially produce a large set of class charts, and later proceed to generate templates for the corresponding typed class interfaces, while another project may start directly with the typed versions, but still be able to generate the class charts for documentation purposes.

What is perhaps even more important is that reversibility allows the mechanism used for creating a given BON deliverable to change during the course of a software project. A typical way of working may be to start with the high-level untyped charts combined with some partial static diagrams and dynamic scenarios. Later, when the requirements have become more stable and

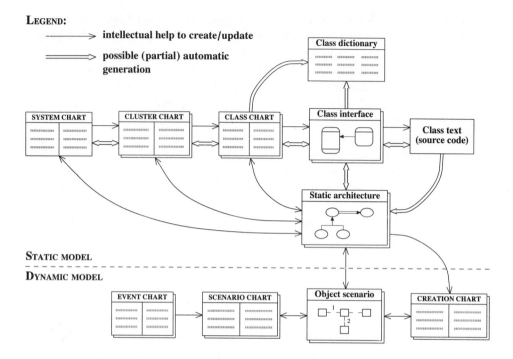

Figure 7.2   Dependencies between BON deliverables

the problem is better understood, typing will be needed to advance the system model. The intellectual effort is then usually shifted to the formal class interfaces, and subsequent updates carried out directly on these.

At that point in time (after the initial class charts have been converted into class interface templates) there is a choice. We may choose to discard the untyped static charts as we move into a more precise typed system description, or we may choose to keep them as documentation. In the latter case, automatic support is needed to maintain consistency between the charts and the evolving interfaces.

Several BON deliverables thus have dual roles in systems development. They may initially act as intellectual guides for finding a good architecture with corresponding typed class interfaces, and later as high-level documentation of the system.

Roles of deliverables

To make it clear how the deliverables are meant to be used in BON, we now look in more detail at the dependency arrows in figure 7.2, and begin with the static model. The chain of single line arrows extending from the system chart, over cluster charts and class charts, into formal class interfaces (and eventually implementation) indicates that manual creation of these deliverables and the corresponding input of modeling information should proceed from left to right. The same set of deliverables is also connected through a chain of double line arrows, indicating that automatic generation is possible in both directions.

The idea is that information entered in one deliverable may be used as the intellectual basis for creating or modifying the next deliverable to the right in the chain. Templates can be automatically generated, but since deliverables to the right represent refinements, new information needs to be added manually. However, when changes are to be reversed (propagated right to left) in the chain, a much higher degree of automatic support is possible and should be used. This is why the single arrows only go in one direction.

As a project progresses, the deliverables directly modified by the development team tend to be further to the right in the chain (typically formal interfaces during design and source code during implementation). Automatic reverse generation then becomes more essential for maintaining consistency, particularly because of the increased volume and level of detail. The class dictionary, for example, which contains an alphabetically sorted class index, should always be created automatically from the class charts and/or the formal interfaces.

The static charts are also connected with the static architecture through single arrows in both directions. Typically, initial charts give rise to partial static diagrams, which may then be independently elaborated giving rise to new or modified charts. Since feature names correspond to labels in static diagrams, and inheritance as well as different types of client relations are part of both the static architecture and the class interfaces, automatic propagation and consistency checking is possible between them.

The double arrow from the class text to the static model indicates that it is possible to generate unlabeled client links between classes to show a relation that occurs for implementation reasons, but is not part of the public interface of any class. Although BON is not concerned with *how* implementation will be carried out, it may sometimes be essential to show that a certain set of important implementation classes—for example, encapsulating an external database interface that may be part of the system requirements—will be used behind the scenes without specifying any details.

Finally, we look at the dynamic model. Here there are only single arrows, since no automatic generation is possible. The event charts serve as complementary help to select and describe scenarios of typical system usage, which are collected in scenario charts. The scenario charts and the creation charts (whose content is guided by the static architecture) then jointly form the basis for the object diagrams. The construction of these diagrams may, in turn, lead to changes in both event charts and creation charts.

Although the static and dynamic models are two very different types of system description, they are closely related since the communicating objects in the object diagrams correspond exactly to the classes in the static architecture describing the behavior of each object. It is therefore possible to alternately work on the static architecture and the object scenarios—whichever seems most likely to yield new insights depending on the current degree of problem understanding—and then propagate any additions and changes to the other model.

7.2 CHARACTERISTICS OF THE PROCESS

Thus, having discussed the BON deliverables, we may turn to look at the system development process whose aim it is to create them. A summary of the process tasks is shown in figure 7.3. The tasks are listed in an *approximate* order of execution, and represent the ideal process referred to in [Parnas 1986]. However, the BON user is free to change the order of the tasks or make any other deviation from the ideal process that will help fulfill the goals of a particular project, as long as the required static and dynamic models are eventually produced.

Risk-driven development strategy

In fact, there are always aspects of a system development project that must be allowed to take priority over any predefined work procedures. After all, the direct aim of such a project is nearly always to deliver a product with adequate functionality and performance to a customer on time and within budget.

Therefore, all software development procedures should be *risk driven*. This means that the level of depth and detail in various parts of a problem investigation should always be adapted to the potential future cost of misunderstanding or modeling something incorrectly. Good high-level early descriptions, particularly for large and complex systems, are therefore often highly unbalanced in terms of elaboration of their different parts.

Instead of falling into the trap of modeling well-known concepts in great detail during the early phases (and get a false sense of rapid progress), we should take a deep breath and dive straight into the tricky problems. Eventually, we will have to deal with them anyway, and postponement only increases the risk of unpleasant surprises or even catastrophe later in the project.

Although this book is not about project management, we would like to emphasize the importance of continually assessing and controlling the high-risk elements in software development projects; see for example [Charette 1989]. In the USA, the Department of Defense and NASA have long been strong

TASK		DESCRIPTION	BON DELIVERABLES
G **A** **T** **H** **E** **R** **I** **N** **G**	1	**Delineate system borderline**. Find major subsystems, user metaphors, use cases.	SYSTEM CHART, SCENARIO CHARTS
	2	**List candidate classes**. Create glossary of technical terms.	CLUSTER CHARTS
	3	**Select classes and group into clusters**. Classify; sketch principal collaborations.	SYSTEM CHART, CLUSTER CHARTS, STATIC ARCHITECTURE, CLASS DICTIONARY
D **E** **S** **C** **R** **I** **B** **I** **N** **G**	4	**Define classes**. Determine *commands*, *queries*, and *constraints*.	CLASS CHARTS
	5	**Sketch system behaviors**. Identify events, object creation, and relevant scenarios drawn from system usage.	EVENT CHARTS, SCENARIO CHARTS, CREATION CHARTS, OBJECT SCENARIOS
	6	**Define public features**. Specify typed signatures and formal contracts.	CLASS INTERFACES, STATIC ARCHITECTURE
D **E** **S** **I** **G** **N** **I** **N** **G**	7	**Refine system**. Find new design classes, add new features.	CLASS INTERFACES, STATIC ARCHITECTURE, CLASS DICTIONARY, EVENT CHARTS, OBJECT SCENARIOS
	8	**Generalize**. Factor out common behavior.	CLASS INTERFACES, STATIC ARCHITECTURE, CLASS DICTIONARY
	9	**Complete and review system**. Produce final architecture with dynamic system behavior.	Final static and dynamic models; all BON deliverables completed.

Figure 7.3 The BON process: initial version of deliverables underscored

advocates of risk analysis and management as a major instrument to control software development.

The above does not mean we cannot start by modeling the more familiar parts of a system. On the contrary, this is often a good way to reduce initial complexity so we can begin to see the wood rather than just trees. However, the easy modeling should only be taken far enough to cleanly separate certain familiar patterns from the more difficult parts.

Once we understand these patterns, we can set them aside and return to them later when the hard parts are also under control. This strategy increases the chances of detecting potential trouble spots early in a project, so they can be nipped in the bud.

Process tasks

As shown in figure 7.3, the tasks are loosely grouped in three phases with the following aims:

- Gathering analysis information (tasks 1–3).

- Describing the gathered structure (tasks 4–6).

- Designing a computational model (tasks 7–9).

The partial ordering for some of the tasks is clearly fixed. For example, it would not make sense to complete the final architecture before we have delineated the system borderline or define features before the corresponding classes have been selected. But some of the tasks are often reversed in practice, depending on the nature of the problem at hand. The following tasks are flexible in this respect:

Task 1 (delineate system borderline) is sometimes postponed to after task 3 when the idea of what the system is supposed to do is initially very vague. In such cases, we may need to design a first preliminary object model before it can be decided what should fall within the scope of the system and what should not.

Task 4 (untyped class definition) is often skipped in projects where all parties involved have high technical skills and long experience and is instead replaced by a typed, more formal definition. If desired, the class charts may then be later generated from the formal interfaces.

Task 5 (sketching system behavior) is sometimes done very early, perhaps already as part of task 1, for systems where a large part of the initial requirements are expressed as complex global actions.

Task 8 (generalization) may be applied already in the early analysis phase in case a fine grain abstract view of the problem domain is crucial for subsequent system design and implementation.

Each task in the BON process has a set of *input sources,* is controlled by *acceptance criteria,* and produces a set of *deliverables* that become part of the analysis and design documentation. The deliverables that are created or updated as result of each task being carried out are listed in the rightmost column of figure 7.3 (with the initial version of each deliverable underscored).

As was pointed out in the introductory chapter, BON concentrates on the general aspects of analysis and design and does not address the full development life cycle of object-oriented software engineering. Instead, the method is kept small, while still covering the issues that are central to a wide variety of applications in both large and small projects. Once these are understood and mastered, it should not be difficult to extend or modify parts of the method to meet specific needs.

Besides analysis and design, there are also many more important issues involved in conducting successful object-oriented software development projects, many of them highly enterprise dependent. Therefore, the BON process is meant to be integrated with other processes and tailored to suit the specific rules and policies of the software production environment in which it is going to be used. For example, since formal quality assurance procedures will be highly variable from one project to another, the acceptance criteria listed in the boxes accompanying the description of each process task (see the following sections) are to be understood only as simple reviewing hints.

For the rest of this chapter, we will discuss each process task in more detail with the emphasis on *what* should be produced and in what order. The next chapter will then examine the typical analysis and design actions involved, and will be more concerned with *how* to find the abstractions and structures needed to produce the deliverables.

Although (as was argued at some length in the previous chapter) drawing a precise line between analysis and design can only be done arbitrarily, we will use a simple definition to roughly discriminate between the two:

1. As long as we only deal with classes that can be considered directly related to the problem domain and restrict ourselves to the public features of these classes, we are doing analysis. We call these classes *analysis classes.*

2. When we begin adding classes and features that are not directly related to the problem domain, design has begun. We call the new classes *design classes.*

With this definition, tasks 1–6 focus on analysis and tasks 7–9 deal with design.

The above view on analysis and design seems to work reasonably well in practice, but the definition is of course cheating. In general, there is no way of telling for sure whether a certain class can be considered "directly related to the problem domain" or not. This is a matter of judgment, since there is no objective reality to compare with—just as in politics, every view of a problem domain is related to what you want to achieve.

However, even if we are not always sure whether we are doing analysis or design (or implementation for that matter), so be it. We should still be able to apply the same powerful principles of abstraction and not worry too much. After all, it is the usefulness of the resulting models that counts, not what we think we did to achieve them.

We will now define and discuss each of the nine process tasks in more detail. Each task description will start by displaying a standardized box summarizing the general results produced by the task, what specific BON deliverables are affected, and what input sources and acceptance criteria to use. (The latter are only hinted at, since quality assurance requirements vary greatly from one organization to the next.)

7.3 TASK 1: DELINEATE SYSTEM BORDERLINE

GENERAL RESULTS
- Major subsystems
- User metaphors
- Incoming and outgoing information flow
- Major system functionality
- Typical use cases
- Reused libraries and reuse policy

BON DELIVERABLES

SYSTEM CHART	SCENARIO CHART

INPUT SOURCES
- Customer requirements
- Domain experts, end-users
- Knowledge of implementation platforms and run-time environments
- Comparable systems or prototypes
- Available reusable components
- General rules and regulations

ACCEPTANCE CRITERIA
- Customer acceptance procedure
- Quality assurance plan

This task is concerned with *what* is going to be modeled and what will be our principal *view* of the world that we are trying to understand and formalize. It is an extremely important task, since it sets the stage for everything else in the subsequent modeling work, and should not be taken lightly. Particularly since the initial difficulties may be quite different depending on system size and modeling purpose, we will spend some time discussing various aspects of the task.

System borderline

Analysis is the study of concepts and procedures in a problem domain. What constitutes the problem domain in a certain modeling situation depends entirely on the purpose of the investigation. As discussed in the previous section, object-oriented analysis may be used to model with the intent of producing software, or just to increase the understanding in some area of interest.

If we produce a very general analysis model of some business operations, it would make perfect sense to talk about "design" and even "implementation" of various organizations by elaborating this analysis model in different directions, even if no software or computers were ever to be involved. Since design has to do with finding a form that suits a certain purpose, the borderline between it and "the problem" is really just a matter of convention.

However, using design and implementation in this broad sense would probably not serve any useful purpose when describing the BON process (although it may certainly do so in other contexts). Therefore, when discussing the process tasks and the corresponding standard activities in BON, analysis will mean creating an object-oriented model of the problem, and design will mean realizing this model in a computerized environment.

Implementation, finally, will mean translating design into program text using a selected programming language. Usually, however, this language is known already during design and is then likely to influence the design model chosen. When BON is just used for enterprise modeling, design or implementation will not be considered.

Delineate the system borderline means to decide what aspects of a problem area should be modeled at the highest level, and what will be the communication between elements in this model and the external world. It may include modeling views of external systems, such as database management systems and GUI packages, or this may be left to design. It all depends on what is considered fixed and what may change.

Subsystems

For small systems, possible partitioning into loosely coupled subsystems can often be postponed to the general class clustering of task 3, but if the system is large, the organizational question regarding work groups becomes an important issue already from the start. Since massive communication between many people is extremely costly and error prone (even worse when geographical distances are involved), having small groups of people working on separate parts of a system is always a major principle for large developments.

Sometimes it even takes precedence over other principles, so that, for example, a certain amount of fine grain reuse may be sacrificed in order to achieve more independence between groups working in parallel. Software production is a series of compromises, and being a good engineer means having a nose for which compromises pay off and which ones do not. This kind of knowledge does not come from books, but from a combination of talent and the right sort of experience.

Thus, when analysis and design of a large system is to proceed concurrently, the major subsystems should be decided already as part of the initial task, so an appropriate work organization can be found. It is then important to make the system parts as logically independent as possible to minimize group interdependencies and facilitate final system integration.

Since there is always a risk of premature decisions if the problem is not very well understood, it is usually better to produce a high-level model of a large system first. When this model has been iterated several times, it will be much easier to select the best partitioning into subsystems and then scale up and proceed with a number of parallel developments.

In creating the initial model, we must be careful not to advance the design "breadth first" without having fully investigated the most difficult parts of the problem. This often means we need to go very deep on some parts of the system, and often take one or two central ideas all the way down to implementation (on a small scale) to make sure they will work.

The initial modeling should be carried out by a small group chosen from the best people available. (What often happens when you try to gain time by violating this rule may be read in Fred Brook's classical essay collection *The Mythical Man-Month* [Brooks 1975].) When a core design has been produced and tested we are much safer, and the risk of steering in the wrong direction when many people come aboard and costs really start to accelerate is greatly reduced. This is precisely in line with the risk-driven development strategy discussed before.

User considerations

One of the major factors to consider when outlining the system borderline is the prospective computer user. Below are some guiding principles taken from [Marmolin 1993].

- *Identify usage.* Describe the situation in which the system will be used: goals of the enterprise, roles, tasks, resources, flows of information, work processes, social relations. Try to understand the interplay between the computer-supported activities and other tasks to be carried out.

- *Identify user groups.* Describe the different types of users involved in terms of: knowledge, competence, experience, attitude, frequency of usage. Are the groups homogeneous or variable? It may be necessary to design alternative dialog forms depending on user type, variable help levels, allow personalized configuration, plan for selective user training, etc. Is the system a central part of the user's tasks or just peripheral? Physically straining (long hours of terminal input), or just a complement to more demanding intellectual work?

- *Worst case principle.* Design the system interface particularly for the users who are expected to be in most need of assistance. The problem is of course to strike a balance between the extreme simplicity required by some groups and the rich functionality needed by others.

- *Metaphor principle.* Base the design model on one or more metaphors from the users' professional environment or cultural background [Booth 1989]. These should be documented early, and used as input for the searching and selection of candidate classes in the problem domain. (Be sure to also document all important *differences* between the system model and what the metaphors would indicate.) Some would regard selection of user metaphors as design, but in our view it is clearly analysis (in the new sense of the word), because the concepts involved will nearly always be close to either the problem domain or some other external reality which is familiar to the user.

- *Minimality principle.* Include exactly the functionality needed to solve user tasks—no more, no less. This recognizes the importance of striving for a small number of orthogonal functions, which will be perceived as relevant by the users and therefore often used. Functions seldom or never used yield a more complex system model making the simple functions also more difficult to understand.

   The principle is of course a guideline rather than a strict rule. In practice, a set of specialized functions is often needed for certain situations or by advanced users, but these functions should then be kept in separate layers in both the user interface and the documentation, so they do not interfere with normal usage.

- *Identify potential semantic errors.* Try to think of possible semantic misunderstandings that may cause the user to misinterpret the effect of a function. Making the design model explicit and using metaphors decreases the risk of semantic errors, but the problem is generally difficult. Mismatches between the design model and the user's mental model is one cause for misunderstandings; semantic inconsistencies in the system is another.

   Common semantic errors may be countered in three ways: better education, better documentation (including on-line help), or modified metaphors. Continuous feedback regarding current processes and system state is important to help users detect errors. A problem is the inherent conflict between providing enough information, on the one hand, and not disturbing the user's work by supplying useless information or forcing unnecessary confirmation of intentional operations, on the other.

   A feasible compromise in many situations is to concentrate on decreasing the risk of irreparable damage by providing stepwise "undo/redo" facilities, and possibilities to interrupt and resume ongoing processes.

- *Use transparent modeless dialogs.* Transparency means that the dialog has a natural and direct relation to the interface. Ideally, the user should not be aware of any interface, but only of objects that can be directly manipulated in obvious ways [Shneiderman 1983]. Modeless means that the meaning of a user function is the same regardless of system state. If modes are necessary to structure a large set of different system behaviors, they should be naturally related to the user task. The principle is to permit the user to do anything at any time, since humans do not solve problems sequentially according to well-defined plans.

The goal is not really to remove modes, but to remove what appears to be modes to the user. For example, if the user must explicitly toggle between modes (like drawing mode, text mode, and command mode) to make subsequent input be interpreted as intended, this may lead to confusion and difficulties in learning the system.

If, instead, there are three types of window, whose purposes are obvious by their graphical appearance (like canvas, editor, and command interpreter), all the user needs to do is place the pointing device in the desired environment (which is then highlighted as confirmation) and start performing actions natural in this context. The modes, which are still there logically for the system to interpret, have disappeared from the user's perception.

An analogous example is the ordinary telephone whose interface is so familiar to people in the industrial world that it has become invisible (that is, until you try to remember the baroque sequences of stars and number signs needed to redirect your phone, or order a wake-up call).

External communication

When we have chosen what parts of the problem domain to model and what general viewpoint to use, we should look at the communication between the elements in the chosen model and the external world. This includes listing major data flows coming into and leaving the system. Frequency rates and sizes are important for systems that will handle heavy loads of on-line transactions or capture large amounts of external sensory data in real time.

Data typically enters the system through terminal input (keyboard or mouse), pipes, files, distributed objects, sensory devices, or notifications from other systems, and leaves it through terminal output (screen, printers, or multimedia), remote calls, pipes, files, and drivers for electronic devices. Data flows will be part of the incoming and outgoing events that represent the abstract stimuli and corresponding responses from the system viewed as a black box. These are documented in an initial version of the system *event chart*.

Only the basic information content is considered at this stage, since the exact form of data communication should not be decided too early. Major aspects of the user interface, such as which user metaphors to choose, should be dealt with early since this may have a strong influence on the overall design of the system, but the data flow details as well as what specific widgets and dialog sequences to use are best postponed.

Major functionality

Starting from the user requirements and guided by the identified external communication and user metaphors, we produce structured lists of desired system functionality. Even if we have not yet decided on classes, most of the functionality can often be grouped into sections relating to different concepts of the system—user metaphors are particularly helpful here, since their elements are obvious candidates for future classes.

A certain number of clusters are defined and documented in the *system chart.* These represent subsystems or other groups of classes to be defined later, which are separated according to various criteria. For large systems this work may be very substantial and constitute the first real structuring of our model, while small systems may initially contain only one cluster. We will discuss clustering in more detail later under task 3.

Typical scenarios

From the listed data flows and initial event chart we also identify a number of typical examples of system usage, or *object scenarios.* These are documented in a first version of the system *scenario chart,* and will be used later to build the corresponding dynamic scenario diagrams as complement to the static diagrams. Depending on the nature of the problem, we may choose to do the dynamic modeling already at the very beginning, and in that case we will also produce first versions of the *creation chart* and the *object scenarios* in this task.

Incremental development

The initial requirements are often vague and inconsistent since customers rarely know exactly what they want. This is not because customers are generally stupid or unable to make firm decisions, but because the software to be developed is mostly aimed at supporting rather special activities. Unless there already exists a completely analogous system to compare with, only clairvoyant people will know beforehand how useful certain initial ideas will turn out to be when implemented in practice, and how much you can get at what cost.

If the modeling can be followed to its logical conclusion through use of a good object-oriented language, there are great opportunities to provide early feedback to users and customers. Instead of spending six months negotiating the details of a 2000 page requirements document, and then proceeding for two years to implement a system where half of the functionality is inadequate because of early misunderstandings having been cast in concrete (and the other half possibly obsolete at the time of delivery), a much more adaptive approach is possible.

By implementing only small portions at a time, starting with a very general framework and proceeding to elaborate and flesh out functionality in the directions shown by experience to be the most fruitful, enormous amounts of wasted effort can be avoided; see for example [Boehm 1981, Gilb 1988]. This approach is in complete harmony with the object-oriented philosophy of finding well-defined reusable abstractions at all levels.

Look for reusable components

The project team should always search actively for possible libraries to reuse, since it is there that the future potential lies for increasing productivity by an order of magnitude. A decision to reuse is of course always a tradeoff between how well the available functionality fits the current problem, what general quality it has, how its future maintenance is taken care of, and so on. This must be weighed against the corresponding factors and extra cost of developing new software.

As the availability of reusable software increases, it becomes more and more important to have a good knowledge of where to search for suitable components. Being connected to a global network like the Internet [Quarterman 1990, Krol 1992], both for general inquiries on product information and for easy access to the very impressive stock of high-quality freeware that is currently being built by universities and non-profit organizations (for example, MIT, Stanford, and the Free Software Foundation), will soon become a strategic necessity for many developers.

Establish reuse policy

We should make a conscious decision as early as possible regarding the level of investment in the future reusability of the system we are going to design and eventually build. This is important, since a high degree of reusability demands much more effort in terms of careful design, generality, robustness, extensive testing, and thorough documentation than is needed for a piece of software that is only to be part of one particular context.

Reuse within a project should always be standard practice, since it pays off directly and serves to foster the needed software culture. Reuse between projects is of course a matter of the overall life cycle costs of the systems involved—now and in the future. Heavy reuse of mediocre components is dangerous, even if money appears to have been saved in the beginning, since it may create dependencies that will delay production of the good abstractions.

Often, a compromise works well here: build as much reusable software as possible within the budget of the project, but with the emphasis on meeting the specific requirements of this contract. This often means that many ideas are sketched with only parts of their potentials realized, but care is taken to pave the way for future generalization. Then, when the product has been delivered and accepted, devote a special investment budget for capitalizing from the project by turning the best ideas produced into reusable libraries.

Scaling

The system we are modeling may be very small or very large. A large system will probably have to be split into many subsystems, but this does not necessarily mean that modeling becomes more complex. If we can build a top-level structure in which the subsystems are viewed only at a very high level, a model of the whole system may still be understandable enough to be managed by a small group of people. Reasonably independent subsystems can then be given complete BON processes of their own, and only the uppermost level of each subsystem need affect the behavior of the total system.

Depending on the goal of a project, the top-level modeling can be very different. If the underlying implementation platform is fixed for the foreseeable future, details of its architecture will probably affect the analysis model. There is nothing *a priori* wrong or too specialized about this, since what is special in one context may be quite general in another. The aim is to be as resilient as possible to future requirement changes, but the nature of those changes will vary depending on the type of development.

On the other hand, if you are designing a public service like a mobile telephone system, what you want to model at the top level should probably be completely independent of both the underlying platforms and their physical distribution. Instead, it becomes all important to have a strong user metaphor, which may survive the technological advances for a long time and will lend itself to many highly different realizations. The model will then be expressed in terms of the metaphor, and even if the underlying design and implementation may lead to huge subprojects, the model can still be kept manageable.

As with all problem solving, the key to mastering complexity is scalable layers of abstraction, enabling the thinker to concentrate on one thing at a time.

Environmental restrictions

Before proceeding to concentrate on the internal modeling of the delineated system, make sure that the basic capabilities and limitations of the external environment in which the system will run are well understood. An elegant analysis and design model which is based on certain assumptions about available services from an underlying operating system or database manager may suddenly prove unimplementable in practice when it is later discovered that the assumptions were wrong.

This is particularly dangerous when moving into a new type of environment. For example, developers who have only been exposed to highly flexible operating systems with few limitations, such as UNIX, may easily consider certain basic facilities so fundamental that the thought of checking never occurs to them.

7.4 TASK 2: LIST CANDIDATE CLASSES

GENERAL RESULTS
- First list of classes based on problem domain terminology
- Glossary of technical terms and concepts used in problem domain

INPUT SOURCES
- Problem space
- User metaphors
- Specifications of implementation platform(s) and external interfaces

BON DELIVERABLES

ACCEPTANCE CRITERIA
- Approval by end-users and domain experts

This task is the real starting point of the object-oriented development process. From the problem domain we can often extract a number of *de facto* concepts that are candidates to become classes. We will say more about this when the BON activities are discussed in the next chapter. The various actors in the user metaphors as well as documented interfaces to external systems are also obvious class candidates.

What we produce here is a list of *candidate* classes, which means we should not be too critical about including a concept from the problem domain—better to have too many concepts than risk missing some of the important ones. In fact, it is sometimes possible to choose between several disjoint sets of concepts, each representing a different way of partitioning the problem space. Seeing the overlapping candidates listed together can then make it easier to pick the best consistent set. So the list will nearly always contain some candidates that will not become classes, and others that will perhaps become several classes.

Classes vs. objects

You sometimes hear people argue that early analysis should concentrate on the *objects* and not worry too much about the *classes*. Primarily, the reasoning goes, we detect a number of actors in the problem domain (the objects) and only later does it become clear how these objects may be grouped into classes. However, this is a misunderstanding of what objects and classes stand for.

In object-oriented analysis we are not concerned with objects *per se*. On the contrary, our aim is to describe them only indirectly—through their behavior. Everything else is irrelevant and should be excluded from the analysis model. In an object-oriented context, we have one and only one way of describing object behavior, and that is through classes (disregarding the hybrid approaches, against which this book is trying to make a case). This means that even if there is only one object of a certain type, the description of its behavior will still be called a *class*. The name is well chosen, because no matter what object is modeled, it is always possible to envision more objects of the same type—now or in the future—and the class will then automatically cover the behavior of these objects as well. (The class actually describes a *pattern* of behavior, since two individual objects of the same type may behave differently depending on system state.)

So when we do not know initially whether two objects behave according to the exact same rules or not, we simply model them as different classes until we know better. Our initial attempts at classifying the problem domain will have to be iterated many times anyway, and merging several classes into one is no worse than splitting up a class found to represent more than one abstraction, or changing the inheritance structure.

Since object-oriented development downplays individual objects (of which there are often a great many) and instead concentrates on the different types of behavior (of which there are much less), the term is really a misnomer. However, starting to push *class-oriented technology* as a solution to the problems of modern society might be misunderstood in some circles.

Glossary of terms

Besides a list of candidate classes, we also produce a glossary of technical terms. This is particularly important in problem domains that use special terminology whose meaning is not obvious to the analysts and designers. The glossary should stress points where misunderstandings may occur, and will be used later as a guide for naming the features of problem domain classes.

It is vital that analysts and users/domain experts understand each other's terms precisely, otherwise wrong interpretations may easily lead to incorrect system requirements. In most cases, it is probably easier for the computer professional (being familiar with applying modeling to widely different areas) to adjust the terminology to that of the problem domain than vice versa. However, sometimes common problem domain terms contain ambiguities or connotations that may be necessary for discussing complicated matters between domain experts, but will only be a hindrance in the abstract model. Then it may be better to agree on some alternative terms to use in the joint work between analysts and domain people.

7.5 TASK 3: SELECT CLASSES AND GROUP INTO CLUSTERS

GENERAL RESULTS
- Problem-domain-related classes grouped into clusters
- First static architecture with some inheritance and client relations

INPUT SOURCES
- Possible subsystems
- List of candidate classes
- Glossary of technical terms

ACCEPTANCE CRITERIA
- Class and cluster management system with automatic consistency checks

BON DELIVERABLES

SYSTEM CHART

CLUSTER CHART

Static architecture

Class dictionary

In this task we start working with the raw material collected in task 2. Beginning with the list of candidates, we form an initial set of concepts to model as classes.

High-level class properties

At this point we may also start thinking about certain key properties of the classes. Some objects may need to be *persistent,* which means that they must not be deleted when the system execution terminates, but instead be saved for later retrieval. Use of an external database for this may have been specified in task 1 (delineating system borderline) or we may decide storage form later, during design.

Some of the selected classes may be *deferred* (in some circles called *abstract*), which means they will never be fully implemented but instead rely on descendant classes to fill in the necessary details. Deferred classes cannot be instantiated and will therefore not be part of the object scenarios. The corresponding actors at system execution time will be instances of *effective* descendant classes.

Some classes may be *externally interfaced,* which means they encapsulate some external communication (function calls, data retrieval, etc.).

Some classes may be *parameterized* (also called generic), which means they give rise to different types depending on a set of type parameters. This is common for various types of container classes.

Similarity and collaboration

Some of the classes are usually easy to select, while others are more difficult. When we get stuck, the best way to proceed is usually to start grouping the classes we have selected according to the two main aspects supported by object-oriented classification: *similarity* and *collaboration.*

Similarity refers to common patterns of behavior, and is captured by *inheritance* relations. Collaboration, on the other hand, refers to objects using the services of each other, and is expressed by *client* relations.

Do not be misled by those who claim that inheritance is implementation oriented and should be postponed to later phases. On the contrary, inheritance is classification of behavior just as much as is the grouping of objects into classes. If the behavior pattern of two objects is exactly the same, we describe them by one class; if it differs only slightly, we describe them by two classes related through inheritance. In both cases we are reducing the amount of behavior description, which helps us master complexity and get a clearer understanding of the problem space. Of course inheritance can be used prematurely to reflect things that are in fact solution oriented and should not occur in the analysis model, but so can any other modeling facility.

Possible system views

Local modeling of smaller groups of classes to find relations between them will often help us detect patterns that can guide us in selecting clustering criteria. A given set of classes may be grouped into clusters according to many different aspects: subsystem functionality, concepts of a certain application domain, subparts of the same whole, children of a common ancestor, encapsulation of external systems or devices, and so on. Figure 7.4 shows a possible *system view* (partitioning into clusters) of a set of classes representing different cars and their tires.

The same set of classes may also be viewed as in figure 7.5 without changing any relations between the classes or any class interfaces. However, in practice it is usually too much trouble to maintain several independent system views, so only one is chosen. The retained view represents a compromise between possible aspects that could be of interest. The grouping criteria are thus chosen for each individual cluster, depending on what is deemed most important with respect to the particular classes involved. Some clusters will represent subsystems, others general libraries, yet others simple groupings of parts or descendants of a common ancestor.

Note that *system views* in BON are views that may be expressed as a hierarchical partitioning of the classes making up the system. There are also other views of interest to the developer, which cannot in general be expressed as

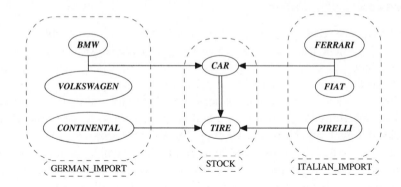

Figure 7.4   Trade-oriented view of cars and tires

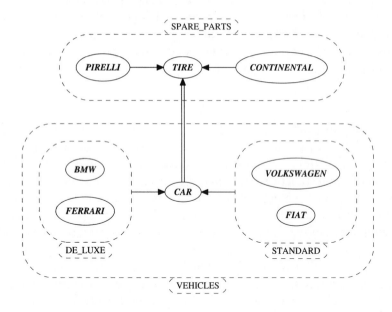

Figure 7.5   Repair-oriented view of same classes

a single hierarchy. For example, the process structure of a system is orthogonal to the classes and their relations, since each process may be built from various overlapping subsets of the same set of classes making up the behavior components.

An object-oriented process execution means instantiation of a root object and the execution of its initialization routine. Each root object thus gets a separate thread of control, and will in most cases trigger the creation of a series of new objects before its execution terminates. Some of these objects may in turn start other processes by instantiating new root objects using the same or different root classes. (For a thorough discussion of the object-oriented execution model, see [Meyer 1988a].)

A single partitioning of the classes to show system structure is usually not enough when many processes are involved, since the same class may be used and viewed differently in different processes. Therefore, each process usually gets its own static and dynamic model. However, it is also possible to let a number of root classes share the same static diagram if a partitioning can be found that suits them all.

Process structure is related to the general issue of object-oriented concurrency, whose research is still in its infancy. Until more is understood about what is really needed in concurrent modeling, BON does not try to invent yet another *ad hoc* notation to be used in all cases. Instead, the BON user is encouraged to employ complementary notations adapted to the particular project to show more complicated concurrent behavior and process structure. A very interesting attempt to merge the process and class concepts can be found in [Meyer 1993b].

Gradual evolution of a good model

The method of first selecting some initial groups of classes, then trying to gain more understanding by working locally with classification within each group, is reminiscent of the common strategy for doing jig-saw puzzles. First you walk around the table collecting pieces of a certain color, a certain pattern, a certain shape, and so forth. Then you sit down and try to relate these pieces to each other. Some of the pieces will turn out to belong elsewhere, but others will fit and little by little the outline of a rose bush, a stone wall, an old castle will become visible. Then a glimpse of the bigger picture may flash by. Since a red petal can be detected in one of the cracks of the stone wall, you begin to suspect that the rose bush is in fact close to the wall...

After modeling the local groups for some time, new insights have been gained and it may be possible to go back and select some more classes from the candidate list and fit them into one of the groups. Then, gradually, some of the groups may be joined into larger groups, while others become clusters of their own. The initial cluster charts and set of static diagrams are built successively, and the system chart updated to reflect the current status.

The clustering criteria will often change several times before a final model is laid down. Some clusters may be there already from the first task (delineating system borderline), because certain reasonably independent subsystems were identified early from the system requirements. But most clusters will grow out of the increased understanding that comes from refining the initial model, and represent views that were not initially apparent.

In the puzzle analogy, we might start to connect sets of pieces based on various criteria (a certain mixture of color nuances, certain interlocking shapes, etc.), which may allow us to build rather sizable structures in the form of disjoint islands. After some time, however, we may see quite different patterns emerge, some within groups (a pond in the meadow, a cottage in the wood), and some extending across groups (a cart track passing the pond into the wood, the blue sky partly visible through the foliage), and these may then be viewed as more important than the initial criteria for completing the global picture.

The analysis and design task is of course different, since its pieces can be combined in so many ways resulting in pictures ranging from the grotesque to the divine. The risk of going in the wrong direction is therefore greater, but we also have the advantage of being able to carve the individual pieces to make them fit.

The static architecture at the end of this task will still be fragmentary, since there is no point in trying to connect everything too early—better to gradually refine the modeling of each cluster until the corresponding roles have become clear. The global picture will be decided later.

7.6 TASK 4: DEFINE CLASSES

GENERAL RESULTS
- Classes defined by *queries, commands,* and *constraints*
- Updated glossary of terms

BON DELIVERABLES

CLASS CHART

INPUT SOURCES
- System and cluster charts
- Typical use cases
- Glossary of terms

ACCEPTANCE CRITERIA
- End-user/customer acceptance

Having selected and grouped an initial set of classes, the next task is to define each class in terms of the *information* it can be asked to return, the *services* it can be asked to provide, and the general *rules* that must be obeyed by the class and its clients.

This is done by filling in the BON class charts, where the above translates to *queries* which are functions that return information about the system state without changing it, *commands* which do not return any information but may instead alter the state, and *constraints* listing general consistency conditions and business rules to be obeyed.

A short class description along with brief indexing information is also entered (see the class chart layout in chapter 3). Naming conventions are quite important for class features, and we will return to this issue in the next chapter.

Class charts may initially be used as structured memos to collect information for further elaboration into typed descriptions, and later as documentation kept up to date through automatic extraction from the formal interfaces.

Analysis and polymorphism

A typical sign of the hybrid character of most object-oriented analysis and design methods published to date is their neglect of the real hallmark of object-oriented technology, namely *polymorphism*. Since polymorphism and dynamic binding are what really distinguish true object-oriented languages from the ones merely supporting modularization and data abstraction, like Ada and Modula 2, one would expect any object-oriented method to give this issue the attention it deserves.

However, looking closer at the literature reveals that little attention is paid to it. Readers may easily get the impression that inheritance and dynamic binding are implementation issues, when nothing could be further from the truth. In fact polymorphism is a very important aid by which the complexity of requirements specifications can be reduced.

Without polymorphism, descriptions of similar system functions applicable to many different but related objects need to be repeated in the class of each specific object type. Furthermore, clients of such related classes need to have one separate static client relation for each of the related object variants it may call during execution. With polymorphism, the dependencies can often be reduced by an order of magnitude (cf. figure 4.24).

So we should actively look for polymorphism of operations as early as possible in analysis and design to increase clarity and enhance maintainability. Since names in the class charts are inherited through the "Inherits from:" clause, polymorphism may already be expressed in these charts. Both the static and the dynamic diagrams in BON support polymorphism and dynamic binding (cf. figures 4.20, 5.17, 5.22).

Glossary of terms

The glossary of technical terms produced earlier serves as a general guide for naming features of the analysis classes. However, sometimes a problem domain term corresponds to several features or some other name is chosen for reasons of better clarity or consistency with other classes. Such deviations from the feature names that would normally be expected by end-users and problem domain experts should be documented to facilitate communication.

7.7 TASK 5: SKETCH SYSTEM BEHAVIORS

GENERAL RESULTS
- Object creation chart
- Event and scenario charts
- Object scenarios

INPUT SOURCES
- Early scenario charts
- Major system functionality
- Typical use cases
- Incoming and outgoing information flow

ACCEPTANCE CRITERIA
- Consistency with static model
- End-user/customer acceptance

BON DELIVERABLES

EVENT CHART

SCENARIO CHART

CREATION CHART

Object scenario

In this task we start elaborating the dynamic model of our system. As a result of task 1 (delineating system borderline) we already have an initial scenario chart capturing the most important types of system usage. A vague idea of this usage is always a prerequisite for finding initial candidate classes and selecting between alternative views of the problem domain. At some point, however, a more detailed and exhaustive picture of potential system usage can be of great help in refining and advancing the growing static model.

Depending on the nature of the problem, this task is of variable importance and may also be carried out very early. Therefore, as was pointed out at the beginning of this chapter, task 5 is often merged with task 1 when the initial requirements are expressed through many complex actions, but with less apparent structure.

Object creation

Executing an object-oriented system means starting up one or more processes in some operating system environment. Initially only one class instance exists for each process—its root object. The root objects will then, directly or indirectly, create all other objects needed to serve the requests issued by the system users. Investigating which classes are responsible for creating new instances of which other classes serves as a link between the static and dynamic models. Finding out when new objects are created may help the developer spot new static dependencies and hint at possible realizations of system operations in the dynamic scenarios. The result is entered into the system *creation chart.*

Checking for object creation may be done using two approaches, and it is often best to use both in parallel. First, go through all classes and for each class think of situations in which an instance of the class may be created. For all such situations, find out which class will act as creator and add the class of the created instance to the corresponding entry list of the creator. Second, start at the root class(es) and try to decide which other objects may be created by the corresponding root object. For all classes of the created objects, try to decide which other instances they may create, and so forth.

The potential creation of a certain type of object by a group of related classes can sometimes be factored, so that this creation is always handled by a common ancestor. If this is the case, the class of the created objects is inserted into the creation entry only for the ancestor, to avoid unnecessary repetition. This applies also when the ancestor is a deferred class with no instances of its own.

Objects are introduced in a system execution in two different ways: by creating new objects or by retrieving old persistent objects, that is objects that were created by an earlier system execution and saved in a database or file system. For an introduction to object-oriented databases, see [Cattel 1991].

Event and scenario charts

A system *event chart* is produced and the first version of the *scenario chart* from task 1 (delineating system borderline) is refined. For large systems, it may be desirable to split these charts into several groups depending on context (type of user, subsystem). This may also be done for the creation chart.

Since the partitioning of a chart is not necessarily tied to a specific cluster or user group, we have no special entry for the context in these charts. Instead, a parenthesized word or phrase indicating the context may be added to the system name in the headers of charts that are split into several groups.

Finding scenarios

The BON method concentrates on object-oriented analysis and design, and does not cover activities in the very early phases of feasibility studies and domain analysis often necessary to obtain the initial requirements of the system [Prieto-Diaz 1987, Arango 1989]. Structured interviewing techniques applied to users and domain experts are often helpful here [Scott 1991] as well as familiarity with the current research results in the field of man–machine interaction [Marmolin 1993].

A technique to find the desired system behavior called *Object Behavior Analysis* (OBA) is described in [Rubin 1992]. It starts by first identifying what needs to take place in general, the system *behaviors,* and proceeds to assign this behavior to *initiators* and *participants.* These play different roles in the system, which will help us understand which parts of the system need to take responsibility for providing various services and managing system information. The result is recorded in *scripts* and *glossaries.*

How many scenarios?

Except for extremely specialized systems, the primitive requests that may be issued by a user can be combined in an (at least for practical purposes) infinite number of ways. So our aim when listing scenarios is certainly not to try and capture every possible usage. Rather we group them into sets of significant *types* of usage, and let each type be represented by a scenario entry in the scenario chart. By selecting an appropriate level of abstraction for the scenarios, it is always possible to cover the full system usage in this way even if many of the details will be ignored for each category.

The number of different scenarios selected depends very much on the type of system and how the requirements are expressed. If a flat scenario structure is not enough, grouping by context may be used as indicated above. Some of the scenarios will later be illustrated by one or more *object diagrams,* but not necessarily all. We should make sure to list each principle type of usage in the scenario charts even if later we do not consider it worthwhile to illustrate them all by object diagrams. Less ambitious pencil and paper checking covering a larger number of scenarios may also be a good way of ensuring completeness and improve the static structure.

Scenarios to guide static modeling

The study of object scenarios is closely related to static modeling. As recalled from the discussion on use cases in the previous chapter, scenarios are mainly used in BON as complementary guides to choosing a proper view of the world and to continuously keep modeling on the right track. Although meeting the requirements embodied in the scenarios is necessary for a successful project, the emphasis should always be on the evolving static model populated with increasingly stable and flexible abstractions that will solve not only today's problems, but also some of tomorrow's.

Planned reuse is of course important, and not preparing at all for changes that seem likely to occur in the future should be as unthinkable for an object-oriented developer as stubbing out a cigar on somebody's living room carpet. How much effort to invest in each case is another matter, but ignoring the issue is just not part of good engineering behavior. However, the future changes envisioned are always more or less limited to simple analogies with what we already have. Only a few human beings are capable of producing truly original thoughts, and then only occasionally, so we must realize that many changes will never be anticipated.

To meet this we must strive to develop an instinct for the kind of abstractions that will increase the probability of unexpected reuse. This is somewhat like the sense of positional strength that good chess players acquire. Although they have no chance to sort out all possible ways in which they may be attacked in the future, they still know that certain formations of forces give great advantages.

7.8 TASK 6: DEFINE PUBLIC FEATURES

GENERAL RESULTS
- Typed class interfaces with public feature signatures and software contracts (pre- and postconditions, class invariants)
- Updated static architecture

BON DELIVERABLES

INPUT SOURCES
- Class charts with *queries, commands,* and *constraints*
- System and cluster charts
- Glossary of terms

ACCEPTANCE CRITERIA
- Consistency with static architecture
- Features cover external events in event charts and selected scenarios in scenario charts

In this task, the informal class descriptions found in the class charts resulting from task 4 (define classes) are translated into fully typed class interfaces with software contracts. The queries become functions which return information, while the commands become procedures which may change the system state. The constraints translate into pre- and postconditions on the operations and class invariants for the whole class. The signature of each public operation is specified (types of input arguments, if any, and type of returned value in the case of functions).

Since we are still dealing with the public features of the problem domain classes, this task is considered the last part of analysis. In practice, most contracting details will be elaborated during design, since it is often much easier to express exact formal assertions about classes and operations when a more refined structure has been decided.

However, quantifiable facts regarding the problem domain that are known already at the analysis stage should if possible be expressed formally, since it helps communicate a more exact picture of what is going to be needed to meet the system requirements. But in most cases there will not be that many quantifiable facts very early in the process.

Typing of features leads to client relations being discovered "for free", since an input argument or a function return value of a certain class type automatically means there is a static client dependency between the class containing the feature and the corresponding supplier class. This may in turn lead to remodeling and updating of the static architecture. Moreover, thinking through possible return types of queries usually increases problem understanding considerably.

The typing is in fact very important for advancing the static model, so unless close collaboration with many users and other problem domain representatives dominates the analyst's work (and sometimes even then), a simplified typed notation is often used very early on as a supplement to (or replacement for) the class charts. Also, since the BON graphical notation for class interfaces was designed with case tools in mind, it needs automatic support. Therefore, if no tool is available the user is free to use any hybrid form of textual and graphical notation that feels comfortable. The underlying specification is what is important.

7.9 TASK 7: REFINE SYSTEM

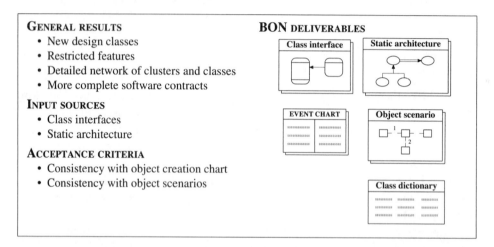

This task begins the design part of the BON process, and will therefore include a repetition of many activities already performed for the analysis classes, now applied to new design classes.

As we have pointed out several times before, there is no clear difference between analysis and design, because it is always a matter of opinion which classes should be considered modeling the problem domain (analysis) and which are part of the solution space (design). Sometimes the concepts used by people in the problem domain carry over more or less completely to an analysis model, and then the distinction may seem obvious.

However, the feeling is deceptive since there is no objective reality to "discover"; every analysis model is a conscious choice of viewing the problem domain in a way that is believed favorable to achieve certain purposes (and is in fact the first step towards a solution). Therefore, if the analysis model corresponds very closely to the problem domain, it may mean we have a natural straightforward mapping, but it may also mean we have superficially accepted too many concepts without thinking through their roles in a software system.

Compressed design tasks

Judging by the amount of text and number of BON process tasks devoted to analysis, the reader may get the impression that this is the overshadowing part of the work that needs to be done before implementation. However, this is just a result of the iterative nature of object-oriented development. Sometimes, when the problem domain is unknown to the analyst and the resulting design job— once the problem is understood—turns out to be small, there may of course be a bias towards analysis. But usually more time is spent on design compared to analysis, since many more details have to be taken into account.

However, the reason we only have three design tasks in BON is that many of the general techniques of finding new abstractions, elaborating old ones, refining the class relation structure, and adding more software contracts, have already been applied during the analysis tasks, so we do not need to describe them again in connection with design. Also, the tasks that need most guidelines are probably the initial ones, when the developer is still overwhelmed by seemingly unstructured complexity in the problem area and requirements text. Once a system model begin to stabilize, much more insight has been gained and work can often continue by analogy with what has already been accomplished.

Proceeding into design

Refinement of the analysis model into design is done by adding new design classes and working out more detail:

- new design classes with detailed interfaces
- new class relations
- more detailed contracting conditions
- possibly restricted features in highly interdependent classes
- refined clustering

The system behavior descriptions may be complemented by design-oriented scenarios, especially for larger subsystems. Sometimes essential parts of the system's interface, such as which GUI packages to use, are postponed until design. Initial feedback from end-users may then again become important, once such decisions are taken.

As the system structure grows larger, more detailed consistency checking can be made between static model and dynamic scenarios, including the life cycles of important objects. If an object-oriented language with a good garbage collector is to be used, the developer need usually not worry about destruction of the transient objects during design, but for persistent objects destruction is a logical problem which must be accounted for as part of the system behavior.

7.10 TASK 8: GENERALIZE

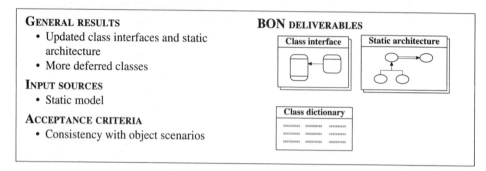

Generalization is a continuous procedure that should always go on in the back of the developer's mind, since it is so closely related to pattern detection. Much of it must be applied very early in the process, since having enough generality built in from the outset affects the basic flexibility and understandability of the system model. However, there is also strong pressure to produce working results in a project, and some of the early class structures may have to be altered many times before the model becomes stable.

Therefore, it is often too expensive to do all generalization work very early in the process, because the frequent changes may render much of this work useless. The best way to proceed is often not to use a very deep inheritance structure at the beginning, while many alternatives may still be tried. Later, when the set of classes and operations become more clear, a better structure can usually be inferred as several superimposed patterns become visible. Multiple inheritance often requires the developer to choose between many different possible combinations, where it is not obvious which view is best. Having a more complete picture of what is needed in the system often helps when making such decisions.

There are two important types of generalization. The first type yields a structure that pays off immediately by making the current system smaller, easier to understand, or more efficient, while the second type is an investment for the future by yielding a more robust system. How much effort to spend on the second type must be a conscious decision, since its payoff is very much dependent on the expected lifetime of the product, what kind of changes can be envisioned, and the overall generality of the system components considered.

It may often be a good idea to have a fully separate generalization phase applied to a product directly *after* release and acceptance by a customer. That way it will not interfere with the project time schedules, but still be applied before the project members are scattered into new assignments and gradually forget the finer details of the system.

Such a separate phase requires a budget of its own, and of course a general appreciation in the organization for an act that may on the surface seem to have negative productivity in terms of produced source code; the resulting system will often be smaller after a successful generalization process. However, it can be an excellent opportunity to capitalize upon the otherwise volatile knowledge gained by the development team, and to do it without too much time pressure.

Another possible point in time for a generalization phase is just *before* a new project is scheduled to begin. The project members will then be likely to have a high motivation, since the results will be immediately useful in the new development.

7.11 TASK 9: COMPLETE AND REVIEW SYSTEM

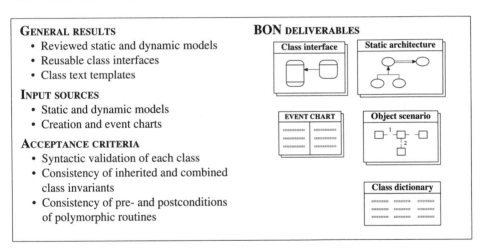

In this final task we polish and complete the evolving models. The overall system consistency is thoroughly checked, and the final documentation produced. What language or languages to use for implementation is usually decided before design starts, since it is important to have this knowledge as early as possible. Hybrid object-oriented languages may limit the design approaches that can be used without breaking the seamlessness. For example, heavy use of multiple or repeated inheritance during design is not a good idea if the implementation language will only support single inheritance.

Class text templates are often generated from the BON specifications as part of this final task. Such generation should be as automatic as possible, preferably done by a case tool, and future changes to the class text should be fed back to the specifications to achieve reversibility.

Root classes

Definition of the root class (or root classes, if many executable processes are involved) is usually postponed until the end of design. Root classes should normally be small and easy to change when systems requirements change. A typical extension that should always be considered is the inclusion of the initial system as a subsystem to some other system.

When this occurs, it is of great help if the system top level was already structured to facilitate such a transition. Ideally, one should only need to change one or more root classes to make the system start in its new role as a subsystem and perhaps add a few classes for communication with the new environment.

Merging and splitting classes

We make a final check that our classification has not been taken too far. If some classes are found to be redundant, they should be removed or merged with other classes. Very large classes or routines should be split using intermediate classes. Implementation dependencies between classes are examined, which may indicate that some public features should instead be selectively exported (only to a group of related classes). Such decisions are of course highly dependent on the kind of support offered by the implementation language.

Contracting consistency

We also go through all classes and corresponding features to finalize their software contracting clauses and check for consistency. Care should be taken that multiple inheritance does not violate the contracts by combining abstractions that do not fit together. In the case of polymorphic features, possible redefinitions must abide by the contracting laws; that is, preconditions may only be weakened and postconditions may only be strengthened.

Completeness and minimality

By going through the event chart, creation chart, and object scenarios once again, we convince ourselves that all behavior needed to take care of user requests is embodied by the classes in the static model, and that no unnecessary classes or features are specified.

If a class or an operation is not used in the system it does not automatically mean it should be removed; we could be developing reusable libraries or some unused features could be included for reasons of symmetry and abstractional balance. However, anything that cannot by traced back to at least one scenario should be questioned.

User documentation

Finally, we stress the importance of producing high-quality user documentation for all aspects of the system which are visible to the external world. This is not an easy task, and is usually quite expensive in terms of time and skill needed, but it is still well worth the investment. Particularly for an elegantly designed complex system, this documentation is the only guarantee you have that at least some of the users will actually understand and use what you have spent so much sweat and creativity to design.

Use the most talented writers you can find among the people who know enough about the system. Better to have a good writer with a reasonable technical background to create the manuals, guided by an expert, than put a technical guru with low writing skills on the job. (And we are not talking about writers who are used to producing a six foot stack of formal documentation conforming to current military standards here, but the ones whose letter to the editor of the local newspaper will cause the politicians to install a bump in the road in front of the day care center first thing next morning.)

Requirements traceability

To facilitate the tracing of functional requirements on a system into various parts of its design and implementation, a requirements cross-reference should be maintained. For each individually identifiable requirement, the classes and clusters realizing the behavior needed to fulfill the requirement should be listed.

8 BON standard activities

This chapter discusses nine standard activities that a developer will be involved with as part of performing the tasks defined by the BON process. The activities are as follows:

1. **Finding classes**

2. **Classifying**

3. **Clustering**

4. **Defining class features**

5. **Selecting and describing object scenarios**

6. **Working out contracting conditions**

7. **Assessing reuse**

8. **Indexing and documenting**

9. **Evolving the system architecture**

These standard activities are orthogonal to the process in the sense that they may all occur to some degree as part of many of the BON process tasks. The first four are continuously repeated during both analysis and design. The fifth occurs mostly during analysis, but may also be repeated during design of large systems. The last four, finally, are chiefly part of the design tasks. We will look now at each activity in turn.

8.1 FINDING CLASSES

A common question asked by many newcomers to the field of object-oriented development is something like: "Well, this encapsulation stuff—inheritance, polymorphism, and all—sure seems powerful, but how do I find the classes?" Our first reaction when faced with this question, often at the end of introductory courses on object-oriented concepts, was one of astonishment. The question might as well have been: "I am thinking of starting this company; I do not know yet what it is going to do, but I want it to be successful. How do I find the basic ideas of the enterprise?"

It seemed strange that anybody would hope for a simple answer. (No doubt there are many books and courses which are more than willing to share their secret of how to enter the Fortune magazine's Global 500 list, but the only detectable correlation between them and practical success is probably the authors' royalties.)

Object-oriented abstraction is completely neutral; it will carry out any kind of encapsulation—good or bad, abstract or concrete—with full discretion, no questions asked. What it can provide is a very clear and structured way of expressing and gradually evolving good ideas, but the semantic content of good ideas for realizing system behavior remains the result of talented and experienced engineering. Only superficial details can be captured by rigid procedures, while the hard parts—the ones that really count—can only be mastered through deep understanding of the problem combined with careful selection among many possible approaches.

However, there are a great number of partial solutions to common problems and other tricks of the trade that should be familiar to any developer. Knowing about them as early as possible will help speed up the long period of hard work and study which is a prerequisite for becoming a good designer. (The other prerequisites of talent and general attitude are more difficult to change, but exposure to powerful ideas may sometimes have a deep effect on the latter.)

Each partial solution addresses a certain aspect of a problem and may serve as guideline or general principle when problems of a similar type are encountered. Familiarity with a large number of such principles and standard solutions to small problems enables the designer to detect many common patterns during problem analysis and re-examination of the evolving system model. This will then provide constant feedback about how to proceed.

Precisely because they focus on different problem aspects, many guidelines and principles are contradictory, and the basic engineering task is to decide which aspect is more important in a given situation. We will try to cover some of the principles and guidelines in this chapter, and we now return to the question of how to find the classes, which is the same as finding good abstractions.

What is an abstract data type?

When we say that an object-oriented system is viewed as a structured collection of abstract data types (implemented as classes), it is important to understand the essence of the term. An abstract data type is an encapsulation of behavior—the emphasis is on "abstract", not on "data". Therefore, one should not fall into the trap of viewing abstract data types as protected data records with accessing operations attached, which may be tempting for people used to traditional data modeling.

On the contrary, the main purpose of an abstract data type is to remove all trace of internal structure by defining data *exclusively* through behavior, that is by defining the semantics of applicable operations [Guttag 1977]. And the word *abstract* means that the available operations should not reflect the internal structure, but instead capture the external properties of the underlying concept. Only those aspects of an object that you are willing to let all clients depend on should be part of the public interface, otherwise the class will just implement a *concrete* data type.

The principle of hiding internal structure and concentrating on external behavior when defining classes has been called "responsibility-driven design" in contrast to "data-driven design" [Wirfs-Brock 1989].

The importance of names

So a class, viewed as an implementation of an abstract data type, should capture the essential properties of a concept through precisely defined external behavior (rather than by information stored). As in all other disciplines, consistent naming of the concepts handled by a system is a major key to proper understanding and efficient communication between its users and developers. Good names act as helpful guides which automatically coordinate human thoughts in the right direction, while inappropriate or misleading names are constant distractors highly increasing the risk of misunderstanding, no matter how brilliant the underlying concepts.

In fact, the names of the classes and their operations make up the words and phrases of the language in which the application is expressed. And anybody who has been involved in language design knows how important even small details can be for the resulting clarity and ease of expression. Therefore, naming is an important part of systems design which should not be taken lightly. Designing software means producing a description aimed for others to read and understand, both humans and machines. Machines will not get confused by bad naming, but humans will (and not just other people but also the designer six months later).

So understandability is always the first concern and is directly tied to the resulting quality of the software. The personal egocentric naming style must yield once and for all, and be replaced by a reversed attitude. It is not the reader who is responsible for understanding what a program or a design is all about, it is instead the responsibility of the *writer* to make sure that everything is expressed so clearly that it will be impossible for any reader to get the wrong impression.

Of course a certain background must be assumed from readers and there is always a cost and a limit associated with everything. The importance of precise understanding will also vary from one case to another, but the paradigm shift is crucial. Describing software should be like writing a political article for a daily newspaper: it had better be convincing to make a difference.

Consistency of style is extremely important for understandability. Therefore, when you are maintaining someone else's text, unless you are prepared to rewrite everything, it is usually better to adopt the general style of the document even if you consider it inferior to your own.

Naming classes

Classes describe objects that encapsulate behavior. An object does not represent *a behavior* but should be thought of as an actor that will respond to various messages with well-defined behaviors. In rare cases a class may only define one public operation, but we should then always be able to envision more in the future. If not, the class is probably not an independent concept and should instead be merged with other classes.

For this reason, class names should be *nouns* with or without qualifying adjectives, like *WINDOW*, *BUTTON*, or *RED_BUTTON*. Sometimes single adjectives could be used as abbreviations, but then there is always an implicit noun in the background. However, since class names are usually global to a system, names like *HELPFUL* or *LAST* are almost always too general to be appropriate. Clearly, this type of qualifier may be applied to more than one concept in a system. For class features, on the other hand, where the enclosing class defines a local context, names like the above are common.

Class names should always represent *one* object of the corresponding type, and thus use singular form. The reason is simple: since every class describes a possible set of objects, the alternative would be to *always* use the plural form. This would not make sense, since it would only yield longer names without adding any information. Also, since signature types are often specified one entity at a time, using the plural form for class names would make normal type declarations look utterly confusing:

favorite_book: *BOOKS*

gives the impression that not just one but a whole set of books are preferred. (It is still possible to use the name *BOOKS* to signify a class handling a whole collection of books, but in such cases *BOOK_SET* or *SET* [*BOOK*] is more clear.)

Much more can be said about how to choose good and consistent names for classes, but most of it applies to any naming used to classify concepts in some problem domain (in fact, this is exactly what the classes are supposed to do). For a general text on classification principles see for example [Ogden 1923].

Analysis classes and design classes

A class can represent any concept that may be viewed as a black box with a specified behavior. In the analysis phase we form a perception of the problem domain, which will then serve as a basis for subsequent design. This is the analysis model and the classes are called the *analysis classes* of the system. They should normally be expressed in problem domain terminology and the corresponding concepts along with the visible operations defined should make sense to users and domain experts with respect to the activities modeled.

As was pointed out before, this is not an objective model of reality but a subjective view chosen with the intent of facilitating future design and implementation of a system whose basic behavior is known. It is in fact the beginning of a design. If too little is known about the desired system behavior, we will not have enough information to decide how the problem domain should be viewed, and then we must instead continue our study of the general requirements.

The new classes that are added during design and implementation are background classes, which deal with concepts that are not of immediate relevance to the user's perception of the system. These may be called *design classes* and *implementation classes* respectively. If the separation of analysis from design is not always easy (since analysis always encompasses an element of design), drawing the line between design and implementation is even more arbitrary. Since both activities deal with finding a suitable representation for an analysis model on some computing equipment, any precise separation is mostly a matter of taste.

Tangible objects

Some authors seem to imply that the analysis classes linked to the problem domain should reflect *tangible* objects. Tangible objects (things you can perceive with your physical senses) are important in the physical world, since they convey a sense of reality and may affect us in a very direct way.[9] However, in the electronic world this difference disappears; a class representing a car is no more tangible than one that models the job satisfaction of employees. What

---

[9] In a deeper sense, a bus is of course also an abstract concept made up by the human mind for practical reasons, but when it hits you crossing the abstract street without looking at the abstract lights, you will know the difference.

counts is how important the concepts are to the enterprise, and what you can do with them. The assumption that tangible objects should be generally more stable than non-tangible objects is also false. You only need to take a look at the piles of last year's models of physical products at the city dump to see how stable they are.

Moreover, tangible objects are very often manifestations of more abstract underlying ideas which are easily missed if modeling is centered on physical appearance. Of course, software may be directly in control of expensive or dangerous physical equipment whose classes may then play a special role in the system, but this is no different from classes in charge of abstract information whose correctness may be life-critical in, say, an intensive care unit of a hospital.

Deferred classes

Deferred classes, that is classes specifying one or more features without providing implementation for them, serve as design skeletons to be completed by descendant classes. These may then tailor the partially defined behavior in desired directions. Specifying strong postconditions for such *deferred* features restricts the semantics of the tailored versions, ensuring that important principles will still apply in the descendants. Using correspondingly weak postconditions will exert less control, but instead leave more room for variation.

The general principle is not to overspecify, but include as postcondition only what must be expected of every conceivable version implementing this feature. On the other hand, whenever such constraints do exist we should take care to specify them since they represent important semantic information.

If all features are deferred, the class comes very close to an abstract data type. As the system model evolves, more deferred classes tend to be added (usually by insertion of more levels in the inheritance hierarchies), since this provides more generality and makes it easier to meet future requirement changes.

The dual roles of a designer

It is important to realize that designing object-oriented software implies that two very different roles have to be fulfilled at the same time: the client role and the supplier role. Like the right and left hand of a pianist they must work in concert, but at the same time independently.

The client role deals with selecting the basic building blocks to use, and the supplier role deals with how to combine these building blocks to achieve a desired behavior. Designing means constantly switching between these two roles. Let us examine the implications a little closer.

Design usually proceeds by refining several classes at a time, collectively representing some layer of abstraction. However, to get the general idea it suffices to look at a single class. Assume the external behavior of this class has been fully specified, and our job is to design its internal workings. A typical approach would be the following.

Assume the supplier role. Look at the operations of already available classes and try to tentatively combine them to see if they are sufficient as basic components for the behavior we are trying to build. If we can envisage a reasonably simple implementation using only these operations, we are done, else we switch to the client role. (The duration of this first attempt may be anything from days for a complicated class when we already have a large stock of suitable supplier classes, down to less than a second if we have nothing appropriate.)

As client we now try to think of what new abstractions would be suitable for conveniently expressing the missing parts of the behavior. As argued in a previous chapter, this can be viewed as designing a mini-language for the type of behavior we are modeling. Depending on the generality and potential power of the new language we come up with, our focus of interest will switch from the problem to the new abstractions for a longer or shorter period.

Recall that an essential part of object-oriented development should always be investment for the future. Therefore, we should actively seek abstractions that do at least a little more than just solve the present (mostly rather special) problem. This means that refinement of new abstractions to take advantage of their future potential is a natural part of the process. We must of course take care not to spend a large part of the project budget on costly deviations from our basic task, but even the short-term revenue is often enough to finance a little extra work. In the long run, this attitude will pay off handsomely.

In fact, after some elaboration many such independent abstractions will yield insights and new potentials that may even affect the initial requirements. If the new outlook enables a whole new set of facilities more or less for free, which will solve the user's problems equally well or much better, even the most hard-headed customer may rapidly switch attitude.

So after working locally with the abstractions until they are reasonably understood, we again assume the supplier role and start combining the new operations to fill the holes in our behavior model. If the behavior we are designing for belongs to the analysis classes, part of our activities in the supplier role will be to sketch object scenarios. We then keep switching roles back and forth until we have completed the desired behavior.

When we think of new abstractions in the client role, an important point is not to strive for an optimal solution to every single problem (as in traditional design by stepwise refinement [Wirth 1971]), but to always take into account what we already have. First, we need to take care not to solve the same problem twice with only slight variations—much better then to invest some effort obtaining one version general enough to be used in both cases. Second, choosing abstractions is always a tradeoff between quality and the cost of development. "The best is the enemy of the good," as observed by Voltaire.

A world of recursive behavior

Abstract data types transform data into behavior, and as client we deal exclusively with the external behavior of our building blocks. In this role, we should therefore never think of data as bits stored in fields inside various objects, but only as something abstract which will manifest itself indirectly, through well-defined behavior. Where the knowledge comes from that enables our supplier objects to behave in the proper way is none of our concern as client.

Since we are also familiar with the supplier camp (our second nature as developers), we do know what usually goes on behind the scenes: our suppliers are in fact jotting down pieces of information here and there. However, if some of them were able to use divine inspiration instead, we would not care as long as they fulfill their contracts.

As suppliers, on the other hand, we are concerned with combining what we have into some behavior that we have undertaken to deliver. This is a very different role. To fulfill it we need two things: a set of references to a number of useful objects to call, and the knowledge of how and when to call them. This is the only information each object must have—nothing else is needed.

We will use an analogy with telephone calls as an illustration here, and we will also allow ourselves to become anthropomorphic for a while (viewing the objects as intelligent creatures). Contrary to Edsger Dijkstra's well-known assertion that "the use of anthropomorphic terminology when dealing with computing systems is a symptom of professional immaturity" [Dijkstra 1982], we believe it can be very useful at times.

So think of the set of recorded object references as numbers in the supplier's personal telephone book. Its content will be the information stored in each object. Invoking an operation on an object corresponds to picking up the receiver and dialing a number in the phone book, either to ask the answering object to do something or just to receive a new telephone number. If required, we start the conversation by reading some of the other numbers in our phone book to the answering object.

Amazingly, the only thing an object ever does (inside the system) is call other objects and exchange telephone numbers—*nothing else*. At first, this does not seem to make any sense at all—where is the useful work? What benefit can we possibly get from a system that can do only one thing: juggle telephone numbers—albeit with stunning dexterity?

Well, the answer lies of course in the external communication. A completely isolated object-oriented system is no more useful to the surrounding world than a configuration of elementary particles that have never been measured and thus never confronted by laboratory workers. Therefore, some telephone calls will actually be answered by special kinds of objects that have some magic way of making things happen in the physical world.

If asked to, some of them may convert a telephone number into patterns visible to the human eye as glowing fluorescence on a video display screen or traces of carbon powder burned into paper. Others will sound the lunch bell; yet others may send a whole battery of missiles to sink a hostile fleet of warships. So the system's juggling of phone numbers has but one purpose: to make these externally connected objects do the right things at the right time.

But what about internal value representation? Whatever happened to our familiar integers, floating point numbers, and strings? The answer is that various value representations are only useful concepts when thinking about internal implementation algorithms. Every implementation has to choose some basic representation, but when a system is viewed from the outside, there is no reason to treat basic values any differently from other objects. They can only be experienced indirectly anyway—through the physical behavior of some externally connected device.

Encapsulated behavior

The reader may consider the last subsections as a deviation from the main discussion of this first BON action, which is how to find classes. However, we think the view presented helps to get a deeper understanding of what is really behind the object-oriented ideas.

One thing that should be clear after this discussion is that it is very dangerous to talk about object-oriented encapsulation as being centered on data, unless it is perfectly clear to the audience that *data* is to be interpreted in the *abstract* sense, as well-defined behavior. This is something entirely different from the view of encapsulated records of data fields, which focus on internal structure.

Since data is nothing but potential behavior, there is nothing strange or stylistically wrong with encapsulating a typical process in a class, even if the system state affected by the process is not maintained by the objects of this class. A class is not obliged to record hidden information to become a respected citizen in the object world; if it can fulfill its behavior without taking notes, all the better.

For example, if a parsing operation for some language syntax is needed, it is not reasonable to make it a feature of a general string handling class, since the fairly specialized parsing facility can hardly be regarded as a natural operation that should be part of any string. On the contrary, an important principle of class design is to include only features that are intimately linked with the abstraction maintained by the class. Mixing several abstractions in one makes reuse more difficult.

One possibility would be to put the specialized behavior in a descendant class, say *PASCAL_STRING*, which inherits from *STRING* and adds the ability to parse Pascal syntax. However, this is not the natural way to view things, since one of the main purposes of a parser is to decide whether a string actually conforms to the given language. Therefore, the parser must be able to analyze any string, not just those that are already known to be correct. (The parser would actually have to be called already at object creation in order to ensure the class invariant!)

There are many cases like this, where behavior is best encapsulated with no internal data, and services instead applied to objects passed as input arguments. Such classes may be termed *tool* classes, as they supply general facilities applicable to objects that need them (cf. facility inheritance in 8.2). Of course the most common classes are still those which maintain some internal information, but we are covering the less obvious cases here.

How many features?

The appropriate number of features in a class may vary a great deal. It all depends on what abstraction is encapsulated. Some classes maintain information that is often requested in many different forms by clients and may need quite a few features to do it. This does not necessarily mean that such classes become difficult to understand, since understandability is more a function of how many different concepts you are faced with than sheer volume.

For example, a document handling class that contains 100 separate operations to set various font options (we are not saying this is the right way of encapsulating fonts, but not necessarily wrong either) may in fact only be dealing with one or a few underlying concepts which are quite familiar and easy to grasp. Ease of selecting the right operation is then reduced to having nicely organized manual pages.

On the other hand, a class with an order of magnitude fewer features whose semantics depend on each other in some intricate manner may be much more difficult to understand and maintain. The most important principle is not to mix separate abstractions in the same class. The average size may be 10–20 features per class. If you have 50 features it may still be acceptable, but you should be prepared to defend your position with good arguments.

A class should not contain too few features either, since this is often a sign of weak abstraction. Either vital features may be missing, or the class should in fact be merged with other classes. If a class has only one feature, something is nearly always wrong. We are of course referring to *effective* classes here; top-level *deferred* classes may have perfectly good reasons to have only one feature, or even none at all.

Completeness and layered design

A class should be complete in the sense that enough operations are provided to effectively use all aspects of the underlying abstraction. If a container class has an *insert* operation, it must also have a corresponding *remove* operation,[10] even if that feature is not needed by the system giving rise to the new class. The extra effort is a small price to pay for the enhanced future reusability.

A good principle is to design a basic layer of primitive features which are sufficient to guarantee completeness of the class, but which are also necessary in the sense that they cannot easily be expressed in terms of each other. This gives a lower bound for what must be implemented right away, and a solid base for understanding the abstraction.

For many classes, however, the basic layer will not be enough to express commonly wanted behavior without tedious repetition of primitive operations. Then we should add a second layer of convenience features, which are exclusively phrased in terms of the primitives. These should be visible in the class interface layout as a separate group, which are not logically needed to understand the class.

Following the principle of layered design also makes it much easier to redefine features inherited from complicated classes and to add new ones.

Class or operation?

A common decision which is not always easy to take is whether a certain behavior should be implemented as a separate class or just as an operation in a class. There is no simple answer to this question, since so many factors may influence the choice. Some criteria are suggested in [Halbert 1987]. For example, any of the following may be a sign that a new class should be created:

- The behavior can be shared and reused by more than one class.

- The behavior is complex and difficult to relate naturally to an already existing class.

- The behavior is very specialized, and even if it could be related to an existing class only some clients of that class will want to use it.

In the last case the behavior should probably be put in a descendant class.

---

[10] Unless, of course, we are modeling a special container from which nothing should ever be removed, like for example a (non-political) history log.

Classes for high-level specification

Already at the topmost analysis level we need some basic concepts to describe how things in the problem domain are structured. Support for this must be included in any analysis notation, and BON uses the clustering mechanism combined with client and inheritance relations. However, much of the additional notation included in other approaches, such as semantic labeling or multiplicity markers, is not necessary in an object-oriented approach.[11] Since the class concept (whose main purpose is to capture abstraction) is already there, it can be used directly to express more detail. Therefore, we should define a standard set of generic classes, such as

$$SET\,[T],\,SEQUENCE\,[T],\,SORTED\_LIST\,[T],$$

$$TABLE\,[T,\,KEY],\,QUEUE\,[T]...$$

for use as specification elements for very high-level information structures. As we have seen in chapter 4, such generic classes may then be attached as labels to relations between other classes in BON static diagrams. Other candidates for high-level specification are classes dealing with:

- finite state machines: $STATE\,[T],\,TRANSITION\,[T]$

- commands: $COMMAND$

- units of measurement: $TIME,\,DATE,\,UNIT,\,AMOUNT$

- various types of value: $VALUE,\,NUMERIC,\,BOOLEAN$

- domain-specific general categories

The precise set chosen depends very much on the application, but it is important to make it consistent, orthogonal, and well defined. The great advantage of this approach is that the specification elements are easily extensible and can be given a precise definition through assertions in the corresponding classes, as opposed to ambiguous labels expressed in natural language.

8.2 CLASSIFYING

The classification activity consists of combining a set of selected classes to see how they may be related in terms of similarity and collaboration. This means finding inheritance and client relations between classes that we already have.

---

[11] BON allows semantic links as structured comments in more complicated cases, but these are used sparingly and are not very important.

(Finding classes in the first place is of course also classification, but that is considered an activity of its own and is not included in the BON classifying activity.)

Inheritance vs. client usage

Very often we have a choice between reusing the facilities of some class by either inheriting from it, or using it as client. The question of when to do which is by no means trivial, since both have their pros and cons. The basic rule is that when you are satisfied with the services offered by a class you should just use it as client, while if you need to alter part of its behavior you should inherit from it.

As client you are comfortably shielded from the implementation of a supplier class. You know that as long as the supplier interface (including the software contract) does not change, its internal workings may evolve without affecting you at all. On the other hand, the specified behavior is then all you get, while inheritance gives you the possibility to tailor inherited features (as long as your modifications do not violate inherited contract clauses).

Inheritance therefore implies greater freedom, but as a consequence you are no longer protected from changes in the ancestor's internal structure (freedom with responsibility). Some object-oriented languages offer special mechanisms that can be used by a class to limit the freedom of descendant classes (called *private* mode in C++). However, using such protection mechanisms may do more harm than good. As was argued in chapter 6, if we limit reuse to what can be foreseen we are in trouble. Therefore, an ancestor should not try and figure out beforehand in what ways its basic concepts may be reused in the future.

Prohibiting descendant classes from accessing certain parts of the ancestor's internal structure introduces restrictions that may easily lead to code repetition or unnecessarily complicated circumventions in future classes. A descendant class must still know exactly what it is doing and take full responsibility, since it is not possible to modify inherited features in a safe way if the ancestor's implementation is treated like a black box. Important principles that should never be violated by any descendant class are instead put in the contract clauses of inherited specifications.

A typical situation when it is more advantageous to inherit rather than be a client is when several features implemented by some other class are to be offered directly by the new class as well. If we are just a client of the old class, every reused feature that is going to be part of the new interface needs to be reimplemented, since it is not possible to re-export features from a supplier class. Even if each implementation is only a few lines (since it can call the corresponding features of the old class), the repetition of many features can be detrimental to clarity and future maintenance.

This often occurs in connection with multiple inheritance. A common example is a class *WINDOW* that inherits both from *TREE* and *RECTANGLE*, the first ancestor implementing the structural properties needed for nested windowing, and the second implementing graphical properties like *move*, *resize*, and so forth.

The effect of using inheritance here (even if none of the features inherited is changed in any way) is that all the reused properties can be exported by *WINDOW* without a single line of new code. Being client, on the other hand, would imply reimplementation of a large number of features. (Such repetitions are quite common with single inheritance, since only one aspect of a many-faceted concept may then participate in an inheritance structure.)

Facility inheritance

Another typical situation in which inheritance may be preferable occurs when a class encapsulates a set of functions whose results depend only on the input arguments, not on any recorded internal state. For example, the standard trigonometric functions are often contained in a class that is simply inherited by any class requiring the facilities (which again assumes multiple inheritance). The alternative—to declare and instantiate a dummy object just to use it for calling these functions—is somewhat awkward.

p: *TRIGONOMETRY*
<create a new instance and attach to p>
$\vdots$
$a := p.cosine\ (b)$

The required qualification and extra lines of code look confusing, and the unnecessary object creation may be resource consuming if the encapsulated feature is called in a tight loop. Inheriting from classes that add only functions but no data fields may cause some extra work for the compiler, but should not cost anything at run-time.

Since inherited operations become part of the local name space of a class (and of all its descendants), the names of such general utility functions should be easily recognizable to prevent confusion with names of features of the main abstraction encapsulated by the class. If this is not the case, either renaming or the dummy object approach should be considered.

When a class is designed for heavy reuse, it may also be important to limit the amount of facility inheritance. Clients to the class will not be affected (unless the inherited facilities are reexported), but the corresponding names must be taken into account by descendant classes and may interfere with later extensions in new directions.

Inheritance for grouping

It is often a good idea to isolate interface details to external software (such as database systems and graphical packages) in separate classes to facilitate future alternative implementations. However, the model offered by the external operations may have to be completed by system abstractions before it can serve as a coherent encapsulation of the external facilities in a class. These added abstractions are probably not entirely independent of the external model, but often independent of many of its smaller details.

Therefore, encapsulating the features that contain direct calls to the external operations in a separate implementation class, and letting this class be inherited by another class containing the necessary additional abstractions, can often enhance clarity. Inheritance is then used for grouping rather than for potential reuse, but if the external system is for example ORACLE version 6, having a common prefix for each of the implementation classes, like for example *ORACLE_CURSOR* and *ORACLE_WARNINGS*, makes it easy to see which classes must immediately be checked when version 7 is later installed.

Inheritance of secondary properties

The possibility to inherit secondary properties from other classes is an essential advantage. By secondary, we mean that these properties are not the ones primarily associated with the abstraction encapsulated by the class. They may nevertheless be important.

For example, if class *FIGURE* inherits from class *PRINTABLE*, this means the instantiated graphical objects will know how to print themselves. Using the name *PRINTABLE* rather then *PRINTER* for the class specifying the *print* operation indicates that we do not really view classes inheriting from it (like *FIGURE* above) as little printers, but as objects which among other things also can take care of their own display.

The distinction is important, because a property like being printable is seldom something we want to use as a main classification category for our classes. Keeping a somewhat low profile is therefore essential so as not to disturb the main conceptual structure, particularly since there may be quite a few such properties around. (Classes inherited to acquire secondary properties are called *mixins* in Common Lisp Object System, CLOS, environments [Gabriel 1991].)

Because the secondary properties are so general, the ancestor classes will often just contain a specification for them, while their implementations are left to descendant classes. In typed notations, such abstract specification plays an additional major role by permitting *constrained* generic derivation.

Consider a general list class which stores its elements in sorted order. Such a class must require that the elements to be stored have an order relation among them, otherwise sorting will not make sense. To ensure this, it can be specified as a constrained generic class *SORTED_LIST* [*T* –> *COMPARABLE*]. The actual generic parameter *T* must then be a descendant of class *COMPARABLE* known to contain the required feature "<" (infix form of *less_than*), which will guarantee that sorting is possible. The "<" operation will be deferred in class *COMPARABLE*, and later defined for each descendant class. So by simply inheriting from *COMPARABLE* and defining one small operation, classes like *PASSENGER_AIRLINER* and *AIR_FREIGHTER* may each take part in sorted lists very elegantly. The first may, for example, define order by number of seats and the second by tons of load capacity.

Beware of reverse modeling

A common trap that beginners in the object-oriented field sometime fall into is modeling the world upside down. Figure 8.1 shows a typical case.

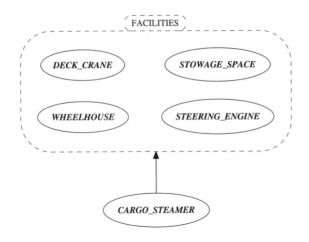

Figure 8.1   Incorrect modeling of attributes

Since multiple inheritance makes it possible to easily merge properties from other classes, some designers may be tempted to use inheritance as a means of gradually including all facilities needed in a class. This is somewhat tricky, because it might actually work by accident (all the way through to implementation), until future enhancement attempts show that something is very wrong in the model.

So why is the design in figure 8.1 so wrong when we have just discussed legitimate inheritance of secondary properties and general utilities? Well, the crucial difference is that although we considered the earlier inherited properties as secondary, they were still properties of the *whole objects* described by the class. When class *AIRLINER* is made a descendant of class *COMPARABLE*, the inherited features define an order relation applicable to the whole aircraft, while the features inherited by *CARGO_STEAMER* were certainly not meant to apply to a whole ship.

For example, if class *DECK_CRANE* has a public operation *turn*, this will become part of the interface of *CARGO_STEAMER*. Therefore, when trying to avoid an iceberg suddenly emerging out of the thick mist, all the skipper will have time to see before being thrown head first into the Labrador Sea is the crane cheerfully turning its jib across the deck.

The classes of the *FACILITIES* cluster represent *parts* of the freighter rather than *aspects* of it, and should of course be used as suppliers instead of ancestors. The *turn* operation in class *CARGO_STEAMER* would steer the vessel, while another operation *turn_crane* is implemented by calling *turn* on an attribute of type *DECK_CRANE*. In this way, the freighter is modeled as an aggregation of its parts, which is the correct view.

Note that keeping the inheritance and fixing the name clash by renaming *turn* into *turn_crane* would only hide the modeling error temporarily. Inheriting from a set of classes means it must be reasonable to view the descendant as a special case of *each* of the ancestor classes simultaneously. All inherited contractual obligations (feature postconditions and class invariants) must also be fulfilled by the descendant. Thus, the risk of conflict is high when combining abstractions that do not represent orthogonal concepts.

However, there may not be that many contract clauses specified initially to sound the alarm, and this makes the reverse modeling trap dangerous (particularly if the situation is a bit less obvious than in the example above). Things may seem perfectly normal at first, just as several people can work at the same desk with entirely different problems until they start mixing things up and use each other's private notes as a basis for their own decisions—then the seemingly innocent procedure suddenly turns into chaos.

8.3 CLUSTERING

Object-oriented structuring is a way of organizing functionality. Any large set of concepts needs to be structured in several levels to be comprehensible to the human mind. The first and most fundamental level is the class, which encapsulates a set of related functions in such a way that the resulting group can be viewed as describing a whole new concept. Such concepts, corresponding to abstract objects with well-defined behavior, can then be used as larger mental pieces by which to understand the world.

The human brain has an amazing capacity to relate different behaviors to each other by detecting patterns of similarity and inventing new names for whatever is behind such similarities. Therefore, matching this capacity requires a very large set of highly overlapping abstract concepts captured by classes. If each of the overlapping classes were to be described from scratch, the resulting descriptions would become too large, and we would not be able to remember enough of them to explain a complicated scenario.

Here is where the second structuring level comes in, namely inheritance. By describing the behavior of a new object type only in terms of differences from the behavior of existing types, large groups of related abstractions can be understood with an order of magnitude less effort. This already goes a long way towards what is needed to build complicated systems, but is still not enough. We need a third structuring facility to group sets of collaborating object types (not only similar types) into smaller recognizable units, which can be used as elements of a higher-level system description.

In BON, this unit of description is the cluster. Recursive clustering can be used to impose a hierarchical structure on the set of classes in a system, which we call a system view. Hierarchies have proven very useful in many classification areas as an effective and simple way of organizing large sets of concepts for easy overview and reference. Even very large sets require relatively few hierarchical levels for complete classification of their elements.[12]

However, since the classes in a system need to be used freely by other classes (the more general the abstraction, the more important the reuse), we cannot let the hierarchical partitioning be strict. Doing this would mean letting in again many of the drawbacks of traditional approaches through the back door. Therefore, the system view of hierarchical clusters is imposed on the classes independently of the basic client and inheritance relations between them.

Compared to classes and their relations, the clustering represents a much looser structure that should be easy to modify from one system version to another. This enables the combination of systematic order and adaptive freedom needed for flexible systems. With a relatively small effort and perhaps some new or modified classes as additional glue, clustering may be used for *programming-in-the-large* [DeRemer 1976] using sets of existing classes.

---

[12] For example, to classify 10,000 elements with an average of 22 elements per cluster, only 3 levels are needed.

Cohesion and coupling

That clustering is not bound by class relations does not mean there is no connection between the two. On the contrary, several important principles apply, but none of them is absolute. One such principle (mentioned already in 1968 in a short essay by Larry Constantine [Constantine 1968]) is to maximize cluster *cohesion* and minimize cluster *coupling*.

Maximizing cohesion means putting classes which collaborate closely in the same cluster, while minimizing coupling means having as few dependencies as possible between classes in different clusters. The rationale behind the principle is obvious: a cluster defines a local context in some sense, and it is desirable that local contexts can evolve in parallel without interfering too much with each other. On the other hand, to be comprehensive as a whole, related abstractions should be kept together.

However, we stress again that the principle is only a guideline. Some commonly needed abstractions (notably the fundamental data structures) need to be easily available in many contexts and should therefore not be hindered by any rule of low coupling. This calls for extra high quality and stability of such abstractions, since large parts of any system are likely to become dependent on them, but the resulting reuse is much more important in this case.

A general coupling rule which is less difficult to follow is to restrict cycles between classes (where both classes use facilities from each other) to occur only within the same cluster.

Interface classes

A good way to decrease dependencies between clusters (and emphasize the needed ones more clearly) can be to collect all externally accessible features in one or more classes serving as the cluster interface. This is particularly useful for clusters encapsulating subsystems or black-box frameworks (see below).

The interface classes may also serve as the subsystem specification, which is an advantage when clusters are assigned to parallel work groups. The rest of the classes in the cluster are support classes whose purpose is to provide additional internal abstractions needed by the interface classes. (If, as is often the case, generally useful classes are discovered among the internal abstractions, these can be moved to some library cluster for use in other parts of the system as well.)

Client—server interfaces

When even greater separation is desirable, as is becoming more and more important in large distributed applications, the whole subsystem may be viewed as just one class by all other system parts. An instance of this class becomes a server object with a set of visible operations available, and these operations may be invoked through some standardized mechanism used for all client–server communication in the system.

Such invocation is typically implemented by symbolic message passing, and may involve general dispatcher objects known as traders or brokers [Marshak 1991, OMG 1991] as well as client and server proxies if the application is distributed. In the latter case, proxy classes can make communication completely transparent to application classes, whether data just passes between adjacent objects in the same address space or is in fact converted up and down the communication layers and passed between heterogeneous applications in a wide area network. In either case, the subsystem will only appear as one abstract object to the rest of the world, and what happens behind the scenes will not affect the clients at all, as long as each party obeys the server contract.

Same level of abstraction

The classes in a cluster should usually be kept on roughly the same level of abstraction with respect to the concepts they handle. If a cluster *VEHICLES* contains the classes *CAR*, *TRUCK*, *BUS*, *ENGINE*, *BODY*, and *WHEEL*, one might consider breaking out the last three and putting them in a separate cluster *VEHICLE_PARTS*. If the classes of the *VEHICLE* cluster then turn out to be the only users of the *VEHICLE_PARTS* classes in the system we are modeling, the latter cluster may be nested inside the first.

To obtain uniform levels of abstraction, we usually need to create several clusters that represent only conceptual groupings of classes. This is often good during early analysis to render more visibility to the roles played by the analysis classes. However, during detailed design and implementation this rule should not be taken too far since the resulting fragmentation at lower levels may do more harm than good.

Frameworks

Encapsulating common types of behavior in subroutine libraries only works for behavior that can be expressed by simple combinations of fixed algorithms selectable by a small number of input arguments. Whenever common patterns are instead, as is often the case, more intricately laced with the surrounding behavior, the only way to avoid complete repetition of the pattern—in traditional approaches—is to copy some program skeleton and edit it manually.

The problem of course is not the editing, which is easy enough using modern programming tools, but the fact that the borderline between the common pattern and the adaptation disappears the moment we edit the skeleton. From then on, the resulting code must be maintained as a separate whole, and we can no longer benefit from the fact that most of it just represents standard behavior.

However, with inheritance we can keep the pattern intact, and still be able to do all the required incremental modifications. A reusable object-oriented design capturing a higher-level pattern will in most cases consist of several classes working as a unit to achieve a certain type of tailorable behavior. Such a design is called a *framework,* and contains a deferred class for each major component viewed by the user, who is then supposed to tune the behavior by defining the deferred operations in descendant classes.

Often a library of effective classes is also supplied for use when default behavior is enough for some of the components. There are essentially two types of frameworks each representing a different degree of maturity of the design. The types may be called *white-box* and *black-box* frameworks, and are discussed in a Smalltalk context by Johnson and Foote in an article proposing a set of design rules, many of which agree with the BON approach [Johnson 1988].

In a white-box framework, tailoring is done by replacing chosen operations by any new behavior seen fit. This gives fine grain control but often makes it difficult to modify the default behavior without detailed knowledge of the internal design of the framework classes.

In a black-box framework the user may only supply new behavior using visible features defined in the framework. This gives less control, but makes the user independent of the internal structure of the framework. Only the visible interface of its components must be understood.

8.4 DEFINING CLASS FEATURES

Assignment of features never starts with a blank set of classes. In fact, if it does, this is a sign of incorrect modeling. Since classes are only to be defined in terms of behavior, unless we have at least a vague idea of some of the basic features of a class (perhaps not yet written down), we do not know enough to decide whether it should be a class. Classes and very basic operations go hand in hand.

However, our initial idea about the features will not necessarily be the best or the only reasonable one. Therefore, trying to define in more detail the features that lurk at the back of our mind—choosing names and signatures, writing down their constraints—will give us more insight. We may then proceed to define more features, either needed to fulfill system behavior or to make the abstraction complete. The whole process becomes an iteration, shifting between finding new classes, moving behavior between classes, and defining more and more features and contracting details. The classification and clustering will also be a natural part of this "multiple tactics" approach.

Initially, we should concentrate on what may be called the basic layer (cf. 8.1), that is features that are essential for using the abstraction encapsulated by the class, and which cannot be easily expressed in terms of other features. Later, when the classes have stabilized, we may start adding convenience features. Such features may in fact be essential for practical use, but are not necessary for understanding the class and can therefore be postponed.

Naming features

The feature names are part of the language chosen for expressing an application. In 8.1 we already stressed the importance of choosing appropriate names for our abstractions, and we now proceed to give some rules for how to name various types of behavior.

Since natural language is such an integrated part of our intellectual culture carrying with it so many useful common connotations, we should only depart from it when we have good reasons. One reason may be the greater precision needed in formal languages (for example, when expressing contracting clauses), another may be brevity. However, since the object-oriented model is particularly good at capturing concepts usually expressed in natural language, the naming of classes and operations generally does not need to depart very much from normal description. This is a particularly important point for the analysis model (which needs to be understandable by non-computer professionals), but also for the subsequent design.

We should take advantage of this opportunity to stay close to natural language when choosing our naming conventions. This does not mean our ideal should be the style of the great epics, whose richness will be too much for our purposes, but rather the terse dialect used in newspaper headlines. There, the phrases are often carefully chosen to trigger very precise associations from the shortest possible text.[13]

The style guidelines of Eiffel [Meyer 1992a] contain many good principles on how syntactic conventions, spatial layout, and grammatical categories can be used to balance the desired degrees of precision, brevity, and consistency. A number of such principles are discussed in the following subsections.

Distinction from class names and clear word separation

There should be a clear syntactic difference between class names and feature names, so that readers do not have to hesitate for a second about whether a name

---

[13] The reader may not agree that conveying correct information is always the first concern in headlines, but the potential is there.

refers to a type or to the *use* of a type. This distinction is extremely important, since grave misunderstandings may result if the concept of class is confused with the concept of class instance. The BON convention is to use only upper case letters for type names, and only lower case for feature names.

There should be a way to incorporate the blanks of multiple word concepts into names, so the individual words are still visible. Without this possibility, expressive naming becomes very difficult. BON recommends using underscores to signify blank spaces between words. Other common conventions use in-word capitalizations, dashes, or combinations of these.

Of the three possibilities in figure 8.2, the second is very confusing in arithmetic expressions and requires blanks to surround minus operators, while the third deviates very much from natural language text.

easy_to_read_name: *SOMETYPE*	-- BON standard
harder–to–read–name: *SOMETYPE*	-- Not recommended
MuchHarderToReadName: *SOMETYPE*	-- Not recommended

Figure 8.2 Possible naming syntax

Avoid abbreviation—but do not overqualify!

Since classes may collaborate with other classes representing entirely different concepts, their names should be complete enough to avoid ambiguity. Feature names always have the context of their class, and so can sometimes be made shorter; on the other hand features are often more specialized and may therefore require longer names. (We are talking about visible feature signatures here; local variables with their limited scope may often use shorter names for simplicity without risk of confusion.)

The overall goal is clarity and ease of reading. Therefore, we should make names as long as needed to avoid ambiguity, but then always strive for short names since excessive length *per se* is also one of the worst enemies of clarity.

One very important principle is never to include in a name facts that are already clear from context. For example, if a class *IBM* includes a list of its employees the feature could be named *employees*, but under no circumstances *ibm_employees*. The IBM prefix is redundant and should not be used (unless of course the class for some reason happens to also contain an employee list of some competitor).

This type of error is rather common among beginners in the object-oriented field who are used to global name qualification. We also strongly disagree with the rules employed in many of Grady Booch's earlier books, recommending names like:

theSensor
aRoom
itsSemaphore

In our opinion, this is extremely bad style and can only decrease readability and increase confusion when used routinely. (We are pleased to see that in the latest edition describing the Booch method [Booch 1994] the number of names of the above type has been reduced by an order of magnitude.)

Grammatical categories

Features that are commands represent actions taken, and should use *verbs* in imperative form as names: *enter, quit, remove.* Queries, on the other hand, represent access to information and should describe the result rather than the process of fetching the information. Therefore, a *noun* possibly qualified by an *adjective* should be used: *speed, temperature, red_light.* In contrast to class names, feature names always have a type as local context and so may often omit the noun of a qualified item without losing clarity: *last, next, shortest.*

Queries returning a boolean value representing a simple "yes" or "no" can use two forms, either an interrogative phrase, *is_full, is_empty,* or just an adjective, *full, empty.*

How many arguments?

If many input arguments are needed for a feature to fulfill its contract, this is usually a sign that something is wrong in the system structure. A major principle of object-oriented design is to reduce the need for heavy information flow between local actors in the system (and do it without resorting to global variables!). Therefore, the number of arguments of a class feature should normally be fewer than for a corresponding subroutine in a traditional language.

Also, the calling syntax used by most object-oriented notations further decreases this number by 1, since typical function calls like $f(a, b)$ will instead have the form $a.f(b)$.

If many arguments still seem to be needed after several restructuring attempts, a solution may be to create a new class as an aggregation of some of the arguments, thus reducing the number of objects passed in one call. Also, never use optional values as arguments, but instead define separate features to set desired options.

As a result, the average number of feature arguments in an object-oriented system can often be kept below one (the ISE Eiffel Base library of fundamental data structures containing 1823 features reports an average of 0.4 arguments to a feature [Meyer 1994a]).

Naming consistency

There is always an inherent conflict in any naming: should a name emphasize the specific or the general properties of the concept it refers to? There is no simple answer to this question; it all depends on what will usually give the most relevant information when the name is presented to a user. Squeezing too much detail into a name may be just as bad as having too little or useless information.

In UNIX environments, files are organized as directory hierarchies with local naming within each directory. Software products are routinely distributed as single directories (containing as many sublevels as needed) and then plugged into a larger customer structure. When installing a specific product it may be difficult to know what to do, since products are so heterogeneous. Some of them may be directly executable, while others require several hours of detailed configuration and compilation before they can be used.

The *de facto* standard that has evolved is to always supply a file named *README* at the top level. This is an extreme example of a situation where generality means everything and specificity will only come later. The name in all its simplicity represents an enormously powerful semantic concept. Whether the product consists of a few files that may be used to print an aphorism each time a user logs off for lunch, or a fully fledged language environment whose correct installation may be of the utmost importance to the organization, the installer will know exactly what to do: just read the file and follow the instructions!

In object-oriented systems, especially large ones, we are often faced with similar problems. Scanning through the features of many classes to select the appropriate ones for a particular task usually requires discarding many names, while only picking out a few. If too much detail is part of the names (or worse, only detail) it becomes difficult to find quickly the interesting categories.

Therefore, when naming features in libraries with many related types or in frameworks, the higher-level category aspects are often far more important for ease of use than detailed precision. This may require some unorthodox naming at times.

Notable examples are the naming schemes in the data structure libraries of Smalltalk-80 [Cook 1992] and Eiffel [Meyer 1990b, Meyer 1994a]. Some standard names chosen in the latter environment capturing higher-level behavior shared by many container classes are shown in figure 8.3.

It may seem strange, at first, to be faced with names like *put* and *remove* instead of the usual *push* and *pop* when dealing with stacks, but the advantages are usually grasped soon enough by programmers. In fact, once the power of this principle has been understood, people will often start promoting it in many contexts.

Name	Behavior
item	element access
count	number of significant items in the structure
has	membership test for given item
put	insert or replace item
force	like *put* but will always succeed if possible; may for example resize structure if full
remove	remove item
wipe_out	remove all items
empty	test for emptiness
full	test for lack of space

Figure 8.3   Some standard feature names for container classes

8.5   SELECTING AND DESCRIBING OBJECT SCENARIOS

The amount of work needed to find representative object scenarios depends very much on the type of system to be developed. In new situations, where there is no previous manual task or users that can be studied, a more elaborate scenario analysis may be required. The essence of such an analysis is to start from existing technical and organizational conditions and try to envisage in detail how a supporting system could be used.

First, a number of probable situations are selected and described as concretely as possible in terms of a series of activities, user tasks and goals, input/output requirements, and presentation formats. One or more of these descriptions are then elaborated with respect to roles, tasks, and needs for computer support. A systematic procedure described in [Gould 1988, Marmolin 1993] is shown in figure 8.4.

Scenario analysis is chiefly used as a general help to generate or test new ideas, particularly in new and unfamiliar situations. Therefore, it is very important to choose representative scenarios that really show how the users interact with the system. An advantage of this approach is that it gives a complete picture of the situations chosen, while the disadvantage of course is that it will be based on just a few, possibly irrelevant examples. An excerpt from a scenario analysis is shown below.

The conditions are the following: a multi-media system providing information about available traveling destinations is to be developed. This system (called the *travel guide*) will be available for customers at travel agencies, so they may browse among alternatives and make a first selection while waiting to be serviced at the front desk.

- Determine technical and organizational conditions for the scenarios
- Identify tasks to be supported and possible system functions
- Describe concretely and in detail three imagined situations of system use
  - one containing common simple tasks
  - one containing common difficult tasks
  - one containing rare but critical and difficult tasks
- For each situation
  - describe the scene
  - describe the actors
  - describe who does what
  - describe important events in the external world
- Describe concretely and in detail how the users might use the system
  - describe the various working operations
  - describe user roles, goals, tasks, actions, how these are controlled, etc.
  - describe for each operation the system support, function, commands, etc.
  - describe the course of events and system support using pencil and paper simulation
- Analyze the scenarios and adapt the system support to derived requirements
  - analyze work flows, information flows, and interaction
  - analyze tasks and form subtasks (make a task model)
  - analyze system usage problems and define support requirements
- Repeat with new situations and new tasks, and adapt the system continuously to new requirements

Figure 8.4   Scenario analysis: a systematic approach

...On a cold day in January Mr P decides to surprise his wife on her birthday with a week of unplanned vacation in a warmer climate. He enters the local travel agency and walks up to the travel guide. The message "Where would you like to go? (press here)" flashes on the screen with a picture of a finger pointing to the text.

Mr P puts his finger on the message and a menu labeled "Select by..." pops up. Mr P picks the alternative "Weather" and a panel showing various weather conditions is displayed. Mr P then realizes that besides romance the financial side is also a major factor, so he presses "Cost" and a new panel consisting of several price groups emerges. He chooses 2 weeks and 2 persons for < $2000 and then returns to the weather panel. There he selects 95% probability of sunshine and > 20 °C day-temperature.

He then tries his combination by pressing the "OK" button. After a few seconds of background music the message "Sorry, nothing available" appears on the screen. Mr P then tries 75% sunshine and > 18 °C, and the system answers with a list of possible travel destinations and the text "For more information, select destination". He presses "Mallorca" and picks the first alternative from the resulting menu "Major sights, Hotels, Recreations". A video recording with samples of the island's cultural attractions appears on the screen...

Roles of scenarios

Scenarios can be of very different complexity. A scene like the one just described illustrates how a complete problem, which we may called a *user task,* is solved. Such scenarios can be broken down into more primitive pieces called *user actions* (selecting weather conditions, submitting a choice).

Some scenarios representing major user tasks will often be worked out already during task 1 in the BON process, since these can be of great help in guiding the initial static modeling and convey a better understanding of what general view of the problem domain to adopt. If the user problems to be solved are reasonably understood at a bird's eye level, the initial user task scenarios will hopefully be realistic even if some of their details may change. So being as complete as possible is of major importance here.

Later, when the basic class structure begins to stabilize, more scenarios representing user actions will be added, enough to cover all types of primitive user behavior at some level of abstraction. This can be done, since we now understand the details better (usually during task 5 in BON).

However, the best partitioning may not always be two fixed levels—user tasks and user actions. For simple systems there is perhaps no reason to separate the two, while more complicated behavior may require more levels. Grouping according to other criteria, such as user categories or subsystems, may also be helpful.

Therefore, no explicit structuring is enforced by the BON charts—there is only one type of scenario chart and scenario diagram. When a tailored structure is needed, we simply recommend adding a category name in parentheses to the name field of each scenario chart.

8.6 WORKING OUT CONTRACTING CONDITIONS

The BON approach focuses on the theory of software contracting, which we consider the most important principle in existence today for constructing correct, reliable software. No other technique proposed so far has the potential to turn software development into the long-awaited discipline of engineering envisioned by Douglas McIlroy in his contribution to the now famous NATO conference in 1968 [McIlroy 1976], and meet the challenge for an, as yet unrealized, software components industry.

The theory, called design by contract [Meyer 1988a, Meyer 1992c], is actually an elegant synthesis of the essential concepts in three major fields of computing research: object-orientation [Nygaard 1970],[14] abstract data types [Guttag 1977, Gougen 1978], and the theory of program verification and systematic program construction [Floyd 1967, Hoare 1969, Dijkstra 1976].

Design by contract

Most pieces of software text in today's systems are only partially understood by their developers. The central task of each subprogram may be clear enough (and sometimes even documented), but as every experienced programmer knows it is the unusual cases, or even the ones that are never supposed to occur, that present the real problems. Since it is never exactly spelled out who is responsible for the exceptional cases—the supplier of a subprogram, or its clients—important prerequisites for various algorithms are often either checked in many places, or not checked at all.

The general feeling of distrust resulting from this practice has lead to a desperate style of blind checking known as *defensive programming*, which leads to even less understandable software with more errors because of the complexity introduced by the added redundant code. So the only solution is to create instead an atmosphere of mutual trust by specifying precisely who is responsible for what part of a complex system behavior. This is what design by contract is all about.

The idea is to treat each subprogram as a subcontractor who undertakes to deliver some service (specified by a postcondition), but only if certain prerequisites are fulfilled (the precondition). The key opening the gate to future trust and order—so that you can finally *know* that you are right when designing a program instead of just guessing [Mills 1975]—is not as one may think the postcondition (which specifies what the supplier will do), but instead the precondition (which specifies what the supplier will *not* do).

To take an example, suppose you are to define a subprogram to calculate the square root of a real number. If you expect this program to work under all conditions, you are in fact mixing two completely different tasks into one:

- Finding and returning the square root of a non-negative number.

---

[14] Simula, the first object-oriented language, not only introduced the remarkable concepts of inheritance and dynamic binding already in 1967, but was also the direct inspiration of almost all later work on abstract data types. It included the strong typing of Algol 60, but had generalized the single stack model into a multiple stack machine, which enabled encapsulation of autonomous objects.

- Returning something reasonable when the input turns out to be negative (assuming the output must be real).

For the first task we have a number of well-understood and efficient numerical methods dating all the way back to Newton to choose from as supplier. For the second task, we do not have a clue. Obviously the client has made a mistake, and there is no way we can know what is a reasonable response.

Therefore, the only approach that makes any sense is to lift the second problem off the shoulders of the supplier (who is not competent to handle it anyway) and instead let it be the responsibility of the client not to ask impossible questions. This may sometimes require explicit testing on the client side, but if it does, there is no better place to do it. Usually the context will lead the client to know without testing that the precondition is indeed fulfilled, something which is never true for the supplier.

Contracting as a mutual benefit

The software contracting model has much in common with standard practices in human society. For example, suppose you are in Stockholm and must deliver an important package to an address at the other end of the city.[15] Then you may either deliver the package yourself, or engage a mail carrier to do it for you. If you choose the latter alternative and employ the services of "Green Delivery" (Stockholm's bicycle courier), the standard agreement between you and the courier looks like the one shown in figure 8.5. When two parties agree on something in detail, the resulting contract protects both sides:

- It protects the client by specifying *how much* must be done.

- It protects the supplier by specifying *how little* is acceptable.

The obligations of one party become the benefits of the other. As an aside

Party	Obligations	Benefits
Client	Provide package of maximum weight 35 kg, maximum dimensions parcel: $50 \times 50 \times 50$ cm, document: 60×80 cm. Pay 100 SEK.	Get package delivered to recipient within central city limits in 30 minutes or less without having to worry about bad weather or traffic jams.
Supplier	Deliver package to recipient in 30 minutes or less, regardless of traffic and weather conditions.	No need to deal with deliveries too big, too heavy, or not prepaid.

Figure 8.5   A contract

---

[15] The example is a slight modification of the one used in [Meyer 1992c].

(provided the contract covers everything) each obligation will also bring an additional benefit: if the condition says you must do X, then X is *all* you need to do. This may be called the No Hidden Clauses rule: sticking to the minimum requirements of the contract is always safe for each party.

Regardless of the No Hidden Clauses principle there are usually external laws and regulations whose purpose it is to prevent unfair contract clauses. For example, if your package happens to contain a famous oil painting by Anders Zorn the courier service is not permitted to drop it in the nearest garbage container simply because it violates the precondition by measuring 80 by 90 centimeters.

Such external regulations, which are part of the general context in which the contractors work, correspond to the class invariants of software contracts.

Laws of subcontracting

Polymorphism with dynamic binding is the main key to software flexibility. It has the power to remove most of the discrete case analysis so error prone and vulnerable to future changes—yet so abundant in traditional software. However, flexibility is meaningless unless the resulting software is correct, and polymorphism can be very dangerous in this respect.

Unless we are very careful when redefining an inherited operation, we may easily end up with a system where only some of the implementations that may be dynamically invoked will actually produce the expected result. What is there to prevent a redefined *area* function from returning, in some cases, the diameter instead? Without clear semantic rules, nothing but fuzzy naming conventions and the folklore of software engineering.

The problem is more subtle than it may appear at first sight, because even if every descendant class has a fully visible and correct specification of its behavior, chaos may still ensue. For example, if we need to compute the area of a list of geometric figures referred to by an entity of type *LIST* [*FIGURE*], all we can look at as client is the specification of the *area* operation as it appears in class *FIGURE*. During execution many different specialized versions of *area* may be called dynamically, but we cannot check their corresponding specifications when writing the list traversing code, if for no other reason than because some of the corresponding classes may not yet exist!

Therefore, we must have strict rules that guarantee that *any* future descendant class (whose operations may be invoked on our behalf whether we like it or not) must fulfill the promises that were given by its ancestors. This leads directly to the laws of subcontracting:

- A descendant class must fulfill the class invariant of the ancestor.

- A descendant class may never *weaken* the postcondition of a redefined feature (since this would mean delivering less than specified by the ancestor).

- A descendant class may never *strengthen* the precondition of a redefined feature (since this would mean imposing restrictions on the client not specified by the ancestor).

Note that nothing prevents a descendant class from strengthening postconditions (doing even better than promised) or weakening preconditions (imposing even fewer restrictions).

Note also that the above rules must be obeyed for every ancestor in the case of multiple inheritance, and will therefore prevent the combination of incompatible abstractions. This is extremely important for building the complicated inheritance lattices needed by, for example, the general data structure libraries of strongly typed language environments.

Where to put consistency checking

Design by contract offers an alternative to the blind checking of defensive programming by specifying a clear division of responsibility between client and supplier regarding the checking of various details of system consistency:

- The *client* is responsible for guaranteeing the precondition when calling.

- The *supplier* is responsible for guaranteeing the postcondition when returning.

Therefore, we have to choose where to put our tests for consistency. Either a condition is part of the precondition and must be ensured by the client, or it is removed from the precondition and must then be handled by the supplier.

Which alternative to choose must be decided case by case based on many factors, but the guiding star should always be the resulting simplicity and understandability of the system architecture. A rule of thumb is that if most clients need their own special treatment depending on some condition, it is better to put it in the precondition, while if the behavior alternatives are more or less standard for most clients, it may be simpler for the supplier to deal with them.

Classes as specification elements

As was argued in chapter 2, we should not strive to make the specification of an object-oriented system independent of its design, since this would defeat its purpose. Maintaining two entirely different descriptions (one for the system specification and one for its implementation) does not make sense, because specifications of large systems become large no matter what language we choose. Therefore, separating the two worlds will only give us inconsistency problems and more difficult maintenance for rapidly evolving systems.

So the specification elements used must in the end be translatable into object-oriented expressions, involving feature calls on objects of the classes which are part of the system design. These classes are the only abstractions that can capture the complex behavior of the system through simple notation (provided the design is good) as using an independent system specification would necessitate starting from scratch. Instead, specification and implementation must share *the same abstraction base,* since the executable code should only be the innermost part of a layered design of abstractions.

Partial recursive specification will not tell us the whole truth about a system, but it will tell us nothing but the truth, and it has the flexibility and incrementality we seek. Any other approach breaks the seamlessness and is in our view doomed to fail as a road to mastering the industrial development of large and complex systems.[16] Complete specification of large industrial systems will probably never become feasible anyway, if only because of the constant changes involved.

Run-time monitoring of assertions

An important side effect of the recursive specification approach described is that assertions may be translated into procedural code and monitored during execution. Basic boolean expressions map directly to programming language primitives, while the first-order quantifications of BON assertions may be implemented as functions. We take the simple class *PERSON* in figure 8.6 as an example. Its invariant expresses that if you are a person, then each of your children has you for one of its parents. (@ is the BON graphical symbol for current object.)

The corresponding Eiffel code, which may be generated by a case tool, is shown in figure 8.7. The control structure of Eiffel, from–until–loop–end, should be self-explanatory and the *LINKED_LIST* class is a cursor structure, which may be traversed by invoking features *start* and successions of *forth* until the state *after* is reached (meaning the cursor is positioned just after the list). The standard feature *item* returns the list element at the cursor position and *Result* is a predefined local variable containing a function's return value. (Entities of type *BOOLEAN* are initialized to **false** by default, so *Result* can be used directly in the second function of figure 8.7.)

---

[16] We are talking about general systems development here; certain critical or highly specialized software may of course still at times benefit from other techniques.

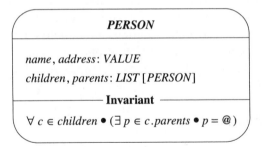

Figure 8.6   Consistency requirement: your children are really yours

```
class PERSON
feature
    name, address: VALUE

    children, parents: LINKED_LIST [PERSON]

    generated_assertion_1: BOOLEAN is
    do
        from
            children.start; Result := true
        until
            children.after
        loop
            Result := Result and generated_subassertion_1 (children.item)
            children.forth
        end
    end

    generated_subassertion_1 (c: PERSON): BOOLEAN is
    do
        from
            c.parents.start
        until
            c.parents.after
        loop
            Result := Result or (c.parent.item = Current)
            c.parents.forth
        end
    end
invariant
    generated_assertion_1
end
```

Figure 8.7   Class with generated assertion routines

When specification elements are implemented using procedural code, we must be extremely careful not to introduce any side effects, since this may change the semantics of the system when the assertions are monitored. Moreover, since *any* feature returning interesting information about the system state is a potential specification element, the rule of side-effect-free functions acquires an even greater importance.

Systematic exception handling

The contract theory also enables a very powerful exception handling mechanism to be applied during system execution. Since routines are not just small pieces of reusable software text, but precisely specified individual implementations, it is possible to introduce a notion of *failure.* Failure occurs when an execution of a routine is for some reason unable to fulfill its part of the contract.

An exception in a routine can be triggered in one of three ways: a supplier returns failure, an assertion is violated, or a signal is received from the surrounding hardware/operating system. (Note that assertion violation includes violation of the postcondition just before returning, as well as violation of a supplier precondition just before calling, since the latter is the *client's* responsibility.)

Exceptions may be processed by *handlers,* which will restore the class invariant for the current object and then either admit failure or else execute the whole operation again (after, for example, setting some flags). Admitting failure means triggering, in turn, a failure exception in the caller.

Since this book focuses on analysis and design and the details of exception handling are closely linked with the programming environment, we will not go further. The interested reader is referred to [Meyer 1992c, Meyer 1992a].

Finally, the violation of an assertion means that some implementation did not behave according to the specification. It is important to understand that this is a sign of a software (or possibly hardware) error. Things that may be expected to happen, no matter how seldom, must be part of the system specification and should therefore be handled in the main logic of the class features.

8.7 ASSESSING REUSE

Since BON is directly targeted at promoting reuse, we have chosen to view various work related to it as a standard activity when completing the tasks outlined in the BON process. This entails both the assessment of when existing software may be reused for parts of the product under development, and decisions regarding how much effort should be invested in future reusability of the new software produced.

A changed attitude

An extremely important driving force in making large-scale reuse come true in software projects is the general attitude of the developers and (perhaps even more importantly) managers involved. A designer must actively seek reuse as part of the routine work. Normally, as much time should be spent on reading old code, looking at design descriptions, browsing through component indexes, reading related literature, as is spent creating new code or designs.

Just as building an extensive network of human contacts has long been a main strategy in many professions, we must learn how to make the most of available channels to reduce the amount of new software development. In fact, for any *complex* functionality needed there should be only two alternatives: either reuse (and possibly adapt) existing software or, if this is not possible or feasible, develop something which may be reused in the future. One-shot developments should be restricted to the *easy* parts within a system.

Make the complex parts reusable

It is clear that large parts of the systems developed to support human activities will always be very special and not worth the effort to be made highly reusable. This is natural, since human endeavors are constantly changing and many ideas (perhaps most) will just be abandoned before long in favor of others. But behind every complex problem—no matter how special—there are always aspects of more general patterns.

The trick is to detect these patterns and capture them as class abstractions. With this strategy, every complex special problem will instead be viewed as a less complex (non-reusable) combination of general (reusable) patterns, where the latter will take care of the complexity. There will still be a substantial amount of non-reusable code, but the important point is that this code is comparatively straightforward, and we can afford to throw most of it away later.

In fact, for general systems, it is an important point of minimizing development effort that significant amounts of trivial code *should* be thrown away between releases of rapidly evolving products! This is the essence of *programming-in-the-large* [DeRemer 1976], where the non-reusable code is viewed as temporary glue to configure the high-quality standard units used to build systems in a certain domain.

The alternative would be to develop too much in advance, without really knowing whether it will ever be used in the future. Potentially reusable but never used components developed at high cost represent as much waste of money as the old tradition of doing the same things over again. However, solving a complex problem without making at least some classes also applicable in more general contexts should be looked upon by any developer as a failure.

Not only reuse of classes

The object-oriented technique is a very powerful vehicle for capturing and reusing concepts. This means that not only existing classes, but any kind of earlier effort in the problem area may have the potential for reuse, because reuse is anything that will reduce the intellectual effort and time required to produce a software system.

The traditional scavenging of old software to try and find useful pieces of code and/or designs still applies. In fact, it may sometimes be more fruitful to go through well-designed traditional programs solving related problems and re-engineer the solutions found into class abstraction than to start from a mediocre class library. Good designs in non-object-oriented languages tend to use (albeit not always consciously) the ideas of encapsulation and virtual machines brought forward by Dijkstra [Dijkstra 1972] and Parnas [Parnas 1972, Parnas 1979], and are usually straightforward to carry over into the object-oriented world.

However, in the case of more obscure designs the benefits gained can easily be offset by the effort needed to understand and rework. As expressed in [Krueger 1992]:

> For a software reuse technique to be effective, it must reduce the cognitive distance between the initial concept of a system and its final executable implementation.

Cognitive distance is defined as "the amount of intellectual effort that must be expended by software developers to take a software system from one stage of development to another."

Encapsulation of non-object-oriented software

An especially important reuse technique, which may very well turn out to be a major strategy in many application areas for gradual migration from old technologies, is object-oriented encapsulation of existing components written in traditional languages. This can be done in several ways, for example:

- by external subroutine calls from class features

- by calling class features from traditional software

- by invocation of external programs from class features

The first alternative is particularly suitable for well-documented and stable external subroutine libraries. (A class that encapsulates a set of external routines is often called a *class wrapper*.) It is often quite easy to make a first encapsulation, which directly mirrors the conceptual model represented by the library routines. As a side effect, the quality of the old software may often be improved by including contracting elements. Depending on how well the encapsulated concepts fit the problem area, these may then be extended by more or less elaborate object-oriented models, using the primitive features as building blocks. The second, inverted, approach may be advantageous when it is desirable to let an old application keep central control, but facilitate the addition of new functionality. Both approaches permit successive replacement of old parts by new object-oriented ones.

The third alternative is very important in connecting already existing local systems in networks using client–server techniques. Object-oriented languages with good interfaces to other languages can act as a very efficient gluing mechanism between heterogeneous components. With relatively little effort, an object-oriented system can tie together the complex behavior of a large number of existing products, and present a user interface that effectively removes the conceptual walls between them. What used to be a world of completely separate products, often with baroque historical interfaces, is then turned into one uniform system with automatic information exchange behind the scenes.

Assess impact of future changes

An important principle in designing reusable software is to constantly make thought experiments as to what would happen if certain requirements currently taken for granted were to change in the future. This gives an idea of the robustness of the product.

Possible areas to investigate include the information structure, the user interface, the number and categories of users, speed requirements, persistency requirements, security, platforms. Of course we cannot afford to take every far-fetched possibility into consideration, but sometimes small preparations to facilitate future changes in certain directions can be made at low cost if they are already built in during the initial design.

8.8 INDEXING AND DOCUMENTING

Another important aspect of software reuse is the problem of selecting the proper components from the base of available software. In this connection there are two obvious truths (also pointed out in [Krueger 1992]), which may effectively prevent reuse in practice:

- To select an artifact for reuse, you must know what it does.

- To reuse an artifact effectively, you must be able to find it faster than you could build something of comparable quality.

The first truism shows the importance of abstract documentation (above the source code level), which is of course equally important for maintenance. In fact, maintenance is only a special case of reuse because whenever a change in system behavior is contemplated, one must always consider what is most cost effective: to modify the existing system or redesign it from scratch.

The second truism shows the need of various classification indexes, ranging from very simple to very refined depending on the size and complexity of the available software base. Because of their importance, we consider indexing and abstract documentation a standard activity in BON.

Abstract documentation

Useful documentation needs to be *abstract,* which means that many details of what is described are omitted. This is the only way to communicate complicated ideas between people, since the human capacity of keeping many things in mind simultaneously is extremely limited [Miller 1956, Miller 1975]. However, the difference between being abstract as opposed to just incomplete is that the details to be skipped are chosen with care. The idea is to find concepts that can be used to group various similarities, so that details do not need to be individually enumerated. Moreover, the concepts chosen must be easy to understand in relation to the expected backgrounds of readers, and have enough precision for the type of description.

At the heart of the documentation of an object-oriented software system are the class interfaces. They are the final components that define the system behavior and whose correctness is a prerequisite for usable software. Therefore, the classes need abstract documentation to be understandable, and, what is more, the documentation needs to be precise. The precision aspect becomes gradually more important as more software is reused and systems grow larger. Without it, we cannot see any possibility of a successful large-scale software components industry.

Software contracting with strong typing has the potential to attain the required precision, and do it without breaking the all-important seamlessness of software development. The core of the documentation of a class should therefore be the software contract between client and supplier. The specification of the contract should be an integral part of each class, and not something maintained on the side.

Besides class documentation, we also need documentation at the cluster level (for those clusters representing subsystems or frameworks) and of the general system architecture at yet higher levels for large systems. Such additional technical documentation, as well as the various kinds of user manuals needed, may be attached to the respective cluster levels in the system static architecture by a case tool.

Class interface documentation

Two important tools are needed to produce useful class interface documentation from class texts: a class *abstractor* and a class *flattener*. The first one removes all implementation details leaving only the signature, the pre- and postconditions and descriptive comments for each feature, and the class invariant. The second eliminates the inheritance structure of a class by including all inherited features (with possible renaming and redefinition taken into account) so that its full interface becomes visible. Combining the two produces a complete abstract interface for a class which is guaranteed to be correct.

Without the class flattener a user may have to scan through a large number of ancestors and compile the interface mentally. Doing this in a multiple inheritance environment with 10–20 ancestors, with some renaming and redefinition needed, and still hoping to understand everything, would seem optimistic indeed.

Among the object-oriented languages, only Eiffel [Meyer 1992a] and Sather [Omohundro 1991] include assertions as fully fledged language features, which in combination with the strong typing makes it straightforward to implement the abstraction tools mentioned above. To some extent, assertions can be emulated by preprocessor macros in C++ [LeJacq 1991], but full run-time monitoring— including enforcement of the laws of subcontracting—requires direct language support.

Documenting frameworks

Object-oriented frameworks, often encapsulating fairly complex designs that can be tailored by users, are generally quite difficult to document in a way that is both precise and easy to comprehend. They often contain many layers of abstraction and a large number of details that need to be understood at times by some users, while a typical user may only need to know about a small subset. The problem is how to structure the documentation in such a way that an inexperienced user can get the required information without being disturbed by too much detail, yet be able to go deeper whenever the need arises.

The possibility of improving current practice of framework documentation by using an idea developed in another domain by the British architect Christopher Alexander is currently being investigated [Johnson 1992]. Alexander used the term pattern for a description of how to solve a particular type of problem. He then designed and carefully structured a set of such patterns (253 design precepts connected to urban development) into a "pattern language" that would capture enough professional architectural knowledge in a document to enable laypersons to use it for designing their own homes and communities [Alexander 1977].

Instead of describing all the facilities and concepts of a framework as a map of its static structure, the pattern language technique focuses on standard ways of using the framework to solve typical user problems. By choosing patterns that cover the most important aspects of what users may want to do, a user can combine these primitive patterns to solve more complex problems.

Within each pattern, the details believed to be needed most often by users are described first, and special usage only later. The reader may choose how far to go with each pattern before moving on to the next. When specialized behavior concerning some system aspect is later needed, the corresponding pattern can be read again in more detail.

Indexing guidelines

Each index entry in an indexing clause consists of a keyword serving as an index, and a list of attached words serving as index values. The choice of indexes and values is left open for a given library or installation to define its own conventions. Some guidelines for such conventions taken from [Meyer 1994a] are listed below:

- Keep indexing clauses short (3 to 8 entries is typical). May change in the future as the needs of cataloging and retrieval tools are better understood.

- Avoid repeating information that may be automatically extracted from the rest of the class.

- Use a set of standardized indexes for properties that apply to many classes (such as choice of representation).

- For values, define a set of standardized possibilities for common cases.

- Include positive information only. For example, the indexing clause of a class that does not have any representation should not contain the entry *representation*: N/A, but simply no entry with keyword *representation*. A reasonable query language will still make it possible to use query pairs like *<representation, NONE>*.

The following are some examples of standard index terms and typical values for a general data structure library. Index term *description* gives a short overview of the abstraction represented by the class. Index term *names* records alternative names for a structure. The abstraction implemented by a class *LIST*, for example, may also be known as a "sequence". Index term *access* records the mode of access to the data structures. Standard values include one or more of the following:

- *fixed* (only one element accessible at a time, as in a stack or queue)

- *fifo* (first-in-first-out policy)

- *lifo* (last-in-first-out)

- *index* (access by an integer index)

- *key* (access by a non-integer key)

- *cursor* (access through a client-controlled internal cursor)

- *membership* (availability of membership test)

- *min*, *max* (availability of operations for accessing minimum or maximum)

Index term *size* indicates size limitation. Common values include:

- *fixed* (size fixed at creation, cannot be changed)

- *resizable* (initial size fixed; explicitly resizable possibly at some cost)

Index term *representation* indicates choice of representation, for example:

- *array* (contiguous, direct access)

- *linked* (linked structure)

Style of comments

Every class feature should have a header comment attached as part of the abstract feature specification. The header comment should be informative, clear, and concise. Brevity is in fact an extremely important quality for comments in general (as well as for most text). To be effective, comments need to have a very high signal-to-noise ratio, otherwise they lead to inattentive reading and thus loss of information. Quoting one of the main rules in Strunk and White's masterpiece *The Elements of Style* [Strunk 1979]: "Omit needless words!"

The following rules taken from [Meyer 1992a] should help achieve brevity without losing vital information. Avoid repeating information which is obvious from the signature or from contract details already specified by the pre- and postconditions. For example, the header comment should not have the form

> *tangent*: *LINE*
>   -- Tangent to circle c through point p
>   → *c*: *CIRCLE*
>   → *p*: *POINT*

but simply

>   -- Tangent to c through p

Avoid noise words and phrases such as "Return the..." explaining the purpose of queries, or "This routine updates..." explaining a state changing command. Instead of

> -- This routine updates the display according to the user's last choice.

use

> -- Update display according to last user choice.

Header comments should begin with a capital letter like a regular sentence, and not contain word abbreviations. They should have the following syntactic form:

- For commands: imperative sentence ending with a period, as in the last example.

- For non-boolean functions: nominal phrase, such as "Tangent..." above.

- For boolean functions: interrogation phrase ending with question mark, as in "Is current node a leaf?"

Use consistent language; if one comment refers to "Length of string..." the next should not say "Update string width...".

8.9 EVOLVING THE SYSTEM ARCHITECTURE

System design proceeds by the gradual refinement of an initially incomplete, abstract structure. This is the essence of object-oriented modeling: not to decide too much too soon. However, refinement means not only working out more detail and filling in missing parts—going from the abstract to the concrete—but also changing parts of the model as our understanding increases. The system will usually have aspects whose modeling is less obvious, and the best way to gain more insight is then often to pick one possible approach and elaborate it in more detail.

So the modeling can be viewed as a succession of iterations between reasonably "consistent" system stages, each hopefully representing a better view than the previous one, until we reach a point of acceptance. In this concluding section on the last of the BON standard activities, we will discuss some general principles for evolving an initial system model.

Avoid premature abstraction

Abstraction is strong medicine, which means that the view of the world represented by the set of abstractions available to us has a very profound influence on the way we think. Therefore, just as good abstractions will act as experienced local guides in their respective problem domains, automatically showing us the best views, misleading or *ad hoc* abstractions can be very dangerous.

Instead of trying to obtain as *many* layers of abstraction as possible, we should search for the *powerful* abstractions. This may sound trivial (or void of content, since we cannot objectively measure what is powerful) but it is still a crucial point in modeling.

Each time we introduce a new abstraction by encapsulating some behavior (or some data, which the reader should at this point be convinced is the same thing), we protect its users from changes behind the scenes. But we do it at a cost: from now on this new concept needs to be part of our vocabulary and will influence our decisions on how to structure the software (in this, as well as in future versions of the system). If the concept is a *strong* abstraction, which means it can be used to solve many interesting variations of some problem and has intuitively clear semantics, then this cost is more than offset by the benefits it brings. In fact, having to remember and take new strong concepts into account in future situations will be a strength rather than a burden, since they may very quickly indicate solutions that are otherwise not easy to see. But for mediocre concepts the payoff is not at all clear, and for weak concepts the net effect of encapsulation is often negative.[17]

It is therefore often better to initially model a problem directly in terms of somewhat lower-level strong abstractions than to prematurely introduce a set of intermediate-level weak abstractions. The reason is that if we start thinking in terms of the weak abstractions and reuse them heavily, it will distort our view of the system and make it more difficult to find the higher-level strong abstractions later.

If, on the other hand, we continue to employ lower-level strong abstractions as long as we only see weak abstractions at the higher level, common usage patterns of the small building blocks will eventually emerge, and indicate how higher-level strong abstractions can be built to encapsulate them. Prematurely introduced weak abstractions may prevent us from ever seeing these patterns.

Strong design means strong dependencies

System design cannot be, and should not try to be, equally flexible in all directions. The characteristic of good design is precisely that it is expressed in

---

[17] Note that a strong concept does not have to be potentially reusable in other systems. Since system evolution (hopefully) means heavy reuse of the components of the previous system version, a very special concept can still be a strong abstraction in the context of the system in which it was conceived.

terms of a small number of well-defined strong concepts capturing the essence of some problem area. Consistent modeling in terms of these concepts (and consequently strong dependence on them) is what enables future requirement changes to be met by simple incremental adaptation instead of extensive redesign.

Trying to guard against all types of changes, on the other hand, will only lead to weak design or no design at all, since the only order equally easy to modify in all directions is random order. Therefore, minimizing the number of client dependencies for each class by systematically encapsulating all collaborative behavior needed in just a few supplier classes, as for example advocated by the Law of Demeter [Lieberherr 1989], represents a driving force towards less consistent global design. Instead of gradually leading to a system in which many classes trust a smaller number of strong abstractions enough to call them directly, the evolution tends to favor many weak abstractions each calling only a small number of other weak abstractions.

Superficially, such a system may seem easier to maintain, since from a local standpoint each class appears less vulnerable to changes in other classes, but this is an illusion. Taking a look at the bigger picture will reveal that most classes contain too many features (often representing flexibility in directions not needed) which duplicate similar behavior and mix several abstractions. There will be much more code to maintain, and the general building blocks, instead of being small, clear, and orthogonal, tend to be large, fuzzy, and overlapping.

Specialization and generalization

There are an infinite number of strong concepts that may be potentially useful in systems development. However, only a very small fraction of them will ever be needed. Therefore—since we are not equipped with divine foresight—we should resist the temptation to develop too much too soon, and instead let experience guide the direction of our evolving conceptual base. A typical technique, directly supported by object-oriented abstraction, is successive specialization and generalization of the concepts found to be most useful in practice.

The corresponding classes will often start by offering an initial set of basic behavior, which may be adapted in descendant classes (specialization). This is the least painful process, since it requires no change at all to the old software. After some time, however, it often turns out that some descendant class C only needs part of the behavior inherited from B. The solution is then to isolate this behavior in a separate class A, which now becomes an ancestor of both B' (containing what is left of B after the extraction) and C.

This is an example of generalization capturing the common parts of two classes. It is more of a corrective action than specialization, since some source code must be changed. However, if the external interface of B can be kept intact (which is often the case) only minimal changes are needed, since old client code using B will continue to work as before.

Deferred classes as program templates

Another important empirical input regarding what abstractions to choose is the discovery of common patterns of behavior, not only in connection with specialization/generalization as above, but also between previously unrelated classes. Behavior patterns that are closely intertwined inside highly variable behavior are often not possible to capture by traditional subroutines. It is therefore common practice in many environments to use templates or skeletons—pieces of software text representing the fixed parts of some behavior—and then add the variable parts through a copy and edit procedure.

In object-oriented environments such templates can often be represented by deferred classes with the variable parts filled in by descendant classes defining implementations for the deferred features. This is a great advantage, since the pattern can be maintained in one place and only the variable parts need to be addressed individually.

Reuse through discovery rather than invention

Software design of well-understood small problems may often profit from the technique of stepwise refinement [Dijkstra 1972, Wirth 1971], going from the abstract to the concrete (provided an eye is kept on what abstractions are already available, so we do not invent them again in slightly different form). But a major part of large systems design, and particularly of system evolution, is to proceed in the reverse direction: from the concrete to the abstract.

There are two good reasons for this. First, we need the benefit of reusing classes already developed and proven in practice, which necessarily has a flavor of "bottom-up" design to it. Second, many common patterns will only emerge after several concrete problems have been implemented (or designed) and the resulting behavior compared. This is to say that a large part of the reusable abstractions in a system (perhaps the majority) will, in the long run, have been *discovered* rather than invented.

This "empirical reuse" has the great advantage of being based on reality instead of foresight, so the corresponding abstractions do not risk being left unused. Of course we should always try to go beyond what is immediately needed and find more general concepts behind the common patterns observed, but not to look too far, because reality may soon enough take a new and unexpected direction.

Implementation as a road to abstraction

Implementation is an extremely important vehicle in the search for reusable designs, because most abstractions are not born in their final form, but rather evolve gradually. We will have to accept working with software in a constant state of evolution, and this fact must not be disregarded by languages and methods.

Therefore, the implementation of a class should not be viewed as an arbitrary low-level solution with no abstractional value for reuse. On the contrary, if done properly, it is a great guide to how similar behavior can be implemented. As opposed to many abstract designs on the drawing board, it also often stood the test of actual usage.

Therefore, separating specification from representation in implementation languages, by providing one inheritance mechanism for subtyping and another for code sharing, as advocated by some researchers, does not promote reusability. The inheritance of concrete classes without code sharing means missing one of the main points of object-oriented development: solving each particular problem only once.

This is perhaps even more apparent when several classes are involved. A white-box framework is defined in [Johnson 1988] as a reusable object-oriented design where the reusing developer is granted access (through inheritance) to the internal structure of a set of classes, while in a black-box framework only visible features may be used (cf. 8.3).

Most frameworks need to start in white-box form to permit fine grain adaptation of behavior by using also the private routines of the inherited classes. As a heavily reused design matures, it is often possible to evolve a white-box framework into black-box form, and achieve the advantages of stronger encapsulation and clearer abstraction. However, this is not possible or worthwhile for all frameworks.

Nevertheless, inheriting a good implementation means getting access to an abstract interface. Although this interface is at a somewhat lower level and somewhat less clearly specified than the corresponding external client interfaces (because of its greater level of control), it is still a substantial abstraction representing a good deal of accumulated knowledge of the problem at hand. As noted in [Johnson 1988], denying the value of sharing representation means denying the value of white-box frameworks, both as a means for reuse and as a vehicle for discovering more powerful abstractions.

Make regular conceptual summaries

Systems development is no easy task, at least not if the ambition is to find good and clean solutions. Often the situation will be perceived as chaotic, but this seems to be a necessary ingredient in all complex problem solving and should not be feared. However, when all the central concepts are in doubt and the general confusion among the designers seems greater than ever, this could be the sign of two very different states:

- The design process could be very close to a point where the thick mist will suddenly disperse to reveal a new-born, clean solution in all its splendor.

- The process could be very far from a solution, perhaps pursuing a dead-end route.

The trouble is, there is no easy way to tell which one. Therefore, as a means of speeding up the process in the first state, or discovering and escaping from the second state, a comprehensive overview of concepts and problems agreed upon should be performed in writing at regular intervals.

To assure a globally consistent view (albeit subjective), this should be done by one or a few designers, each covering a relatively independent set of concepts. When the rest of the group compare the view to their own, previously unknown disagreements will surface. Writing down design thoughts for others to read is an excellent means of testing their degree of maturity; things you cannot explain, usually you do not fully understand. Much of the error detection and corresponding improvements of designs often results from merely systematic documentation.

Seek polymorphism

Polymorphism with dynamic binding is the acid test for object-orientedness. It provides the unique capability of eliminating case analysis before applying an operation to an object in a family of related types, where each member may need a slightly different version of the operation. This permits the application of a whole group of similar operations to a set of similar objects in just a single feature call, letting the system worry about connecting each object to the correct implementation at run-time.

Polymorphism is the natural thing to use when we are only interested in the *similar* aspects of a set of operations (which is very often the case). The similarity is captured by giving each version the same name, and then thinking in terms of applying *one* operation to one or more objects instead of the actual set that may be involved behind the scenes.

A common ancestor of the object types, specifying this name and corresponding signature, is enough to achieve the desired effect. Pre- and postconditions capturing the essence of the similarity addressed will assure the correct semantics for each version, present and future, through the laws of software subcontracting.

This makes it possible to apply an important rule for maximizing the separation of concerns in a system, which has been named the single choice principle by Bertrand Meyer:

> Whenever a software system must support a set of alternatives, the exhaustive list should be known by only one component in the system.

Following this principle as closely as possible leads to considerably smaller systems which are easier to maintain and understand. We can only do this by actively promoting polymorphism as early as possible in the development process.

On library design

We conclude this chapter by touching briefly on some library design principles. An object-oriented library is meant to be used by many developers, and to cover some problem area (small or large) in a reasonably complete, yet flexible way. This automatically implies higher demands on correctness, documentation, robustness, ease of use, and efficiency, than for systems developed with a special environment and user group in mind. Great as the potential benefit of good libraries may be, equally much damage can be caused by a heavily reused low-quality piece of software, so extra effort has to be invested.

Precondition checking

Since heavily reused libraries are (hopefully) of better quality than average software and are extensively tested, one may jump to the false conclusion that run-time monitoring of assertions is not of much value once a library has stabilized. However, what is then forgotten is that a violated precondition is not a sign of error in the supplying feature, but in the *client*.

Therefore, it is extremely profitable to specify formally as many of the precondition clauses as possible in library routines, and leave the checking on, since this is a very effective way of catching errors in the applications that use them. As opposed to postconditions, the checking of preconditions tends to be cheap in terms of memory and CPU power consumed, since many conditions can be expressed as simple boolean expressions.

Consistency

As mentioned earlier in 8.4, consistency becomes all important for large libraries regarding naming, concepts, user metaphors, and functionality. Here, similarity of related operations by choosing the same name for them extends beyond polymorphism. When searching through a large number of partially unknown abstractions for some desired functionality, we need a way to first do a quick categorization in order to come up with a crude selection. Then we can afford to look a little closer at the specifications of the candidates in this smaller set.

Defining a basic layer of operations to cover the functionality of a complicated class, and then complementing these by convenience features, may also be important in this context.

Inversion of control

The purpose of a library is to capture and reuse knowledge of how certain types of problems can be solved. Most libraries act as passive but resilient toolboxes containing good abstractions that the user can choose from, combine, and adapt in desired directions (for example, data structures, graphical figures, GUI widgets, mathematical functions). The idea is that only the user—who has the big picture—knows enough to select and combine the right components for the job.

However, for certain well-understood problems the outline of a whole component, or in some cases a whole application, can be captured as reusable knowledge in a library, then often called a framework. In frameworks, the top-level control is often reversed, so that the user instead plays the passive part. The basic behavior is then furnished by the framework, but can be adapted by information passed from the user, or by the framework calling user-supplied routines. Such frameworks can play the role of structured templates for solving complex problems using standard methods.

Toolkits

Some frameworks addressing complex problems require many similar details to be supplied by the user. When a large number of classes need to be defined, even if each one of them is straightforward enough, the sheer quantity may soon become unmanageable.

Therefore, one may need to go a step further and use a dedicated application that will generate most of the information required by the framework from much simpler input (either interactively or from stored files). Such applications may be called object-oriented toolkits. Typical areas that may benefit from toolkit-generated class text include GUI applications, finite state machine applications, and object-oriented parsers. We conclude this chapter with a few examples.

In Glazier [Alexander 1987], Smalltalk classes and methods are generated using the MVC model to create new types of windows from interactive user specifications combining a set of primitive window elements. The user does not need to know the rather complicated details of the Smalltalk windowing framework supporting the MVC paradigm to use Glazier.

In EiffelBuild [Meyer 1994b], complete Eiffel applications can be generated using the EiffelVision encapsulation of Motif and OpenLook and an extensible set of standard command classes. The user builds a GUI window hierarchy interactively by selection and placement of standard widgets, and then connects mouse and keyboard events in respective widgets to corresponding commands by graphical drag-and-drop. A user extensible set of standard commands are available as icons on a palette. Commands can be made state dependent and the corresponding state transition graph defined using a graphical FSM editor.

In both these cases, a large number of tedious and error-prone details can be hidden from the user, who can still tailor the result by editing the resulting classes. This is particularly important when the requirements change constantly, as they do in rapid prototyping or research applications. The third example problem area, parsing, is perhaps even more typical in this respect.

The Eiffel parsing library [Hucklesby 1989, Meyer 1994a] supports automatic parsing of languages expressed in LL(1) grammar form. Each grammatical construct becomes a separate class, which gives interesting possibilities for the clean separation between the syntax and semantics of a language.

However, the resulting number of classes for a realistic language is much too large to maintain by hand, particularly when the language itself is evolving and each version may be described using several alternative grammars. The toolkit PG [Grape 1992] automatically generates classes directly from grammars expressed in a compact extended BNF notation.

Finally, a whole object-oriented programming environment may also be viewed as a toolkit whose purpose it is to support the generation of general applications. Some interesting new principles for such a toolkit can be found in [Meyer 1993a].

Part IV
Case studies

9 A conference management system

This and the next two chapters will be devoted to showing the use of the BON method and notation for object-oriented modeling in three significant case studies coming from different problem areas. Two of them were inspired by working systems, and partly extracted from effective implementations.

The three areas exemplified will be a simple information system, a high-level hardware encapsulation, and the mapping between an object model and a relational data model. This chapter contains the first case study, whose objective is to model an information system to support the management of a technical conference.

The system should help the organizers follow up a series of events taking place during the preparation of the technical program, and to handle incoming contributions and attendee registrations. The basic tasks of the conference system are the following:

- Monitor the scheduled events and check that all actions required are carried out in time.

- Automate the process of most conference tasks avoiding duplication of effort, and produce warnings to make sure deadlines will not be missed.

- Serve as a repository of information useful to both the technical and organizational committees.

The typical conference we have in mind consists of three main parts: a set of technical sessions presenting recent research and development results, a number of half-day lectures (tutorials) on various topics related to the conference theme, and an exhibition part featuring industrial applications in the area, mostly commercial products. The technical presentations are usually bound and published in conference proceedings, which are distributed to the attendees upon arrival at the registration desk, and also sold separately.

9.1 SYSTEM BORDERLINE

Users

It is customary to split the conference tasks between three reasonably independent parties:

- A *program committee* responsible for the technical program. This includes inviting researchers and developers in the field to contribute material (call for papers), assigning contributed papers and tutorials to suitable reviewers, selecting the contributions to include in the final program, and grouping them into sessions and subject tracks.

- An *organizing committee* responsible for general policies and logistics. This includes advertising and general mailings (invitations to attend), decisions on pricing and capacities, sponsor negotiations, rental of suitable premises, conference lunches and special evening arrangements, accommodation prebookings, registration handling (attendees and exhibitors), confirmation letters, publishing, tutorial notes, participation lists, and attendee badges.

- An *accounting department* taking care of the financial side. This includes invoicing, follow up on payment, and subsequent balance statistics on gross sales and expenditures.

In many disciplines the major conferences are international, which means that committee members as well as speakers and attendees may come from any part of the world. It is then very unlikely that the people responsible for the conference will all share the same geographical location. Particularly the program committee is in most cases a highly distributed group and will for practical reasons usually have only one common meeting to decide what papers to include in the final program. The organizing committee may be more homogeneous, but is usually separated from the program committee. Finally, the financial side may use a standard system already present at one of the organizing parties, or leave the task to an independent commercial service bureau.

This usually results in the use of unrelated software by the different groups. An invoicing and accounting system with conference add-ons will perhaps satisfy the administrative people, while the program committee members may use some generally available software, like a spread-sheet program, to record submissions and review reports.

The program committee receives contributions and sends letters of acceptance or rejection. Even if in practice the organizing committee may take over the bookkeeping, duplication of information and parallel updates without careful synchronization inevitably lead to oversights resulting in the wrong letter being sent, duplicate letters, or no letter at all in some cases.

To counter this, a more rigorous system may define exact formats for data interchange between heterogeneous systems along with orderly procedures for keeping all distributed data consistent. In this example, however, we will just assume one single support system, which will have all facts available and be responsible for the overall consistency. This may be achieved if distant committee members only communicate messages to the central system, which then handles all correspondence with attendees and contributors.

Incoming information

Typical information entering the system is:

- registration form

- payment (bank wire, credit card slip, check)

- submitted paper or tutorial

- purchase order

- reviewer report

Figure 9.1 shows an example of what to expect of a registration entry format.

<Title>	Dr
<Last name>	Maugham
<First names>	Julia Rachel
<Affiliation>	Advanced Spacecraft Intl.
<Country>	USA
<Postal address>	1010 Bourbon Street
<City zip code>	New Orleans LA 70100
<Telephone>	504 333 22 11
<Facsimile>	504 444 55 10
<Electronic mail>	maugham@asi.com
<Selected tutorials>	T3, T13, T21, T10
<Conference days>	2
<Amount paid>	$ 1675.00
<Entitled rate>	A
<Registration number>	341
<Registration date>	1993-12-30

Figure 9.1   Registration sample

Outgoing information

Typical information leaving the system is:

- call for papers, invitations, promotional material
- letters of confirmation, acceptance, rejection
- attendee tickets
- preliminary and final program
- invoices, reminders
- proceedings, tutorial notes
- evaluation forms, badges
- session signs and posters
- list of attendees, financial status

Figures 9.2 and 9.3 show examples of an invoice and a financial report. In order to find risk areas, we might ask ourselves what could go wrong in a poorly designed support system. Possible negative effects include low credibility

---

Participant: Adams Matthews Stefenson
Reference: 301
Date: January 5, 1994

INVOICE

ooooooooooo

WaO–Oh! '94 Registration – Regular Rate			
Quantity	**Description**	**Unit Price**	**Total**
1	Conference 2 days	$ 495.00	$ 495.00
4	Tutorials	$ 295.00	$ 1180.00
		TOTAL AMOUNT	$ 1675.00

Payment:

- by check to the order of Intl. Conference Management Service Inc.
- by bank wire to the following banking references: *ICMS – LA County Bank, Burbank, California, account number:* 00T9486Q094

Figure 9.2 Invoice sample

STATISTICS – January 15, 1994	
Number of registered persons:	890
Number of exhibitors:	62
Number of registered persons to Tutorial T1:	55
Number of registered persons to Tutorial T2:	62
⋮	⋮
Conference fee gross sale:	$ 445,000
Exhibition fee gross sale:	$ 124,000
Expenditures:	$ 375,000
Current Balance:	$ 194,000

Figure 9.3   Report summary sample

(conflicting information sent to speakers), loss of revenue (poor handling of registrations), incorrect estimates regarding the number of luncheons, simultaneous translation headphones, accommodation needs, and so on.

Well-identified functionalities of the system correspond to specific user roles with assigned responsibilities. Some of them will be captured by representative scenarios and illustrated through dynamic diagrams. The aim of our analysis and design is roughly to decide what concepts in the problem domain are important enough to be modeled as classes (thus affecting the software architecture), and what should just be mapped into object states.

A conference support system may range from a quite simple system with limited functionality to quite ambitious software addressing a considerable amount of things perhaps not directly related to the event itself. One of the major benefits in using the object-oriented approach is that it often enables a continuous evolution without invalidating anything related to the initial requirements and the working implementation.

Therefore, we will deliberately accept incomplete specifications and will see that despite the fuzzyness of our initial set of requirements, we can still organize our development around a few simple abstractions. Even for a small system used by a limited number of people, we can design and release a first self-contained functional version, and then gradually extend it with add-ons in much the same way as is often formalized in large-scale industrial developments through incremental deliveries [Gilb 1988].

9.2 CANDIDATE CLASSES IN THE PROBLEM DOMAIN

When looking for our first list of classes to start the modeling, our main concern is to review *de facto* classes observed in the problem space and try to capture the most significant ones. There is no ideal world to discover here, but a bit of modeling practice will help us develop a feeling for what kind of problem domain abstractions are worth considering at the highest analysis level, and which decisions should definitely be postponed till later.

For example, although CONFERENCE_ROOM may be a tangible object in the problem domain, it is not important enough to start working with, whereas REGISTRATION and COMMITTEE seem to capture profound roles with major effects on the task of organizing a conference. The first candidate classes are shown in figure 9.4. They are ordered alphabetically by name, because in real situations when the number of candidates tends to be larger than in this example, grouping by affinity does not work well and only makes it more difficult to quickly find a class in the chart.

Different user groups have different views of the system, and some problem domain concepts will be important to some users and ignored by others. For example, exhibitor booths with their various sizes and prices will be of interest to the organizing committee (as they represent a considerable source of income), while the program committee may not even worry about whether there will be an exhibition or not.

Other concepts may be shared by several user groups, but we must not forget that such concepts are then never viewed in exactly the same way. For example, a tutorial may be viewed by the program committee as a piece of structured information of a certain technical quality, which belongs to a certain educational track.

The same tutorial may primarily be viewed by the organizing committee as a commercial offering, whose degree of success (and corresponding revenue) depends on the number of enlisted participants and the resulting scores of the evaluation forms. Finally, the people in the copy shop preparing the tutorial notes will probably view it as a stack of documents whose important properties are things like master copy quality, time of arrival, single or double paged printing, binding method, and relative popularity (more work for successful tutorials).

For concepts like this, we must decide which user viewpoints to support, since this may highly affect the corresponding class abstractions. (In our example, class TUTORIAL will be defined from the conference management viewpoint ignoring the documentation aspects.)

9.3 CLASS SELECTION AND CLUSTERING

From the first identified set of classes, we may now start considering candidate partitions dividing our system into different clusters. These upper-level clusters represent the internal model of the basic system functionalities. We choose four

CLUSTER	*CONFERENCE MANAGEMENT SYSTEM*	**Part:** 1/1
PURPOSE General conference administration support.	**INDEXING** **keywords:** conference system, first gathered analysis classes	

Class/(Cluster)	Description
ATTENDEE	Registered person attending the conference.
COMMITTEE	Peers organizing the conference and performing a fair evaluation of the contributions to obtain a well-balanced program of high-quality technical presentations reflecting the major directions of the current research and industrial development in the field.
CONFERENCE	System for managing a selected domain event of a few days' duration, consisting of technical presentations, a choice of short tutorial courses lectured by domain experts, and a commercial trade show displaying industrial advances in the field.
CONTRIBUTOR	Person listed in the final conference program.
PAPER	Authored technical paper submitted to the program committee chairperson.
PROGRAM	Description of conference events.
REFEREE	Program committee member refereeing submitted technical papers for possible acceptance in the technical conference program.
REGISTRATION	Record of attendee participation keeping track of affiliation, selected sessions, and registration fees.
SEND_OUT	Message sent from the committees to anyone involved in the event, such as attendees, speakers, staff, and conference suppliers, regardless of the physical media used (electronic mail, postal letter, or facsimile).
TASK	Elementary action performed by the management system upon receipt of an external event, or because of some information contained in the agenda.
TUTORIAL	Short training course submitted to the program committee chairperson addressing a specific topic in the field.

Figure 9.4   First candidate classes

clusters, as shown in figure 9.5, to capture what we view as fairly distinct responsibilities of the system. We also provide a textual description for each introduced cluster, which will be the basis for any further discussion between the users of the system and its designers.

The clusters are iconized according to the BON notation, and will be expanded later when more is known about the classes contained in each cluster. With this

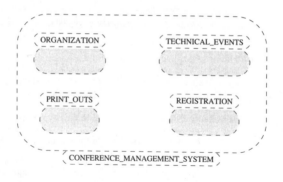

SYSTEM	CONFERENCE MANAGEMENT SYSTEM		Part: 1/1
PURPOSE General conference administration support.	**INDEXING** **domain:** information system **functionality:** conference organization, registration follow-up **keywords:** conference, course, trade show, attendee registration		
Cluster	**Description**		
ORGANIZATION	Handles all major events occurring during the organization of the conference, from the initial decision of its title, date, duration and estimated budget, all the way to successful completion.		
TECHNICAL_EVENTS	Is responsible for putting together the program, recording the status of all contributions, checking in referee reviews, and following a precise timetable for what has to be done and when.		
REGISTRATION	Collect any registration data needed for invoicing, production of lists, printing of badges, and automated sending of formatted letters. Store every piece of information related to whatever may change the cost/benefit ratio of the conference: attendee registrations, exhibitor registrations, cancellations, room booking, catering, etc.		
PRINT_OUTS	Record every possible format used to print out something of interest to the conference: preformatted letters, badges with registration information, final program listing selection and filtering criteria, up-to-date final program description, and session signs to post on conference doors.		

Figure 9.5 First cluster definition sketch

cluster partitioning, we may now attempt to assign the first identified set of classes to the chosen clusters. This will still be somewhat tentative, since no class chart has yet been written. Only a more systematic description of the class properties and constraints may confirm the appropriateness of our choice.

Since all classes so far, except *CONFERENCE* and *PROGRAM*, seem to represent concepts that can have several variants and therefore perhaps result in inheritance hierarchies, we mark them as deferred until we know more. The result is shown in figure 9.6, where *CONFERENCE* has been selected as the root class. A common ancestor *PRESENTATION* of classes *PAPER* and *TUTORIAL* has also been introduced (the heirs are not shown in the figure).

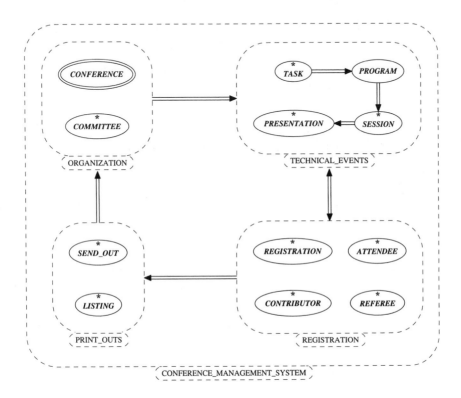

Figure 9.6 Management and registration close-up

At this point, it becomes possible to outline dependencies between the clusters. It is worth noting that the cluster dependencies in figure 9.6 imply an order relationship that could help in staffing and scheduling a "cluster-based" software development. We may therefore plan to benefit from a layered approach. In a good design, it is often possible to direct the client relations from the application specific clusters, through intermediate clusters, down to the utility clusters. General utilities can usually be made application independent, whereas application-dependent clusters are more closely related to the corresponding problem domain.

Clearly, cluster *PRINT_OUTS* encapsulates capabilities that are potentially reusable in a system that does not have anything to do with conference management and organization. The cluster can be designed and implemented with facilities such as:

- formatting text according to predefined format templates (used for printing badges, poster signs, etc.)

- automatically laying out a letter selecting from a number of predefined styles: kind invitation, acknowledgment of receipt, friendly reminder, etc.

- selecting ready-to-use text substitution elements according to letter recipient: male or female, attendee or speaker.

Classification

Looking closer at our first general classes reveals there are numerous variants that may have to be considered, for example:

Registrations
>advance registration, discount registration, complementary registration (press, exhibitors, VIPs)

Contributors
>conference speaker, co-author, keynote speaker, tutorial speaker, panel moderator, panel speaker, session chairperson

Committees
>program committee, organizing committee

Send outs
>contributor send out, attendee send out, supplier send out

Paper
>rejected paper, selected paper

To model systematic variations between similar objects we basically have two different strategies to choose from: either rely on classification by inheritance, or translate adaptations into object states using client relations. If similar objects will often be handled together but still require different treatment depending on the exact variant, then inheritance is often preferable since it allows dynamic binding of tailored operations.

An extremely important principle in systems development is to get rid of as many case discriminations as possible, since these are very sensitive to system changes and therefore make maintenance much more difficult. However, inheritance is not always feasible, particularly when many variants can be combined or when the roles played by an object can change dynamically. While client relations can vary over time, inheritance relations are fixed.

If we try to use inheritance to classify the roles of people attending the conference, as illustrated in figure 9.7, we soon witness a combinatorial explosion. We find that even multiple inheritance is not enough to model all

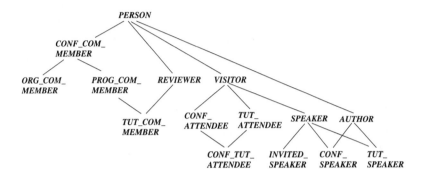

Figure 9.7 Partial classification attempt

possible role combinations, because:

- most program committee members are probably reviewers, but maybe not all

- a program committee member can also be a speaker

- some speakers are probably reviewers, etc.

Looking back at classes such as *REFEREE*, *CONTRIBUTOR*, and *ATTENDEE* introduced in the first candidate list, we realize that we cannot keep all these roles as classes. Instead, we replace them with one simple class *PERSON*, whose objects will have registration properties to model the various attendee profiles needed.

The same situation comes up with registrations. The numerous combinations of registration types would pollute an attempted inheritance classification with fork and join cycles, similar to what we saw in figure 9.7. So we will once again rely on internal properties and stick with a single class *REGISTRATION*. Fortunately, these problems do not arise with simpler classification schemes, involving for example presentations and committees.

However, before committing ourselves any further as to what classification structures to use, it is now time to sketch a set of analysis class charts in order to gain more insight into the properties of the corresponding abstractions.

9.4 CLASS DEFINITION

This task, involving untyped class specifications on our way to more formal interfaces, is usually required when a system is delivered to end-users or customers who do not have a very clear idea of what they want. Although the chart format suggested by BON is designed to help further translation into class specifications based on abstract data types, it also resembles a formatted memo used to record major aspects of the problem.

One way to start defining the classes is to go back to the first class descriptions (candidate list in figure 9.4) and outline a more elaborate version of each entry, taking the changes discussed so far into account. Usually each class description raises new abstractions that may in turn become class charts.

Organization

The first two charts address the conference as a whole and the committees in charge of steering the event technically and practically, as shown in figure 9.8.

CLASS	CONFERENCE	Part: 1/1
TYPE OF OBJECT Generic conference		**INDEXING** **cluster:** *ORGANIZATION* **keywords:** conference, scientific meeting
Queries	Name, Location, Conference capacity, Organizing committee, Program committee, Program, Budget, Attendees, Insurance policy	
Commands	Prepare. Close down.	
Constraints	Run only once a year. Total registrations ≤ conference capacity. Location serviced by an international airport. Accommodation capacity ≥ conference capacity. Insurance policy subscribed. Organized in collaboration with sponsors.	

CLASS	COMMITTEE	Part: 1/1
TYPE OF OBJECT Conference committee		**INDEXING** **cluster:** *ORGANIZATION* **keywords:** reviewers, experts, managers
Queries	Chairperson, Members	
Commands	Set up. Select chairperson.	
Constraints	Chairperson is committee member.	

Figure 9.8 Conference and committee class charts

We see that the *CONFERENCE* class has a number of constraints attached. Some of these may later be turned into assertions in a typed class interface (pre- and postconditions and class invariants), but there are also facts, intentions, rules, etc., that do not translate into formal specifications but are still interesting to record.

For example, easy access to an international airport is an important consideration when choosing the conference premises. But it may not be meaningful to express this formally in a system, since what should be considered "easy access" may require human judgment on a case-by-case basis to balance between measurable properties such as number of international flights to this airport, commuting distance from airport, frequency of shuttle buses, taxi capacity at bus terminal, etc. This type of constraint may instead become part of an on-line set of guiding instructions in an implementation to help system users make the right decisions.

Note that there is a difference between constraints of the type just described and constraints that are in fact absolute rules, only too complicated to be expressed formally. The latter kind may still be part of formal assertions in the form of comments. After all, the main purpose of assertions is specification, while the possibility of run-time checking is a great asset but no prerequisite.

Although we need to model committees with different responsibilities (like program and organizing committees), they will all have members and a chairperson, so we begin by encapsulating these features in a general class *COMMITTEE* to be used as ancestor.

It is common to let a separate group of people handle tutorials, since the educational aspects (and also commercial—successful tutorials can be a substantial help in financing the conference) may need somewhat different skills compared to selecting which scientific reports to include. The tutorial group is often a subset of the program committee, but could be formed separately. Since several of its tasks are similar to handling the scientific contributions (registering incoming proposals, accepting or rejecting, grouping into subject tracks), it seems natural to model the group as a committee of its own.

However, handling the scientific part does require formal procedures, such as peer reviewing and transfer of copyrights, which are not needed for tutorials, so we cannot use the exact same class. Figure 9.9 shows a feasible static architecture to capture what we have just discussed.

The class *TECHNICAL_COMMITTEE* encapsulates what needs to be added to the general *COMMITTEE* abstraction in order to also handle submitted presentations, while *ORGANIZING_COMMITTEE* instead adds a great deal of administrative features. Finally, class *PROGRAM_COMMITTEE* adds features for sending out call for papers and for supervising a formal reviewing process. It will also contain a tutorial subcommittee of type *TECHNICAL_COMMITTEE*.

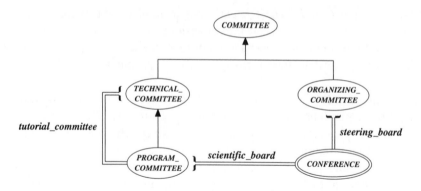

Figure 9.9 Committee classification

Note that it would not be appropriate to name the latter class *TUTORIAL_COMMITTEE*, since that would model program committees as special kinds of tutorial committees, which is clearly wrong. On the other hand, since the features that will be in any technical committee (of which the program committee is a special case) seem enough to fulfill the behavior of a tutorial subcommittee, we see no need for a separate *TUTORIAL_COMMITTEE* class. If more specialized tutorial needs come up later during design, the latter class may be added as a sibling to *PROGRAM_COMMITTEE*.

As a consequence of our discussion, all the committee classes are effective classes. Even if we do not yet see any need for direct client use of the top class *COMMITTEE*, it may become useful as a simple encapsulation of a set of members with a chairperson, so there is no reason to mark it as deferred. We therefore remove the deferred marker introduced in figure 9.6. The class charts for the committees are shown in figure 9.10.

The size of the program committee has been limited by constraints to 40 members. To achieve a good balance between theory and practice, we have also decided to spread the committee members evenly between industry and academia so that the numbers differ by at most four. Moreover, publishing limitations, the capacity of the conference premises, the number of parallel sessions wanted, and the duration of each talk and of the whole conference will jointly restrict the number of papers that may be accepted. As seen in the chart, this limit has been set to 30 in our example.

Finally, the last committee chart found in figure 9.10 shows the behavior needed for the organizational part. Although the substance of the program is prepared by the program committee, the final mailing is channeled through the organizing committee, so consistency may be ensured and duplication avoided. Since committee members are just *SET* [*PERSON*], the same person may belong to any number of committees.

CLASS	TECHNICAL_COMMITTEE	Part: 1/1
TYPE OF OBJECT Conference technical committee	**INDEXING** **cluster:** *ORGANIZATION* **keywords:** scientific community	

Inherits from	*COMMITTEE*
Queries	Received submissions
Commands	Define submission guidelines. Register submission. Accept submission. Reject submission. Group submissions.

CLASS	PROGRAM_COMMITTEE	Part: 1/1
TYPE OF OBJECT Conference program committee	**INDEXING** **cluster:** *ORGANIZATION* **keywords:** scientific community, reviewers, peers	

Inherits from	*TECHNICAL_COMMITTEE*
Queries	Tutorial subcommittee, Acceptance standards, Review meeting, Referees
Commands	Prepare call for papers. Dispatch submission to reviewers. Enter review results. Select session chairs. Prepare final program.
Constraints	Members ≤ 40. Industrials − Academics ≤ ±4. Final selected papers ≤ 30.

CLASS	ORGANIZING_COMMITTEE	Part: 1/1
TYPE OF OBJECT Conference organization committee	**INDEXING** **cluster:** *ORGANIZATION* **keywords:** non-profit organization, steering committee	

Inherits from	*COMMITTEE*
Queries	Contracted exhibition services, Contracted publisher, Regulation policy, Sponsors
Commands	Mail call for papers. Mail final program. Mail exhibition kit. Handle registrations. Send final papers to publisher. Print and bind final tutorial notes. Schedule paper and tutorials sessions. Print attendee list. Collect evaluation sheets.

Figure 9.10 Specialized committee class charts

Conference program

With the committee responsibilities and corresponding classification sorted out, we may now proceed to take a closer look at the conference program. A program consists of tutorials and technical presentations selected by the program committee members during their unique and timely review meeting ending with heartbreaking decisions (a rejection rate of 2/3 or more is often necessary to achieve good technical quality at a popular scientific conference). Often, for reasons of time and travel expenses, only a small part of the program committee will in fact attend the meeting, while the rest of the members make their contributions as reviewers.

The definition of the conference program directly yields its constituent parts. The chart for class *PROGRAM* (figure 9.11) defines two queries, *Agenda* and *Contributions*, to access the sessions and the selected papers and tutorials. The general *PRESENTATION* class encapsulates common properties of technical papers and tutorials. We have chosen to move class *PROGRAM* to the *ORGANIZATION* cluster (cf. figure 9.6), since putting a program together

CLASS	*PROGRAM*	Part: 1/1
TYPE OF OBJECT All information pertaining to the final conference program and its related preparation	**INDEXING** **cluster:** *ORGANIZATION* **keywords:** agenda, program of sessions	
Queries	Paper and tutorial submission deadline, Final contribution deadline, Preliminary program, Contributions, Agenda	
Commands	Update. Print.	
Constraints	Final deadline = submission deadline + 4 months. Contributions accepted by program committee.	

CLASS	*PRESENTATION*	Part: 1/1
TYPE OF OBJECT Submitted paper or tutorial	**INDEXING** **cluster:** *TECHNICAL_EVENTS* **keywords:** scientific result, technical achievement	
Queries	Presentation code, Title, Authors, Status, Speakers	
Commands	Accept. Reject. Hold.	
Constraints	Presentation code and title must be unique.	

Figure 9.11 Program and presentation class charts

involves keeping track of deadlines, sending reminders, and so forth, while class *PRESENTATION* remains in the *TECHNICAL_EVENTS* cluster.

Usually, there are many types of presentation: tutorial, technical paper, keynote address, invited talk on a special topic, panel session, poster session, "birds of a feather" session, workshop, and so on. For the sake of simplicity we will only detail two specific cases here: technical paper sessions and tutorial sessions. We define the special behavior needed for papers and tutorials, respectively, as shown in figure 9.12.

CLASS	*TUTORIAL*	**Part:** 1/1
TYPE OF OBJECT Submitted tutorial	**INDEXING** **cluster:** *TECHNICAL_EVENTS* **keywords:** speech, lecture, training, public seminar	
Inherits from	*PRESENTATION*	
Queries	Capacity, Number of attendees, Technical prerequisite, Track, Duration	
Constraints	Number of attendees ≤ capacity.	

CLASS	*PAPER*	**Part:** 1/1
TYPE OF OBJECT Submitted paper	**INDEXING** **cluster:** *TECHNICAL_EVENTS* **keywords:** contribution, publication, article	
Inherits from	*PRESENTATION*	
Queries	Review reports, Average score	
Commands	Award best paper. Transfer copyright to publisher.	
Constraints	Not already published when submitted.	

Figure 9.12 Tutorial and paper class charts

Note how the constraints section is again used to record business rules. In this case, class *PAPER* states that a submitted paper must not have been published before (or even submitted to another conference, to be more restrictive). Even if this cannot be automatically checked, it is an important piece of information that may perhaps be made part of the author and/or submission guidelines.

We may now sketch the static architecture of the analysis classes associated with the technical program: its published incarnation and its presentation-based format (figure 9.13). Note that all classes containing dynamically interesting

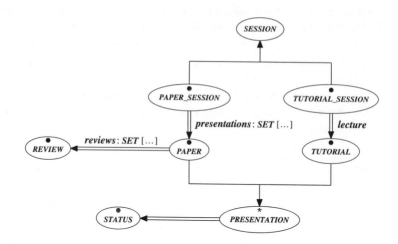

Figure 9.13 Technical events classes

data have been marked as *persistent*, which means that at system shut-down the corresponding instances must be saved on secondary storage (object or relational database, file system, etc.) for later retrieval. In a typical information system, such as this, many classes tend to be persistent.

Class *PRESENTATION* is marked as deferred because it contains commands for accepting or rejecting a submission, which needs to be done differently depending on type of presentation. Class *SESSION*, on the other hand, might be sufficient for workshops, panel sessions, etc., and is therefore not deferred. We do not show the charts for the session classes, nor status and review (we will return to them when we look at the formal class interfaces).

Registration

The next cluster to examine is the registration part of the system. We can model registrations and their connections with attendees in several ways. One possibility is to mirror the incoming pre-registrations, which often list several participants from the same organization, and enter only one registration per received order (group registration). This may seem nice and simple, but a moment's reflection reveals that it would in fact be a very inflexible solution.

If individual attendees can only be found through the corresponding registration numbers, we will be in trouble each time a company calls to change or cancel the registration for one person in a group registration. Each attendee may also choose a combination of tutorials, so one registration for each attendee with a two-way client relation between classes *PERSON* and *REGISTRATION* seems a smarter choice (figure 9.14).

Figure 9.14 Registration and person static coupling

The *PERSON* class solves the classification problem raised earlier regarding attendee roles. Each instance represents a person who is entitled to visit all or parts of the conference, and will be attached to a corresponding registration recording the terms. This will automatically lead to the proper badge being printed, and a speaker will therefore not risk being refused entry to his own technical session because an official prepaid registration was never issued! (This actually happened to one of the authors some years ago in San Diego.) Figures 9.15 and 9.16 show the corresponding class charts.

CLASS	*REGISTRATION*	**Part:** 1/1
TYPE OF OBJECT Record of attendee participation, keeping track of affiliation, selected sessions, and registration fees	**INDEXING** **cluster:** *REGISTRATION* **keywords:** conference registration, permission to attend, authorization	
Queries	Attendee, Conference days, Selected tutorials, Date, Amount paid, Invoice sent, Confirmed	
Commands	Confirm participation. Invoice referred to attendee. Send practical information documents.	
Constraints	Invoice has no effect for free access attendees.	

Figure 9.15 Registration class chart

CLASS	*PERSON*	**Part:** 1/1
TYPE OF OBJECT Person whose address is kept track of by the conference: committee member, (potential) attendee, referee, speaker, etc.	**INDEXING** **cluster:** *REGISTRATION* **keywords:** conference attendee, speaker, exhibitor, lecturer, visitor, participant, authorized person	
Queries	Name, Title, Affiliation, Address, Country, Registration	
Commands	Register. Cancel registration. Substitute other person.	
Constraints	Anyone entitled to visit the conference is registered.	

Figure 9.16 Person class chart

Printed material

During the preparation of the conference program and incoming registrations, different types of letters are sent out by the conference management system: invitations, confirmations, acceptance and rejection letters, and so on. A great deal of other material is also printed before and during a conference, such as address labels, evaluation sheets, attendee badges, and invoices. A deferred class *PRINT_OUT* encapsulates general facilities for formatting and printing documents, which in turn use a set of predefined templates describing the general layout of different types of printed material, as illustrated in figure 9.17.

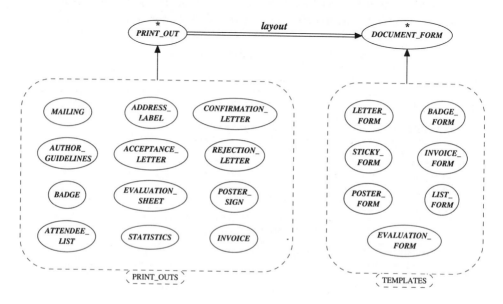

Figure 9.17 Print support

Typically, the template classes will specify fonts, point sizes, logos, line drawings, etc., used for the various blocks of information in a document of a certain type, while the information contents of each block will be supplied by the specific printout class.

Conference management

Arranging a conference means a great deal of interaction with other parties (authors, attendees, exhibiting companies, conference sites, hotels, travel agents, exhibition service contractors, publisher, reviewers, committee members). Having a successful program with satisfied participants requires a lot of interdependent tasks to be carried out, agreements to be checked, deadlines to be met, and logistics to be planned.

Trying to go a little further in our sketch of the initial set of classes, we may now take a design decision, which is to introduce a dedicated class to help collect and keep track of various important time-related activities. The class, which we call *TIMETABLE*, will act as a data repository that is checked by the top-level class at regular intervals to help follow up scheduled events and produce warnings if important deadlines are about to be missed. This results in the partial architecture shown in figure 9.18.

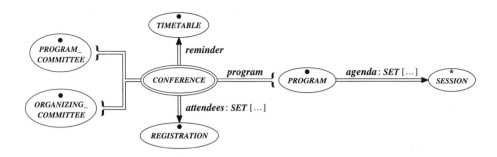

Figure 9.18 Conference management

When the system is restarted each morning, say, the root class *CONFERENCE* checks the timetable to see if anything pressing needs to be done first. It then issues warnings, prints recommendations, invokes appropriate actions in the committee classes, or whatever the level of ambition in the implementation calls for. The normal operation would then typically be to enter some kind of standard command input loop, and let the users input registrations, select papers, schedule sessions, etc., at their choice.

The class chart of the timetable is shown in figure 9.19. The submission and final contribution deadlines were moved from the *PROGRAM* class into *TIMETABLE* in order to have a comprehensive overview of all important time-related events that need to be followed up. No commands are specified, since the interface to *TIMETABLE* is not yet decided. One reasonable solution is to store the time information in a plain parameter file, and simply use a text editor to dynamically change entries when circumstances call for it.

Deadlines in relation to conference sites, hotels, caterers, etc., are mostly open to discussion and may thus change several times during the conference preparation, and if not enough good-quality papers and tutorials have been received, it may be necessary to extend submission deadlines. The automatic checking will probably need to be done more frequently as certain important dates get closer.

CLASS	TIMETABLE	Part: 1/1

TYPE OF OBJECT
Keep track of important dates and
deadlines
	INDEXING
	  cluster: *ORGANIZATION*
	  keywords: conference events, deadlines,
	    reminder, control, follow-up	

Queries	Today's date, Frequency of checking, Last checked date, Advertising dates, Call for papers mailing dates, Invitation mailing dates, Manuscript submission deadline, Formal review deadline, Review meeting date, Final paper deadline, Final program at latest, Lunch orders at latest, Hotel reservations at latest, Author notification at latest, Early payment discount deadline	
Constraints	Checks performed at regular intervals.	

Figure 9.19   Timetable class chart

9.5 SYSTEM BEHAVIOR

Events and scenarios

Using our initial sketchy description of the system and the first set of gathered analysis classes, we may now outline a set of significant incoming external events that will lead to interesting system behavior. These events (incoming stimuli) result in the creation of new objects, or the passing of information between active objects, or the entry and propagation of external data into active objects. Some of them will also cause significant outgoing system responses to be produced by internal actions.

A set of incoming events are collected in the chart shown in figure 9.20. A second chart captures outgoing events that are system responses triggered after a chain of external incoming and internal events is activated (figure 9.21). In practice, it is usually not worthwhile to try and provide a complete set (in any sense) of all possible event and scenario types. The aim is to select some examples illustrating the most typical and important usage (concentrating on potential trouble spots), and see how they map to the static architecture. Since there is always a cost involved in working out a scenario and scenarios represent some of the things most volatile to system architectural changes, they should not be overdone.

Particularly for an evolving system with fuzzy requirements, as in this case, the scenarios should mainly be viewed as a set of throw-away elaborations that will help us check and improve the evolving static model, and not, for example, as the formal basis of a future system test batch. System testing and long-term documentation have many other aspects, and should be addressed separately.

EVENTS	CONFERENCE MANAGEMENT SYSTEM	Part: 1/2
COMMENT Typical incoming events triggering interesting system behavior.	**INDEXING** **keywords:** external events, incoming stimuli	

External (incoming)	**Involved object types**
A contribution is registered	*CONFERENCE, PROGRAM_COMMITTEE, PRESENTATION**
The formal review results of submitted paper are entered	*CONFERENCE, PROGRAM_COMMITTEE, PAPER, REVIEW*
A contribution is accepted or rejected	*CONFERENCE, PROGRAM_COMMITTEE, PRESENTATION*, STATUS*
An accepted contribution is attached to a session	*CONFERENCE, PROGRAM_COMMITTEE, PROGRAM, SESSION, PRESENTATION**
A session chairperson is selected	*CONFERENCE, PROGRAM_COMMITTEE, PROGRAM, PAPER_SESSION, PERSON*
An attendee is registered	*CONFERENCE, ORGANIZING_COMMITTEE, REGISTRATION, PERSON*

Figure 9.20 Incoming events

We will limit ourselves to four scenarios in this example, while in a real development we would probably select some more. The chosen scenarios are listed in the scenario chart shown in figure 9.22, which acts as the front page of the dynamic model, summarizing the dynamic object diagrams to follow.

What relations to emphasize

Whenever a message is expected to be exchanged between two objects, it is necessary to verify that the calling object can reach the receiver object. This means there must be transitive closure on client/supplier links between the classes of the sender and receiver objects, respectively.

However, this does not necessarily mean it will be possible to follow public query links from the sender to the receiver class. Several client dependencies will arise through private features and through local variables used in the implementation of public features. Whether such implicit client relations are shown in the corresponding static diagrams or not, is a question of what we want to emphasize and must be left to the designer's good judgment.

Several considerations come in here. First, even when client relations between clusters may be derived from the types of public features, we do not necessarily

EVENTS	CONFERENCE MANAGEMENT SYSTEM	Part: 2/2

COMMENT
Typical outgoing events.
	INDEXING
	  keywords: internal events, outgoing
	       responses	

Internal (outgoing)	Involved object types
Call for papers is sent	*CONFERENCE, ORGANIZING_COMMITTEE,* *PERSON, MAILING*
Invitations are sent	*CONFERENCE, ORGANIZING_COMMITTEE,* *PERSON, MAILING*
A paper is sent to referees	*CONFERENCE, PROGRAM_COMMITTEE, PAPER,* *STATUS, REVIEW, PERSON*
Warning issued for exceeding tutorial session capacity	*CONFERENCE, REGISTRATION, TUTORIAL*
An author notification is sent	*CONFERENCE, PROGRAM_COMMITTEE,* *PERSON, PRINT_OUT*, LETTER_FORM*
An invoice is sent to a prepaying attendee	*CONFERENCE, ORGANIZING_COMMITTEE,* *REGISTRATION, PERSON, INVOICE,* *INVOICE_FORM*
A badge is printed	*CONFERENCE, ORGANIZING_COMMITTEE,* *REGISTRATION, PERSON, BADGE, BADGE_FORM*
The conference attendee list is printed	*CONFERENCE, ORGANIZING_COMMITTEE,* *REGISTRATION, PERSON, ATTENDEE_LIST,* *LIST_FORM*

Figure 9.21 Outgoing events

want to show them in high-level views of the system. This is because different client relations resulting from analysis and design choices are not necessarily equally profound or stable.

Some relations may mirror very deep model decisions, while others are there simply because we have been forced to make a choice between equally feasible alternatives. The latter types are more likely to change over time, and in order to reflect the more fundamental properties of a system architecture, they may be left out of some static diagrams.

On the other hand, there may be a very profound client dependency between two problem domain classes, even if the exact client relations are not reflected by return types of public features. Such client dependencies may be an important part of the high-level views, but cannot be labeled, since we do not want to decide yet how the necessary connection will actually be implemented.

SCENARIOS	*CONFERENCE SUPPORT*	**Part:** 1/1

COMMENT
  Scenarios selected for study.
	INDEXING
	  keywords: paper evaluation, notification,
	  registration, badge printing	

Input review results and compute score:
  The scores found in the formal review reports for a submitted paper are entered into the system, and an average score is computed for later use at the program committee review meeting.

Accept or reject a paper and notify authors:
  A submitted paper is selected and an acceptance or rejection date is entered; a notification letter is sent to the first author.

Register attendee:
  An attendee is registered with his/her address, and selected tutorials are recorded.

Print attendee badge:
  An attendee is selected, and the corresponding badge is printed in the appropriate format.

Figure 9.22 Scenario chart

Since the dynamic connection between two objects will also imply some sort of static chain between them (either before or behind the curtains in an eventual implementation), working with dynamic scenarios often helps clarify modeling questions of the kind just raised.

First scenario

The first object scenario deals with the input of review results, and is illustrated in figure 9.23. The scenario describes the main steps involved in finding a paper

Scenario 1: Input review results and compute score	
1–2	*One of the submitted papers is selected*
3–5	*Formal review scores are input*
6–7	*Score average is computed and stored*

Figure 9.23 First object scenario

and entering its corresponding review results. Since an eventual implementation will involve many details that we still want to keep open, the idea is to include only essential object communication in an object diagram.

For example, to find a desired paper the user might first click on "show submitted papers" in the main menu of class *CONFERENCE*, then repeatedly select "next paper" from a local menu in class *PROGRAM_COMMITTEE* until the sought paper appears on the screen. However, in a different implementation the user may instead click directly on "find paper" in *CONFERENCE* and input a pattern matching string for the desired title.

Since there are so many possible ways to let a user navigate in an information system, there is no point in trying to specify what classes will take care of the successive user control input. Instead, we concentrate only on the information content entering the system at various steps in a scenario.

So the initial user interaction is not included in the diagram, but we assume that the *CONFERENCE* object is somehow told to select a paper. This, in turn, leads to a message being sent to the *PROGRAM_COMMITTEE* object, which is in charge of the list of submissions (1). *PROGRAM_COMMITTEE* then consults its set of papers until the right paper is found (2).

This will typically mean iterative calls to a generic *SET* class to obtain one *PAPER* object after the other, telling each of them to present some identification (title, authors, etc.) and let user interaction decide when to stop. However, as we have just argued, the details of such interactions are better left to later phases. Moreover, we normally do not want to clutter object diagrams with messages to standard container objects. Instead, we use stacked object icons to imply lists and sets.

So the message labeled 2 in the diagram is actually an abstraction of a navigation within a set of objects, which may eventually involve other objects in a final implementation (not only design objects and general utility objects, but also analysis objects). For example, when presenting information about each paper in order to let the user select the proper one, there are several alternatives. If author names are part of the information, then *PERSON* objects will be involved also in this step, but this will not be the case if only titles are presented during the search.

When the *PAPER* object has been selected, *PROGRAM_COMMITTEE* calls it to obtain the corresponding set of *REVIEW* (3), whose members are then successively called to input the referee scores (4). In the diagram, we represent the user input required to transfer the scores to the system as an external message sent to a corresponding *REVIEW* object (5). This does not necessarily mean that the actual user interaction takes place in class *REVIEW*, since (again) the details of user terminal input are typical implementation issues that should be kept open at this stage.

However, we still want to be able to show the interesting fact that external user data will be entering the system as part of the scenario. Therefore, the convention is to depict the data entry as a user input message directed to the receiving object, even if it may be implemented differently. The input may for example first be accepted by a centralized user input object, whose features will be called by *PROGRAM_COMMITTEE*, which will in turn send the data to *REVIEW*.

Unless there are special reasons, we do not care to illustrate external communication that only results in browsing through a system or running up and down menu hierarchies. Therefore, external incoming messages depicted in object diagrams will correspond to incoming data flow or selections leading to new objects being created or read from secondary storage; that is, interactions that imply some significant change to the system state and its information contents.

Similarly, outgoing messages will correspond to something substantial leaving the system, like data transferred to external media, calls to other systems, printed reports, etc., and not just trivial things like writing a prompt or an error message on a user's terminal.

Finally, when all reviewer scores have been entered, the set of *REVIEW* is again consulted by *PROGRAM_COMMITTEE*, which computes an average score (6), and sends it to the *PAPER* object for storage (7).

Second scenario

The next scenario, which illustrates the acceptance procedure for an individual paper, is in figure 9.24. The first part of the scenario shows the messages involved in recording the acceptance status of a paper. Steps 1–2 first select the proper paper (same as in previous scenario). *PROGRAM_COMMITTEE* then sends an accept or reject message to the paper (3), which in turn tells the corresponding *STATUS* object to change the paper status (4).

This will need user input for setting the date of acceptance or rejection (5). Again, we use the convention to depict user input as directed to the object which will hold the information (*STATUS* in this case), regardless of the way it is going to be implemented.

The second part of the scenario shows the author notification procedure. First, *PROGRAM_COMMITTEE* sends a message to *PAPER* (6) to get the authors, which is a *SET* [*PERSON*], and then consults this list to obtain the first author (7). Depending on the decision reached, *PROGRAM_COMMITTEE* then creates the proper form of notification letter (8), which involves a conditional choice between two alternatives: rejection or acceptance. Both are covered by passing the message to an object group rather than to individual objects.

Scenario 2: Accept or reject a paper and notify authors	
1–2	A paper is selected
3–5	Acceptance or rejection date is entered
6–7	The first author of the paper is selected
8	A notification letter is created
9–11	The letter is sent to first author

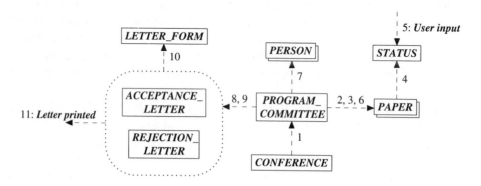

Figure 9.24   Second scenario

Finally, the notification letter is told to print itself (9), which makes it consult the proper format template (10), and then the formatted letter leaves the system, probably directed to some external print spooling system (11). The actual mailing is assumed to be done manually. The inclusion in the final program is postponed until the final version of the article is received for inclusion in the proceedings.

Note that the reviewer scores do not enter the picture here, because these have already been scrutinized at the program committee's formal review meeting. Scenario 2 only effects the decisions taken at that meeting.

Third scenario

This scenario shows the registration of a conference attendee (figure 9.25). The user directs the system to enter registration information, which transfers control to the *ORGANIZING_COMMITTEE* (1), which in turn creates a new *REGISTRATION* object (2). The registration data is input (3), which is marked as a message from the external world to the *REGISTRATION* object, again regardless of how the data entry will actually be implemented.

Based on the input data, a *PERSON* object is either created or reused from the existing set of persons in the conference database and the corresponding address

Scenario 3: Register attendee	
1–3	*A new registration is created*
4–5	*Attendee references are recorded*
6–7	*Selected tutorials, if any, are registered*

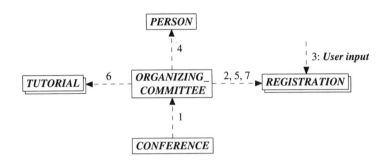

Figure 9.25 Third scenario

information is entered or updated (4). (In accordance with our earlier design decision, each listed person in a group registration from an organization will be registered separately to enable individual changes for each participant.) The *PERSON* object is then recorded in the *REGISTRATION* (5). Then, again based on the received input, possibly selected tutorials are recorded in the same *REGISTRATION* (6–7).

Fourth scenario

The last scenario (figure 9.26) shows an attendee badge being printed for a person who is entitled to visit some part of the conference. The attendee is selected from the registration database (any person with permission to visit the conference in any capacity must already have been registered), and a badge is printed according to the information stored in the corresponding registration, using the proper format description.

Besides printing the attendee name tag, the badge object may also output instructions requesting some manual attachments to the badge, such as ribbons of various colors stating the title of attendees with special functions: conference chair, speaker, session chair, staff, program committee, etc. A registration category code could be used to discriminate between the roles of different attendees, and prevent, for example, a keynote speaker being invoiced for visiting the conference.

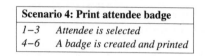

Figure 9.26   Fourth scenario

9.6 FORMAL CLASS DESCRIPTION

Each class can now be described in a more thorough and formal manner, deciding the signature of each *query* and *command*, starting from the first definitions in the class charts. For each feature in a formal class interface, the type of each input argument as well as the return type (in the case of a query) is specified as either a user-defined class type, or a predefined analysis class type.

Besides signature specifications, which give the abstract syntax of the corresponding feature calls, formal assertions are used to specify semantic properties through pre- and postconditions and a class invariant. The bulk of these semantic specification elements will usually be created during detailed design and implementation.

Predefined types for analysis and design

Predefined types are very general abstractions that can be reused in a wide variety of analysis models, and each development organization working with BON should define a standardized extensible set of such types with well-defined semantics. In this example, we assume the basic predefined types *BOOLEAN*, *VALUE*, and *SET*.

The *BOOLEAN* type has value semantics, which means it is always attached to an object and can therefore never be void (the attached value is either **true** or **false**). The same is true for very basic numeric types, such as *INTEGER* and *REAL*, but these are normally considered too special to be used at the highest analysis level. Since we want to keep the representation of various values open as long as we can, we only use the familiar low-level types in case they are actually part of the requirements (such as when re-enginering existing software where already specified interfaces must be kept unchanged).

However, *BOOLEAN* is a notable exception, since although it will probably map directly to some type in most implementation languages, it represents a fundamental concept in logical reasoning and is therefore in fact extremely general (in a sense, much more general and high level than typical top-level abstractions such as airplanes and hospitals).

The *SET* type is a general generic container class that can be used to hold any specified type of elements. Note that we are referring to very general data abstractions without committing ourselves to any implementation. Therefore, abstract data containers also represent high-level concepts that may be used to reason about any kind of analysis objects.

While *BOOLEAN* and *SET* may often map directly to specific implementation classes or to basic types, *VALUE* has more a flavor of TBD (To Be Decided) about it. At the early stages of modeling, we often come across a large number of queries returning various pieces of interesting information, but whose exact format we do not yet want to fix.

For example, the *capacity* query in the *CONFERENCE* class (figure 9.27) may return just an *INTEGER* stating the maximum number of attendants. However, we may also find more specific information useful: how much latitude before the crowding level becomes unacceptable vs. absolute limit (local fire regulations), all available space already included or possibility to increase capacity (last minute rental of adjacent annexes), etc.

Using a *STRING* would mean freedom to express more such details to a human user, but instead prevent easy automatic comparison. Using a dedicated analysis class *CAPACITY* could solve both problems, but also means increased complexity. Since the capacity considerations are not part of the fundamental system structuring questions, we would like to leave the corresponding decisions for later.

One possibility would be to just leave *capacity* untyped (which is the standard approach in many other methods), but the BON spirit is to use a very general type instead. By specifying *VALUE*, we express that the information returned will not be any of the high-level analysis classes modeled so far, that it could (and often will) be a very basic type, but also leaves open later refinement into a new type defined by a design or implementation class. The idea is to encourage the analyst not to make premature decisions, but still maximize the possibility to express and reason about things that should be decided.

Therefore, use of the *VALUE* type is very common, particularly in typical administrative information systems like our conference example. If we know we are dealing with a piece of numeric information, we could use the basic type *NUMERIC*, which guarantees that the standard arithmetic operations will be defined for the corresponding object (but still does not preclude a string representation, if so desired).

We will now look at the translation from charts to formal interfaces, one system area at a time.

Organization cluster

We begin with the organizational part of the conference, and look first at the root class with its associated program and list of important dates. The interface specifications for these classes are shown in figure 9.27. The organizing and program committees as well as the conference program are seen as integral parts of the conference. This is emphasized by using the aggregation variant of the corresponding client relations.

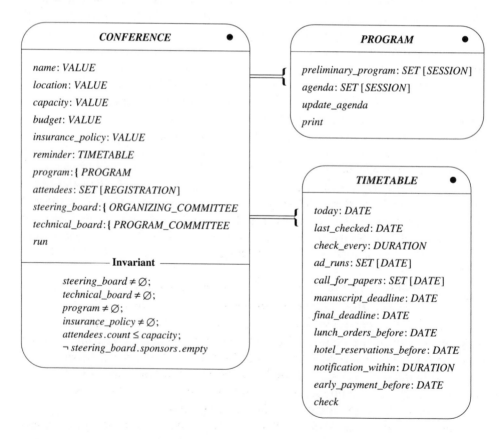

Figure 9.27 Conference and program

In the invariant of class *CONFERENCE*, this is emphasized by specifying that the references to these parts must not be void, and so must be set up already at object creation time. Since the committee members may not all have been selected when the system is first started (and the program is usually empty or just contains a preliminary sketch), the parts may of course be gradually filled with content. The invariant just specifies that the conference object must always be attached to the corresponding objects, empty or not.

Two features of class *SET*, the queries *empty* (returning **true** if there are no elements in the set) and *count* (returning the number of elements), are also used to express assertions about sponsors and number of attendees. We have chosen to delegate the responsibility of maintaining a set of sponsors to the *ORGANIZING_COMMITTEE*, but the constraint stating that the conference should be organized in collaboration with sponsors (see the class chart in figure 9.8) belongs to the conference proper rather than the committee class.

This is the reason why the assertion $\neg$ *steering_board.sponsors.empty* is placed in the conference class, and not in the organizing committee class. Generally, if every object of a class must obey certain rules under all circumstances, these rules belong in the invariant of the class. But if the rules are just imposed because the class is being used by other classes in a restrictive context, then the rules belong in assertions about the client classes.

Looking at the class chart (figure 9.8) again shows that of the three commands defined there (*prepare*, *run*, *close down*) only *run* was kept. This is not unusual, and again shows the hybrid character of the class charts serving both as initial class definitions and as generalized memos. They often contain operations which mirror actions in the problem domain, but which may later turn out to have no counterpart in a computerized system.

As a conference organizer, we may have a clear view of three distinct phases regarding the tasks to be carried out. First we prepare everything during a period of several months (marketing, program preparation, pre-registration, etc.), then we actually run the conference during some usually extremely hectic days, and finally we close it down and take care of the aftermaths.

However, for a support system this division hardly makes any sense, since the same system should be run on a day-to-day basis for as long as it may help its users. So it becomes natural to have a single *run* command that will execute at startup time each day, read in whatever persistent objects were saved in previous system sessions, check important deadlines, output reminders, and then accept general user commands.

In the reminder class *TIMETABLE*, we have assumed the existence of two basic temporal classes, which may be part of a general reusable time utility cluster, as shown in figure 9.28. Class *DATE* represents an absolute point in time, while *DURATION* represents a relative time period. The timetable is

Figure 9.28   Temporal utilities

supposed to be checked at regular intervals (expressed by the query *check_every*) and author notifications must be sent within a certain time limit after the formal decisions have been reached.

The class interfaces of the committees with their classification are shown in figure 9.29. The reader may have noted that there are no input arguments in the feature signatures of our high-level analysis classes specified so far. This is no coincidence, since the input information required at the upper system levels often needs user interaction whose details it would be premature to specify already in the analysis model.

Therefore, when modeling interactive systems, input arguments usually start to appear in BON formal class descriptions only during design. In the case when we model a system that mainly interacts with other systems, or develop reusable class libraries, things may be quite different.

In figure 9.29 we see that the class *ORGANIZING_COMMITTEE* has some queries whose return types are *SUPPLIER* objects or sets thereof. However, we are not going to define the supplier class in our analysis model, so one might question its use. Why not just specify *VALUE·* at this point, and then refine the type later in the process, when more is known?

The reason is that although it may not be possible (or desirable) at an early stage to decide any interface details for a certain group of values, we may still suspect that they will have enough things in common to warrant separation by choosing a special ancestor type for them. Simply assigning *VALUE* as the type would not capture that similarity.

In the *PROGRAM_COMMITTEE* interface (figure 9.29), we have an example of feature redefinition. Any *TECHNICAL_COMMITTEE* object has a set of sessions attached, since what makes the corresponding class different from a general *COMMITTEE* is the handling and selection of presentations to be included in a program. In class *PROGRAM_COMMITTEE*, we add the formal reviewing process and a subcommittee feature as a further specialization. Since we know that the elements in the *sessions* set must be of type *PAPER_SESSION*, we can redefine the feature to return this type of set. The redefinition is specified by two plus signs, signifying that the feature is "twice implemented".

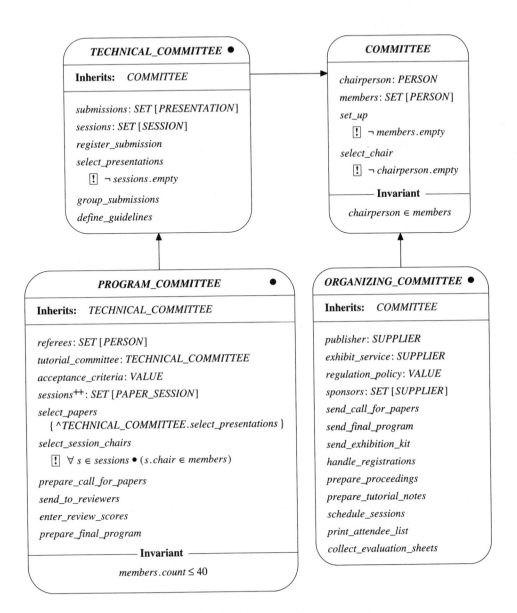

Figure 9.29 Committees

Since *tutorial_committee* uses the general class for technical committees, there is no corresponding specialization in which to redefine the *sessions* feature for the tutorial committee. Instead, *PROGRAM_COMMITTEE* becomes responsible for ensuring that the elements in the set *tutorial_committee.sessions* will always have type *TUTORIAL_SESSION*. In the first case, redefinition permits static checking by a compiler that the session elements will have the correct subtype, while in the second case only dynamic checking is possible.

Finally, we note that feature *select_presentations* has been renamed *select_papers* to better reflect its usage in this subclass. (See section 3.8 for a description of the BON graphical class interface symbols.)

Registration cluster and technical events cluster

The coupling between the persistent classes *REGISTRATION* and *PERSON* is detailed in figure 9.30.

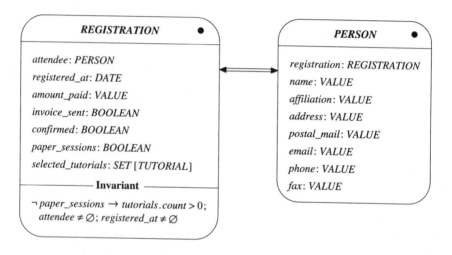

Figure 9.30 Registration

Each registration is attached to one, and only one, person. This permits us to easily specify a different set of tutorials and to make individual changes also for attendees that were collectively enlisted by one organization. Applicable company discounts and the like will be distributed on each attendee.

Conversely, each person entitled to visit all or parts of the conference will automatically have a registration created and a registration attribute may be added, if desired, to record the reason for complimentary non-paid access rights (invited speaker, sponsor representative, committee member). The invariant states that a registration must imply access to either the scientific program or some tutorial (or both).

The interfaces for the classes which are part of the technical program are shown in figure 9.31, and the final static architecture of the conference system in figure 9.32. The invariants of the session classes state that all presentations

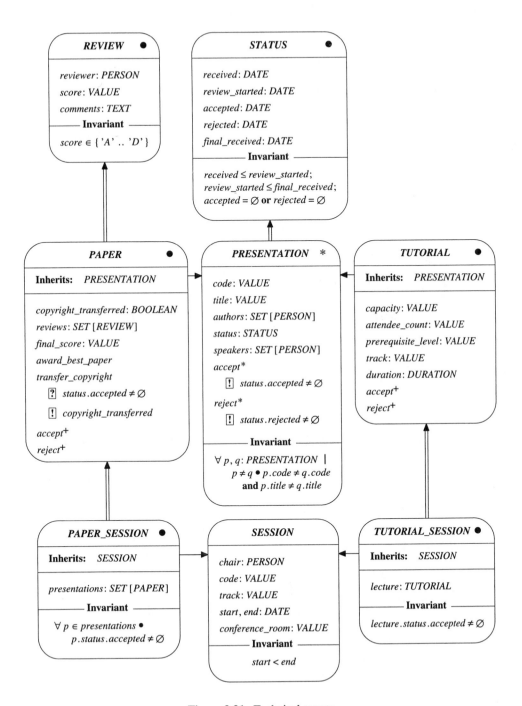

Figure 9.31 Technical events

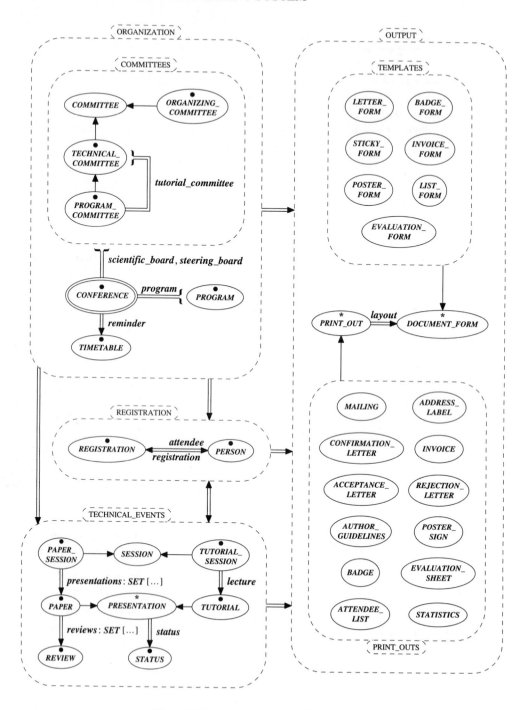

Figure 9.32   Complete static architecture

attached must be accepted, while the more complicated invariant of the presentation class says that the *code* and *title* of each submission must be unique.

To express the latter, we let p and q range over all pairs of *PRESENTATION* objects, and assert that the corresponding attributes are different. The invariant of class *REVIEW* asserts that the score is always one of the four characters 'A' through 'D' expressed as membership of an enumerated set. (See section 3.12 for a full description of the BON predicate logic.)

10 A video recorder

In this case study, we will model the software control system for a simple video tape recorder. The purpose is to show the danger of concentrating too much on the underlying hardware to be modeled. Classes that reflect tangible hardware objects may occur at some point during detailed design and implementation, but they may not be the ones to use at the topmost level of a system if we want to achieve reusability.

10.1 SYSTEM BORDERLINE

Most standard hardware components in a modern video cassette recorder (VCR) can be controlled by micro computer logic, thus enabling easily tailorable operation for different needs. Our task is to produce a high-level design of the control program to be installed in the Micro Computer Unit (MCU) of the new, simple, but reliable and aggressively priced model Multronic 2001, currently being developed at the Bonasonic company.

The technical manager of the Home Video Division has just returned from a three-day seminar on object-oriented abstraction and software contracting, and is very enthusiastic about its potential for reuse of knowledge and increased product quality. Although the hardware and main functions have already been completed, there is still time to apply the new ideas to the controlling software, whose implementation is just about to start.

Knowing the dangers of rushing into new technology without adequate background, the manager has engaged a consultant for in-house training in object-oriented analysis and design, and to support the software engineers during the initial system modeling.

Internal operation

The principle mechanical components of the video recorder are sketched in figure 10.1. The model has four heads: two rotating video heads, a fixed

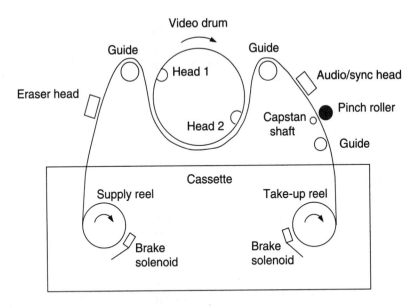

Figure 10.1   Video recorder: tape in read/write position

audio/sync head, and a fixed eraser head. The audio head handles recording and playback of sound, and also reads sync pulses telling the current location of a moving tape. The identical video heads are mounted on a rotating drum and are used for playback or recording of a video signal, depending on current mode.

The rotating heads scan the tape, receiving or recording one picture frame per revolution. Since the two heads are mounted at 180°, they can take alternate turns: when one head is about to leave the tape, the other enters and takes care of the next frame. The rotation makes it possible to scan and show a still picture also when the tape is stopped in load position (pause function). The fixed eraser head is used to demagnetize the tape just before recording.

The machine has five separate motors: a cassette motor, a load motor, a drum motor, a reel motor, and a capstan motor. When a cassette is inserted in the machine, it is pulled in by the cassette motor in two steps: first in, then down. Sensors report cassette-in and cassette-down respectively, and a time-out is used to eject a tape that has not reached the down position within 5 seconds.

When a cassette is down, the tape position is controlled by the load motor. The tape has three positions reported by sensors: released, sync only, or loaded. To eject the cassette, the tape needs to be in the released position. For fast forward or rewind, the load motor brings the tape into contact with the audio head so recorded sync pulses can be read. For playback or record, it brings the tape to the loaded position shown in figure 10.1 by moving the two guides inwards on each side of the video drum.

On playback or recording, the pinch roller is pressed against the capstan shaft by a pinch roller solenoid, and the capstan motor moves the tape. The winding and unwinding of the tape reels in the cassette is controlled by the reel motor. A reel idler is pressed against either reel depending on direction, and the reel motor thus rotates the corresponding take-up reel.

The tape tension at each reel is reported by sensors and used to control the reel speeds through the reel motor on the take-up side, and through the reel brake solenoid on the supply side. Sensors also detect write-protected mode and beginning and end of tape, so the reel motor can be safely stopped and full reel brakes applied in time.

The Multronic 2001 includes a data bus that is used by the MCU to address the ICs controlling various hardware components.

External operation

The front panel of the VCR is shown in figure 10.2. Besides the standard playback and recording functions, up to 32 channels may be preset for easy reception of satellite stations, and up to eight recordings can be programmed in advance.

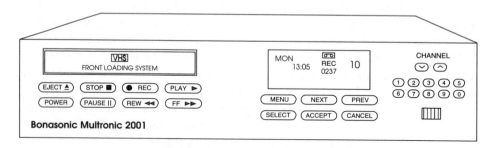

Figure 10.2 Video recorder: front panel

The channel is selected by the UP and DOWN channel buttons or by the numeric keyboard. The current time is shown in the left upper part of the display window, and the current channel in the right upper part. When a cassette is loaded, a tape-in indicator lights up in the middle part of the display, and the current mode of operation and tape position is shown. In figure 10.2, the VCR is recording from channel 10 and the position counter has reached 237. The buttons below the window are used to control tuning of channels, setting the clock, and programming recordings. Pressing the MENU button displays a selection list in the lower part of the window, as shown in figure 10.3. In this case there was no cassette in the machine, so the upper middle part of the display is off.

Figure 10.3   Video recorder: selection menu

Setting the clock, tuning a station, or programming the timer at position 1–8 can now be done by first positioning the rectangular cursor using the NEXT and PREV buttons and then pressing the SELECT button. Programmed recordings are marked by a small dot below the corresponding position.

The left part of figure 10.4 shows timer programming and the right part shows how to set the clock. Both dialogs can be carried out while the tape is operating, for example rewinding as in the right display. Input is entered from the numeric keyboard into the current field, and the rectangular cursor is automatically advanced upon valid completion of a field. The cursor can also be moved using NEXT and PREV to correct individual entries. When a record is completed it is stored by pressing the ACCEPT button, while pressing CANCEL leaves the menu dialog and returns to normal operation.

Figure 10.4   Video recorder: timer and clock dialogs

If tuning is selected, the VCR starts searching for the next available station at the video input, and the tune entry flashes until a station is found. Pressing ACCEPT then stores the tuned frequency at the current channel.

Playback, recording, and tape positioning can also be controlled by the battery-powered infrared remote controller shown in figure 10.5. In the back of the chassis there are some connection sockets to external equipment and a switch to select input from either a video camera or a tuner.

System viewpoint

The enclosing hardware and specified functionality defines the system borderline exactly, so we do not need to spend initial time figuring out what parts of the

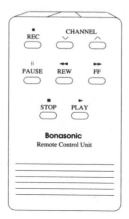

Figure 10.5   Video recorder: remote controller

problem domain should be modeled or identifying external information flow, metaphors, and typical use cases. In this case study, understanding the requirements is enough to start looking for initial classes.

10.2 CANDIDATE CLASSES

An often recommended method to find classes is to look for *de facto* problem domain structure. In a piece of tangible equipment like a video recorder, the separate physical parts which need to be dealt with then become obvious candidates for abstraction. If we can identify the parts that have program interfaces, this will give us an initial structure to work with.

A first attempt

From the requirements in the previous sections we can identify several groups of program-interfaced components: motors, solenoids, heads, sensors, buttons, display window, and remote controller. We can collect this information in a first cluster chart, as shown in figure 10.6.

The first five candidates in the chart represent deferred classes, since the corresponding hardware components will have different interfaces and therefore need to modify the available operations. The button and keyboard classes, on the other hand, will probably only need to return an input code. The cassette slot also works somewhat like a load button, since when a cassette is inserted far enough, this is detected by a sensor which will trigger the rest of the cassette transport.

CLUSTER	VCR_UNIT	Part: 1/1
PURPOSE Controlling software for the Bonasonic Multronic 2001 video recorder.	**INDEXING** **keywords:** video recorder, first candidate classes	

Class/(Cluster)	Description
MOTOR	Device to control various movable parts in the VCR: cassette transport, tape path, tape movement, drum rotation, capstan shaft rotation.
SOLENOID	Magnetic coil to attract or repel certain movable parts: reel brakes, pinch roller.
HEAD	Electromagnet for reading, writing, or erasing information on the tape: video heads, audio head, eraser head.
SENSOR	Detector reporting certain physical conditions: start or end of tape, tape path position, cassette inserted, cassette down, tape protected, signal sent from remote controller.
DISPLAY_WINDOW	Device displaying visible information to user: current time and channel, tape-in, mode of operation, winding position, menu selection, timer dialog, clock dialog.
OPERATION_BUTTON	Button pushed by user to operate the VCR: playback, record, stop, pause, rewind, fast forward, eject, channel up or down.
CONTROL_BUTTON	Button for selecting options: enter menu, program recording, set clock.
KEYBOARD	Set of buttons for entering numeric input: 0–9.
LOAD_SLOT	Slot for entering tape cassette.
TIMER	Hardware clock that can deliver interrupts at certain preset points in time.
TUNER	AFC device that can search for tunable stations and switch between a number of frequencies stored in memory.
FRONT_PANEL	VCR front containing buttons, display, and cassette slot.
REMOTE_CONTROLLER	Device transmitting an infra-red light signal when one of its buttons is pushed by the user.
MCU	Micro computer unit housing the control program.

Figure 10.6   First candidate classes

10.3 CLASS SELECTION AND CLUSTERING

In the next task, we proceed to select analysis classes from the candidates, then classify and possibly group them into a cluster structure. The deferred candidates, except *DISPLAY_WINDOW*, each have a distinct set of candidate subclasses identifiable from the requirements. The corresponding set of classes can be grouped into clusters, as shown in figure 10.7.

The subclasses to *DISPLAY_WINDOW* cannot be inferred from the text, since we do not know what distinct LED matrixes or other display elements the front panel display window consists of. Several types of displayed information may

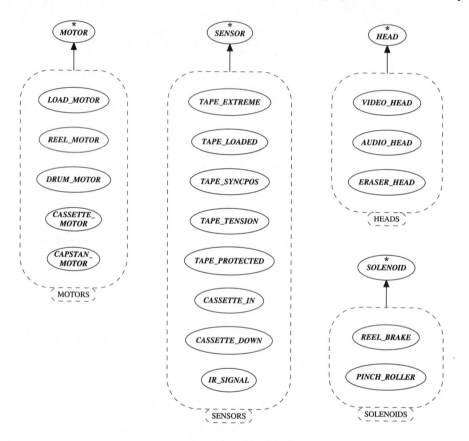

Figure 10.7 Similarity grouping

share the same physical components, while more complex information (for example the menu dialog) probably needs to use several physical components.

The *LOAD_SLOT* class is not needed, since the sensor *CASSETTE_IN* will detect the user inserting a tape. The remote controller has a set of operational buttons, while the front panel also has a set of control buttons to set options. This can be expressed with aggregation relations. Grouping the button classes into a *BUTTONS* cluster and then enclosing what we have plus the *TIMER* and *TUNER* classes in a *VCR_UNIT* cluster produces the architecture shown in figure 10.8. The *VCR_UNIT* comprises the hardware components which are used by the *MCU* to control the home video system.

Assessing the architecture

Now it is time to take a look at the analysis classes arrived at so far, and try to assess their potential reusability with respect to future changes. We seem to have encapsulated the current hardware components fairly well, so that low-level interface details may be hidden from the upper layers of the MCU logic. Instead of deciding directly what particular IC pins should go high or low to start motors, set video signal directions, apply brakes, etc., higher-level operations can be applied to abstractions of the components.

However, if we start thinking of what operations the selected classes should have, we realize that we are in trouble. The class *MOTOR* should probably have a *stop* operation, but that is just about all we can say at this level of generality. Some motors have only two modes, constant speed in one direction or off, others have several speeds and may reverse the direction. The speed might be fine tuned by varying the input voltage, or by applying brakes to increase the resistance. Motors may be mechanically combined to perform several functions as one unit. There are even recorders that use only one motor to replace all five in our example.

Moreover, motors that need exact speed control, like drum motors, reel motors, and capstan motors, are usually controlled by servo systems in separate

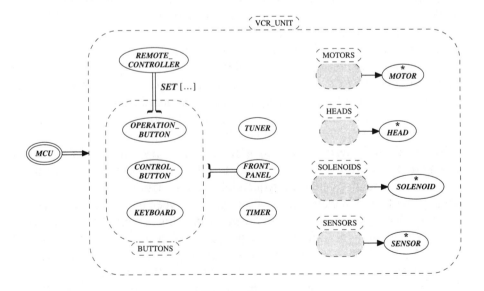

Figure 10.8 First static architecture

ICs. Similar variability holds for tape heads, sensors, and solenoids. Also, the *BUTTONS* cluster, *REMOTE_CONTROLLER*, and *FRONT_PANEL* classes mirror the physical structure of the recorder, but since buttons represent extremely simple abstractions, the chosen classification will probably not help system maintenance very much.

Although our classes represent general components that are widely used in many video recorders, they are (with the exception of *TIMER* and *TUNER*) either not very interesting or else too special to use at the earliest analysis level. We should look for something more general.

A second attempt

So we forget about specific hardware components for the moment, and look instead at the main services offered by a video home system (VHS). Our aim is to avoid the conceptual straitjacket resulting from choosing too special abstractions at the highest level, but still impose some useful structure that can be reused in future versions of the Multronic model and perhaps also in other Bonasonic VCR products.

It seems reasonable to separate two parts: one for magnetic signal handling and one for the mechanical transportation of tape and heads. We call these classes *VIDEO_CONTROLLER* and *TAPE_CONTROLLER* respectively. The *TIMER* and *TUNER* classes of our previous attempt also seem general enough for most video systems.

Another general service, which will be more and more important for future models, is user control of options. All modern video systems offer special functions like programmable recordings, programmable tape editing, simulated stereo on playback, audio dubbing, child locking, and so on.

Using these functions requires an interface that is somewhat more complicated than just pressing one button. On the other hand, since we have no direct pointing device or fully fledged alphanumeric keyboard (too space consuming to be useful), we need some simple consistent metaphors to let the user input all required information without too much difficulty.

The Multronic interface has simple menus with some navigational buttons and a numeric keyboard as the physical interface for option control. We can use this to create a general concept of sequential menu containing a set of entries and some predefined commands to shift the focus between entries, select a submenu, input a value to an entry, leave the menu, etc. This is captured by the deferred class *MENU*, and the effective subclasses in the Multronic system are called *OPTIONS*, *PROGRAM*, and *CLOCK* respectively. The new static architecture is shown in figure 10.9. As we can see, it is entirely different from our first attempt in figure 10.8. The corresponding cluster charts are found in figure 10.10.

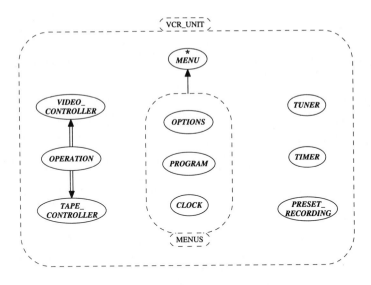

Figure 10.9   Second static architecture

10.4 CLASS DEFINITION

Having selected and grouped the analysis classes, we now proceed to look at
their operations. The class chart for *OPERATION* is shown in figure 10.11; it
has one command for each operational button on the front panel.

The corresponding buttons at the remote controller lead to codes transmitted to
the IR sensor. We do not model any button classes, but instead let the
EVENT_HANDLER class take care of all panel button events and signals from
the timer, tuner, and sensors, and direct them to the proper objects. This scheme
therefore includes the remote controller, whose trivial program is not modeled.

Each button may yield a unique code, or perhaps a group code coupled with a
position number within the group, depending on the hardware component used.
The event handler may use tables or other means to trigger corresponding
operations in the *VCR_UNIT* classes (FSM modeling is a typical candidate here).
We do not care about the details, but prefer to leave things open not to preclude
different strategies.

The interface of the class *OPERATION* is very close to the user metaphor
about what goes on in the VCR. No particular hardware components are
assumed at this level. There will probably be more operations to take care of
various sensor events, but since we do not know how much of this will be
handled by local ICs and what will have to be dealt with by the micro processor,
they are left out until future detailed design.

CLUSTER	VCR_UNIT	Part: 1/1
PURPOSE Controlling software for the Bonasonic Multronic 2001 video recorder.	**INDEXING** **keywords:** video controller classes	

Class/(Cluster)	Description
OPERATION	General operation of the video recorder.
VIDEO_CONTROLLER	Operates the magnetic signal handling part of the recorder, such as directing the heads to amplify the signal from tape or from input channel depending on recording or playback.
TAPE_CONTROLLER	Operates all movable mechanical parts to position the tape, move the cassette, rotate the drum and capstan, etc.
TIMER	Keeps track of programmed recordings and returns a signal when the hardware clock reaches preset times.
PRESET_RECORDING	Stores one programmed recording with channel number and start/stop time.
TUNER	Searches for receivable stations and stores their frequencies for easy selection.
MENU	Deferred class containing a sequence of entries and a number of standard commands to move between entries, select alternatives, input values, etc.
EVENT_HANDLER	Handles all external events, like interrupts from sensors, clock interrupts, buttons pressed on front panel, or signal received from remote controller. Directs each event to the object responsible for taking care of it.
(MENUS)	Subcluster containing classes inheriting from class *MENU*.

CLUSTER	MENUS	Part: 1/1
PURPOSE Different types of menu classes encapsulating user selections.	**INDEXING** **keywords:** video recorder, user menus	

Class/(Cluster)	Description
OPTIONS	Menu for tuning stations and selecting submenus to set clock or program recordings.
PROGRAM	Menu interface for programming.
CLOCK	Menu interface to reset system clock.

Figure 10.10   Analysis clusters, second attempt

CLASS	*OPERATION*	**Part:** 1/1
TYPE OF OBJECT Main VCR operation.	**INDEXING** 　**cluster:** *VCR_UNIT* 　**keywords:** video recorder, main operation	
Commands	Load cassette. Eject cassette. Playback. Record. Stop. Pause. Fast forward. Rewind. Forward cue. Reverse cue. Channel_up. Channel_down. Input a digit.	

Figure 10.11 Main operation

The display details in the requirements text are also considered too special for the analysis model, and are left until we know more about the hardware display elements to use. The cueing operations *forward cue* and *reverse cue* stand for medium speed tape transport, allowing a user to skip over sections of a recording while still viewing its contents (rapidly moving frames, usually with significant distortion). The next charts are the controller classes in figure 10.12. These

CLASS	*VIDEO_CONTROLLER*	**Part:** 1/1
TYPE OF OBJECT Handler of the magnetic part of a VCR.	**INDEXING** 　**cluster:** *VCR_UNIT* 　**keywords:** video recorder, magnetic signal	
Queries	Is VCR in playback mode? Is VCR in recording mode? Current channel	
Commands	Playback. Record. Set channel.	
Constraints	Memory for 32 channels.	

CLASS	*TAPE_CONTROLLER*	**Part:** 1/1
TYPE OF OBJECT Handler of the mechanical part of a VCR.	**INDEXING** 　**cluster:** *VCR_UNIT* 　**keywords:** video recorder, mechanical part	
Queries	Tape in read/write position? Tape in sync position? Tape released? Cassette loaded? Tape stopped? Tape normal forward? Tape fast forward? Tape rewinding? Tape cueing forward? Tape cueing reversed?	
Commands	Move tape to read/write position. Move tape to sync position. Release tape. Load cassette. Stop tape. Eject cassette. Run tape normal forward. Run tape fast forward. Rewind tape. Cue tape forward. Cue tape reversed.	
Constraints	Move to read/write or sync position requires loaded cassette. Inserted cassette which has not reached bottom in 5 seconds is ejected.	

Figure 10.12 Subsystem controllers

classes have boolean queries reporting on the various modes of the mechanical and magnetic subsystems of the VCR. Since the operational buttons all correspond to potential mode changes, the commands and queries come in pairs: to enter a mode and to check whether a mode is in effect or not.

Next, we turn to the menu classes. We choose a number of standard operations encapsulated in the abstract class *MENU*. The names of the operations are fixed, but they need to cover a fair amount of variable behavior, so we keep their semantics flexible. Each of them is defined for each specific menu type to produce the desired behavior. The class chart for *MENU* is shown in figure 10.13.

CLASS	*MENU*	Part: 1/1

TYPE OF OBJECT
    Menu navigation and data entry.
	INDEXING
	    cluster: *VCR_UNIT*
	    keywords: video recorder, abstract menu	

Queries	Is this menu open?	
Commands	Open this menu. Shift focus to next entry. Shift focus to previous entry. Select. Accept. Cancel. Delete. Input numeric value.	

Figure 10.13 Menu class with standard operations

The abstract menu keeps a list of entries, and the commands to open the menu and shift focus between its entries should be defined to display whatever user feedback is suitable. The class structure is independent of what type of hardware display is used, if any. *Select*, *accept*, *cancel*, and *delete* are standard commands that often make sense in menus, but do not always have to be used.

For example, in the options menu of the Multronic, *select* means tuning a station or opening the clock or one of the program positions, depending on current entry, *accept* means storing the last tuned frequency if the current entry is tune, *cancel* always means leaving the menu and returning to normal operation, while *delete* means clearing the current programmed recording or last stored frequency.

In the clock setting and programming submenus of the Multronic, the entries are fields in the user input record, and *accept* means accepting a completed value and resetting the clock or program position. To facilitate class definition, we could implement the commands as no-operations rather than deferred in *MENU*, so subclasses only need to define those actually used. The free implementation of the commands combined with the mapping from the event handler into desired class operations can cope with quite a few variations of user input in future Bonasonic models. The remaining classes, *PRESET_RECORDING*,

TIMER, and *TUNER*, are straightforward, and the corresponding class charts are not shown. We will return to them briefly in task 6 on formal definition.

10.5 SYSTEM BEHAVIOR

With the classes defined, the next task is to describe system behavior in terms of communicating objects. The primitive events are easy to identify, since they are all related to very distinct buttons. We group them into categories, as is shown in the event chart in figure 10.14. We then select some scenarios to describe with object diagrams. There are not that many interesting variants of behavior among the top-level analysis classes in our model, so three scenarios seems enough. The corresponding scenario chart can be found in figure 10.15.

EVENTS	*VCR_SYSTEM*	**Part:** 1/1
COMMENT External events are either from the user or from the timer.	**INDEXING** **keywords:** video recorder, multronic 2001	

External (incoming)	**Involved object types**
User inserts or ejects a cassette.	*EVENT_HANDLER, OPERATION, TAPE_CONTROLLER*
User presses a tape operation button: play, record, stop, pause, forward cue, reverse cue, rewind, or fast forward.	*EVENT_HANDLER, OPERATION, VIDEO_CONTROLLER, TAPE_CONTROLLER*
User switches channel: channel up, channel down, or numeric input in normal mode.	*EVENT_HANDLER, OPERATION, VIDEO_CONTROLLER*
User presses menu in normal mode.	*EVENT_HANDLER, OPERATION, OPTIONS*
User presses a control button in menu mode: menu, next, prev, select, accept, cancel.	*EVENT_HANDLER, OPTIONS, CLOCK, PROGRAM*
User presses a numeric button in menu mode.	*EVENT_HANDLER, OPTIONS, CLOCK, PROGRAM*
User presses a button on the remote controller.	*EVENT_HANDLER, OPERATION, VIDEO_CONTROLLER, TAPE_CONTROLLER*
A programmed start or stop time is reached.	*TIMER, PRESET_PROGRAMMING, OPERATION, VIDEO_CONTROLLER, TAPE_CONTROLLER*

Figure 10.14 Significant event types

SCENARIOS	*VCR_SYSTEM*	**Part:** 1/1
COMMENT Typical behavior triggered by user and/or built-in timer.	**INDEXING** **keywords:** video recorder, multronic 2001	

Program a recording: User enters the options menu, selects a program position, and sets time interval and station to record.
Execute programmed recording: A preset time is reached and a station is recorded for the chosen time interval.
Find recording, play, and rewind: User inserts a cassette, finds a program and plays it, then rewinds the tape and restores the cassette.

Figure 10.15 Three scenarios

Any button pressed is caught by the *EVENT_HANDLER* class, which will direct the event to the proper object depending on button and VCR mode. Some user actions have no effect in certain modes, such as pressing ACCEPT in normal (non-menu) mode or pressing REC when the recorder is already recording. Whether this is detected in the event handler or in the corresponding controller object is kept open. The object diagram for the first scenario is shown in figure 10.16. We do not model exactly how numeric values are input, since various shortcuts may be applied to reduce the number of keystrokes.

The second scenario could be thought of as triggered by an internal event, but we prefer to view the event as external (coming from the hardware clock). We assume the clock interrupt is caught directly by the *TIMER* class without passing

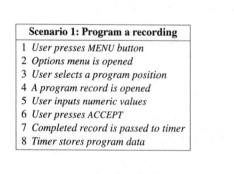
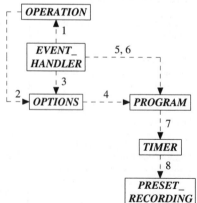

Figure 10.16 First scenario

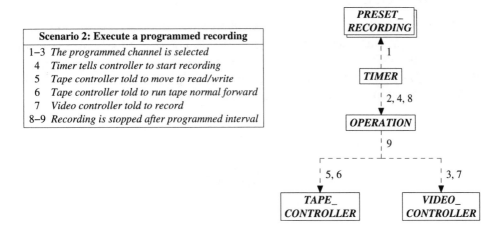

Figure 10.17   Second scenario

through *EVENT_HANDLER*. The resulting object diagram is in figure 10.17.

Finally, the third scenario is shown in figure 10.18. When the tape is stopped, both controllers may or may not be involved depending on whether the magnetic signal should be affected. Therefore, we put message label 11 before the fork point in the diagram. This concludes the dynamic modeling, and we turn again to the static architecture to look in more detail at the class features.

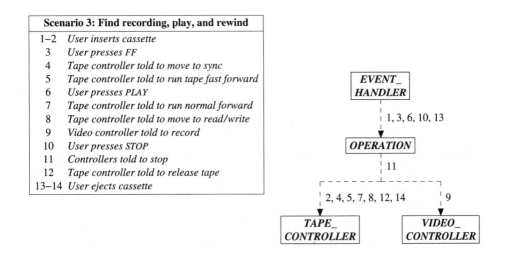

Figure 10.18   Third scenario

10.6 FORMAL CLASS DESCRIPTION

What remains is the last analysis task: to translate the class charts into more
formal class interface descriptions. Since we do not want to specify too many
details for the VCR at the analysis level, there are not many contracting clauses
to fill in. They will come later during detailed design and implementation. The
classes for programming and tuning are shown in figure 10.19.

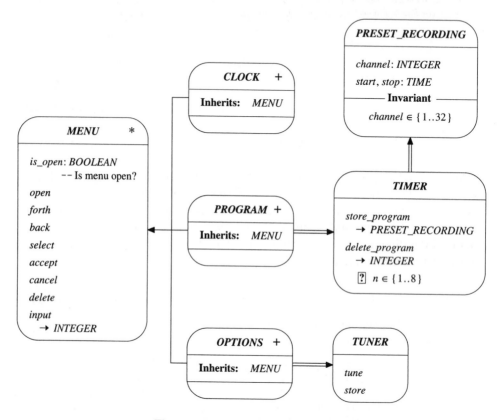

Figure 10.19 Menus, timer, and tuner

Figure 10.20 shows the interfaces of the top-level operational class and the
two controller classes. We see that at this general level, there is not (yet) much
more information in the formal class interfaces, as compared to the
corresponding class charts. However, they are much more compact, allowing
more comprehensive views of groups of classes with some of their relations.

We show in figure 10.20 that class *OPERATION* will be a client of the two
controller classes, but we do not know at this stage what features will cause the
corresponding relations.

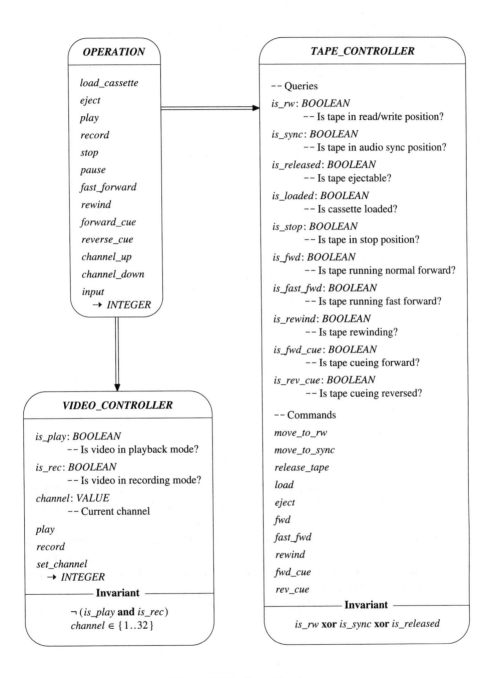

Figure 10.20 Controller classes

10.7 FINAL STATIC ARCHITECTURE

This concludes the analysis part of the BON process. To proceed further with this case study we would need more information on the hardware used for the Multronic model. Therefore, we will stop here, and the final static structure of our VCR system is shown in figure 10.21.

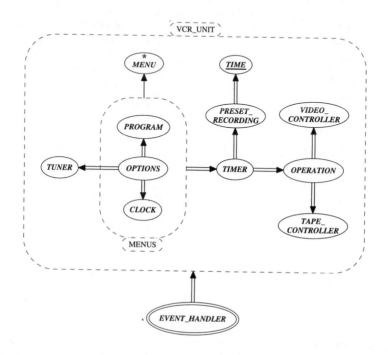

Figure 10.21   Final static architecture

Comparing this architecture with our first analysis model in figure 10.8 gives us a clear illustration of the important insight that there is no objective reality. Models only exist in relation to what you want to do with them. Useful as tangible objects may be for providing a starting point for building a system model, they must always be treated with suspicion precisely because they are tangible and therefore in most cases somewhat special. What tend to survive in the long term are often the more abstract underlying ideas.

11 Relational and object-oriented coexistence

How should one model persistent objects and relationships between them in an object-oriented system? This question often arises in application domains where information systems play a central role. As argued in chapter 2, a strong case can be made against entity–relationship modeling and its variations in object-oriented contexts, since it breaks the inherent seamlessness of the approach. However, even if object-oriented technology is now rapidly moving towards commercial acceptance on a broad scale, relational databases will most likely continue to play an important role as data repositories for a long time yet, including many object-oriented applications.

There are several reasons for this. First of all, statistics have proven that the average lifetime of stored data is far greater than the average lifetime of applications handling the data. Thus while applications are being modified and replaced, corporate data, although extended and updated, tends to remain where it sits. Therefore, many information systems have grown extremely large and the cost of a complete data conversion may not always be justifiable.

Moreover, databases are often accessed and manipulated by many different applications in heterogeneous environments (often geographically distributed), and it may not be worthwhile to rewrite all of these applications to comply with a different database organization. Other reasons may have to do with company policies, previous investment in database software and expertise, performance requirements (transaction processing, concurrent updates, average uptime), and data security (consistency controls, recovery/rollback, authorization).

The conclusion is that bridges are often needed between the relational and object-oriented worlds. The purpose of this last case study is to discuss how object models and relational models can be made to coexist in a system. The approaches illustrated are drawn from actual working implementations, but since a full discussion could easily fill a book of its own, they have been considerably simplified.

11.1 FROM DATA STORAGE TO OBJECT PERSISTENCE

Let us first recall what is needed by an object-oriented execution model. Object-oriented applications handling massive quantities of data often end up using and creating large numbers of objects. Most existing object-oriented environments still run on top of operating systems that do not support the basic run-time requirements of an object-oriented approach: built-in object allocation, automatic reclamation of unreachable objects (garbage collection) regardless of physical location, and transparent paging at the object level of both transient and persistent objects. Until basic facilities like these become widely available as part of standardized families of operating systems, each object-oriented environment needs to implement all or part of them as a separate virtual machine (run-time system).

Not to burden applications with implementation details, object-oriented environments must offer powerful means to handle both transient and persistent objects. Large quantities of transient objects can often be taken care of by traditional garbage collection in combination with virtual memory management at the operating system level. Small amounts of persistent objects, in turn, can be encapsulated by the run-time system using database library classes interacting with an ordinary file system. However, to handle a potentially very large number of persistent objects, more complete database capabilities are usually required. A mapping is needed whenever object-oriented applications interface with legacy systems or with databases that do not interoperate with an object-oriented environment.

Interoperability in this context means more than just a basic coupling. Owing to the high level of object integration required (object type and format, polymorphism) distribution transparency of objects with implicit access via the development environment is rapidly becoming an important issue. Some technical approaches addressing the problems involved are beginning to emerge, whose aim is to support the notion of an "object bus" and connect heterogeneous object-oriented applications directly at the object level [OMG 1991].

Seamlessness between execution model and persistent data means that values and types directly map the class instances used by the execution model; there is no "impedance mismatch" between primary memory and disk-resident data. An ideal solution completely frees client applications from storage details and permits virtual addressing of an infinite object space. In such cases, the object-oriented run-time system transparently pages in or out clusters of objects according to their status and behavior in the application: frequency of access, reachability, expected lifetime, and so forth.

Consider the following program fragment from a developer's standpoint. The declaration and qualified call translate at execution time into: "apply routine *register* defined and exported by class *CUSTOMER* to an instance of *CUSTOMER* (or one of its descendant classes) attached to an attribute called attendee."

> *attendee*: *CUSTOMER*
> ⋮
> *attendee.register*

In a fully transparent persistent environment, the above is complemented by: "regardless of the effective location of the object referred to by *attendee* at the time the call is executed."

An object is persistent if its existence is independent of the system session in which it was created. A persistent object continues to exist until it either becomes unreachable or is explicitly deleted. Various techniques can be employed in object-oriented environments to make an object persistent. Figure 11.1 depicts some possibilities.

1	*customer* := **new persistent** *CLIENT*
2	*customer*: **persistent** *CUSTOMER*
3	**persistent class** *CUSTOMER* ⋮ **end** *customer*: *CUSTOMER*
4	**class** *CUSTOMER* **inherit** *PERSISTENT* ⋮ **end** *customer*: *CUSTOMER*
5	*persistent_collection*: *PERSISTENT_UNIVERSE* *customer*: *CUSTOMER* ⋮ *persistent_collection.put* (*customer*)

Figure 11.1   Various persistency schemes

The first three examples in figure 11.1 introduce specific language constructs: (1) extended object creation mechanism, (2) extended type declaration of entities referring to objects, and (3) extended class declaration mechanism. The last two examples use predefined classes to achieve persistency: (4) all children to a common ancestor become persistent, and (5) a persistent object container accepts any object reference, and all objects inserted into the container automatically become persistent.

Regardless of the specific mechanism used, we may adopt the following *deep persistency* principle: all objects reachable through successive references from a persistent object also become persistent. This ensures consistency of the system state (class invariants). Unless the transitive closure of objects referred to by a persistent object is also stored, some objects may become invalid.

Objects explicitly made persistent through some scheme like the ones in figure 11.1 are sometimes called *persistent roots* (not to be confused with root objects starting up system executions). All other objects may dynamically be or not be persistent, depending on whether they can be reached from a persistent root or not.

Persistency in BON is defined as a class property and persistent classes can be marked as such by a special class header annotation (bullet). This is often of interest during analysis, since figuring out what objects need to survive system sessions may be a good way to increase problem understanding. However, it would be too restrictive to require that only persistent objects can be instantiated from a class marked as persistent.

There may be situations in a system where a temporary object needs to behave exactly like a persistent one, and forcing the creation of two nearly identical classes in such cases does not make much sense. Therefore, marking a class as persistent in BON means that its objects are *potentially* persistent.

We conclude this section by stating two principles regarding persistency, which are important for the seamlessness and reversibility of the BON approach. The aim is to keep analysis and design models simple and consistent, independently of where the objects will ultimately reside.

Principle 1

> There should be no syntactic distinction between persistent and transient data in terms of how they are defined and used.

Principle 2

> The persistent object model should be designed as a seamless part of the full static model.

With these preliminaries we are ready to take a look at the problems involved when object persistency (or part of it) is to be based on an underlying relational model. We will discuss an approach for achieving a high degree of transparency with regard to object retrieval and update—in spite of the structural differences between object models and relational databases. The focus will be on the dynamic construction of queries to reduce as much as possible the static dependency of applications on the actual database schema.

11.2 OBJECT MODELS AND RELATIONAL MODELS

Our objective is to design an integration layer that can access data in different storage formats and automatically convert between them. This layer may also have its own local repository, which may be used for caching to avoid constant data transfer through a gateway. The kind of environment envisioned is illustrated in figure 11.2.

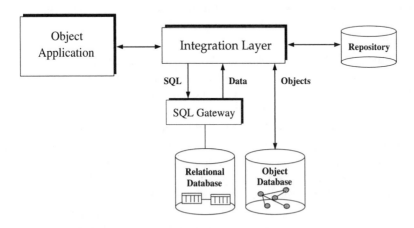

Figure 11.2 Transparent integration of heterogeneous storage

Different forms of coupling are possible. At the highest level of integration, persistent class instances are stored along with their features and class descriptions. With a more pragmatic approach, only the data part (state variables) of persistent objects is stored. In both cases, the database needs to be closely integrated with the execution model.

However, when the logical structure of the available persistent storage is totally unrelated to the object model (relational databases, flat files, indexed files) a separate interface layer is needed to do the necessary transformations. In figure 11.2 a SQL interpreter is used as backend to retrieve and store data in a relational database.[18]

In either case, it should be possible to define application object models, where the persistency decisions are kept completely free from any implementation choice, and all application objects are accessed the same way whether transparently constructed from external data or not.

---

[18] The relational data language SQL was earlier named SEQUEL and is usually pronounced as though it still were. We therefore write "a SQL..." rather than "an SQL...".

Integrity constraints

A number of data integrity rules are usually enforced in a relational system to prevent certain types of inconsistencies from entering the database. These rules, commonly known as integrity constraints, address various aspects of the semantic content of stored data. We will mention a few of them below, and see how they translate to a BON object model.

Domain integrity refers to type checking between the values used in query expressions and the declared types of the corresponding entities. All RDBMS provide the necessary level of checking to avoid any violation of the type system rules. Since BON is statically typed, it is assumed that the supporting environment (CASE tool at the analysis and design level, and programming system at the implementation level) will detect any type error.

Referential integrity has to do with the consistency of references between schema elements. Whenever an entry in a relational table refers by a foreign key value to an entry in another table, that other table must exist and have an entry with matching primary key value. Any modification of the database content must keep all related tables consistent and prevent the introduction of unmatched references. These checks are usually supported at the RDBMS level. It is assumed in BON that referential integrity is captured by assertions in class descriptions. In the example given in figure 11.3, integrity is guaranteed by the postconditions associated with the routines *bid_farewell* and *retire*.

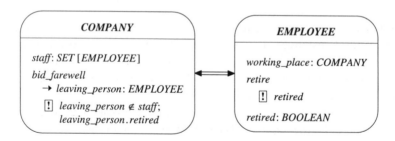

Figure 11.3   Referential integrity in class contracts

User-defined integrity is usually taken care of by *stored procedures* or *triggers* in relational databases. With BON it is part of the object-oriented data description. The creation routines of a class are responsible for ensuring that each object of the class is created in a consistent state. Any operation changing the state of the object will, if necessary, trigger other monitoring operations to ensure that the consistency is maintained.

At execution time, depending on the supporting environment, integrity violations may invoke exception handlers, rollback procedures, and other recovery mechanisms.

We now turn to the design of an integration layer coupling an object model with a SQL gateway. There are three aspects of such a layer that need to be addressed:

- How to retrieve data from an existing relational database.

- How to regenerate application objects from the retrieved data.

- How to design a relational schema suitable to store and retrieve a given persistent object model.

Our aim is to find a generic model to tackle the problems, which is as independent as possible of both the object-oriented application and the relational database system used.

11.3 A RELATIONAL DATABASE WRAPPER

Short overview of the relational model

In relational databases, information is modeled as *relations* defined on finite sets of data values called *domains.* A relation is a set of ordered lists of data values called *tuples.*

Each tuple is an element of the cartesian product of domains *D1×D2×D3...* (set of all possible ordered lists of values with one element drawn from each domain). Each occurrence of a domain in the definition of a relation is called an *attribute,* and the same domain may occur several times. Note the difference between domain and attribute: a domain is a basic pool of permissible values, while an attribute represents the *use* of a domain within a relation.

Domains and relations are implemented as tables with *m* rows and *n* columns. Each row corresponds to a tuple (an element in the set), and each column to a relational attribute. For this reason, RDBMS vendors usually use the terms *table, column,* and *row* instead of relation, attribute, and tuple.

The great majority of relational systems are *normalized,* which means that all domain elements must be atomic values. All values in a given domain have the same type chosen from a small set of predefined basic types, such as: *INTEGER, FLOAT, DOUBLE, DATE, CHAR, STRING, MONEY.* Each attribute (or column) of a relation has a name, so it can be referred to without using its relative position, and a type, which is the basic type of the corresponding domain.

Relations are usually defined with constraints imposed on the tuples to avoid data duplication or cross-dependency. A common constraint on a relation is to require that each tuple be uniquely identifiable by a subset of the attribute values. Such a subset is called a *primary key.* Often one attribute is enough to identify tuples, in which case we have a *single-attribute* primary key.

Access to relational data is achieved through general set operations: *selection, projection, product, join, union, intersection,* and *difference.* In addition to tables predefined in the relational schema, new tables may be created dynamically through such operations. The data access set operations are expressed in a relational database language called SQL (Structured Query Language) used to store, retrieve, and modify information in the database. (SQL has become the *de facto* standard in the relational database world, and was accepted as an international standard by ISO in 1987. The latest ISO version, SQL/92, became ratified in 1992 [Date 1993].)

In figure 11.4, three example tables are shown: *CUSTOMER, INVOICE,* and *PRODUCT.* The header of each table shows the table name and the names of each attribute. Below the double line are the tuples, whose values conform to the basic type of each attribute (these types are not shown in the table).

The most frequently exercised operations in relational database applications are usually simple selections of tuples whose attribute values satisfy certain conditions, insertion or deletion of tuples, and change of attribute values in

CUSTOMER			
Client_Id	Name	Address	Zip_Code
A45	Jack's Snack	899 Ventura Blvd, La Cienaga	CA 92340
L20	Red Lobster	9B Nathaniel Hawthorne, Tauton	MA 02780

Primary key: (Client_id)

INVOICE			
Purchase_Order	Product_number	Qty	Client_Id
940120-010	1022	500	A45
940322-093	1024	80	Y89

Primary key: (Purchase_Order, Product_number)

PRODUCT		
Product_number	Description	Unit_Price
1022	Corned Beef 1.54 oz can	0.99
1023	Snails in garlic butter 0.8 oz bag	4.99
1024	Peeled tomatoes 1.9 oz bottle	1.99

Primary key: Product_number

Figure 11.4 Tables from a relational schema

tuples. Selection is mostly combined with projection, which means that only a subset of the attribute values are retrieved.

The *join* operation is important for more complex retrieval. For example, assume we want a list of all customers who ordered products with a unit price of at least five dollars. The result should be presented as a table with the following attributes: client id, client name, client address, product description.

The combination of these attributes does not exist as a table *per se* in our schema, but it is possible to join our three tables to obtain the requested information. Using SQL syntax, the selection can be expressed as follows:

```
select CLIENT.client_id, name, address, description
from CLIENT, INVOICE, PRODUCT
where CLIENT.client_id = INVOICE.client_id and
        INVOICE.product_number = PRODUCT.product_number and
        PRODUCT.unit_price >= 5.0
```

The result of a selection query is generally a set. Therefore, SQL provides facilities to iteratively fetch each matching row. A cursor maintained by the database server points to the currently retrievable row, and standard operations can be used to move the cursor from one row to another within the result.

The relational model for database management, originated in the late 1960s by E. F. Codd, has a strong mathematical foundation [Codd 1970]. It has been thoroughly researched and a large number of rules and criteria for relational data organization and manipulation have been proposed [Codd 1985a, Codd 1985b, Codd 1990]. For good comprehensive overviews of the area, see [Date 1990, Date 1983, Date 1993].

Designing a database interface cluster

Any cluster layer interfacing a relational database and an object-oriented system would be responsible for managing server sessions, maintaining the relational schema, performing queries and updates, and doing the mapping between rows and objects. To summarize this, let us define the major abstractions of such a layer and group them as shown in the cluster chart of figure 11.5.

We can also display the classes in a first static architecture sketch as shown in figure 11.6. The implementation of each model class will encapsulate a set of external calls to the database server. The *DATABASE_INTERFACE* cluster is a client of class *ANY* because any type of object may become persistent and thus need to receive external data.

Our first aim is to outline the interface of a general reusable cluster for accessing a relational database. The specification of this cluster is at a rather technical level, so we will skip the class chart definitions and move directly to the formal class descriptions.

CLUSTER	DATABASE_INTERFACE	Part: 1/1

PURPOSE
    Layer to make relational database
    manipulations transparent.
	INDEXING
	    keywords: object and relational
	    coexistence, rdbms interface	

Class/(Cluster)	Description
DB_SESSION	Session manager responsible for handling the connection to the database server and for tracking the proper or non-proper completion of all transactions.
DB_QUERY	SQL wrapper sending selection commands to the database server.
DB_CHANGE	SQL wrapper sending store, update, and delete commands to the database server.
DB_RESULT	Representation of one matching row returned by the database server in response to a SQL selection.

Figure 11.5   First candidate classes in interface layer

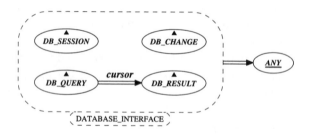

Figure 11.6   First cluster sketch

Class *DB_SESSION* encapsulates the most important primitives to handle transactions between an application and the database server. Its interface is outlined in figure 11.7.

Class *DB_QUERY* sends SQL selection queries to the database server and stores the resulting table rows. Clients can then iterate on the result supplying a callback routine to process the table rows, one by one. The interface description of class *DB_QUERY* is shown in figure 11.8.

Typically, the callback object will be the client object itself, inheriting from *ACTION* and defining the *execute* feature. Since the client already has a reference to the *DB_QUERY* object on which the iteration was invoked, the *execute* routine will be able to access the database cursor of the corresponding selection.

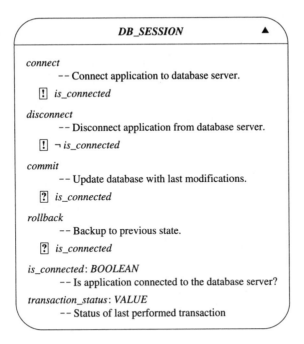

Figure 11.7   Encapsulation of a database session

Class *DB_RESULT* represents the database cursor pointing to the current table row returned by the database server. It is responsible for the conversion of data fields from the SQL structure on the server side into corresponding basic object attributes that may be accessed in a normal way by the object model. Any of the fields can thus be inspected, which gives clients full control to do whatever processing is needed.

However, in many cases the main part of the action for each returned row will be to transfer some or all of the data fields into the corresponding attributes of some result object. Therefore, the *load_object* command of *DB_RESULT* (see figure 11.8) will automatically convert and load data from the fields of the current row into an object supplied as an argument.

Each *basic* attribute of the argument object that has a name and a type which matches an attribute of the table row will be set to the corresponding value. An object attribute is considered basic if its type corresponds directly to a type defined in the relational database. The mapping from one type system to another can be preset in a utility class and accessed when needed.

It is the client's responsibility to ensure that each basic object attribute which is to receive a value corresponds exactly (by name and type) to one of the table

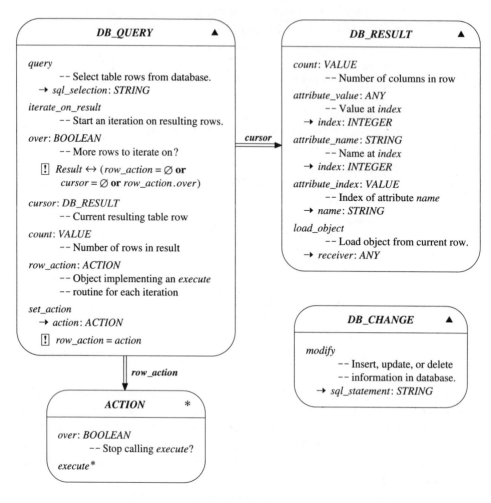

Figure 11.8 Encapsulation of relational storage and retrieval

row attributes. Furthermore, the names and types of the attributes of an object must be dynamically accessible at execution time for the automatic data transfer to work. In object-oriented environments where this information is not available, a corresponding table (preferably generated from the corresponding class description by some tool) may have to be attached to each persistent class.

Note that the automatic loading does not require all basic attributes of the receiving object to match columns in the table row, nor all columns to correspond to an object attribute. Only basic attributes with matching name and type will be transferred. This convention has two advantages:

- Some basic object attributes may be left out of a query if they are considered uninteresting in some context (perhaps given default values).

- Several objects of different type may be loaded, one at a time, from the same query result. This will be important for our design of the higher-level layers.

Class *DB_CHANGE*, finally, is simply used to pass a SQL statement requesting an update, deletion, or insertion in the relational database.

Mapping non-basic object attributes

So far, we have only discussed storage and retrieval of basic object attributes. Usually, however, the attributes of most objects in an object model will be a mixture of basic and non-basic types. If we look at the class *REGISTRATION* from the conference case study, whose interface is repeated in figure 11.9, we find two attributes that relate to other model classes, namely *PERSON* and *TUTORIAL*.

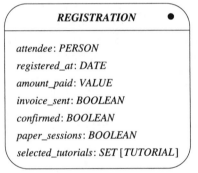

Figure 11.9 A persistent class description

These attributes represent object references which cannot be mapped directly to relational attributes. (In this case study, we will assume that all typed features of persistent model objects represent class attributes rather than functions, unless otherwise stated.)

However, we can use the automatic data transfer previously described to have the basic attributes of a *REGISTRATION* object (*registered_at, amount_paid, invoice_sent, confirmed,* and *paper_sessions*) automatically initialized from the database rows. In an eventual implementation, general types such as *VALUE* in figure 11.9 will have been specialized to a basic type of the programming language making the correspondence to the relational types clear. A possible mapping could be the one in figure 11.10.

The *PERSON* and *TUTORIAL* objects corresponding to *attendee* and *selected_tutorials* can then be initialized separately with rows coming from other relations, and the corresponding references filled in by the application object responsible for restoring *REGISTRATION* objects.

Name	Type
REGISTERED_AT	DATE(MM/DD/YY,HH24.MI.SS)
AMOUNT_PAID	FLOAT
INVOICE_SENT	CHAR(1)
CONFIRMED	CHAR(1)
PAPER_SESSIONS	CHAR(1)

Figure 11.10   Relational table representing class *REGISTRATION*

When a persistent object structure is stored in the database, we must capture the unique identity of each object through primary keys in the database tables. Sometimes basic attributes already exist, whose values can be used to fully identify each object. In our case, it might be possible to use *registered_at* as the primary key, provided that time information of enough granularity is included and that registrations are not entered simultaneously.

If such an attribute (or group of attributes) does not exist, we need to add an extra field containing a unique identifier. Such an extra field may also be useful for efficiency purposes when the existing primary key is long and many other persistent objects will refer to this one.

Object reference attributes may be stored as fields pointing to other tables representing the referenced objects (so-called foreign keys). Different strategies may be used to represent references between model objects, depending on the corresponding instance multiplicity.

- If the reference is *one-to-one* (as for *attendee* in class *REGISTRATION* above), an extra field in either one of the tables REGISTRATION or PERSON containing a primary key to the other is enough.

- If the reference is *one-to-many* (as for *children* in a class *MOTHER*), an extra field in the table representing the "many" pointing to the table representing the "one" will do.

- If the reference is *many-to-many* (as for *selected_tutorials* above), we may need to represent the relation as a joint table TUTORIAL_ATTENDENCE containing two primary keys: one pointing to table REGISTRATION and one to TUTORIAL.

  However, if the maximum number of instances referred to by either side is low, another possibility is to map the reference into a fixed number of extra fields containing either a zero reference or a primary key value.

For example, if the maximum number of tutorials each person may attend is four, a separate table can be avoided by adding attributes *tutorial1, tutorial2, tutorial3,* and *tutorial4* to table REGISTRATION.

There are also various strategies for mapping inheritance relations to relational database schemas. For overviews, see [Rahayo 1993, Premerlani 1994, Blaha 1994].

A scenario

We conclude this section with a scenario illustrating how an application may use the query facility with automatic data transfer. The dynamic diagram is shown in figure 11.11.

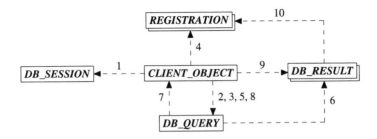

Scenario: Query database and load result	
1–3	*A client object starts a database session, creates a query object, and invokes a SQL query on it.*
4–7	*The client creates a new registration and starts an iteration on the query result, supplying itself as action object. The query object resets the cursor to point to the next resulting row, and invokes the client action routine.*
8–10	*The action routine obtains the cursor object and tells it to load the registration object from the table row.*

Figure 11.11   Scenario showing access and automatic load

11.4 INTERFACING AN EXISTING RELATIONAL SCHEMA

Another important issue for the database encapsulation is the structure of the relational schema (what precise tables and attributes we need to access). Various factors affect the design of such a schema.

Factors determining the schema

Basically, there are two situations regarding choice of data organization:

- The relational schema mapping the object model will not be used for any other purpose.

- The relational schema is also used by other applications that do not necessarily have exactly the same view of the world.

In the first case, the database can be used as an implementation vehicle with relational tables replacing flat files, indexed files, or any other data storage facility. This situation leaves a great deal of freedom in designing the relational schema, and data administrators may capture the object model in a way that best fits the application. The goal is then to find a suitable tradeoff between a mapping giving good performance and one that is easy to understand and maintain.

In the second case, many additional factors must be taken into account. Often the schema and associated database (or a significant part of it) is a legacy to our system, which we may not be able to do anything about. The way attributes are distributed in the object model may then be very different from the organization of the corresponding data on the relational side.

This may result in SQL queries performing complicated joins across numerous scattered tables, which may degrade performance. Often the solution is to perform a number of pre-joins on selected tables and store them temporarily during an object-oriented session. The initial cost at session start is then offset by the improved performance during data transfer between the models.

With a growing number of heterogeneous applications sharing persistent information across networks, the ability to adapt to existing structures is important. In fact, even if the schema can be optimally tailored to an object model (no initial legacy), the database organization tends to become much more rigid once it has been filled with large amounts of data.

As time passes, the object model will gradually change (perhaps even faster than with traditional models, because of the inherent flexibility of the object-oriented approach). The impedance mismatch may then make it too expensive to continually modify the relational structures to keep up with the changes. This means we may have to face the legacy situation soon enough, even in cases where the only applications ever accessing the data are object oriented!

The rest of this case study will be devoted to a detailed discussion of how existing schemas can be mapped to model objects. We will design a set of clusters of reusable classes enabling applications to become independent of the exact database organization, and show how this cluster fits in with the general database encapsulation presented in the previous section.

We will see how the design can be done gradually in layers raising the level of abstraction to overcome the structural differences between the relational and object models.

Schema dependency

If a typed implementation language is used, making static changes in the object model implies recompilation of the application. This is reasonable, and usually corresponds to a new version of the software. However, updates of the relational schema in a database shared by many applications may occur frequently (new columns added to tables, new tables added, minor reorganizations for efficiency). A solution which forces recompilation and reinstallation of an application each time a schema change occurs is therefore too rigid in most cases.

For this reason, we should strive to keep our applications free from exact knowledge of the mapping between the object model and the relational database. Rather than placing complete information directly in the static class structure about the names of each database column accessed and the table it resides in, the mapping should be dynamically reconfigurable by modification of data in some repository. But how can we obtain adequate performance without integrating the relational structure in our object-oriented applications?

A virtual database

One solution is to define a *virtual database* containing a set of *virtual tables,* and then make applications statically dependent only on this database. (Such virtual tables are known as *views* in RDBMS terminology.) If the virtual database is chosen reasonably close to the real database, the conversion between the two schemas will be straightforward, and can be effected by SQL statements dynamically maintained as stored procedures or persistent strings. This gives freedom to rename and create new tables in the database and to rename and move around columns between them without changing the static structure of the applications.

Regarding the logical representation of each column in the database, the amount of freedom depends of course on the complexity of the mapping. If the database stores temperature in degrees Fahrenheit and the object model uses the Celsius scale, we cannot expect SQL to hide this fact. Also, even if the SQL dialect provided by the database server would allow expressions to retrieve two database columns *given_names* and *last_name* and directly return a concatenated attribute *name* to the object model, it will hardly be possible to do the reverse on update.

Therefore, the logical structure of the real database must usually be mirrored by the virtual database, and applications must be statically dependent on the representation form chosen for each column interacted with. However, independence of the exact tables in which the columns reside, as well as of any table or column renaming, is still a great advantage.

Each virtual table is represented by a class encapsulating a set of basic attributes. The virtual table classes (which collectively represent the database visible to the application) will be named *row classes*. Instances of row classes are called *row objects* and each row object will act as a gateway to the real database.

Each virtual table is chosen so that there is a simple mapping between its attributes and the attributes of the real database tables. The persistency classes will encapsulate operations to do the conversion using a SQL database server. However, the corresponding SQL statements will be maintained outside the application to always reflect the current state of the real database schema. An application can load the correct SQL mapping at startup time or, in case it needs to run continuously for a long time, be triggered to reload any change that may occur during execution.

An example application

To illustrate the above approach, let us select four of the persistent classes from the conference case study (chapter 9). The corresponding class descriptions, showing only the features which we assume will be implemented as attributes, are repeated in figure 11.12.

We also assume there is a corporate database which is to be used for mapping relevant parts of our object model. In the corporate database, we find four tables containing information that can be used to. represent the basic attributes of classes *PERSON* and *REGISTRATION*. These are shown in figure 11.13. There are no existing tables corresponding to classes *TUTORIAL* or *PRESENTATION*.

The CUSTOMER and AFFILIATION tables come from the company's general customer register and the INVOICE table from its accounting system. The REGISTRATION table is assumed to have been designed as part of an older system which handles conference registrations but not the technical program. We also assume that at present there is nothing we can do to change the formats of these tables. This represents a kind of legacy situation not uncommon in practice.

Since some objects are more difficult than others to map to a relational system, it may be an advantage to have a relational and object-oriented persistency mix. In this case, we choose to store and retrieve *PERSON* and *REGISTRATION* objects in the relational database, while *TUTORIAL* objects will be stored using some object persistency mechanism provided in the language environment.

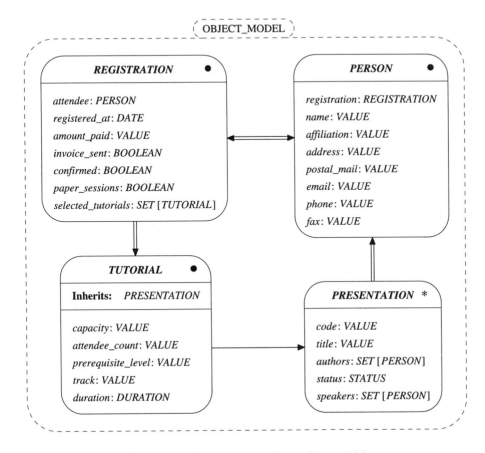

Figure 11.12 Simplified persistent object model

This strategy also fits well with general performance considerations. Since the tutorial objects are relatively few and frequently accessed, they should remain in main memory during system execution. Person and registration objects, on the other hand, may occur in great numbers but only the ones currently being processed need fast access.

The general access, manipulation, and update of our object model and corresponding relational data can now be outlined as follows:

- *Creation of new tutorial objects.*
  These objects must be present before any registrations can be accepted, since choice of tutorials is part of the registration data. Before the reference to *speakers* and *authors* is filled in, the CUSTOMER and AFFILIATION tables are searched to check whether some of the persons

CUSTOMER

Name	Type
CUSTOMER_CODE	INT
SALUTATION	CHAR(4)
LAST_NAME	CHAR(32)
FIRST_NAME	CHAR(32)
MIDDLE_INITIAL	CHAR(1)
COMPANY	INT
EXTENSION	CHAR(16)
POSITION	INT
DEPARTMENT	CHAR(32)

REGISTRATION

Name	Type
PERSON_CODE	INT
ENTRY_DATE	DATE
DISCOUNT_RATE	FLOAT
CONFERENCE	CHAR(1)
TUTORIAL1	CHAR(8)
TUTORIAL2	CHAR(8)
TUTORIAL3	CHAR(8)
TUTORIAL4	CHAR(8)
CONFIRMATION	DATE
INVOICE	INT

AFFILIATION

Name	Type
COMPANY_CODE	INT
COMPANY_NAME	CHAR(32)
ACTIVITY	INT
COMPANY_SIZE	INT
STREET	CHAR(32)
BUILDING	CHAR(32)
ZIP_CODE	CHAR(8)
CITY	CHAR(32)
COUNTRY_CODE	INT
COUNTRY_NAME	CHAR(32)
FAX	CHAR(16)
PHONE	CHAR(16)
EMAIL	CHAR(16)

INVOICE

Name	Type
INVOICE_CODE	INT
CUSTOMER	INT
ISSUED_DATE	DATE
PAYMENT_DATE	DATE
PAYMENT_TYPE	CHAR(8)
AMOUNT_PAID	FLOAT
AMOUNT_RECEIVED	FLOAT
VAT	FLOAT

Figure 11.13   Relational tables in an existing database

are already present in the corporate database. If this is the case, all
attribute values of the *PERSON* objects are initialized with the
corresponding values from the database. Persons not found in the database
will be created and initialized from the input data on the object model side.

- *Creation of new registration objects.*
  These objects are created from registration input data and will refer to the
  already defined tutorial objects. As above, assigning the reference
  attendee will either retrieve an old *PERSON* object from the database, or
  create a new object.

- *Update relational database.*
  Database updates may be performed at regular intervals, or when
  requested by an operator. Unless some personal data needs to be

corrected, the CUSTOMER and AFFILIATION tables will only be updated if new persons have been entered in the object model. The REGISTRATION table will be updated for each new registration and when existing ones are modified. The latter occurs, for example, when a letter of confirmation has been sent or a tutorial selection is changed.

A virtual database interface

We are now in a position to start putting things together and sketch a general design for mapping persistent objects to relational systems whose tables are not in direct accordance with the object structure. We will use the architecture depicted in figure 11.14.

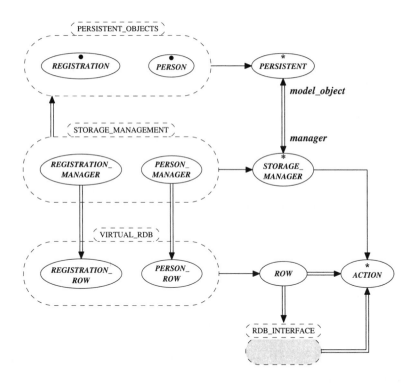

Figure 11.14 Persistent object management (outline)

The two row classes of the virtual database are defined in figure 11.15. They are the virtual relational representation of the corresponding persistent objects. A row class encapsulates the interface of the RDB cluster. It may be given a SQL selection, in which case it will create a *DB_QUERY* object, attach itself to it, and forward the query.

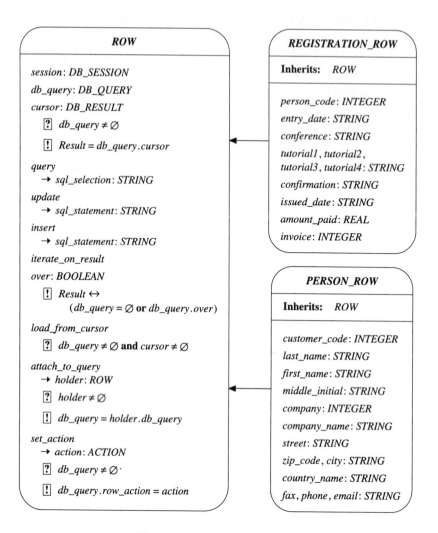

Figure 11.15 Table row classes

The *set_action* and *iterate_on_result* commands can then be used to scan through the resulting table rows and *load_from_cursor* will load the current row object, so it can be further processed. The resulting rows must of course contain all columns corresponding to the attributes of the row object, so it can be loaded. This is the responsibility of the client passing the SQL query.

Each persistent class will have two other classes corresponding to it: a *row* class representing the object in the virtual database, and a *manager* class to do the conversion between the representations. Each manager will only know the internal format of the row objects it is responsible for.

Comparing the columns of figure 11.13 with the row classes shows that the attributes of *PERSON_ROW* correspond directly to a subset of the columns of CUSTOMER and AFFILIATION, which can easily be obtained by join and projection using SQL. The same is true for *REGISTRATION_ROW* with respect to tables REGISTRATION and INVOICE. Note, however, that the clients of the virtual database know only about the virtual tables, and not even the row class knows about the scattering in the real database. There is no static trace of tables CUSTOMER, AFFILIATION, and INVOICE.

Since we are using a corporate customer base to store personal data about all conference attendees, one may ask what to do with participants who have no company affiliation. Such questions are typical for legacy situations where structures are reused for purposes slightly different from the initial intention. In this case we assume that we can invent and store a special COMPANY_CODE representing private participants and simply leave the corresponding COMPANY_NAME column blank for these entries.

We will return in the next section to the issue of how queries can be formed in the object model to retrieve persistent object structures. For now, let us just assume that the proper SQL requests will at some point be supplied as an argument to the *query* feature of the row object.

As already mentioned, it is perfectly legal for a query to return more columns than what is needed to load a given row object. First, there may be a need for the client (in its row action) to check certain data in the cursor structure that will not be transferred to the row object. Second, if a suitable naming convention is used so that the destination of each attribute can be inferred dynamically from its name, a client can use the result of a single SQL query to fill several row objects, one at a time, without the need for unique attribute names across the row classes.

Since non-matching attributes are ignored in each transfer, no conflicts will occur. A standard solution would be to use the SQL renaming facility (SELECT ... AS) to give each resulting column a name related to the proper row object attribute, regardless of what names are used in the database tables.

For example, if the data for both a *REGISTRATION_ROW* and a *PERSON_ROW* were to be returned by the same SQL query, we could use names "REGISTRATION_ROW$ENTRY_DATE" etc. for columns whose destination is the former object and "PERSON_ROW$FIRST_NAME" etc. for those aimed for the second object.

If the object to be loaded is of type *NAME* and has an attribute *attr* the conversion routines would look for columns named "NAME$ATTR" and transfer the corresponding value. (A SQL statement of type "SQL NAMES ARE ...$..." introducing some character not used for other purposes would ensure unambiguous interpretation.)

11.5 QUERYING A PERSISTENT OBJECT MODEL

Besides a basic mechanism for the retrieval and storage of persistent objects, we need a way to express what objects we want. The general issues of object-oriented query languages are still at the research stage with different directions favoring procedural or declarative approaches. Most concrete proposals from the latter school, so far, have been based on relational algebra (Object SQL); see for example [Kim 1990, Loomis 1991].

However, many commercial applications (probably the majority) do not need the full power of relational algebra to fulfill their functionality, since the types of retrieval performed are pretty much known in advance. Therefore, simplicity and flexibility is often more important than complete generality.

In this section, we will look at a simple approach that can be incorporated with our relational database encapsulation to express a fairly broad class of queries in a very natural way. It can also be used as a basis for automatic translation into SQL statements, provided that the queries are not too complex.

Query frames

The idea is to transpose the technique of Query-by-Example [Zloof 1977] to the object-oriented world. Rather than passing a query as a string expressed in some query language, we may simply supply a template describing the retrieval criteria for each attribute of a persistent object. The storage manager responsible for retrieving the corresponding type of object may then inspect the template and return the objects matching the criteria.

A possible scheme would be the following: the client creates a new object of the required persistent type, fills in the attributes that will serve as retrieval criteria, and calls a retrieve operation on the object. The supplier side will then fill in the missing attributes by returning all matching objects, one by one, using the iteration facilities described earlier.

However, there are some disadvantages with this approach. First, basic attributes that are not of reference type (like *INTEGER* or *REAL*) always have values. Therefore, there is no obvious way to signal whether an attribute of this type has been set or not.

If a query result contains a real attribute *temperature,* a value 0 in the template could mean either null (all objects wanted), or zero (only objects of temperature zero wanted). This can be circumvented by defining special values (usually the largest representable negative numbers) and letting clients use these to signify null values for reals and integers.

However, a more severe drawback is that the selection criteria are limited to exact equality. If this is all we need, the approach is nice and simple, but more expressiveness is usually required. So we are going to use a more general approach, which is to define for each persistent class a corresponding *query frame*.

The query frame of a class is a class containing attributes with the same names, but where all basic types have been replaced by *ANY* (a predefined type to which all other types conform), and all class types have been replaced by the type of its corresponding query frame. The query frame class corresponding to class *REGISTRATION* is shown in figure 11.16.

Using objects of this kind to set up a query frame structure, rather than the objects themselves, opens up new possibilities for expressing criteria.

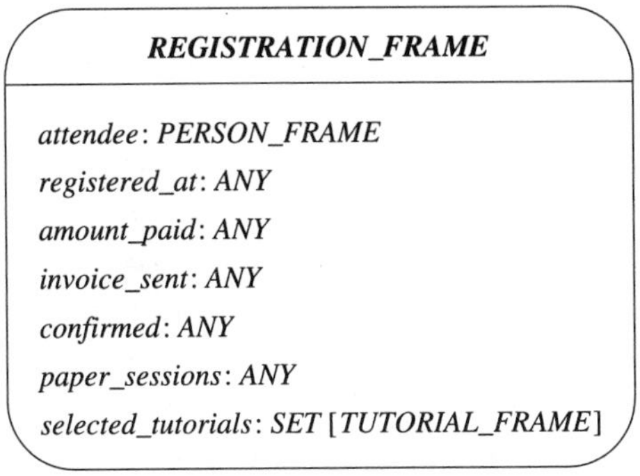

REGISTRATION_FRAME

attendee: *PERSON_FRAME*

registered_at: *ANY*

amount_paid: *ANY*

invoice_sent: *ANY*

confirmed: *ANY*

paper_sessions: *ANY*

selected_tutorials: *SET* [*TUTORIAL_FRAME*]

Figure 11.16   Query frame for class *REGISTRATION*

Retrieval by example

For each basic attribute of the query frame, there are two choices:

1. The frame attribute is set to a value of the same type as that of the corresponding attribute in the model object, in which case the selection criterion becomes exact equality on this value. This is an important option, since we may want to compute the corresponding value dynamically without being forced to convert the result into a string.

2. The frame attribute is set to a string, in which case the criterion may be an expression in any language chosen. For attributes in the model object of string type, we are then faced with a small ambiguity: string values will always be interpreted as criteria expressions rather than as literal values. So if the expression "> 'Johnson'" normally means "all values sorted after 'Johnson'", some escape conventions are needed to express a literal match of the same string. However, this is not much of a problem, since even very simple string matching languages will need facilities for resolving such situations anyway.

The two types of attribute initialization may be freely mixed in a query. As an illustration, consider the query frames set up in figure 11.17 for the selection of a set of registrations. The query asks for all registrations entered after March 15, 1994, where an invoice was sent, less than $500 has been paid, and the attendee lives in the USA.

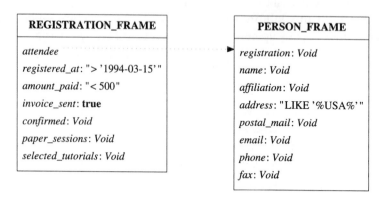

Figure 11.17   Selection of registration objects using query frames

It is also possible to allow lists of query frame structures, each representing a possible selection on the attribute values of the object and its supplier objects. Such a list would then represent logical **or** of the selection criteria set up by each frame structure.

Retrieval by key

It is important for a client to be able to cut off the retrieval of deep structures, so that not everything needs to be transferred at once. Particularly, there may be recursive object structures that simply cannot be retrieved in just one SQL statement. To this end, we employ the convention that whenever an attribute of class type (representing a reference to another object) is set to *Void* in a query frame, the corresponding object is not retrieved. This is the case for *selected_tutorials* in figure 11.17. If the attribute had been initialized with an empty *SET* [*TUTORIAL*], the tutorial objects would have been retrieved too for each registration.

When an object reference is cut off in a query frame by initializing an attribute of class type to *Void* in a retrieval by example, it does not necessarily mean that the client will not be interested in the corresponding object. It may be wanted after some inspection of the retrieved data.

Assume a terminal operator scans through a large number of registration objects without retrieving the corresponding *attendee* fields until a particular registration is reached, at which point the personal data suddenly becomes interesting. It would then be awkward if the application had to have a provision for reinitializing a parallel *REGISTRATION_FRAME* object (this time with the *attendee* reference initialized to an empty *PERSON* object rather than *Void*), and then retrieve the same registration once more in order to get the personal data.

However, this will not be needed, since even if the *PERSON* object was not retrieved the first time, the *REGISTRATION_MANAGER* has the key information in the corresponding *REGISTRATION_ROW* object to get it directly from the database.

11.6 PERSISTENT OBJECT MANAGEMENT

We will now take our design one step further, and establish enough detail to outline a full scenario from start to end of a simple persistent object retrieval. To this end, we extend the upper level of the preliminary sketch in figure 11.14 and introduce a few more classes as shown in figure 11.18 to capture the general principles involved.

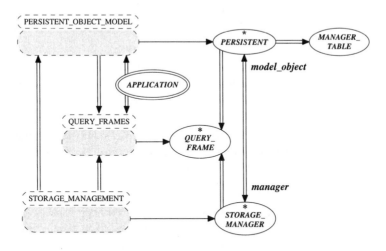

Figure 11.18 Persistent object management

Our aim is to keep as much persistency detail as possible out of the class definitions of the model objects. Therefore, the only static differences between a class whose objects are potentially persistent and one whose objects are just transient are the following two.

First, a persistent class must inherit from the class *PERSISTENT* (see figure 11.18). This will enable clients to invoke retrieval operations on the objects and iterate through sets of matching instances. Second, it will need to redefine the signature of *retrieve_by_example*. The argument supplied as retrieval criteria for a persistent *REGISTRATION* object, for example, must be defined as *REGISTRATION_FRAME*.

Each type of persistent object is retrieved and stored in the underlying database by a corresponding manager class, and all manager classes inherit from *STORAGE_MANAGER*. The idea is not to build static knowledge into the persistent classes by specifying the exact type of manager needed to take care of the corresponding objects. Instead, there will be a dynamic mapping available, so that persistent objects can invoke their proper manager by simply stating their own type. Since the class name is already a unique type identification, a mapping from class name strings to the corresponding manager will be enough (to keep the discussion simple, we assume that the persistent classes are non-generic).

The class name of an object can often be obtained dynamically from predefined system classes in many object-oriented environments. One of two standard techniques may then often be used for manager routing:

- If there are facilities in the environment to create a new instance of a class directly from the class name, we only need a mapping to the class name of the manager.

- If this is not possible but there is an "object cloning" facility available, we may instead use object templates. At system initialization, one instance of each persistent manager class is created to serve as a cloning template, and a table of type *TABLE* [*STORAGE_MANAGER*, *STRING*] is set up to map each persistent class name into a reference to one of the template objects. The returned reference is then forwarded to a cloning facility, which will instantiate a new copy of the object,

The class *MANAGER_TABLE* in figure 11.18 is assumed to take care of the mapping, using some suitable technique. When called upon to access persistent data, the features of *PERSISTENT* will thus look up the proper manager and establish the bidirectional client link between the object and its manager.

It is important to note that although the two classes *PERSISTENT* and *STORAGE_MANAGER* depend on each other, they are independent of which subtype the other party will have. The specific manager class that will do the actual conversion work must of course have full access to the attributes of the persistent object, so *REGISTRATION_MANAGER* will statically depend on *REGISTRATION*, but not the reverse (see figure 11.18).

Also, in this design we have assumed one manager for each persistent object type. However, this is not necessary when dynamic routing is used. If there are a large number of persistent classes in a system, their management will probably tend to repeat typical patterns, and it may then be desirable to have fewer, more general, managers to take care of groups of persistent object types.

We now proceed to look at the collaborating features of the two common ancestors of persistent classes and storage managers respectively.

Persistent objects

The interface of class *PERSISTENT* is shown in figure 11.19. The first time a persistency operation is called on a persistent object, the appropriate manager template will be located through a routing table shared by all persistent objects. A new storage manager will then be created and attached to the *manager* attribute of the persistent model object, and a back reference assigned in the manager object.

Three forms of retrieval, *retrieve_by_example, retrieve_by_command,* and *load_from_cursor,* are available for persistent objects. All three commands will be transparently forwarded to the appropriate storage manager without any processing. Note that the only thing that needs to be changed when the feature *retrieve_by_example* is redefined in a persistent class is the type of the query frame argument. All implementation logic will reside in the corresponding manager.

The first retrieval form implements the high-level selection criteria suitable for application clients, which should be independent of any lower-level access details. However, even the storage managers should know the low-level details only of the objects they manage. Note that this includes what is defined by the corresponding persistent class, but does *not* include what is defined by any of its supplier classes.

For example, to retrieve a *REGISTRATION* object, the registration manager will (in most cases) need to retrieve a corresponding *PERSON* object referred to by *attendee*. However, it would be most unfortunate if the mapping of the attributes of class *PERSON* into attributes of the virtual relational database (or even worse, to the real database) had to be statically known by class *REGISTRATION_MANAGER*.

If this were the case, we would need to create and maintain manager implementations not only for each persistent class, but also for each combination of a persistent class using another one as client. In a system with a large number of persistent classes, the situation would soon become unmanageable.

One improvement would be to let the registration manager call a *PERSON_MANAGER* to have the *attendee* part retrieved and translated.

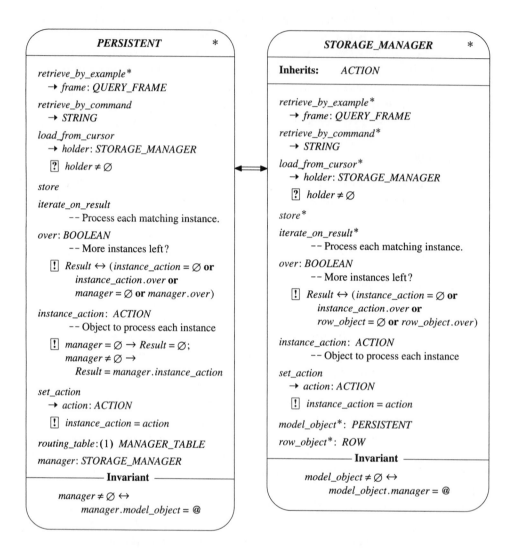

Figure 11.19 Collaborations for persistency management

However, this would create a lot of static dependencies between different managers (somehow mirroring the dependencies between the corresponding model objects, but with enough differences to create maintenance problems). So a better solution is to go a step further, and always channel any persistency operation through the persistent objects themselves.

This is where the alternative retrieval forms *retrieve_by_command* and *load_from_cursor* come in. They are both meant for storage managers rather than application clients. The arguments supplied when invoking these operations can be used for communication between managers, but the routing will be done by the corresponding model object, so that no unwanted static dependencies are created.

The iteration features are similar to the ones already discussed for the lower-level clusters. An application can attach an action object (usually itself) and then receive a callback for each retrieved object instance matching the selection criteria.

Storage managers

A storage manager translates persistent data between a model object and a corresponding virtual relation (in case the instances are stored in a relational database, as for *REGISTRATION* and *PERSON* in our example) or some other storage (in case the instances are stored elsewhere, as for *TUTORIAL*). We will only discuss the relational aspect in this case study.

The three forms of retrieval are different. The first, *retrieve_by_example,* will cause the manager to read the supplied query frame object (or object structure, if "inner" frame objects are also included) and use the attribute information to find a suitable SQL query that will return the data required to set up the matching objects.

As was argued earlier, it is desirable to minimize the static dependencies on the exact organization of the real database, which is why we introduced a virtual relational database represented by the row classes. However, the SQL statements certainly need to be phrased in terms of the current database schema, so how can we avoid becoming statically dependent on that schema when putting the queries together?

We will return to the issue of automatic generation of SQL queries in the concluding section, but for now we will only assume that whatever steering information needed to dynamically construct the SQL statements that may occur in our system (not always that many different types) is somehow maintained outside the compiled executables. Applications will thus not need recompilation when schema changes occur that do not affect the logical organization of the persistent objects, which is our goal.

Unless we come up with a good automatic translation for a broad class of queries, the stored tables may have to be structured *ad hoc* and perhaps not be so trivial to maintain. However, even with a low level of automatic support, we should be better off than if we are forced to change our compiled classes for each minor schema change.

We assume that a class *SQL_MAPPINGS* will encapsulate a set of mapping primitives, which will be used by the managers to dynamically build the required

SQL statements. In an ambitious approach, the mapping data required would probably be stored with the objects in the relational database.

The *retrieve_by_command* feature is mainly used when a manager needs to obtain an object through its primary key. As was explained in an earlier section, a *REGISTRATION_FRAME* query object may be set up to cut off the retrieval of personal data by initializing the *attendee* reference to *Void*. The registration manager will then only retrieve the basic attributes of *REGISTRATION*, but will keep the primary key to the corresponding *PERSON* object in case it is requested later.

A common scenario may be a terminal operator quickly browsing through a large number of registrations with retrieval of the personal data turned off. When certain field values appear on the screen, the operator becomes interested and orders the personal data to be filled in. The registration manager will then typically be in the middle of its callback *execute* routine processing the current instance of an *iterate_on_result,* and have a truncated *REGISTRATION* as *model_object.*

The application object (which receives the order while waiting for input in *its* callback action) then creates an empty *PERSON_FRAME* object, assigns it to the *attendee* attribute of the *REGISTRATION_FRAME* object, and issues a new *retrieve_by_example* on the same registration object.

The registration manager then detects that a new retrieve has been issued in the middle of an iteration, which leads to a different action. Rather than as a request for a new retrieval of model objects, the query is now understood as a request to retrieve more of the deep structure of the *REGISTRATION* instance already available. The degree of depth in such a new retrieval is again controlled by the values (void or non-void) of the non-basic attributes of the frame object and its suppliers, recursively. In the case of *PERSON*, there is no further structure to retrieve.

So the manager rescans the query frame and detects that the *attendee* attribute is no longer void and should be filled in. The registration manager then generates a suitable SQL query to obtain the missing data and invokes a *retrieve_by_command* on an empty *PERSON* object with the SQL string as argument. It then attaches itself as action object and starts a separate *iterate_on_result,* which will only return one *PERSON* object since it was retrieved by its primary key. The translated person object is then assigned to the registration object and control is returned to the application *execute* routine, which displays the missing data on the screen and the operator can continue browsing.

(The conventions just described represent of course a rather special design decision, but the idea is to convince the reader that reasonably clean solutions are indeed possible.)

Finally, the third form of retrieve, *load_from_cursor,* directs the manager to load its *model_object* with relational data obtained by another manager.

When composite objects like *REGISTRATION* are to be retrieved from the database, the most efficient way is usually to let the database server do the required joins to obtain both the registrational and personal data at once. This means that a registration manager will construct the full query and supply it to a *REGISTRATION_ROW* object, which will call the database server and get a set of table rows in return.

The registration manager then invokes a *load_from_cursor* on the row object to load all basic attributes of the registration, and the manager can translate these into the registration object. However, the person attributes for the *attendee* supplier object remain, and they cannot be loaded and translated by this manager, since we do not want cross-dependencies on internal formats.

Instead, the registration manager simply creates an empty *PERSON* object and invokes *load_from_cursor* on it, supplying itself as cursor holder. The person object does not know anything about cursors, but it can propagate the request to a *PERSON_MANAGER*, which will then access the supplied manager argument, extract the corresponding *REGISTRATION_ROW*, and supply it to a *PERSON_ROW* as argument of an *attach_to_query*.

The person manager invokes *load_from_cursor* on the *PERSON_ROW* object, which (since it has been reattached) will then transfer data from the cursor held by the registration row, and then translates the resulting row attributes into the person object. The registration manager can now use the retrieved person object to complete its registration object.

A full retrieval scenario

We are now ready to present a complete scenario describing how a persistent registration object is retrieved from the database. A dynamic object diagram with its accompanying scenario box can be found in figure 11.20. However, for the interested reader, we will also go through each step in more detail below and mention the operations involved.

A typical scenario would proceed as follows.

1. A client initializes a *REGISTRATION_FRAME* with attribute *attendee* attached to a *PERSON_FRAME* object to signify that the personal data of each registration should also be retrieved. The attributes (of both frame objects) whose values are to be part of the selection criteria are set to mirror the conditions. The client then invokes *retrieve_by_example* on a *REGISTRATION* object, supplying the query frame as argument.

   The registration object invokes a corresponding *retrieve_by_example* on its *REGISTRATION_MANAGER* passing the query frame. If the

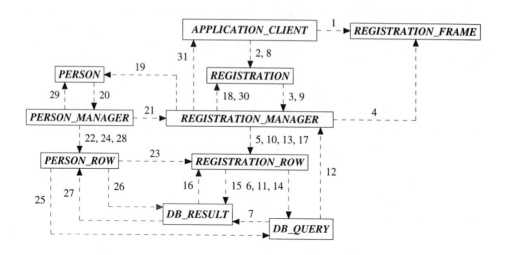

Scenario: Retrieval of persistent registration objects
1–2 The client initializes a query frame with selection criteria, and asks a registration object to retrieve matching instances.
3–7 The registration object calls a registration manager, which inspects the query frame and sends the appropriate SQL statements to a registration row object. The row object forwards the query to the database server, which returns a cursor structure.
8–10 The client tells the registration object to iterate on the result, that is load the matching objects one by one, each time giving the client a callback to process the instance. The request is forwarded to the registration manager, which starts an iteration on the registration row, supplying itself as action object.
11–12 The registration row starts an iteration on the cursor structure, forwarding the manager as action object. The manager action is called with the cursor pointing to the data of the first matching object.
13–19 The registration manager tells the registration row to load itself from the cursor, and sets the basic attributes of the registration object by translating from the corresponding row attributes. It then creates a person object and tells it to load itself from an existing cursor, supplying itself as cursor holder.
20–23 The person object forwards the load request to a person manager, which obtains the registration row from the registration manager argument. The person manager tells a person row to attach itself to an existing cursor structure held by the registration row.
24–31 The person manager tells the person row to load itself from the current cursor and sets the attributes of the person object. The registration manager completes the registration by inserting a reference to the person object, and calls the client action routine for application processing.

Figure 11.20 Typical retrieval scenario

registration object has no manager, a new one is created and attached using the shared routing table.

2. The registration manager then translates the query frame attribute values to appropriate SQL statements, and calls *query* on a *REGISTRATION_ROW* with the query string as argument (see figure 11.15 for the interface of row classes). The *REGISTRATION_ROW* attaches itself to a *DB_QUERY* object and calls its *query* operation passing the SQL string. A set of table rows is then returned from the database server (see figure 11.8 for the interface of the database encapsulation).

3. The client uses *set_action* on a *REGISTRATION* to attach an action object for processing (usually itself) and then calls *iterate_on_result* on the registration, which is passed to the *iterate_on_result* of the manager. The registration manager calls *set_action* on the *REGISTRATION_ROW* supplying itself as action object, followed by an *iterate_on_result* on the row.

4. The *REGISTRATION_ROW* transfers the manager as action object to the *DB_QUERY* and calls its *iterate_on_result*. The *DB_QUERY* creates a *DB_RESULT* representing the first matching table row and invokes the *execute* callback in the registration manager. The manager then calls *load_from_cursor* on the *REGISTRATION_ROW*, which then calls *load_object* through the *cursor* feature of *DB_QUERY*, supplying itself as receiving object.

5. The *DB_RESULT* object loads matching attributes of the first row of the result into the *REGISTRATION_ROW* object. The *execute* routine of the registration manager then proceeds to translate the row object attributes into the *REGISTRATION* object.

6. All basic attributes of the registration have now been loaded, and the registration manager proceeds to retrieve person data while still performing its *execute* callback routine. The registration manager creates a new *PERSON* object and invokes *load_from_cursor* on the empty object. The cursor holder passed as argument to *load_from_cursor* is a reference to the *REGISTRATION_MANAGER* itself.

    The *PERSON* object then invokes *load_from_cursor* on its *PERSON_MANAGER* (attached to the person object via feature *manager*). The *REGISTRATION_MANAGER* reference just received by the *PERSON* object is again passed as cursor holder in this second call.

7. The *load_from_cursor* command in the *PERSON_MANAGER* starts by getting a reference to a *REGISTRATION_ROW* through the *row_object*

feature of the registration manager passed in as argument. It then invokes *attach_to_query* on the *PERSON_ROW* referred to by feature *row_object,* passing as argument the registration row. The effect is to connect the person row to the cursor structure held by the registration row.

When this has been done, the person manager issues a *load_from_cursor* on the *PERSON_ROW*. The person row calls *load_object* on the *cursor* of its newly connected *DB_QUERY* and supplies itself as receiver argument. The *DB_RESULT* object now loads matching attributes of the first row of the result into the *PERSON_ROW* object.

8. The person manager translates the person row object attributes into the *PERSON* object. Control is then returned to the *execute* routine of the registration manager, which finishes its work by attaching the person object to the registration, which then becomes complete. It then invokes the callback routine of the client.

9. The *execute* of the client then processes the returned persistent object. When the routine exits, control is returned to the *execute* of the registration manager, which returns it to the *DB_QUERY*, which moves the cursor to the next resulting table row and again invokes a callback in the manager.

10. The above scenario continues until no more resulting rows remain, or the application client has signaled termination by setting the *over* feature of its action object to **true**. When this happens, the manager will propagate the decision by setting its own *over* feature, and this will make the *iterate_on_result* of *DB_QUERY* return control instead of issuing a callback. The corresponding *iterate_on_result* of the manager also returns, and the client may proceed at the point of its initial iteration call to the registration object.

We will conclude the case study with a discussion on how much automatic support is feasible for the generation of SQL queries.

11.7 AUTOMATIC GENERATION OF SQL STATEMENTS

Since the SQL queries must be expressed in terms of the real database schema, we do not want to have them hard-wired into our software applications. So we are faced with two problems:

- We need to obtain dynamically the mapping between our virtual database and the real database in order to generate a SQL selection statement that will return the proper columns for our row classes.

- We need to find a way for application clients to express selection criteria solely in terms of model object attributes, which can be dynamically translated into SQL statements on the real database.

These are challenging requirements which are not easy to meet. If we were to invent an object-oriented query language completely unrelated to SQL, the dynamic translation would most likely become intractable. However, if we impose some suitable restrictions on the permitted queries and on the relational mappings used, new possibilities open up.

Model queries

The idea is to use SQL syntax transposed to the model object attributes. If the strings assigned to the attributes of a query frame object are valid SQL expressions restricting the corresponding model object attributes, a simple translation scheme is possible. With this approach, the query frames of figure 11.17 are equivalent to the query shown in figure 11.21, expressed in an object-oriented SQL notation.

```
select
      registered_at, amount_paid, invoice_sent, confirmed,
      paper_sessions, attendee.name, attendee.affiliation,
      attendee.address, attendee.postal_mail, attendee.email,
      attendee.phone, attendee.fax
where
      registered_at > '1994-03-15' and
      amount_paid < 500 and
      invoice_sent = true and
      attendee.address LIKE '%USA%'
```

Figure 11.21   An object-oriented SQL query

Such a notation may also be used by application clients as an alternative to the query frames of *retrieve_by_example*. A selection is then passed as a string to *retrieve_by_command*. If all attributes that are part of the selection criteria in the model object are representable as SQL expressions built from columns in the real database, the translation is reduced to simple substitution.

We may still allow some criteria involving object attributes that cannot be transformed to SQL expressions using the database schema, but then these criteria cannot be part of the selection sent to the database server. A correspondingly larger number of table rows will thus be retrieved, and the ones not matching the non-translatable criteria filtered out *a posteriori* by the manager of the persistent object type.

Attribute mappings

The mapping facilities that are needed for storage managers to make automatic conversions are encapsulated in the class *SQL_MAPPINGS*, whose interface is outlined in figure 11.22. All mappings are between strings and can be maintained as simple editable tables and, for example, be stored as persistent strings in the database.

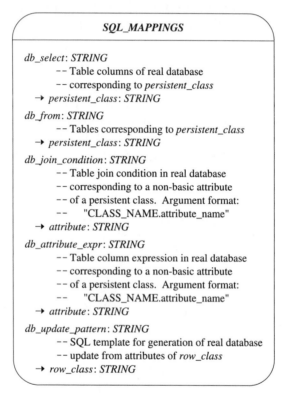

Figure 11.22 Query generation primitives

The first four features return information needed to build queries that can be sent to the database server. A generated query consists of three parts:

- The table columns that need to be selected to provide enough information for building each persistent instance.

- The join conditions for the natural joins to be performed between tables representing a client and tables representing a supplier. For example, class *REGISTRATION* needs to join its tables with those of class *PERSON* to obtain the data corresponding to the attribute *attendee*.

- The selection criteria expressed as SQL conditions on the retrieved database table columns.

The target columns of the selection are precisely the attributes of the corresponding row classes. The call *db_select* ("REGISTRATION") would return:

```
"REGISTRATION.PERSON_CODE as REGISTRATION_ROW$PERSON_CODE,
REGISTRATION.ENTRY_DATE as REGISTRATION_ROW$ENTRY_DATE,
REGISTRATION.PAPER_SESSIONS as REGISTRATION_ROW$CONFERENCE,
REGISTRATION.TUTORIAL1 as REGISTRATION_ROW$TUTORIAL1,
REGISTRATION.TUTORIAL2 as REGISTRATION_ROW$TUTORIAL2,
REGISTRATION.TUTORIAL3 as REGISTRATION_ROW$TUTORIAL3,
REGISTRATION.TUTORIAL4 as REGISTRATION_ROW$TUTORIAL4,
REGISTRATION.CONFIRMATION_DATE as
        REGISTRATION_ROW$CONFIRMATION_DATE,
REGISTRATION.INVOICE as REGISTRATION_ROW$INVOICE,
INVOICE.ISSUED_DATE as REGISTRATION_ROW$ISSUED_DATE,
INVOICE.AMOUNT_PAID as REGISTRATION_ROW$AMOUNT_PAID"
```

If the selection includes personal data, a *db_select* ("PERSON") will also be needed to add the corresponding columns to the format of the retrieved rows.

Besides the selected columns, we need to accumulate all tables that participate in the resulting selection. These could in principle be extracted from the former strings, since we store all column selections qualified by table name to avoid any name clashes. However, sometimes table alias names must be used for unambiguous reference (see the next section).

We therefore store the table reference strings separately, and the calls *db_from* ("REGISTRATION") and *db_from* ("PERSON") yield, respectively:

```
"REGISTRATION, INVOICE"
"CUSTOMER, AFFILIATION"
```

Next, we need to build the restriction clause on the rows initially selected. This must include the corresponding join condition for each "inner" object. Calling *db_join_condition* ("REGISTRATION.attendee") would return:

```
"REGISTRATION.PERSON_CODE = CUSTOMER.CUSTOMER_CODE"
```

In fact, when the *basic* attributes of a class are stored in more than one table, there will be join conditions involved besides the ones introduced by "inner" objects. Therefore, entries may also have to be stored for the class names themselves, not just for each of their non-basic attributes. This is the case for both our classes and the calls *db_join_condition* ("REGISTRATION") and *db_join_condition* ("PERSON") will return the following strings:

```
"REGISTRATION.INVOICE = INVOICE.INVOICE_CODE"
```

```
"CUSTOMER.COMPANY = AFFILIATION.COMPANY_CODE"
```

which must also be part of the restriction clause. Finally, before completing the generated query by appending the selection criteria supplied by the client object, each model object attribute occurring in these criteria needs to be substituted by a corresponding SQL expression in terms of the real database columns. To this end, the calls:

> *db_attribute_expr* ("REGISTRATION.registered_at")
> *db_attribute_expr* ("REGISTRATION.amount_paid")
> *db_attribute_expr* ("REGISTRATION.invoice_sent")
> *db_attribute_expr* ("PERSON.address")

will return the following strings, respectively:

```
"REGISTRATION.ENTRY_DATE"
"INVOICE.AMOUNT_PAID"
"INVOICE.ISSUED_DATE is not null"
"PERSON.STREET || ', ' PERSON.ZIP_CODE || ', ' PERSON.CITY
|| ', ' COUNTRY_NAME"
```

Self-joins

Assume a conference system which also keeps track of alternative arrangements (often called spouse programs) for people accompanying attendees. A possible model is shown in figure 11.23.

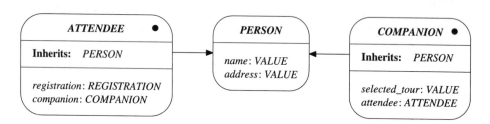

Figure 11.23   Simplified model for *ATTENDEE* and *COMPANION*

An ancestor class *PERSON* contains common attributes, while *ATTENDEE* and *COMPANION* add the needed extensions.

If for some legacy reasons we want to use only one relational table to store both types of object, letting each row represent either a conference attendee or someone accompanying an attendee, such a table containing personal data could look like the one in figure 11.24. A row representing an attendee would leave the selected tour column blank, while a companion row would have companion code zero.

PARTICIPATOR

Name	Type
PARTICIPATOR_CODE	INT
NAME	VARCHAR(50)
ADDRESS	VARCHAR(50)
REGISTRATION_CODE	INT
COMPANION_CODE	INT
SELECTED_TOUR	CHAR(12)

Figure 11.24   Table covering both *ATTENDEE* and *COMPANION*

At first glance, it may seem as though an *ATTENDEE* object would need to be built from two SQL queries: the first selecting the attendee row and the second selecting a possible companion based on the retrieved value of the companion code column. However, this is not necessary.

We could enter a companion row with blank name and address fields, and let it represent the "empty" companion. In each row representing an unaccompanied attendee, the corresponding key value would be used as companion code, thus ensuring referential integrity.

The SQL selection below could then be generated (column renaming omitted for brevity), and the resulting rows would contain all data needed to regenerate the complete *ATTENDEE* objects, one by one.

```
select
    ATTENDEE.NAME, ATTENDEE.ADDRESS,
    COMPANION.NAME, COMPANION.ADDRESS, COMPANION.SELECTED_TOUR
    REGISTRATION.REGISTERED_AT, ...

from
    PARTICIPANT as ATTENDEE, PARTICIPANT as COMPANION,
    REGISTRATION

where
    ATTENDEE.name = 'John Hopkins' and
    ATTENDEE.COMPANION_CODE = COMPANION.PARTICIPANT_CODE and
    ATTENDEE.REGISTRATION_CODE = REGISTRATION.REGISTRATION_CODE
```

The generation scheme

To summarize, the generation of a SQL query using the features of *SQL_MAPPINGS* would proceed as follows:

1. Scan the query frames to find out how many objects must be instantiated from each table row returned by the SQL query. This is recursively controlled by the client, which can either initialize a reference to a non-basic object in the query frame, or leave it as *Void*.

2. Construct the **select**-part by appending the database attribute list of the corresponding row class for each object that is to be loaded from a resulting table row. This is done through repeated calls to *db_select*. (Here, as in the following steps, we implicitly assume that any needed keywords and comma separators are also inserted.)

3. Construct the **from**-part by appending the database tables involved for each object (repeated calls to *db_from*).

4. Start constructing the **where**-part by appending the join condition for each model object, as well as for each attribute referring to a participating "inner" object (like *attendee* in our example). This is done through repeated calls to *db_join_condition*.

5. Translate all selection criteria supplied by the client query frames that are expressed in terms of model object attributes into equivalent criteria understandable by the database server. This is accomplished by substituting the corresponding SQL expressions of the real table columns using calls to *db_attribute_expr*.

6. Complete the **where**-part by appending the resulting criteria strings.

Updating the database

The generation of SQL statements for updates and insertions is much simpler. Since all data, including primary keys, is available in the row objects, we only need to store SQL templates to be filled in with current attribute values. The call *db_update_pattern* ("REGISTRATION") would return:

```
update REGISTRATION set
"ENTRY_DATE = :entry_date, CONFERENCE = :conference,
TUTORIAL1 = :tutorial1, TUTORIAL2 = :tutorial2,
TUTORIAL3 = :tutorial3, TUTORIAL4 = :tutorial4,
CONFIRMATION_DATE = :confirmation_date, INVOICE = :invoice
where PERSON_CODE = :person_code"
```

Preceding a name by a colon is the usual SQL placeholder notation to signify that a value will be dynamically substituted. The manager could either use the pattern to fill in a complete SQL statement for immediate execution, or put it in a stored procedure to be furnished by attribute values using the dynamic SQL conventions for argument passing.

The *issued_date* and *amount_paid* attributes are not part of the pattern, since in our legacy example we assume that these values will only be read by the conference system, while the corresponding updates are done by a separate invoicing system.

Moreover, we have omitted *insert* and *delete* from our design for simplicity, but the mappings for these features can be handled similarly.

11.8 FULL STATIC ARCHITECTURE

Finally, we present the complete architecture of our persistency layers in figure 11.25, showing how it all fits together. As can be seen, the different layers are well separated and the static dependencies between them have been reduced to a minimum.

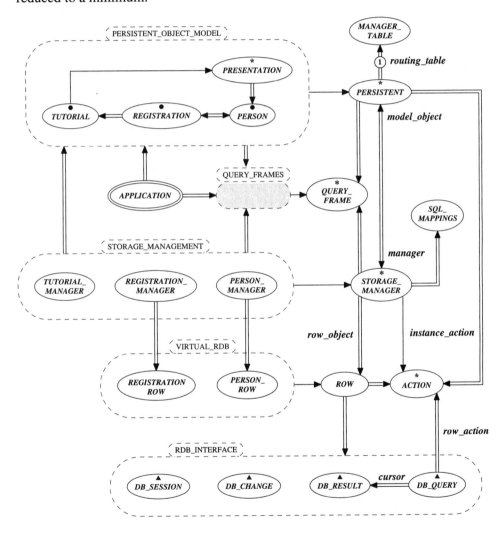

Figure 11.25   Persistent object mapping: full static architecture

12 Exercises

12.1 CLUSTERING A PROBLEM DOMAIN

(This exercise requires the preliminary reading of chapters 3–4.)

Analysis classes relate directly to a problem domain. However, depending on the selected viewpoint, different logical groupings may be defined to satisfy criteria such as high cohesion, low coupling, and a (possibly nested) classification structure emphasizing important aspects of system usage.

1. Partition the cluster *TRANSPORTATION* given in figure 12.1 according to the three alternate viewpoints: *Crew Member*, *Passenger*, *Manufacturer*.

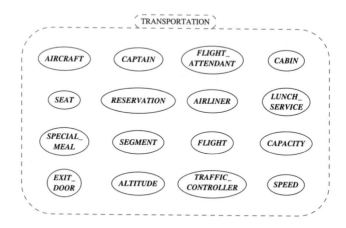

Figure 12.1 Cluster *TRANSPORTATION*

2. The set of analysis classes given in figure 12.2 was inspired by [Rumbaugh 1991]. Suggest appropriate viewpoints corresponding to the two different clusterings, and replace the temporary symbols *C1, C2, …* by self-explanatory names.

Viewpoint 1:

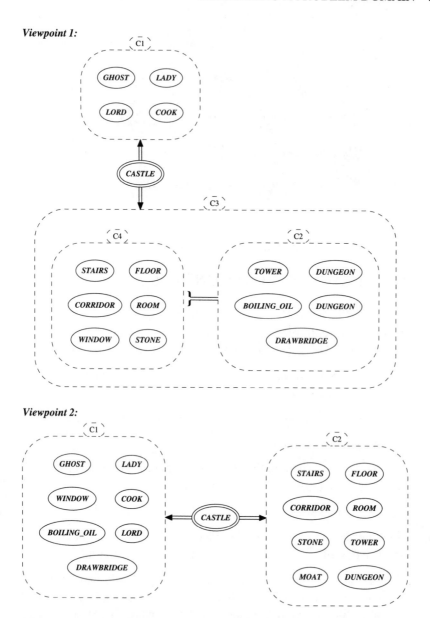

Viewpoint 2:

Figure 12.2 Two alternative cluster partitionings based on different viewpoints

3. The initial analysis of a vacation cruise system has led to a set of classes given in figure 12.3. For each of the three different viewpoints *Travel Agent, Vacationer,* and *Captain,* draw the system borderline that leaves out the classes considered irrelevant in a system based on this viewpoint.

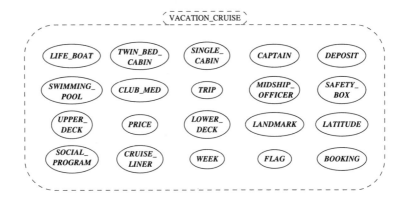

Figure 12.3 Cluster *VACATION_CRUISE*

12.2 DEFINING CLASS RELATIONSHIPS

(This exercise requires the preliminary reading of chapter 4.)

For each numbered requirement, identify candidate classes and define the type of relationship involved between the candidate classes. Argue your choice.

1. All factory rooms have a buzzer triggered by a central clock to signal the end of the working day.

2. Architects are often involved in different concurrent projects.

3. A country has a capital city.

4. Political parties, such as the Republican party, the Democratic party, and the Libertarian party, have voters and supporters.

5. A road connects two cities.

6. Teaching assistants are Ph.D. students and faculty members. They get a monthly payroll check from the university administration.

7. All files are defined as a sequence of bytes. A file can be a text file, a directory, or a special file. A text file can be replaced by a symbolic link to a plain file. A plain file can be either a binary file or a sequential data file. A file belongs to exactly one file system.

8. An undirected graph consists of a set of vertices and a set of edges. Edges connect pairs of vertices.

9. Project planning starts with a list of tasks. Each task is recursively decomposed into subtasks until elementary tasks are reached. Resources

are then allocated for each elementary task. One resource is the task schedule, defined by a starting time and a duration. The resources available for a non-elementary task are determined by looking at the resources for each of its subtasks.

12.3 ASSERTIONS AND CLASSIFICATION

(This exercise requires the preliminary reading of chapters 3–4.)

1. Given the interface of class *PERSON* in figure 12.4, add a precondition to the command *marry* expressing that one can only marry someone who is not already married. Assuming two distinct person references *john* and *helen*, sketch one or more restricted features that may be used by an implementation of *marry* to ensure that

    > *john.marry* (*helen*)

    is strictly equivalent to

    > *helen.marry* (*john*)

2. Write the class interfaces of *BRIDE* and *GROOM* in a way that ensures that each person can only be married to persons of the opposite sex, and only to one at a time.

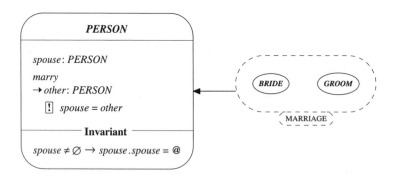

Figure 12.4 Class *PERSON* and cluster *MARRIAGE*

3. Given the utility class *FAMILY* in figure 12.5, make it an ancestor of the class *PERSON* in figure 12.4 and extend the contracts in classes *PERSON*, *BRIDE*, and *GROOM* to keep the parent–child relationship consistent and prevent brothers and sisters from marrying each other.

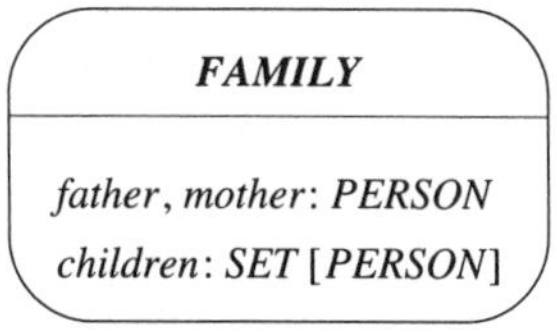

Figure 12.5   Class *FAMILY*

12.4 DYNAMIC BEHAVIOR

(This exercise requires the preliminary reading of chapter 5.)

The requirements for claim processing within a product selling organization leads to the scenario description and dynamic diagram given in figure 12.6. The diagram captures the main control flow of a claim processing system.

A customer's complaint is received by a salesperson and initiates a claim procedure. A claim form is sent to the product manager and to other persons. A copy of the form is routed to the technical services responsible for the defect as indicated by the salesperson.

The technical department makes a report with diagnosis and corrective action taken. The report is passed back to the product manager, who accepts or turns down the claim. The salesperson eventually authorizes reimbursement or replacement products as settlement.

Extend the dynamic model as indicated below. (Recall that message relations signify the flow of *control*, not of data. Therefore, passive information containers have incoming arrows when accessed by active client objects, but outgoing arrows only when calling in turn some other object.)

1. Define a "quick settlement" scenario whereby the customer and the salesperson immediately agree on a settlement over the phone for low-value products.

2. Update the scenario (dynamic diagram and textual description) so that somebody (salesperson, sales manager, or receptionist) phones the customer to explain the settlement when a decision has been reached.

3. Update the scenario to include persons in charge of following each claim through the claim handling procedure. If decisions are delayed, customers should be notified of current status to avoid repeated soliciting.

4. Update the scenario to show shipment of replacement products, or reimbursement checks, respectively.

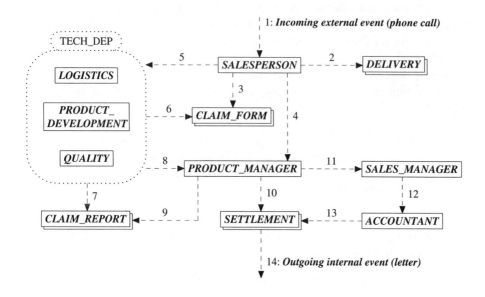

Scenario 1: Process a claim	
1	*A phone call is received by a receptionist and directed to a salesperson.*
2–3	*Salesperson checks delivery, and fills out a claim form according to customer's complaint.*
4–5	*Salesperson sends claim form to product manager with copies to persons in technical department.*
6–8	*Technical department considers the claim, makes a claim report, and forwards result to product manager.*
9–11	*Product manager consults claim report, makes settlement decision, and tells sales manager.*
12	*Sales manager forwards claim report with authorization to accounting department.*
13–14	*Accounting department sends letter with customer settlement: reimbursement or replacement of product.*

Figure 12.6   Dynamic scenario of claim processing system

12.5 PRESCRIPTION AND DESCRIPTION

(This exercise and the following ones require the preliminary reading of chapters 3–5.)

Consider the following problem solving requirement:

A shepherd wishes to move a cabbage, a lamb, and a wolf across a bridge in a carriage. The carriage can only transport one item at a time. If the lamb is left alone with the cabbage, the cabbage will be eaten. If the lamb is left alone with the wolf, the lamb will be eaten.

Assume a scenario where everything is safely transported across the bridge with a minimum number of trips, and infer the following static modeling information.

1. List the analysis classes.

2. Group the analysis classes into clusters and draw the static architecture.

3. Outline class features.

4. Define assertions to ensure that no item will be eaten.

5. Define a class invariant to ensure that the transportation will terminate (finite number of trips).

6. Express the successful strategy using a scenario and a dynamic diagram.

7. Referring to your resulting design, look for a *will_eat* feature that you may have introduced and implement it in your favorite object-oriented language.

12.6 TRAFFIC-CONTROL SYSTEM

The following specification is taken from [Korson 1990].

A software system manipulates the hardware for traffic control located at an intersection. The hardware includes a set of sensors, the traffic lights, and a control box. The software reads the state of the sensors, determines the new state for the intersection, and signals the lights to change. In addition, the system is to have other capabilities, such as a test option to cycle the lights through the set of configurations. The system can also be set to a default state, which might be flashing yellow in one direction and red in the other. The sensor indicates the presence (or absence) of a vehicle in a particular lane.

There are several kinds of sensors with different internal workings, all of them interrupt–driven with a bit set whenever the sensor is tripped. After the decision to change the state of the intersection, every sensor is reset. This particular intersection uses three-color lights for go-straight lanes. Each light has a current state, a set of valid next states, and a default state. The controller physically contains the switches for the lights, the data stores for the sensors, and a clock for timing the state of the poll/decision cycle. The controller software reads the clock, polls the sensors, determines the next state, and sends the signals to change the lights.

1. Delineate the software system borderline and the interface with the hardware.

2. List implementation details that can be excluded from the analysis model.

3. List a first set of analysis classes mapping the problem domain.

4. Define the scenario and associated dynamic diagram describing two vehicles arriving concurrently at the intersection from different directions.

5. Estimate the number of objects (class instances) referred to in your dynamic model.

6. Outline the static architecture and the class descriptions.

12.7 DICE GAME

At the OOPSLA '89 Conference in New Orleans (USA), a contest was organized by Tom Love and presented to different representatives of the object-oriented language community. The aim was to compare designs and solutions resulting from tools, methods, and languages available at that time. The following is an outline of the problem requirements.

A dice game called "Greed" is played between two or more players. Five dice are rolled from a cup, and the winner is the first player to score 5000 points. To enter the game, 300 points are needed on the first roll. If the first roll is greater than 300, the player has the option to stop and keep the initial score or to continue. On continuing, only the dice that have not yet scored may be rolled. If all the dice score (in one or multiple rolls) the player may start a new turn by rolling all five dice. A player may continue rolling as long as a score is made on each roll. An individual roll producing no points is called a "bust". When a bust occurs, all points accumulated during the turn are lost and the turn ends. Three of a kind score 100 times the face value of one die, unless the face value is 1 in which case the score is 1000. Single values of 1 and 5 score 100 and 50, respectively.

1. List candidate classes and define the analysis charts of a system that would monitor the "Greed" game: players, scores, rules, display of results.

2. Outline the class interfaces with public features.

3. Outline a first static diagram.

4. Outline a scenario and dynamic diagram corresponding to a "bust."

5. Look for analysis classes that may be generalized for use in any dice game.

6. Consider the different alternatives for adding a graphical interface to the initial set of model classes.

12.8 CAR RENTAL COMPANY

A car rental company wishes to computerize its car reservation and invoicing system. All vehicles are delivered from and returned to the same location. The system will help keep track of vehicles, making single or block reservations, and issuing invoices based on the pricing structure and running promotions.

The company has several different car models from different manufacturers in its fleet of vehicles. The models are grouped in price categories. Different rental plans are available: daily time and mileage rate, daily rate including unlimited mileage, weekly rates, and a special weekend rate for vacationers.

The price charged by the car rental company is established in advance for a given period. The price for a given model depends on the price category, the type of customer, and the rental plan chosen. Corporate customers get a special discount on normal rates, but not on special weekend rates.

The company finds it important to have information available on the options which may be fitted to certain car models, such as two or four doors, automatic or manual transmission, anti-lock brakes, cruise control, and so forth. The information on what is actually fitted to the cars in the rental fleet must correspond to the information on options provided by the car suppliers. There is no charge for these options, but customers will often request some of them when reserving cars, and the company wishes to try to meet such requests.

In addition to the fitted options there are optional non-fitted extras, such as roof-rack, trailer, snow-chains, and child seats. These extras may be requested at a special additional charge. Different optional insurance plans are also available at extra charge.

A customer may handle a car reservation directly, through a travel agent, or through another company. The reservation may request certain options and extras. The means of payment is usually indicated at reservation time, but may be changed when the car is returned. Reservations are accepted for a given advance period, and cars are tracked daily according to their status: available, booked, rented, under maintenance, being repaired, etc.

1. A first analysis resulted in the static architecture depicted in figure 12.7. Assign possible labels to client/supplier relationships. Look for missing classes and clusters.

2. Draw the associated dynamic model corresponding to a block booking of two cars: a two-door Volkswagen with manual gears and a Chevy with automatic transmission and roof-rack. The selected rental plan specifies

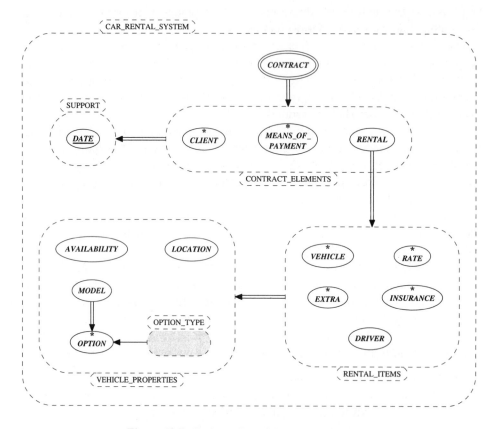

Figure 12.7 Static outline of the car rental system

unlimited mileage, one week rental, corporate rate, and collision damage insurance policy.

3. A smart reuse manager has noticed that an existing corporate component library already includes the classes *PRODUCT*, *STORAGE_AREA*, *PRICING*, *CONSUMER*, *DELIVERY*, and *AVAILABILITY*, resulting from a previous project dealing with stock management for a grocery store. Adapt the car rental classification to take advantage of these classes.

12.9 TRUCK FREIGHT

A system is designed to automate the preparation of freight transportation on trucks. Truck carriers must comply with strict transportation regulations. In addition, they may become liable for any damage caused by an improper delivery in case the regulations were not faithfully observed. The system should

help assess the nature of the transported shipment and produce the legal documents that truck drivers must handle.

The different laws and ordinances regulating the traffic of trucks on roads keep changing: new ones are issued, others become obsolete. A product may be prohibited for road transportation in some country, or in a geographic area. Regulations are based on the type of freight: type of substance, oversized or overweight loads, perishable products.

The regulations constrain the selection of the itinerary and the delivery time frame. For instance, some toxic substances may not be transported across populated areas, or at night; fresh fish must be transported from the harbor to the retailers in less than two days; and livestock may not be transported for a continuous duration of more than 5 hours.

Therefore, the truck carrier company is responsible for assessing the nature of transported products and delivering the freight in good condition, on time, and without violating the regulations.

Each truck load is defined by the properties of the transported goods. The shipping company constantly queries and updates a freight database, and manages the translation between the technical descriptions given by the customer for each freight and their legal counterparts in terms of product classes, restrictions on the itinerary, transportation periods, and the level of qualification required for the truck driver. The system should support the following tasks:

- Perform a formal evaluation of a product to be transported, based on information provided by the manufacturer. For chemical substances, the evaluation is based on physical properties.

- Given the product identification code thus established, define the best possible itinerary from a starting point to a destination with possible restrictions on geographic areas and roads.

- Assign a truck driver with suitable qualifications for the type, weight, and size of the freight.

Products are categorized hierarchically in three levels: the *class* of the substance, the *group* within the class, and the identification *code* within the group. A product may belong to several classes, groups, and codes, but only one is said to be the major criterion while the others are considered minor criteria.

Special attention is paid to hazardous products, which are evaluated according to their physical characteristics such as: flash point, boiling point, solubility, and chemical components. Below are some examples:

- The flash point classifies a product within class 1 (inflammable liquids).

- The toxic effect classifies a product within class 2 (toxic substances).

- The corrosive effect classifies a product within class 3 (corrosive substances).

- The perishability classifies a product within class 4 (rapidly degradable substances).

A substance may be of class 1, 2, and 3, but only one class is retained as the major criterion. Within each class, groups are established and identified by one alphabetic character. Below are some groups defined for class 2 (toxic substances).

- 2.A: Very poisonous products with a flash point below 21 °C and a boiling point below 200 °C, which do not belong to class 1.

- 2.B: Organic substances with a flash point ≥ 21 °C and non-inflammable organic substances.

- 2.C: Metal–organic substances and carbonyls.

- 2.D: Non-organic substances that react with water, water soluble liquids, and acids of poisonous gases.

- 2.E: Other non-organic substances.

Finally, for each group, identification codes are assigned to the product or substance. Below are some codes within 2.C (metal–organic substances and carbonyls):

- 2.C.10: Refrigerated perishable fruits or vegetables.

- 2.C.28: Live stock.

- 2.C.31: Organic lead compounds.

A first analysis produced the cluster sketch in figure 12.8 and one class chart shown in figure 12.9. Continue the analysis by doing the following:

1. List the analysis classes and produce a class dictionary.

2. Define a first static model by completing the initial set of clusters and classes.

3. Define a dynamic scenario describing the assignment of a truck driver to a shipment.

4. Suggest a design that would make it possible to adapt the system to most future regulation changes without the need to modify any source code.

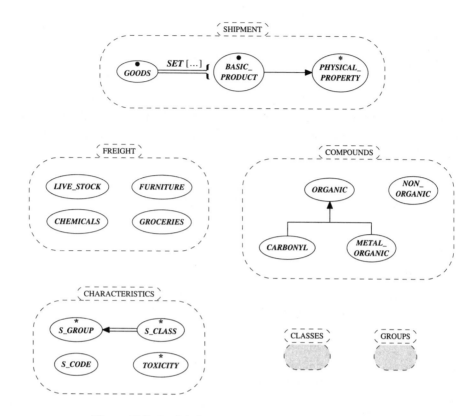

Figure 12.8   Partial cluster partitioning of truck freight system

CLASS	*BASIC_PRODUCT*	**Part:** 1/1
TYPE OF OBJECT Element defined in security data and stored in database.		**INDEXING** **cluster:** *PRODUCT* **created:** 1994-04-06 jmn
Queries	Eatable? Live? Flammable? Corrosive? Water_soluble? Flash_point, Boiling_point, Solubility, Description, Hazardousness, Substance class, Substance group, Substance code	
Commands	Assign substance class. Assign substance group. Assign substance code.	

Figure 12.9   *BASIC_PRODUCT* class chart

5. Assume there are less than 50 class categories and groups, but thousands of identification codes. Investigate how this may or may not impact your design choices.

12.10 REAL-TIME PROCESS CONTROL

In a fragrance company, the industrial production of perfumes employs a chemical reaction controlled by some real-time software. A liquid mixture made from raw vegetal essences is poured into a tank, and the heat is increased until it reaches a certain peak controlled by external sensors.

There is also a feedback of elements flowing out of the boiler. The outgoing steam is kept until it complies with some trade secret combination of essences that are input as control parameters by the company chief executives and by technicians (nicknamed "noses") in charge of maintaining the accuracy of existing or newly created fragrances. When perfection has been reached, the steamed combination is forwarded to a cooling system.

A first analysis of the software resulted in the cluster chart shown in figure 12.10.

The system has several control points, three of which are listed below:

- C1: control point to regulate the liquid valve

CLUSTER	*Fragrance_production*	Part: 1/1
PURPOSE Classes controlling the chemical reactions involved in producing various exact fragrances.	**INDEXING** **created:** 1993-05-23 jmn	

Class/(Cluster)	Description
CONTROLLER	Actor responsible for monitoring the boiling process under normal operational conditions.
HEATING	Device enabling change of temperature accessed through the controller.
PIPE	Incoming and outgoing parts where the mixture is flowing.
SENSOR	Actor retrieving external values.
TANK	Container of mixture (liquid and steam) flowing through pipes and heated with heating system.
STEAM_REACTION	Actor used to record and check the production of steam from the mixed reaction liquid.

Figure 12.10 *FRAGRANCE_PRODUCTION* cluster chart

- C2: control point to regulate the steam valve

- C3: control point to regulate the heating process

Each control point has a corresponding sensor:

- S1: checking the liquid level in the tank

- S2: checking the steam pressure in the tank

- S3: checking the temperature level in the tank

In addition, the system must comply with some physical constraints: the water level, pressure, and temperature in the tank must range between certain lower and upper bounds. The corresponding values (which vary depending on the type of reaction currently in process) are dynamically entered by the system operator.

To optimize the production process, the system must also enforce the following monitoring strategy:

- If the tank becomes too hot, the system should first try to add more cold liquid within a preset time frame. If after that the temperature is still too high, the pressure is decreased during another time frame. If this also proves insufficient, the heat is reduced as a last resort.

- If the tank becomes too cold, the reverse procedure is employed: first increase the heat, then increase the pressure, and then reduce the amount of incoming liquid.

What should be considered too hot and too cold, as well as the lengths of the time frames, are input system parameters entered by the operator or retrieved from a database.

1. Define the first architectural draft of the system.

2. Describe the different classes listed in the cluster chart.

3. How would you express the constraints at the design level? What will be left to the programming phase?

4. Draw a dynamic diagram representing a complete production phase: incoming of fragrance mixture, control of its compound elements, optimization of the process according to the physical sensor values, and transfer of the resulting steam into the cooler.

Part V
Appendices

Appendix A:
BON textual grammar

A.1 INTRODUCTION

This appendix presents a formal syntax specification of the BON textual notation, which is useful for automatic processing and for maintenance of BON designs where no case tool is available. The specification gives a comprehensive overview of all notational concepts in BON, facilitating the construction of parsers for translating BON charts and diagrams into other desired formats.

Communicating BON designs from either case tools or text files to other tools with well-defined interfaces is thus straightforward. Interesting possibilities in this respect include configuration management tools, commercial DBMS environments, and widely available document processors and desktop publishing tools. For example, it is not very difficult to create templates for the informal BON charts, using some of the more advanced word processors. With textual BON it is then possible to mix the interactive input of charts with automatic generation from information stored elsewhere.

The formal description also gives the reader a second chance to resolve possible unclarities that always lurk in natural language descriptions. Nothing can compensate for the precision of a formal notation when it comes to communicating the difficult cases unambiguously.

On the other hand, a language grammar is much harder to read to get a general overview of a notation than are typical examples of language usage. For this reason, and since a fair portion of the BON textual notation has not been shown elsewhere in the book, the next appendix will provide the interested reader with textual equivalents to some of the graphical BON diagrams presented earlier.

The textual version of BON does not include any means for describing the layout of diagrams. This would require an independent set of concepts largely orthogonal to the BON structural elements. Such a language may emerge later as a result of experience with case tools supporting BON.

A.2 THE SYNTAX NOTATION

We will present the BON textual grammar in an extended BNF (Backus Naur Form), where the extensions are very close to the ones used in [Meyer 1992a]. The syntax notation is based on the following concepts.

Any syntactically meaningful part of a BON textual specification, such as a cluster, a class, or an assertion, is called a *component.* The structure of all components of a certain category is described by a *construct,* and an individual component conforming to this description is called a *specimen* of the construct.

Each construct has a unique *construct name,* which is a single word in roman font starting with a capital letter. For example, Class_chart, Feature_clause, and Object_group are construct names, and the corresponding specimens are any individual class chart, feature clause, etc., that may be built according to the rules specified by the grammar.

Every construct is either *terminal* or *non-terminal.* A specimen of a terminal construct is called a *lexical element* or a *token.* The set of tokens make up the basic vocabulary which may be used to construct sentences in the language, and their internal structure is not described by the grammar. The set of tokens are either considered known *a priori,* or else described separately (usually through regular expressions applied to sequences of individual characters, or by informal language).

Non-terminals, on the other hand, are described in terms of other constructs, either terminal or non-terminal. Such a description is called a *production* for the construct, and has the following form:

Construct   ≙   right-hand-side

By convention, every non-terminal construct appears (through its construct name) as the left-hand side of exactly one production. Terminal constructs, on the other hand, may only appear on the right-hand side (by definition). The symbol ≙ means "is defined as".

The right-hand side of a production specifies the structure of the left-hand construct, and since every non-terminal construct has a production attached, the corresponding specimen can always be recursively decomposed into sequences of tokens.

It is not always possible to tell whether a construct is terminal or non-terminal without checking if it occurs as the left-hand side of a production or not. However, two common token types are written using different typography for easy identification: **keywords** (in lower case boldface) and fixed operators (enclosed in double quotes). There are three basic types of production, which have the following forms.

Aggregate

Defines the construct as a fixed sequence of construct parts. One or more elements in the sequence may be marked as optional by enclosing them in square brackets. For example:

Parenthesized	≜	"(" Expression ")"
Inheritance_relation	≜	Child **inherit** ["{" Multiplicity "}"]
		Parent [Semantic_label]

defines Parenthesized as a left parenthesis followed by an Expression followed by a right parenthesis, and Inheritance_relation as a Child construct followed by the keyword **inherit**, then an optional multiplicity part (Multiplicity enclosed in braces), then a Parent construct, then an optional Semantic_label.

Choice

Defines the construct as one of a fixed number of alternative constructs. It is written as a non-empty sequence of constructs separated by vertical bar. The production

Expression ≜	Quantification	Call	Operator_expression	Constant

therefore means that an Expression is a Quantification, or a Call, or an Operator_expression, or a Constant.

Repetition

Defines the construct as a variable length sequence of specimens of another construct, possibly separated (if more than one element) by a given separator. The separator (if any) may be either terminal or non-terminal. A repetition right-hand side is written in one of the two forms below:

$$\{ \text{Element\_construct Separator\_construct} \dots \}$$

$$\{ \text{Element\_construct Separator\_construct} \dots \}^+$$

The first form signals that the sequence may be empty, while the second requires at least one element. Omitting the separator construct means that multiple elements are concatenated without separators in this type of sequence. Below are some examples. The first production defines an Index_list as a sequence of one or more Index_clause, separated by a semicolon. The second defines

Features as a sequence of one or more Feature_clause without any separator. The third production defines a Dynamic_ref as zero or more Group_prefix followed by a Dynamic_component_name.

Index_list	≜	{ Index_clause ";" ... }+
Features	≜	{ Feature_clause ... }+
Dynamic_ref	≜	{ Group_prefix ... } Dynamic_component_name

With these preliminaries, we are now ready to give the full syntax specification of the BON textual notation. The grammar is defined in the following sections and then concluded by a discussion of the lexical components, summing up the keywords and operators used.

A.3 BON SPECIFICATION

Bon_specification	≜	{ Specification_element ... }+
Specification_element	≜	Informal_chart | Class_dictionary | Static_diagram | Dynamic_diagram | Notational_tuning

A.4 INFORMAL CHARTS

Informal_chart	≜	System_chart | Cluster_chart | Class_chart | Event_chart | Scenario_chart | Creation_chart
Class_dictionary	≜	**dictionary** System_name { Dictionary_entry ... }+ **end**
Dictionary_entry	≜	**class** Class_name **cluster** Cluster_name **description** Manifest_textblock

System_chart	≜	**system_chart** System_name [**indexing** Index_list] [**explanation** Manifest_string] [**part** Manifest_string] [Cluster_entries] **end**
Cluster_entries	≜	{ Cluster_entry ... }+
Cluster_entry	≜	**cluster** Cluster_name **description** Manifest_textblock
System_name	≜	Identifier

Index_list   ≙   { Index_clause ";" ... }⁺
Index_clause   ≙   Identifier ":" Index_term_list
Index_term_list   ≙   { Index_string "," ... }⁺
Index_string   ≙   Manifest_string

Cluster_chart   ≙   **cluster_chart** Cluster_name
                      [**indexing** Index_list]
                      [**explanation** Manifest_string]
                      [**part** Manifest_string]
                      [Class_entries]
                      [Cluster_entries]
                      end
Class_entries   ≙   { Class_entry ... }⁺
Class_entry   ≙   **class** Class_name **description** Manifest_textblock
Cluster_name   ≙   Identifier

Class_chart   ≙   **class_chart** Class_name
                      [**indexing** Index_list]
                      [**explanation** Manifest_string]
                      [**part** Manifest_string]
                      [**inherit** Class_name_list]
                      [**query** Query_list]
                      [**command** Command_list]
                      [**constraint** Constraint_list]
                      end
Query_list   ≙   { Manifest_string "," ... }⁺
Command_list   ≙   { Manifest_string "," ... }⁺
Constraint_list   ≙   { Manifest_string "," ... }⁺
Class_name_list   ≙   { Class_name "," ... }⁺
Class_name   ≙   Identifier

Event_chart   ≙   **event_chart** System_name
                      [**incoming | outgoing**]
                      [**indexing** Index_list]
                      [**explanation** Manifest_string]
                      [**part** Manifest_string]
                      [Event_entries]
                      end
Event_entries   ≙   { Event_entry ... }⁺
Event_entry   ≙   **event** Manifest_string **involves** Class_name_list

Scenario_chart	≜	**scenario_chart** System_name
		[**indexing** Index_list]
		[**explanation** Manifest_string]
		[**part** Manifest_string]
		[Scenario_entries]
		end
Scenario_entries	≜	{ Scenario_entry ... }$^+$
Scenario_entry	≜	**scenario** Manifest_string **description** Manifest_textblock

Creation_chart	≜	**creation_chart** System_name
		[**indexing** Index_list]
		[**explanation** Manifest_string]
		[**part** Manifest_string]
		[Creation_entries]
		end
Creation_entries	≜	{ Creation_entry ... }$^+$
Creation_entry	≜	**creator** Class_name **creates** Class_name_list

A.5 STATIC DIAGRAMS

Static_diagram	≜	**static_diagram** [Extended_id] [Comment]
		component Static_block **end**
Extended_id	≜	Identifier | Integer
Comment	≜	{ Line_comment New_line ... }$^+$
Line_comment	≜	"−−" Simple_string
Static_block	≜	{ Static_component ... }
Static_component	≜	Cluster |
		Class |
		Static_relation

Cluster	≜	**cluster** Cluster_name
		[**reused**] [Comment]
		[Cluster_components]
Cluster_components	≜	**component** Static_block **end**
Class	≜	[**root** | **deferred** | **effective**]
		class Class_name [Formal_generics]
		[**reused**] [**persistent**] [**interfaced**] [Comment]
		[Class_interface]
Static_relation	≜	Inheritance_relation | Client_relation

Inheritance_relation	≜	Child **inherit** ["{" Multiplicity "}"]
		Parent [Semantic_label]
Client_relation	≜	Client **client** [Client_entities] [Type_mark]
		Supplier [Semantic_label]
Client_entities	≜	"{" Client_entity_expression "}"
Client_entity_expression	≜	Client_entity_list | Multiplicity
Client_entity_list	≜	{ Client_entity "," ... }⁺
Client_entity	≜	Feature_name | Supplier_indirection | Parent_indirection
Supplier_indirection	≜	[Indirection_feature_part ":"] Generic_indirection
Indirection_feature_part	≜	Feature_name | Indirection_feature_list
Indirection_feature_list	≜	"(" Feature_name_list ")"
Parent_indirection	≜	"–>" Generic_indirection

Generic_indirection	≜	Formal_generic_name | Named_indirection
Named_indirection	≜	Class_name "[" Indirection_list "]"
Indirection_list	≜	{ Indirection_element "," ... }⁺
Indirection_element	≜	"..." | Named_indirection
Type_mark	≜	":" | ":{" | Shared_mark
Shared_mark	≜	":" "(" Multiplicity ")"

Child	≜	Static_ref
Parent	≜	Static_ref
Client	≜	Static_ref
Supplier	≜	Static_ref
Static_ref	≜	{ Cluster_prefix ... } Static_component_name
Cluster_prefix	≜	Cluster_name "."
Static_component_name	≜	Class_name | Cluster_name
Multiplicity	≜	Integer
Semantic_label	≜	Manifest_string

A.6 CLASS INTERFACE DESCRIPTION

Class_interface	≜	[**indexing** Index_list]
		[**inherit** Parent_class_list]
		Features
		[**invariant** Class_invariant]
		end
Class_invariant	≜	Assertion
Parent_class_list	≜	{ Class_type ";" ... }⁺
Features	≜	{ Feature_clause ... }⁺

$$
\begin{array}{rcl}
\text{Feature\_clause} & \triangleq & \textbf{feature}\ [\,\text{Selective\_export}\,] \\
 & & [\,\text{Comment}\,] \\
 & & \text{Feature\_specifications} \\
\text{Feature\_specifications} & \triangleq & \{\,\text{Feature\_specification}\ \ldots\,\}^{+} \\
\text{Feature\_specification} & \triangleq & [\,\textbf{deferred}\ |\ \textbf{effective}\ |\ \textbf{redefined}\,] \\
 & & \text{Feature\_name\_list}\ [\,\text{Type\_mark Type}\,] \\
 & & [\,\text{Rename\_clause}\,] \\
 & & [\,\text{Comment}\,] \\
 & & [\,\text{Feature\_arguments}\,] \\
 & & [\,\text{Contract\_clause}\,]
\end{array}
$$

$$
\begin{array}{rcl}
\text{Contract\_clause} & \triangleq & \text{Contracting\_conditions}\ \textbf{end} \\
\text{Contracting\_conditions} & \triangleq & \text{Precondition}\ |\ \text{Postcondition}\ |\ \text{Pre\_and\_post} \\
\text{Precondition} & \triangleq & \textbf{require}\ \text{Assertion} \\
\text{Postcondition} & \triangleq & \textbf{ensure}\ \text{Assertion} \\
\text{Pre\_and\_post} & \triangleq & \text{Precondition Postcondition}
\end{array}
$$

$$
\begin{array}{rcl}
\text{Selective\_export} & \triangleq & \text{"\{" Class\_name\_list "\}"} \\
\text{Feature\_name\_list} & \triangleq & \{\,\text{Feature\_name "," }\ldots\,\}^{+} \\
\text{Feature\_name} & \triangleq & \text{Identifier}\ |\ \text{Prefix}\ |\ \text{Infix} \\
\text{Rename\_clause} & \triangleq & \text{"\{" Renaming "\}"} \\
\text{Renaming} & \triangleq & \text{"\textasciicircum" Class\_name "." Feature\_name} \\
\text{Feature\_arguments} & \triangleq & \{\,\text{Feature\_argument}\ \ldots\,\}^{+} \\
\text{Feature\_argument} & \triangleq & \text{"->" [Identifier\_list ":"] Type} \\
\text{Identifier\_list} & \triangleq & \{\,\text{Identifier ","}\ \ldots\,\}^{+} \\
\text{Prefix} & \triangleq & \textbf{prefix}\ \text{'"' Prefix\_operator '"'} \\
\text{Infix} & \triangleq & \textbf{infix}\ \text{'"' Infix\_operator '"'} \\
\text{Prefix\_operator} & \triangleq & \text{Unary}\ |\ \text{Free\_operator} \\
\text{Infix\_operator} & \triangleq & \text{Binary}\ |\ \text{Free\_operator}
\end{array}
$$

$$
\begin{array}{rcl}
\text{Formal\_generics} & \triangleq & \text{"[" Formal\_generic\_list "]"} \\
\text{Formal\_generic\_list} & \triangleq & \{\,\text{Formal\_generic ","}\ \ldots\,\}^{+} \\
\text{Formal\_generic} & \triangleq & \text{Formal\_generic\_name ["->" Class\_type]} \\
\text{Formal\_generic\_name} & \triangleq & \text{Identifier} \\
\text{Class\_type} & \triangleq & \text{Class\_name [Actual\_generics]} \\
\text{Actual\_generics} & \triangleq & \text{"[" Type\_list "]"} \\
\text{Type\_list} & \triangleq & \{\,\text{Type ","}\ \ldots\,\}^{+} \\
\text{Type} & \triangleq & \text{Class\_type}\ |\ \text{Formal\_generic\_name}
\end{array}
$$

Unary	≜	**delta** | **old** | **not** | "+" | "−"
Binary	≜	"+" | "−" | "*" | "/" |
		"<" | ">" | "<=" | ">=" |
		"=" | "/=" | "//" | "\\" | "^" |
		or | **xor** | **and** | "−>" | "<−>" | **member_of** | ":"

A.7 FORMAL ASSERTIONS

Assertion	≜	{ Assertion_clause ";" ... }+
Assertion_clause	≜	Boolean_expression | Comment
Boolean_expression	≜	Expression
Expression	≜	Quantification | Call | Operator_expression | Constant
Quantification	≜	Quantifier Range_expression [Restriction] Proposition
Quantifier	≜	**for_all** | **exists**
Range_expression	≜	{ Variable_range ";" ... }+
Restriction	≜	**such_that** Boolean_expression
Proposition	≜	**it_holds** Boolean_expression
Variable_range	≜	Member_range | Type_range
Member_range	≜	Identifier_list **member_of** Set_expression
Type_range	≜	Identifier_list ":" Type

Call	≜	[Parenthesized_qualifier] Call_chain
Parenthesized_qualifier	≜	Parenthesized "."
Call_chain	≜	{ Unqualified_call "." ... }+
Unqualified_call	≜	Identifier [Actual_arguments]
Actual_arguments	≜	"(" Expression_list ")"
Expression_list	≜	{ Expression "," ... }+
Operator_expression	≜	Parenthesized | Unary_expression | Binary_expression
Parenthesized	≜	"(" Expression ")"

Unary_expression	≜	Prefix_operator Expression
Binary_expression	≜	Expression Infix_operator Expression
Set_expression	≜	Enumerated_set | Call | Operator_expression
Enumerated_set	≜	"{" Enumeration_list "}"
Enumeration_list	≜	{ Enumeration_element "," ... }+
Enumeration_element	≜	Expression | Interval
Interval	≜	Integer_interval | Character_interval
Integer_interval	≜	Integer_constant ".." Integer_constant
Character_interval	≜	Character_constant ".." Character_constant

Constant	≜	Manifest_constant | *Current* | *Void*
Manifest_constant	≜	Boolean_constant | Character_constant |
		Integer_constant | Real_constant |
		Manifest_string
Sign	≜	"+" | "–"
Boolean_constant	≜	**true** | **false**
Character_constant	≜	"'" Character "'"
Integer_constant	≜	[Sign] Integer
Real_constant	≜	[Sign] Real
Manifest_textblock	≜	String_begin String String_end
String	≜	{ Simple_string New_line ... }+
Manifest_string	≜	String_begin Simple_string String_end

A.8 DYNAMIC DIAGRAMS

Dynamic_diagram	≜	**dynamic_diagram** [Extended_id] [Comment]
		component Dynamic_block **end**
Dynamic_block	≜	{ Dynamic_component ... }
Dynamic_component	≜	Scenario_description |
		Object_group |
		Object_stack |
		Object |
		Message_relation

Scenario_description	≜	**scenario** Scenario_name [Comment]
		action Labeled_actions **end**
Labeled_actions	≜	{ Labeled_action ... }+
Labeled_action	≜	Action_label Action_description
Action_label	≜	Manifest_string
Action_description	≜	Manifest_textblock
Scenario_name	≜	Manifest_string

Object_group	≜	[**nameless**] **object_group** Group_name [Comment]
		[Group_components]
Group_components	≜	**component** Dynamic_block **end**
Object_stack	≜	**object_stack** Object_name [Comment]
Object	≜	**object** Object_name [Comment]

Message_relation	≜	Caller **calls** Receiver [Message_label]
Caller	≜	Dynamic_ref
Receiver	≜	Dynamic_ref
Dynamic_ref	≜	{ Group_prefix ... } Dynamic_component_name
Group_prefix	≜	Group_name "."
Dynamic_component_name	≜	Object_name | Group_name
Object_name	≜	Class_name ["." Extended_id]
Group_name	≜	Extended_id
Message_label	≜	Manifest_string

A.9 NOTATIONAL TUNING

This will be explained in the next section.

Notational_tuning	≜	Change_string_marks |
		Change_concatenator |
		Change_prefix
Change_string_marks	≜	**string_marks** Manifest_string Manifest_string
Change_concatenator	≜	**concatenator** Manifest_string
Change_prefix	≜	**keyword_prefix** Manifest_string

A.10 LEXICAL COMPONENTS

We conclude this chapter with a discussion of the lexical components, which are used to form BON textual descriptions in accordance with the grammar defined in the preceding sections. These components are the terminal constructs that do not appear as the left-hand side of any production in the grammar, and therefore need to be described separately.

Identifiers

The Identifier construct is defined as a sequence of alphanumeric characters including underscore. An identifier must begin with an alphanumeric character and must not end with an underscore (whose purpose really is to mimic word separation). Letter case is not significant, but using consistent style rules is important.

The recommended BON standard is to use all upper case names for class and cluster names, all lower case for feature names, and lower case beginning with a capital for object groups and constants values. We also strongly recommed using underscore for word separation rather than, for example, in-word capitalization, since this greatly enhances readability.

Free operators

The Free_operator construct represents feature names used as infix and prefix operations. Such operations may be textual keywords, such as the boolean **and** and **or**, but are more often composed of special characters, like "+", "**", "=>", etc.

The purpose is usually to make object-oriented expressions (which are always feature calls in the end) look very similar to the formalisms used in some discipline thus providing a more compact and readable notation for the problem at hand. Since it is difficult to foresee exactly what operator combinations may be needed, BON only defines the Free_operator construct as a sequence of non-spacing printable characters that does not conflict with any of the predefined ones. However, in practice, more restrictions are added by each development environment.

Comments

Major analysis and design elements, such as static diagrams, clusters, classes, object groups, etc., often need to have comments attached to them in order to explain overall modeling aspects that have no natural place among the constituent parts at lower levels.

Therefore, the BON textual notation recognizes comments to major specification elements as part of the grammar, thereby encouraging the standard placement of them. This also provides a parser with the possibility to check and possibly enforce certain strategic descriptions. However, besides the places recognized by the grammar, comments may be inserted anywhere in a BON textual description, except inside strings.

Strings

The construct Simple_string is defined as any string of characters not containing a New_line character. The non-terminal construct Manifest_string is a Simple_string enclosed in the pair of terminals String_begin and String_end. Similarly, the non-terminal Manifest_textblock is a sequence of Simple_string separated by New_line and enclosed by the same pair of terminal constructs (see the grammar above).

These delimiters are defined by default as a string containing one double quote character. The character sequence "show some class, don't treat me like an object" is then interpreted as a Manifest_string. However, to facilitate the accommodation of double quotes inside strings without having to insert escape characters, the delimiting strings may be changed (often to some control characters in connection with automatic processing).

BON also defines a lexical Concatenator construct. If a Concatenator is found inside a Simple_string, it is removed along with all characters (including New_line) up to and including the next Concatenator construct. This makes it possible to embed formatting white space into strings for readability, without making the formatting characters part of the strings.

The Concatenator construct is defined as a single backslash by default, but may be changed by the user. It must not conflict with the string delimiters. An example of its use is shown below.

```
"This is a long simple string, which has been broken into\
                    \ two lines for readability"
```

The basic constructs Integer, New_line, Character, and Real are not further specified, since they may need different definitions depending on the development environment.

Reserved words

Reserved words are terminal constructs which are predefined sequences of letters only, and which cannot be used as identifiers by the user, since this might lead to language ambiguities. The reserved words in BON consist of **keywords** and *predefined names.* There are only three of the latter type: *Current, Result,* and *Void.* The full list is shown in figure A.1.

In a sizable language, there is always the risk that some keywords steal valuable name space from the user, and textual BON, being fairly expressive, is

action	creator	false	not	reused
and	*Current*	feature	object	root
calls	deferred	for_all	object_group	scenario
class	delta	incoming	object_stack	scenario_chart
class_chart	description	indexing	old	static_diagram
client	dictionary	infix	or	string_marks
cluster	dynamic_diagram	inherit	outgoing	such_that
cluster_chart	effective	interfaced	part	system_chart
command	end	invariant	persistent	true
component	ensure	involves	prefix	*Void*
concatenator	event	it_holds	query	xor
constraint	event_chart	keyword_prefix	redefined	
creates	exists	member_of	require	
creation_chart	explanation	nameless	*Result*	

Figure A.1 BON reserved words

no exception. To counter this disadvantage, BON defines a terminal construct Keyword_prefix, which is empty by default.

By defining Keyword_prefix as the string "$", for example, we may change the syntax of BON so all keywords now need to be prefixed by a dollar sign, thus freeing all the corresponding normal words for use in specification of the system under development.

Special symbols

Finally, we collect the complete set of special symbols used in BON with an overview of their meaning (figure A.2). Each of them has been described earlier in the book. The ones marked as operators (except for the type operator ":") can be viewed as class features of infix form that may be redefined by descendant classes.

Conclusion

The BON textual notation is a full specification language for object-oriented system designs, whose purpose is threefold:

- It can be used to communicate exact specifications between various tools and environments, thus taking advantage of the advances in many independent areas of presentation.

- It can be used for better understanding of the concepts underlying the graphical notation and for settling ambiguities. With today's widely available parser generator utilities, the task of writing a parser for the language becomes easy.

- It provides a means of storing and updating a specification in a simple way, using standard text editors, which can serve as an alternative to a dedicated case tool. It may be feasible to copy small whiteboard diagrams with pencil on paper in connection with design sessions, but maintaining larger specifications requires more. Anybody who has experienced the pain of trying to keep evolving graphical figures up to date without strong automatic support knows only too well what we are talking about.

Finally, regarding the different presentations that may be generated from a BON textual description, we have not tried to cover graphical layout in the textual language. The basic graphical appearance of each textual concept has been defined earlier in this book, along with validity constraints and rules for how relational arrows may be combined, labels be positioned, etc. But what valid alternative to choose is left to the strategies of the individual case tool.

SYMBOL	NAME	USE
--	double dash	Introduces comments
'	single quote	Encloses character constants
"	double quote	Encloses prefix and infix operator names
,	comma	General element separator
;	semicolon	Separator for parent lists, assertion clauses, and indexing clauses
( )	parentheses	Grouping of expressions, multiplicity
[ ]	square brackets	Encloses generic parameters
{ }	braces	Encloses restricted export lists, renaming, enumerated sets
+ − * /	plus, minus, times, division	Arithmetic operators
// \\	double slash, double backslash	Integer division, modulo operators
^	up arrow	Power operator, renaming
< >	less than, greater than	Relational operators
<= >=	less than or equal, greater than or equal	Relational operators
= /=	equal, not equal	Equality and non-equality
->	right arrow, implies	Feature arguments, constrained genericity, logical implication
<->	equivalence	Logical equivalence
.	dot	Feature calls, renaming, relational references, object_id
..	double dot	Interval marker
:	colon	Type mark, type operator, index separator
:{	aggregate mark	Indicates aggregate supplier

Figure A.2   BON special symbols

Appendix B:
BON textual examples

B.1 BON SPECIFICATION

In this appendix, we will show the corresponding textual version of some of the graphical BON descriptions presented earlier in the book. This will give interested readers a feeling for the textual language without the need to decode everything from the grammar given in the previous appendix.

A BON textual specification consists of a sequence of one or more of the following types of specification element, which may be given in any order:

- Informal chart (system, cluster, class, event, scenario, creation)

- Class dictionary

- Static diagram

- Dynamic diagram

- Notational tuning

The last type of specification does not address the system being modeled, but may be used to dynamically alter some lexical details regarding the terminal symbols recognized by textual BON. Three operations are available for language tuning:

- **string_marks** to change the default double quote string delimiter

- **concatenator** to change the default backslash string concatenator

- **keyword_prefix** to alter the names of all textual BON keywords into new names, where each old name is prefixed by a given string.

The class dictionary is meant to be generated automatically from the class charts and/or class interfaces, so no corresponding BON chart format is specified for it.

We will look at the informal charts and the static and dynamic diagrams in order, and discuss some of the choices made in the design of textual BON.

B.2 INFORMAL CHARTS

The informal charts are enclosed in *<name>*_**chart** ... **end** blocks, and the keywords delimiting their respective fields correspond closely to the labels used in the graphical forms. The class charts for *CITIZEN* and *NOBLEPERSON* (from chapter 3) are shown in figure B.1, and two cluster charts are in figure B.2.

```
class_chart CITIZEN
indexing
        cluster: "CIVIL_STATUS";
        created: "1993-03-15 jmn";
        revised: "1993-05-12 kw"
explanation
        "Person born or living in a country"
part "1/1"
query
        "Name", "Sex", "Age", "Single", "Spouse", "Children", "Parents",
        "Impediment to marriage"
command
        "Marry", "Divorce"
constraint
        "Each citizen has two parents.",
        "At most one spouse allowed.",
        "May not marry children or parents or person of same sex.",
        "Spouse's spouse must be this person.",
        "All children, if any, must have this person among their parents."
end

class_chart NOBLEPERSON
indexing
        cluster: "CIVIL_STATUS";
        created: "1993-03-15 jmn";
        revised: "1993-05-12 kw", "1993-12-10 kw"
explanation
        "Person of noble rank"
part "1/1"
inherit    CITIZEN
query
        "Assets", "Butler"
constraint
        "Enough property for independence.",
        "Can only marry other noble person.",
        "Wedding celebrated with style.",
        "Married nobility share their assets and must have a butler."
end
```

Figure B.1 Class charts: types of citizen (cf. figure 3.3)

```
cluster_chart ORGANIZATION
indexing
    author: "Kim waldén", "Jean-marc nerson";
    keywords: "organization", "staff"
explanation
    "Handles all major events occurring during the\
    \ organization and completion of a conference."
part "1/1"
class CONFERENCE
description
    "The root class of the conference system."
class PROGRAM
description
    "Information about the final conference program\
    \ and its preparation."
class TIMETABLE
description
    "Repository of scheduled events."
cluster   COMMITTEES
description
    "The committees engaged in the conference organization\
    \ to take care of the technical and administrative parts."
end

cluster_chart COMMITTEES
indexing
    cluster: "ORGANIZATION";
    author: "Kim waldén", "Jean-marc nerson";
    keywords: "committee", "scientific board", "steering board"
explanation
    "Groups all general and special types of committees."
part    "1/1"
class COMMITTEE
description
    "General committee abstraction."
class STEERING_COMMITTEE
description
    "Committee in charge of practical arrangements."
class PROGRAM_COMMITTEE
description
    "Committee in charge of selecting technical contributions."
end
```

Figure B.2   Cluster chart (cf. figure 3.2)

It is possible to include new line characters verbatim in most of the descriptive text fields of the charts, since these are defined as Manifest_textblock in the grammar. However, we have chosen not to do so, because in a case tool with window resizing capabilities we would need to reformat text fields to fit the current window size anyway. Instead, we use the string concatenator "\" to build simple strings from line formatted specification input.

Descriptive text fields consisting of a number of semantically separable phrases, such as **query**, **command**, and **constraint**, are syntactically defined as a sequence of Manifest_string separated by a comma.

B.3 STATIC DIAGRAMS

Cluster structure

The next examples, figures B.3 and B.4, show the nesting of static components.

```
static_diagram First_system_breakdown
component
    cluster CONFERENCE_MANAGEMENT_SYSTEM
    component
        cluster ORGANIZATION
        cluster TECHNICAL_EVENTS
        cluster PRINT_OUTS
        cluster REGISTRATION
    end
end
```

Figure B.3   First cluster definition sketch (cf. figure 9.5, upper part)

Cluster components are enclosed in **component** ... **end** blocks, unless the cluster is empty in which case the cluster name suffices. (An empty cluster will be displayed graphically as an icon, but whether a non-empty cluster will be iconized or not has to do with the presentation format, which is not addressed by textual BON.)

As in the examples, static and dynamic diagrams may have names attached for identification and readability. Since such names are not significant for the modeled system (unlike, for example, class and cluster names), we define them as Extended_id (either Identifier or Integer). This may sometimes be practical for automatically generated textual diagrams.

Class headers

Figure B.5 shows a set of annotated class headers. There is only one syntactic Class construct, so headers are described by omitting the Class_interface part.

Inheritance relations

The next examples show inheritance relations of various types. Multiplicity may be specified by a number enclosed in braces, as seen in figure B.6, where the class *TRIPLE_INDEX* inherits three times from class *INDEX*. The joined

```
                    static_diagram Nested_data_structures
                    component
                        cluster DATA_STRUCTURES
                        component
                            cluster SORTING reused
                            component
                                class LINEAR_SORT
                                class QUICKSORT
                                class RADIX_SORT
                                class INSERTION_SORT
                                class SHELLSORT
                                class HEAPSORT
                                class TOPOLOGICAL_SORT
                                class SORT_MERGE
                            end
                            cluster GRAPHS
                            component
                                deferred class GRAPH
                                class WEIGHTED_GRAPH
                                class DIRECTED_GRAPH
                                class UNDIRECTED_GRAPH
                                class BIPARTITE_GRAPH
                                class DENSE_GRAPH
                            end
                        end
                    end
```

Figure B.4 A nested data structure cluster (cf. figure 3.16)

```
                    static_diagram
                    component
                        root class CONTROL_PANEL
                        class TRANSACTION persistent
                        class MAILER interfaced
                        class HASH_TABLE [T, U]
                        deferred class FLYING_OBJECT
                        effective class HELICOPTER
                        class INPUT reused interfaced
                        class VECTOR [G] reused
                        deferred class SESSION interfaced
                    end
```

Figure B.5 Annotated class headers (cf. figure 3.15)

relational arrows in figure 4.1, on the other hand, have no correspondence in textual BON. Figure B.7 shows the inheritance between classes and clusters. We use dot notation on the cluster names involved to refer to classes residing inside nested clusters, as seen in the figure. This makes it possible to have local name spaces for classes in different clusters at the analysis level, and also

```
        static_diagram
        component
              class COLD_STORE
              class FREEZER
              class REFRIGERATOR
              class INDEX
              class TRIPLE_INDEX
              deferred class FLYING_OBJECT
              effective class AIRCRAFT
              effective class ROCKET
              class SPACE_SHUTTLE
              deferred class VEHICLE
              effective class BICYCE
              effective class BOAT
              effective class CAR
              REFRIGERATOR inherit COLD_STORE
              FREEZER inherit COLD_STORE
              TRIPLE_INDEX inherit {3} INDEX
              AIRCRAFT inherit FLYING_OBJECT
              ROCKET inherit FLYING_OBJECT
              SPACE_SHUTTLE inherit AIRCRAFT
              SPACE_SHUTTLE inherit ROCKET
              BICYCLE inherit VEHICLE
              BOAT inherit VEHICLE
              CAR inherit VEHICLE
        end
```

Figure B.6   Different type of inheritance (cf. figure 4.1)

documents more clearly what cluster interdependencies we have in our diagrams. If the implementation language supports renaming of classes on a cluster basis, possible name clashes may easily be resolved later.

Client relations

Labels attached to client relations are enclosed in braces, as seen in figure B.8, which contains a number of compacted generic links. Here (as in figure B.7) we have split the figure into multiple diagrams. The third diagram in figure B.8 had to be separated to avoid name clashes on the classes involved, which would make the specification ambiguous. The first and second diagrams were separated to obtain the grouping of the static components contained in the figure.

```
static_diagram 1
component
    cluster PARENTS
    component
        class A
        class B
    end
    cluster CHILDREN
    component
        class C
        class D
        class E
    end
    CHILDREN.C inherit PARENTS.A
    CHILDREN.C inherit PARENTS.B
    CHILDREN.D inherit PARENTS.A
    CHILDREN.D inherit PARENTS.B
    CHILDREN.E inherit PARENTS.A
    CHILDREN.E inherit PARENTS.B
end
static_diagram 2
component
    cluster PARENTS component ... end
    cluster CHILDREN component ... end
    CHILDREN inherit PARENTS.A
    CHILDREN inherit PARENTS.B
end
static_diagram 3
component
    cluster PARENTS component ... end
    cluster CHILDREN component ... end
    CHILDREN.C inherit PARENTS
    CHILDREN.D inherit PARENTS
    CHILDREN.E inherit PARENTS
end
static_diagram 4
component
    cluster PARENTS component ... end
    cluster CHILDREN component ... end
    CHILDREN inherit PARENTS
end
```

Figure B.7 Recursive abstraction (cf. figure 4.3)

Although we have had no example so far in the book of nested generic derivation, this does occur in practice not too infrequently. The BON notation therefore supports nested generic type parameters in compacted client relations, so that several levels of indirection through standard container classes can be removed and diagrams concentrated on the essential concepts for the modeling.

```
                    static_diagram 1
                    component
                        class BASEBALL_CARD
                        class SON
                        class LIST [T] reused
                        class PARENT
                        class ACCOUNT
                        SON client {expenses} LIST
                        PARENT client {assets} LIST
                        LIST client {(first, last): T} BASEBALL_CARD
                        LIST client {(first, last): T} ACCOUNT
                    end

                    static_diagram 2
                    component
                        class NURSE
                        class PATIENT
                        class SURGEON
                        class OPERATION
                        class TABLE [U, V->KEY] reused
                        class PATIENT_ID
                        class DATE
                        NURSE client {patients} TABLE
                        SURGEON client {duties} TABLE
                        TABLE client {item: U} PATIENT
                        TABLE client {item: U} OPERATION
                        TABLE client {key: V} PATIENT_ID
                        TABLE client {key: V} DATE
                    end

                    static_diagram 3
                    component
                        class SON
                        class BASEBALL_CARD
                        class PARENT
                        class ACCOUNT
                        class NURSE
                        class PATIENT
                        class SURGEON
                        class OPERATION
                        SON client {expenses: LIST [...]} BASEBALL_CARD
                        PARENT client {assets: LIST [...]} ACCOUNT
                        NURSE client {patients: LIST [..., PATIENT_ID]} PATIENT
                        SURGEON client {duties: LIST [..., DATE]} OPERATION
                    end
```

Figure B.8 Multiple generic derivation (cf. figure 4.14)

Each occurrence of [...] in the label of a compacted link refers to the supplier class. For example,

$\quad\quad\quad$ *FIGURE* **client** {*SET* [*SET* [...]]} *POINT*

expresses that class *FIGURE* has some entity of type *SET* [*SET* [*POINT*]].

Figure B.9 shows some indirect client dependencies resulting from the generic derivation of parent classes. The braces enclose the client entity part, which describes what causes the relation. The entity part may express generic indirection through a parent class as in figure B.9, role multiplicity as in figure B.10, and multiple feature labels as in figure B.11. Aggregation relations are expressed by a corresponding type mark between the client entity part and the supplier.

```
static_diagram 1
component
    class SEQUENCE [T] reused
    class BYTE
    class FILE
    FILE inherit SEQUENCE
    SEQUENCE client { -> [...] } BYTE
end
static_diagram 2
component
    class FILE
    class BYTE
    FILE client { -> SEQUENCE [...] } BYTE
end
```

Figure B.9   Generic client relation through inheritance (cf. figure 4.15)

```
static_diagram
component
    class VISITING_ALIEN
    class LANDING_DOCUMENT
    class APARTMENT
    class ROOM
    class HOUSE
    class ARCHITECT
    VISITING_ALIEN client {2} LANDING_DOCUMENT
    APARTMENT client {3} :{ ROOM
    HOUSE client {1} ARCHITECT
    ARCHITECT client {3} HOUSE
end
```

Figure B.10   Multiplicity markers (cf. figure 4.16)

Since role multiplicity maps to a fixed number of static relationships between a client and a supplier, each playing a different role during execution, the corresponding numbers are just a replacement for client labels. It is therefore syntactically natural to place the corresponding multiplicity numbers in the same

```
        static_diagram
        component
            class VISITING_ALIEN
            class LANDING_DOCUMENT
            class APARTMENT
            class ROOM
            class HOUSE
            class ARCHITECT
            VISITING_ALIEN client {immigration_form, customs_form} LANDING_DOCUMENT
            APARTMENT client {kitchen, bedroom: SET [...], living_room: SET [...]} :{ ROOM
            HOUSE client {designer} ARCHITECT
            ARCHITECT client {summer_house, winter_cottage, main_residence} HOUSE
        end
```

Figure B.11 Naming rather than enumerating roles (cf. figure 4.17)

position as the labels (enclosed in braces, and before the type mark).

Multiple sharing of instances, on the other hand, corresponds to one entity being dynamically attached to a fixed number of possible instances during execution. Therefore, such instance multiplicity is instead enclosed in ordinary parentheses and put after the type mark as can be seen in figure B.12.

In diagram 6 of this figure, we have an example where both types of multiplicity are used simultaneously to express that a PC class has two client relations, each dynamically sharing three instances of class *FILE_SERVER*. The next example shows the static relations between elements inside and between different clusters (figure B.13).

```
static_diagram 1                            static_diagram 4
component                                   component
    class PC                                    class PC
    class FILE_SERVER                           class FILE_SERVER
    PC client {2} : (1) FILE_SERVER             PC client : (2) FILE_SERVER
end                                         end

static_diagram 2                            static_diagram 5
component                                   component
    class PC                                    class PC
    class FILE_SERVER                           class FILE_SERVER
    PC client {server1} : (1) FILE_SERVER       PC client {server} : (2) FILE_SERVER
    PC client {server2} : (1) FILE_SERVER   end
end
                                            static_diagram 6
static_diagram 3                            component
component                                       class PC
    class PC                                     class FILE_SERVER
    class FILE_SERVER                            PC client {2} : (3) FILE_SERVER
    PC client {server1, server2} : (1) FILE_SERVER   end
end
```

Figure B.12 Different ways to express sharing (cf. figure 4.19)

```
static_diagram Graphical_editor
        -- This diagram shows the basic design of a graphical editor with grouping facilities.
component
    cluster DISPLAY_ELEMENTS    -- Contains different display objects
    component
        cluster GEOMETRIC_FIGURES   -- Subcluster with geometric figures
        component
            class LINE
            class ELLIPSE
            class CIRCLE
            class RECTANGLE
            class SQUARE
            CIRCLE inherit ELLIPSE
            SQUARE inherit RECTANGLE
        end
        deferred class FIGURE
        class PIXEL_MAP
        class TEXT
        class GROUP
        GEOMETRIC_FIGURES inherit FIGURE
    end
    deferred class DISPLAY_OBJECT
    class POINT
    DISPLAY_ELEMENTS inherit DISPLAY_OBJECT
    DISPLAY_ELEMENTS.GROUP client {members: SET […]} :{ DISPLAY_OBJECT
    DISPLAY_ELEMENTS.FIGURE client {points: SET […]} POINT
end
```

Figure B.13 Graphical objects with grouping (cf. figure 5.17)

Class interfaces

The textual notation for the technical events classes of the Conference case study is shown in figure B.14. The textual form needs a few more delimiters to become unambiguous than the corresponding graphical form. For example, contract clauses must be terminated by **end**. Finally, we show a textual form of the overall static architecture of the Conference study in figure B.15 and figure B.16.

B.4 DYNAMIC DIAGRAMS

We conclude with some dynamic diagrams. Objects are represented graphically by the respective class name optionally qualified by a parenthesized object id. Usually only a few objects need to be qualified in graphical dynamic diagrams, since the spatial context will be enough to identify most of them; this holds also for multiple instances of the same class. However, since textual descriptions have no positional information available, we always need the qualification

```
static_diagram Technical_events
component
    class REVIEW persistent
    feature
        reviewer: PERSON
        score: VALUE
        comments: TEXT
    invariant
        score member_of { 'A' .. 'D' }
    end
    class STATUS persistent
    feature
        received: DATE
        review_started: DATE
        accepted: DATE
        rejected: DATE
        final_received: DATE
    invariant
        received <= review_started;
        review_started <= final_received;
        accepted = Void or rejected = Void
    end
    class PAPER persistent
    inherit
        PRESENTATION
    feature
        copyright_transferred: BOOLEAN
        reviews: SET [REVIEW]
        final_score: VALUE
        award_best_paper
        transfer_copyright
            require
                status.accepted /= Void
            ensure
                copyright_transferred
            end
        effective accept
        effective reject
    end
    deferred class PRESENTATION
    feature
        code: VALUE
        title: VALUE
        authors: SET [PERSON]
        status: STATUS
        speakers: SET [PERSON]
        deferred accept
            ensure status.accepted /= Void  end
        deferred reject
            ensure status.rejected /= Void  end
```

```
    invariant
        for_all p, q: PRESENTATION such_that
            p /= q it_holds p.code /= q.code and
            p.title /= q.title
    end
    class TUTORIAL persistent
    inherit PRESENTATION
    feature
        capacity: VALUE
        attendee_count: VALUE
        prerequisite_level: VALUE
        track: VALUE
        duration: DURATION
        effective accept
        effective reject
    end
    class PAPER_SESSION persistent
    inherit SESSION
    feature
        presentations: SET [PAPER]
    invariant
        for_all p member_of presentations it_holds
            p.status.accepted /= Void
    end
    class SESSION
    feature
        chair: PERSON
        code: VALUE
        track: VALUE
        start, end: DATE
        conference_room: VALUE
    invariant  start < end
    end
    class TUTORIAL_SESSION persistent
    inherit
        SESSION
    feature
        lecture: TUTORIAL
    invariant
        lecture.status.accepted /= Void
    end
    PAPER inherit PRESENTATION
    TUTORIAL inherit PRESENTATION
    PAPER_SESSION inherit SESSION
    TUTORIAL_SESSION inherit SESSION
    PAPER client REVIEW
    PRESENTATION client STATUS
    PAPER_SESSION client PAPER
    TUTORIAL_SESSION client TUTORIAL
end
```

Figure B.14 Technical_events (cf. figure 9.31)

```
static_diagram Conference_architecture
          -- This diagram shows the overall architecture of the Conference Management system.
component
    cluster ORGANIZATION
    component
        cluster COMMITTEES
        component
            class COMMITTEE
            class ORGANIZING_COMMITTEE persistent
            class TECHNICAL_COMMITTEE persistent
            class PROGRAM_COMMITTEE persistent
            ORGANIZING_COMMITTEE inherit COMMITTEE
            TECHNICAL_COMMITTEE inherit COMMITTEE
            PROGRAM_COMMITTEE inherit TECHNICAL_COMMITTEE
            PROGRAM_COMMITTEE client { tutorial_committee } :{ TECHNICAL_COMMITTEE
        end
        root class CONFERENCE persistent
        class PROGRAM persistent
        class TIMETABLE persistent
        CONFERENCE client { scientific_board, steering_board } :{ COMMITTEES
        CONFERENCE client { program } :{ PROGRAM
        CONFERENCE client { reminder } TIMETABLE
    end
    cluster REGISTRATION
    component
        class REGISTRATION persistent
        class PERSON persistent
        REGISTRATION client { attendee } PERSON
        PERSON client { registration } REGISTRATION
    end
    cluster TECHNICAL_EVENTS
    component
        class SESSION
        class PAPER_SESSION persistent
        class TUTORIAL_SESSION persistent
        deferred class PRESENTATION
        class PAPER persistent
        class TUTORIAL persistent
        class REVIEW persistent
        class STATUS persistent
        PAPER_SESSION inherit SESSION
        TUTORIAL_SESSION inherit SESSION
        PAPER inherit PRESENTATION
        TUTORIAL inherit PRESENTATION
        PAPER_SESSION client { presentations: SET [...] } PAPER
        TUTORIAL_SESSION client { lecture } TUTORIAL
        PAPER client { reviews: SET [...] } REVIEW
        PRESENTATION client { status } STATUS
    end
```

Figure B.15   Complete static architecture, part 1 (cf. figure 9.32)

```
                        cluster OUTPUT
                        component
                            cluster TEMPLATES
                                class LETTER_FORM
                                class BADGE_FORM
                                class STICKY_FORM
                                class INVOICE_FORM
                                class POSTER_FORM
                                class LIST_FORM
                                class EVALUATION_FORM
                            end
                            cluster PRINT_OUTS
                            component
                                class MAILING
                                class ADDRESS_LABEL
                                class CONFIRMATION_LETTER
                                class INVOICE
                                class ACCEPTANCE_LETTER
                                class REJECTION_LETTER
                                class AUTHOR_GUIDELINES
                                class POSTER_SIGN
                                class BADGE
                                class EVALUATION_SHEET
                                class ATTENDEE_LIST
                                class STATISTICS
                            end
                            deferred class PRINT_OUT
                            deferred class DOCUMENT_FORM
                            TEMPLATES inherit DOCUMENT_FORM
                            PRINT_OUTS inherit PRINT_OUT
                            PRINT_OUT client {layout} DOCUMENT_FORM
                        end
                        ORGANIZATION client OUTPUT
                        ORGANIZATION client TECHNICAL_EVENTS
                        ORGANIZATION client REGISTRATION
                        REGISTRATION client OUTPUT
                        REGISTRATION client TECHNICAL_EVENTS
                        TECHNICAL_EVENTS client REGISTRATION
                        TECHNICAL_EVENTS client OUTPUT
                    end
```

Figure B.16   Complete static architecture, part 2 (cf. figure 9.32)

whenever more than one object of the same class occur in a textual diagram.

Again we use dot notation for separation, and require such object names to be suffixed by an Extended_id (either Identifier or Integer) for unique reference. Figure B.17 shows an example where such qualification is needed.

We note that the objects *GROUP.outer* and *GROUP.inner* were qualified already in figure 5.21, while the other object identities could all be inferred from context. In the textual form, these objects had to be qualified by integer suffixes,

```
dynamic_diagram Move_group
component
    scenario "Scenario 2: Move example group"
    action
        "1"        "Next outer group member requested"
        "2"        "Square asked to move"
        "3"        "Next square point requested"
        "4"        "Point asked to move"
        "5"        "Outer circle asked to move"
        "6"        "Next outer circle point requested"
        "7"        "Point asked to move"
        "8"        "Inner group asked to move"
        "9"        "Next inner group member requested"
        "10"       "Inner circle asked to move"
        "11"       "Next inner circle point requested"
        "12"       "Point asked to move"
        "13"       "Text asked to move"
    end
    object SQUARE
    object CIRCLE.1
    object CIRCLE.2
    object TEXT
    object GROUP.outer
    object GROUP.inner
    object SET.1
    object SET.2
    object SET.3
    object SET.4
    object SET.5
    object_stack POINT.1
    object_stack POINT.2
    object_stack POINT.3
    GROUP.outer calls SET.1  "1"
    GROUP.outer calls SQUARE  "2"
    SQUARE calls SET.2  "3"
    SQUARE calls POINT.1  "4"
    GROUP.outer calls CIRCLE.1  "5"
    CIRCLE.1 calls SET.3  "6"
    CIRCLE.1 calls POINT.2  "7"
    GROUP.outer calls GROUP.inner  "8"
    GROUP.inner calls SET.4  "9"
    GROUP.inner calls CIRCLE.2  "10"
    CIRCLE.2 calls SET.5  "11"
    CIRCLE.2 calls POINT.3  "12"
    GROUP.inner calls TEXT  "13"
end
```

Figure B.17   Move example group (cf. figure 5.21)

probably appended by a generating case tool.

Similarly, we need an identification for unnamed object groups in order to refer to it by message relations. This is illustrated in figure B.19, where the name *Group* was assigned to the nameless group.

```
dynamic_diagram Claim_settlement
        -- This dynamic diagram groups typical sequential subtasks.
component
    scenario "Scenario 5: Settlement of claims for damages resulting from car accident"
    action
        "1-3"      "Owner obtains necessary statements and certificates\
                    \ from involved parties, fills in damage report, and\
                    \ sends it to insurance company."
        "4-7"      "Insurance adjuster evaluates damage claims and sends\
                    \ settlement statement back to owner."
        "8-9"      "Owner agrees on car rental and repair details based\
                    \ on settlement."
    end

    object_group Accident_report
    component
        object WITNESS
        object POLICE
        object INSURANCE_INSPECTOR
    end

    object_group Evaluation
    component
        object INSURANCE
        object STANDARD_PRICE_LIST
        object APPROVED_GARAGES
    end

    object_group Repair
    component
        object RENTAL_COMPANY
        object GARAGE
    end

    object OWNER
    object INSURANCE_ADJUSTER
    object DAMAGE_REPORT
    object SETTLEMENT
    OWNER calls Accident_report  "1"
    OWNER calls DAMAGE_REPORT  "2"
    OWNER calls INSURANCE_ADJUSTER  "3"
    OWNER calls SETTLEMENT  "8"
    OWNER calls Repair  "9"
    INSURANCE_ADJUSTER calls DAMAGE_REPORT  "4"
    INSURANCE_ADJUSTER calls Evaluation  "5"
    INSURANCE_ADJUSTER calls SETTLEMENT  "6"
    INSURANCE_ADJUSTER calls OWNER  "7"
end
```

Figure B.18   Grouping into sequential subtasks (cf. figure 5.23)

```
dynamic_diagram Evaluate_paper
component
    scenario "Scenario 2: Accept or reject a paper and notify authors"
    action
        "1-2"     "A paper is selected"
        "3-5"     "Acceptance or rejection date is entered"
        "6-7"     "The first author of the paper is selected"
        "8"       "A notification letter is created"
        "9-11"    "The letter is sent to first author"
    end

    nameless object_group Group
    component
        object ACCEPTANCE_LETTER
        object REJECTION_LETTER
    end

    object LETTER_FORM
    object_stack PERSON
    object PROGRAM_COMMITTEE
    object CONFERENCE
    object_stack PAPER
    object STATUS
    CONFERENCE calls PROGRAM_COMMITTEE  "1"
    PROGRAM_COMMITTEE calls PAPER  "2, 3, 6"
    PROGRAM_COMMITTEE calls PERSON  "7"
    PROGRAM_COMMITTEE calls Group  "8, 9"
    PAPER calls STATUS  "4"
    Group calls LETTER_FORM  "10"
    Group calls Outside_world  "11: Letter printed"
    Outside_world calls STATUS  "5: User input"
end
```

Figure B.19   Paper evaluation (cf. figure 9.24)

Appendix C:
BON quick reference

BON deliverables: dependencies

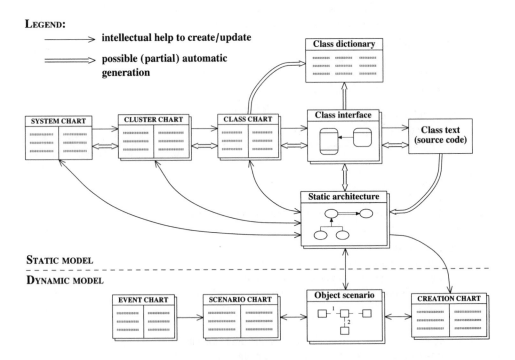

LEGEND:

——————▷ intellectual help to create/update

═══════▷ possible (partial) automatic generation

BON deliverables: description   (◊ indicates the most important ones)

System chart
SYSTEM CHART

Definition of system and list of associated clusters. Only one system chart per project; subsystems are described through corresponding cluster charts.

Cluster charts
CLUSTER CHART

Definition of clusters and lists of associated classes and subclusters, if any. A cluster may represent a full subsystem or just a group of classes.

Class charts
CLASS CHART

Definition of analysis classes in terms of *commands, queries,* and *constraints,* understandable by domain experts and non-technical people.

Class dictionary
Class dictionary

Alphabetically sorted list of all classes in the system, showing the cluster of each class and a short description. Should be generated automatically from the class charts/interfaces.

◊ Static architecture
Static architecture

Set of diagrams representing possibly nested clusters, class headers, and their relationships. Bird's eye view of the system (zoomable).

◊ Class interfaces
Class interface

Typed definitions of classes with feature signatures and formal contracts. Detailed view of the system.

Creation charts
CREATION CHART

List of classes in charge of creating instances of other classes. Usually only one per system, but may be repeated for subsystems if desirable.

Event charts
EVENT CHART

Set of incoming external events (stimuli) triggering interesting system behavior and set of outgoing external events forming interesting system responses. May be repeated for subsystems.

◊ Scenario charts
SCENARIO CHART

List of object scenarios used to illustrate interesting and representative system behavior. Subsystems may contain local scenario charts.

◊ Object scenarios
Object scenario

Dynamic diagrams showing relevant object communication for some or all of the scenarios in the scenario chart.

BON process: tasks and activities

Task		Description	BON deliverables
G A T H E R I N G	1	**Delineate system borderline.** Find subsystems, user metaphors, use cases.	SYSTEM CHART, SCENARIO CHARTS
	2	**List candidate classes.** Create glossary of technical terms.	CLUSTER CHARTS
	3	**Select classes and group into clusters.** Classify; sketch principal collaborations.	SYSTEM CHART, CLUSTER CHARTS, STATIC ARCHITECTURE, CLASS DICTIONARY
D E S C R I B I N G	4	**Define classes.** Determine *commands, queries,* and *constraints.*	CLASS CHARTS
	5	**Sketch system behaviors.** Identify events, object creation, and relevant scenarios drawn from system usage.	EVENT CHARTS, SCENARIO CHARTS, CREATION CHARTS, OBJECT SCENARIOS
	6	**Define public features.** Specify typed signatures and formal contracts.	CLASS INTERFACES, STATIC ARCHITECTURE
D E S I G N I N G	7	**Refine system.** Find new design classes, add new features.	CLASS INTERFACES, STATIC ARCHITECTURE, CLASS DICTIONARY, EVENT CHARTS, OBJECT SCENARIOS
	8	**Generalize.** Factor out common behavior.	CLASS INTERFACES, STATIC ARCHITECTURE, CLASS DICTIONARY
	9	**Complete and review system.** Produce final static architecture with dynamic system behavior.	Final static and dynamic models; all BON deliverables completed.

STANDARD ACTIVITIES	
1	**Finding classes**
2	**Classifying**
3	**Clustering**
4	**Defining class features**
5	**Selecting and describing object scenarios**
6	**Working out contracting conditions**
7	**Assessing reuse**
8	**Indexing and documenting**
9	**Evolving the system architecture**

BON notation: charts and interfaces

INFORMAL CHARTS

SYSTEM	SYSTEM_NAME	Part:
PURPOSE	INDEXING	
Cluster	Description	

EVENTS	SYSTEM_NAME	Part:
COMMENT	INDEXING	
External (in/out)	Involved object types	

CLUSTER	CLUSTER_NAME	Part:
PURPOSE	INDEXING	
Class/(Cluster)	Description	

SCENARIOS	SYSTEM_NAME	Part:
COMMENT	INDEXING	
Scenario 1: Description 1		

CLASS	CLASS_NAME	Part:
TYPE OF OBJECT	INDEXING	
Inherits from		
Queries		
Commands		
Constraints		

CREATION	SYSTEM_NAME	Part:
COMMENT	INDEXING	
Class	Creates instances of	

CLASS INTERFACE

CLASS_NAME

Indexing information

Inherits: *PARENT CLASSES*

Public features
____ A, B, C ____

Features only visible to classes A, B, C

____ **Invariant** ____

Class invariant

FEATURE SIGNATURES

name*, *name*$^+$, *name*$^{++}$	deferred/effective/redefined
name: *TYPE*	result type
name: { *TYPE*	aggregation result type
name: (n) *TYPE*	shared result type
{ ^*CLASS_NAME*.*name* }	rename clause
→ *name*: *TYPE*	input argument
$\boxed{?}$, $\boxed{!}$	pre- and postcondition

ASSERTION SYMBOLS

Δ *name*	attribute *name* may change
old *expr*	previous value of *expr*
@, ∅	current object, void reference
+, −, *, /, ^, //, \\	arithmetic op
=, ≠, <, ≤, >, ≥	relational op
→, ↔, ¬, **and**, **or**, **xor**	boolean op
∃, ∀, |, •	predicate logic op
∈, ∉, { }, ..	set op
: *TYPE*	type op

BON notation: static and dynamic diagrams

CLASS HEADERS

$(NAME)$ reused

$(NAME^{\bullet})$ persistent

$\left(\begin{array}{c} NAME \\ [G, H] \end{array}\right)$ parameterized

$\left(\begin{array}{c} * \\ NAME \end{array}\right)$ deferred

$\left(\begin{array}{c} + \\ NAME \end{array}\right)$ effective

$\left(\begin{array}{c} \blacktriangle \\ NAME \end{array}\right)$ interfaced

$((NAME))$ root

SCENARIO BOX

Scenario:
1   description
2   ...

OBJECT HEADERS

| NAME | one object

| NAME (*id*) | one object (qualified)

| NAME | one or more objects

OBJECT GROUPING

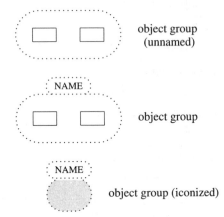

object group (unnamed)

object group

object group (iconized)

CLUSTERING

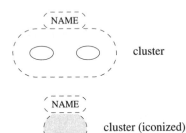

cluster

cluster (iconized)

STATIC LINKS

———▶   inheritance

═══▶   client association

═══{   client aggregation

MULTIPLICITY

⟨3⟩   ⟨2|4⟩   of relation

①   of shared instances

DYNAMIC LINKS

– – – ▶   message passing

DYNAMIC LABELS

1, 2   sequence number

STATIC LABELS

name
name1, *name2*
TYPE [...]
name: *TYPE* [...]
(*name1*, *name2*): *TYPE* [...]
→ *TYPE* [...]

Appendix D:
Other approaches

Below is a list of references to other approaches to object-oriented analysis and design. Only work that presents a distinct method has been included.

ASTS Development Method 3 (ADM3)
[Firesmith 1993]

the Booch Method
[Booch 1994]

Class-Relation
[Desfray 1992]

Class, Responsibility, Collaboration (CRC)
[Beck 1989]

the Fusion Method
[Coleman 1994]

General Object-Oriented Design (GOOD)
[Seidewitz 1987]

Hierarchical Object-Oriented Design (HOOD)
[Robinson 1992]

Methodology for Object-Oriented Development (MooD)
[Siemens 1993]

Methodology for Object-Oriented Software Engineering of Systems (MOSES)
[Henderson-Sellers 1994]

Object Behavior Analysis (OBA)
[Rubin 1992]

Object Modeling Technique (OMT)
[Rumbaugh 1991]

Object-Oriented Analysis/Object-Oriented Design (OOA/OOD)
[Coad 1991a, Coad 1991b]

Object-Oriented Analysis/Object-Oriented Design Language (OOA/OODLE)
[Shlaer 1992]

Object-Oriented Role Analysis, Synthesis, and Structuring (OORASS)
[Reenskaug 1992]

Object-Oriented Semantic Networks
[Berard 1991]

the Object-Oriented Software Development Method
[Colbert 1989]

Object-Oriented Specification (OOS)
[Bailin 1989]

Object-Oriented Structured Design (OOSD)
[Wasserman 1990]

Object-Oriented Systems Analysis (OSA)
[Embley 1992]

Objectory/OOSE
[Jacobson 1992]

Ptech
[Martin 1992]

Responsibility-Driven Design (RDD)
[Wirfs-Brock 1990]

Semantic Object Model (SOM)
[Velho 1992, Velho 1994]

Semantic Object Modelling Approach (SOMA)
[Graham 1994]

Synthropy
[Cook 1994]

Uniform Object Notation/Synthesis
[Page-Jones 1990]

Appendix E:
Glossary of terms

ABSTRACT CLASS.　*See* DEFERRED CLASS.

ABSTRACT DATA TYPE.　A type of data structure (often abbreviated ADT) defined exclusively through its external behavior. An ADT is specified by a number of applicable operations, how each operation may be invoked (the signature), and its effect (the semantics).

ABSTRACT FEATURE.　*See* DEFERRED FEATURE.

ABSTRACTION.　A conceptual model of something, which suppresses details that are less interesting in a certain context and instead emphasizes what is essential. Abstraction is the key tool for humans to understand the world—without it reasoning would not be possible. However, since essentiality is not an objective quality, the value of an abstraction depends entirely on what it is used for.

ACCESS CONTROL.　The selective mechanism by which clients are granted access to the features of a class. Public features are accessible to all clients, while restricted features may only be used by a specified group of clients. A private feature can only be called on the current object, and only by other features in the same class (or recursively by the feature itself). *See also* INFORMATION HIDING.

ACTIVE OBJECT.　An object playing an active role, that is driving a thread of control by calling other objects. The called objects then play the part of passive objects. Since being active is a role, the same object can be active in one scenario and passive in another. The role of acting in both capacities (being called and also calling other objects) is sometimes referred to as agent, and the corresponding objects are then called agents.

ACTOR.　Anything that can call a system object from the outside, such as a human operator, a sensory device, or another system.

Agent.   *See* Active object.

Aggregation.   A composition of a group of objects into an integral unit.

Aggregation relation.   A relation between an object and one of its integral parts. The exact semantics of this relation may vary from one case to another within the same system.

Analysis.   In normal usage, the process of breaking something down into its constituent parts to find out how it works. However, object-oriented analysis is often used in the alternative meaning of building a model of a problem domain.

Ancestor class.   A class from which another class, the Descendant, inherits directly or indirectly.

Application.   An executable system modeling some problem domain.

Architecture.   The major components of a system and the structural relations between them.

Assertion.   A software contracting element expressed as a logical statement (predicate). The assertions discussed in this book are routine pre- and postconditions and class invariants, which are used to define the semantics of a class without regard to implementation details. Complementary assertions, such as loop invariants, loop variants, and free assertions, may be used for reasoning about the correctness of a given implementation.

Association.   A relationship denoting a logical dependency between two classes.

Attribute.   A property of an object manifested as a function returning a value.

Behavior.   The way an object reacts to calls from other objects. The top-level object of a system, the root object (or root objects, in the case of concurrent object execution), is considered called by whatever starts the corresponding process.

Binary association.   A relationship between two entities in an entity–relationship model.

Binding.   The attachment of an object to an entity. An entity, in BON terminology, is any symbol used to refer to an object. *See also* Static binding and Dynamic binding.

Boolean algebra.   *See* Propositional logic.

BOTTOM-UP DESIGN.   The construction of something new from already existing parts. Opposite of TOP-DOWN DESIGN. Extensive reuse implies (by definition) a great deal of bottom-up design.

BROKER.   A special object, acting as mediator between client and server objects in distributed object-oriented applications. The term was introduced in the "Object Management Architecture Guide" published by the Object Management Group and X/Open [OMG 1990], and is an abbreviation for object request broker (ORB).

BUSINESS RULES.   Norms of a business that should not be violated by any system action. Such rules often manifest themselves as constraints on the persistent objects of the system.

CANDIDATE CLASS.   A concept that is a candidate to become a class in an object-oriented model. The first set of candidate classes usually results directly from a study of the problem domain.

CASE DISCRIMINATION.   The explicit enumeration of a set of possible system states and specification of a corresponding action for each case. Much of the potential of the object-oriented approach lies in reducing the number of case discriminations in a system by an order of magnitude through the systematic use of polymorphism and dynamic binding. (*See also* SINGLE CHOICE PRINCIPLE.)

CHILD CLASS.   A class that inherits directly from another class (the PARENT).

CLASS.   A description of the behavior of certain kinds of objects, called *instances* of the class. In this book, a class is viewed as an implementation of an abstract data type, and the semantics of the corresponding operations is specified through software contracts.

CLASS ATTRIBUTE.   A state variable (sometimes called *instance variable*) of a class. In this book, we do not consider the concept of metaclass as used in Smalltalk.

CLASS FEATURE.   *See* FEATURE.

CLASS INSTANCE.   An object built according to the description in a class; any number of instances may be built from the same class.

CLASS INTERFACE.   The collective interface of all the features of a class. The *public* interface is defined by the set of public features.

CLASS INVARIANT.   An assertion about every object of a certain class. The class invariant must be satisfied before and after execution of any public

feature of the class. This is more committing than the contracts of individual features, since not only all existing features but also all features added in the future must obey the class invariant.

CLASS METHOD. In Smalltalk, a class method refers to an operation applicable to the class itself rather than to an *instance* of the class. In this book, however, a class is not viewed as an object but merely as a description of object behavior. Therefore, a class method (or class feature) just means a feature of a class.

CLASSIFICATION. Systematic placement of objects in categories with respect to similarities and differences, often resulting in hierarchical orderings such as the Linnaean system for classification of plants and animals. The science or practice of classification is often called taxonomy after the branch of biology concerned with classification of organisms.

CLIENT. Either a client object calling another object (the supplier object), or a client class encapsulating a call to an object of another class (the supplier class). *See also* SUPPLIER.

CLIENT–SERVER. A general model in which a consumer (the client) can request service from a producer (the server) without knowing where the server is located (apart from its name) or how the services are implemented.

CLUSTER. A group of classes and/or other clusters selected according to some criteria to form a conceptual unit. A system may be partitioned into a hierarchical structure of non-overlapping clusters, called a *system view*. The same set of classes can be partitioned into different system views, but for practical purposes only one is usually maintained for a particular system. Clusters may be related to óther clusters and also to individual classes (in the same, or in other clusters).

CLUSTERING. The act of designing a cluster structure. The selection criteria are usually highly variable from one system to another, and also within the same system. Some clusters may represent fully fledged subsystems, while others merely collect a small group of classes with a common ancestor.

COHESION. A qualitative measure of how strongly the components of a module are related to each other. A highly cohesive module concentrates on a single task, and is therefore much easier to understand and maintain, compared to one with low cohesion, which coincidentally groups many unrelated tasks into one. *See also* COUPLING.

COLLABORATION. A term used to signify the cooperation of a set of objects calling each other to perform some overall task. *See also* RESPONSIBILITY.

COMMAND.   An operation on an object which does not return any value, but which may change the system state. *See also* QUERY.

COMPONENT LIBRARY.   A repository containing reusable components.

COMPRESSION.   In BON notation, most graphical elements can be compressed into less space consuming forms, or hidden completely. A case tool would keep the full information in its internal model, so compressed elements may again be expanded. Compression and expansion can be applied recursively, and the level of detail chosen for each part of a system diagram.

CONCRETE CLASS.   *See* EFFECTIVE CLASS.

CONSTRAINT.   Signifies some rule or restriction that applies to an object type or some of its operations. Complements the queries and commands of BON class charts to capture the semantics of a class, or general business rules. Some identified constraints usually translate into formal assertions during later phases, while others may instead influence the system design.

CONSTRUCTOR.   An operation which is given control directly after the creation of an object (before returning to whatever object issued the creation call) in order to complete the initialization. Constructors are needed when the default initialization values for the attributes of an object are not enough. In particular, a constructor must ensure that the class invariant is satisfied directly after an object is created. Some implementation languages permit the specification of alternative constructors for a given class.

CONTAINER CLASS.   A class representing a data structure that can hold objects as elements.

CONTRACT MODEL.   *See* DESIGN BY CONTRACT.

CONTRAVARIANT RULE.   A rule stating that argument types of a feature signature may be redefined to (and only to) ancestor types. *See also* COVARIANT RULE.

CONTROL FLOW.   The logical paths taken during execution of a system depending on various conditions of the system state.

COUPLING.   A qualitative measure of module interconnection in a software structure. Low coupling means that each module is relatively independent of other modules. This makes the system easier to understand and maintain, since it is possible to investigate one part in isolation without having to deal with the rest of the system concurrently. *See also* COHESION.

COVARIANT RULE.   A rule stating that argument types of a feature signature

may be redefined to (and only to) descendant types. *See also* CONTRAVARIANT RULE.

CURRENT OBJECT. Except for the root object (which is called from the surrounding operating system environment), the only way to invoke a feature of a class is to apply it to an object. While the feature is executing, this object then becomes the current object and is implicitly referred to whenever an unqualified call or an assignment to a state variable occurs.

DATA ABSTRACTION. An encapsulation of data that hides internal structural details and instead presents an external interface to clients.

DATA DICTIONARY. A description of all data types used in a software system. The term is typically used in connection with data modeling and relational database management systems.

DATA FLOW DIAGRAM. A graph showing the major data flows of a system at execution time and the successive transformation of data. Data flow diagrams (DFDs) are part of structured analysis methods.

DATA HIDING. *See* INFORMATION HIDING.

DATA MODELING. A modeling technique concentrating on the central data structures of a system, particularly the persistent parts. The most common approaches used in this context are variants of the entity–relationship (ER) modeling [Chen 1976].

DATABASE. A repository for storage of persistent data. A database could be anything from a flat file to a multi-disk, multi-platform distributed data set.

DBMS. Acronym for database management system. The mainstream DBMS products have developed from hierarchical systems, over network systems, into relational systems (RDBMS) and object-oriented database management systems (ODBMS).

DEFENSIVE PROGRAMMING. A programming style, also referred to as blind checking, where redundant error control is inserted in the program code. This leads to increased complexity and programs which are more difficult to understand and maintain. The reason for defensive programming is generally that no clear division of responsibility between client and supplier exists in the system. By contrast, the software contracting model specifies exactly who is responsible for what, and therefore represents the opposite of defensive programming.

DEFERRED CLASS. A class containing at least one feature which has no implementation (and never will have). Deferred classes cannot be

instantiated, but serve as partial specification for all corresponding descendant classes, which will fill in the missing details. Deferred classes are sometimes called abstract, and if no features are implemented, a deferred class can come very close to the mathematical specification of an abstract data type. *See also* EFFECTIVE CLASS.

DEFERRED FEATURE.   A feature that has no implementation (and never will have). It serves instead as a (full or partial) specification of all implemented versions of the feature that may occur in descendant classes. The opposite is EFFECTIVE FEATURE.

DELEGATION.   Refers to shared behavior in object-oriented systems using prototypes instead of classes [Lieberman 1986]. Delegation enables objects to reuse part of the knowledge stored in a prototype object representing the default behavior of a concept. This approach is adopted by the language Self [Ungar 1987].

DERIVED ATTRIBUTE.   An attribute in ER modeling that can be inferred from other attributes.

DESCENDANT CLASS.   A class which inherits directly or indirectly from another class, the ANCESTOR.

DESIGN.   In normal usage, the process of arranging or building something from a set of components. However, object-oriented design is often used in the alternative meaning of building a computer representation of an analysis model.

DESIGN BY CONTRACT.   A view of software development as a series of documented contracting decisions [Meyer 1992b]. In this book we use the phrase "software contracting".

DESTRUCTOR.   A class feature which is executed when an object of the corresponding class is finally destroyed. May be invoked by an automatic garbage collector or through some other mechanism.

DOMAIN ANALYSIS.   The analysis of a certain problem domain, particularly with the intent of finding common concepts that could be captured as reusable abstractions.

DOMAIN EXPERT.   A person with great skills and experience in a certain problem domain area.

DYNAMIC BINDING.   A mechanism permitting different behavior to result from the same feature call. Depending on the exact type of object attached to the entity on which a feature is called, different implementations may be

invoked at different points in time. The mechanism is crucial to eliminate the abundance of case discriminations that occur in most systems developed with traditional techniques. Dynamic binding is usually combined with inheritance. *See also* POLYMORPHISM.

DYNAMIC CHART. An informal BON chart recording dynamic behavior. There are currently three types of dynamic chart: event chart, scenario chart, and creation chart. *See also* STATIC CHART.

DYNAMIC MODEL. A model capturing a high-level description of the typical execution of a system in terms of time-ordered events. It concentrates on the *how* part to serve as complement to the *what* part represented by the STATIC MODEL.

DYNAMIC TYPE. The actual type of object attached to an object reference at any given moment. *See also* STATIC TYPE.

DYNAMIC TYPING. A typing scheme where each object has a well-defined type, but where the type of each symbol used in a description is not explicitly specified. Type correctness can only be checked at run-time. Smalltalk is an example of an object-oriented language with dynamic typing. *See also* STATIC TYPING.

EFFECTIVE CLASS. A class all of whose features are effective. Objects taking part in a system execution must be instances of effective classes. *See also* DEFERRED CLASS.

EFFECTIVE FEATURE. A feature which has an implementation attached to its specification. Opposite of DEFERRED FEATURE.

ENCAPSULATION. *See* INFORMATION HIDING.

ENTITY. The term entity in BON stands for any symbol used to refer to an object, such as a state variable, a feature argument, or a local variable.

ENTITY–RELATIONSHIP DIAGRAM. A diagram showing the data entities in a system and the relationships between them, usually adorned with semantic labels. Often abbreviated ER diagram or ERD.

ER MODELING. Abbreviation for entity–relationship modeling, which uses ER diagrams to describe the most important data elements in a system (particularly the persistent parts).

EVENT. *See* SYSTEM EVENT.

EVENT TRACE. A graph or table showing a series of events that may occur in a system. Event trace diagrams usually represent time on one axis and communicating objects on the other.

EXCEPTION HANDLING.   The handling of contract violations at execution time. A contract violation occurs when something happens which is outside the scope of the system specification.

EXPANSION.   *See* COMPRESSION.

EXTENSIBILITY.   A system quality permitting many requirements changes to be incorporated in the system without extensive redesign and corresponding high cost.

FEATURE.   An operation applicable to an object. The term feature also covers the concept of class attribute at implementation time, that is state variables.

FEATURE CALL.   The invocation of an operation on an object.

FINITE STATE MACHINE (FSM).   A machine which accepts a sequence of input events and produces a sequence of output events. Each input and output event belongs to a finite set of events, and each output event depends both on the corresponding input event and on the past history of input events. Typical examples of FSMs are telephone switching circuits and vending machines.

FIRST-ORDER LOGIC.   A logic where the formal elements may range over objects in sets, but not over all subsets of sets.

FRAMEWORK.   A set of classes representing an object-oriented abstract design. Typically, a user may tailor the behavior of a framework by client calls to public framework routines, or by definition or redefinition of features inherited from framework classes.

FSM MODELING.   Using finite state machines (FSMs) to describe the dynamic behavior of a system or some of its parts.

GARBAGE COLLECTION.   The reclamation of allocated object space that is no longer needed in a system. Memory management is a central issue in object-oriented systems, since very often large numbers of objects are created which only live for a relatively short time. The primary memory occupied by these transient objects needs to be reused lest the system run out of available object space. Modern automatic garbage collectors can relieve the user of the tedious and extremely error-prone task of manual memory administration with little execution overhead.

GENERALIZATION.   The act of detecting a general pattern in a concrete problem solution and capturing the higher-level essence, so it can be reused to solve related problems. This is often done by introducing new deferred classes in the inheritance hierarchies of a system. *See also* SPECIALIZATION.

GENERIC CLASS.   *See* PARAMETERIZED CLASS.

GROUP.   *See* OBJECT GROUP.

HIERARCHY.   A structure with a top-level component, where each component may have any number of subcomponents, and where each component (except the top component) is a subcomponent of exactly one other component.

HYBRID TECHNIQUE.   A technique mixing different paradigms in the same approach.

IDENTITY.   *See* OBJECT IDENTITY.

IMPLEMENTATION.   The refinement of a software design to the point where the resulting description is directly executable on some supporting platform.

INCREMENTAL DEVELOPMENT.   A software development technique which starts by producing a system with minimal functionality, barely enough to be useful, and then proceeds to gradually add functionality in small increments. Since each successive system version is tested and validated by actual usage, the risk of going in the wrong direction is greatly reduced and the cost estimation for each increment becomes much more feasible compared to large monolithic developments. Incremental development matches the basic object-oriented ideas very well.

INDEXING.   The addition of keywords and index terms to classes in order to improve documentation and facilitate the search for reusable components in class libraries.

INFORMATION HIDING.   A technique whereby implementation details likely to change in the future are hidden from the authors of client modules, who are instead presented with a public interface. In spite of the name, the intent is usually not so much to hide the information as to prevent clients from becoming dependent on it.

INHERITANCE.   A mechanism allowing a module to share the behavior defined in another module, but still be able to modify it and to add new behavior. Some researchers advocate separation between inheritance of *specification* and inheritance of *implementation*, but this book takes the opposite view.

INSTANCE.   *See* CLASS INSTANCE.

INSTANCE MULTIPLICITY.   The number of instances of a given class that may be attached to another object through a named reference. Often expressed as a range and referred to as a "cardinality constraint" in data modeling. *See also* ROLE MULTIPLICITY.

INSTANCE SHARING.   The same object being attached to several other objects, which then share its resources.

INSTANCE VARIABLE.   The Smalltalk name for state variables.

INSTANTIATION.   The process of creating new objects according to the description in a class.

INTERFACE CLASS.   A class serving as (part of) the interface to a cluster of classes. Classes outside the cluster only use the interface classes, while these in turn use the rest of the classes in the cluster to implement the external behavior.

INVARIANT.   *See* CLASS INVARIANT.

LATE BINDING.   *See* DYNAMIC BINDING.

LAYER.   A set of classes and corresponding operations at the same level of abstraction. *See also* CLUSTER.

LEVEL OF ABSTRACTION.   A set of system components representing distinct concepts in a given context. The levels of abstraction in a system are partially ordered so that a given component depends only on components at the same or lower levels.

LINK.   The graphical representation of a relation between elements in BON. Client links and inheritance links relate classes and clusters in static diagrams, while message links relate objects and object groups in dynamic diagrams.

MEMBER FUNCTION.   A class feature in C++ terminology. Corresponds to a query or a command in BON terminology, depending on whether or not it returns a value.

MESSAGE.   A feature call in Smalltalk terminology.

METACLASS.   A Smalltalk concept whose instances are classes. There is no correspondence to metaclasses in BON, since classes are strictly regarded as descriptions of object behavior, and not as objects.

METALANGUAGE.   A language used to reason about another language. Mixing language and metalanguage without a clear syntactic separation between the two levels can lead to severe misunderstandings.

METHOD.   A technique or arrangement of work for a particular field or subject.

METHOD (OF A CLASS).   A class feature in Smalltalk terminology.

METHODOLOGY.   Often used as a synonym for method, but signifies more properly the system of methods used in a discipline, or the general science of method and procedure.

MIXIN.   In CLOS terminology, a class which is inherited to get access to certain utility features.

MULTIPLE INHERITANCE.   A mechanism allowing one class to inherit simultaneously from more than one parent class.

MULTIPLICITY.   *See* INSTANCE MULTIPLICITY and ROLE MULTIPLICITY.

NAMING.   The procedure of giving names to concepts in a system. Proper naming is extremely important for the understandability of a system.

OBJECT.   The basic components of an object-oriented system, exhibiting well-defined behavior in response to a number of applicable operations. Also called CLASS INSTANCE.

OBJECT CLASS.   Sometimes used in data modeling to signify a type of object, as opposed to OBJECT INSTANCE. In object-oriented contexts, the term is confusing and should not be used.

OBJECT DIAGRAM.   A graphical description of a scenario showing message passing between objects.

OBJECT GROUP.   A group of objects that are treated collectively in some context. In a BON dynamic diagram, messages may be passed to an object group signifying that one or more of the objects are called.

OBJECT GROUPING.   The process of finding adequate object groups.

OBJECT IDENTITY.   The concept of a unique identity which distinguishes an object from all other objects, regardless of whether their internal structures and values coincide or not. All objects are created with a unique identity in an object-oriented system, so the user need not worry about introducing access keys.

OBJECT INSTANCE.   Sometimes used in data modeling to signify an instance of a type, as opposed to OBJECT CLASS. In object-oriented contexts, the term is confusing and should not be used.

OBJECT MANAGEMENT.   The storage and retrieval of persistent objects.

OBJECT-ORIENTED.   A term signifying that a certain system or method includes support for abstract data types combined with inheritance, polymorphism, and dynamic binding.

OBJECT-ORIENTED ABSTRACTION.   An abstraction represented as a class, which describes the behavior of a certain type of object through applicable operations.

OBJECT-ORIENTED ANALYSIS.   An object-oriented model of a problem domain—or the process of creating such a model.

OBJECT-ORIENTED DATABASE.   A database and corresponding environment with direct support for storing not only the data parts of an object, but also its operations and references to other objects.

OBJECT-ORIENTED DESIGN.   An object-oriented model of a computer representation of a problem—or the process of creating such a model.

OBJECT-ORIENTED ENCAPSULATION.   *See* OBJECT-ORIENTED ABSTRACTION.

OBJECT-ORIENTED EXECUTION.   System execution viewed exclusively as a set of objects passing messages to each other.

OBJECT-ORIENTED IMPLEMENTATION.   Implementation of software using an object-oriented language.

OBJECT-ORIENTED MODEL.   A model expressed as a structure of classes with specified operations, related through inheritance and client dependencies.

OBJECT-ORIENTED MODELING.   The process of creating an object-oriented model.

OBJECT-ORIENTED PROGRAMMING LANGUAGE.   An executable language which directly supports abstract data types, inheritance, and dynamic binding. The three object-oriented languages attracting most attention in industry today are C++, Smalltalk, and Eiffel.

OBJECT-ORIENTED SOFTWARE DEVELOPMENT.   The process of developing software using object-oriented analysis, design, and implementation.

OBJECT-ORIENTED SPECIFICATION.   The process of specifying a system as a set of cooperating objects with well-defined behavior. Software contracting combined with strong typing can be used to capture the semantics of such a system.

OBJECT-ORIENTED SYSTEM.   A system built using object-oriented techniques. Notice that this is not the same as a system exhibiting object-oriented user metaphors, such as graphical items that may be manipulated by the user, resizing of windows, drag and drop, and so forth. The latter kinds of system need not be object oriented at all (although this is certainly an advantage for their future maintenance).

OBJECT STATE.   That part of the system state that has an effect on the future behavior of an object. Object state often corresponds to one or more ATTRIBUTES of the object, but this does not necessarily mean that data is stored in the object itself.

ODBMS.   Acronym for object database management systems. (This term is gradually replacing the longer name OODBMS as the "-oriented" part is being dropped.)

OOA.   Acronym for object-oriented analysis.

OOD.   Acronym for object-oriented design.

OOPL.   Acronym for object-oriented programming language.

OPERATION.   *See* FEATURE.

OVERLOADING.   A mechanism permitting the same name to be used in different contexts with different meanings.

PARADIGM.   A fundamental way of viewing a problem area which is generally accepted by a large number of people. A paradigm is generally difficult to question, because its perceived truth is often an integral part of a culture and has a profound impact on how we think. Its followers may not be aware of the paradigm at all; they just unconsciously take its implications for granted. Switching to object-oriented modeling means a paradigm shift for some people, notably those heavily trained in the so-called structured techniques.

PARAMETERIZED CLASS.   A class from which a number of related types may be derived, depending on a number of furnished type parameters. *STACK [BOOK]* and *STACK [INTEGER]* are typical examples of two types derived from the same parameterized class *STACK [T]*. Also called generic class.

PARENT CLASS.   A class from which another class, the CHILD, inherits.

PARTIAL FUNCTION.   A function which is not defined for all possible argument values (as opposed to a TOTAL FUNCTION).

PARTIAL ROUTINE.   A query or command which is not defined for all possible argument values and system states (thus having a precondition which is different from *true*). Partial routines play a central role in software development, since in many cases they permit a much simpler and concise solution compared to a corresponding total routine, which has to handle lots of irrelevant cases for which there is no reasonable response. Combining

partial routines with software contracts allows precise specification of who is responsible for checking: the client or the supplier.

PASSIVE OBJECT.   *See* ACTIVE OBJECT.

PERSISTENT CLASS.   A class whose instances are persistent.

PERSISTENT OBJECT.   An object whose life span is independent of any system session. It may reside in either primary or secondary storage.

PHYSICAL OBJECT.   An object perceived as physical by people in a problem domain.

POLYMORPHISM.   A mechanism by which a named reference, also called an *entity*, can be attached to objects of different type at different points in time. Unconstrained polymorphism (as in Smalltalk) permits any entity to refer to any type of object, while in a typed language (such as Eiffel) an entity may only be attached to objects of the declared type or a descendant type. Polymorphism is sometimes used as a synonym for DYNAMIC BINDING.

POSTCONDITION.   A predicate which must be true just after the execution of a public feature, provided the feature's precondition was fulfilled when the execution started. *See also* PRECONDITION.

PRECONDITION.   A predicate that must be true when a public feature is called by a client. *See also* POSTCONDITION.

PREDICATE LOGIC.   A logic that apart from constant objects also uses formal variables ranging over objects in its expressions. Predicate logic is a generalization of propositional (or sentential) logic, and is also known as predicate calculus.

PRIVATE FEATURE.   A feature which is not publicly available to clients. It may only be invoked on the current object by features in the same class.

PROBLEM DOMAIN.   A certain application area or other context, in which a problem is to be solved with the help of computer software.

PROGRAMMING-IN-THE-LARGE.   The act of combining high-level components into tailored configurations to fit the needs of a particular application. The term was coined in [DeRemer 1976], which discusses module interconnection languages.

PROPERTY.   An (abstract) attribute of an object, either accessible directly through some query or else indirectly inferable through system behavior.

PROPOSITIONAL LOGIC.   A logic whose expressions are built from primitive

sentences (considered true or false) and logical connectives, such as *not*, *and*, *or*, *implies*, *equals*. Also known as propositional calculus, sentential logic, or boolean algebra.

PROTOCOL. A Smalltalk term denoting the collective signatures of all features (methods) of a class.

PROXY. An object acting on behalf of another object, but appearing to the client as being that other object. Typically used in distributed object-oriented systems to implement transparent calls across networks in client–server architectures.

PUBLIC FEATURE. A feature which is publicly available to all clients.

PURE TECHNIQUE. A technique which does not mix elements of other paradigms with its own view.

QUERY. An operation on an object which returns a value, but does not alter the system state. *See also* COMMAND. Strict separation of object behavior into state changing procedures (commands) and side-effect-free value returning functions (queries) is of fundamental importance for the ability to reason about the correctness of a class.

RECURSIVE SPECIFICATION. A specification technique in which the conceptual base for expressing specification and implementation is the same. Removing the artificial barriers between specification and implementation (which is possible with object-oriented abstraction) gives developers a chance to keep code and specification consistent during the lifetime of a system, since the two will move in concert.

REDEFINITION. A modification in a descendant class of the implementation of an inherited feature.

RELATION. A dependency between two entities; used in this book as an abbreviation for the term relationship. BON includes three types of relation: inheritance, client, and message.

RELATIONSHIP. *See* RELATION.

RENAMING. A modification of the name of an inherited feature in a descendant class. This is a purely syntactic device, which allows more proper names to be used when the role of an inherited concept is altered.

REPEATED INHERITANCE. The same feature being inherited more than once from a class.

RESPONSIBILITY. A term used to emphasize the behavior of an object rather

than its structure. An object may be responsible for certain system actions and for maintaining certain information, but instead of dealing directly with the processing or data storage, the object may call on other objects behind the scenes to do the job. *See also* COLLABORATION.

RESTRICTED FEATURE.   A feature which is only publicly available to specific clients.

REUSABLE LIBRARY.   *See* COMPONENT LIBRARY.

REUSE MANAGER.   Someone responsible for the component libraries and for maintaining the reuse policy of an organization.

REUSED CLASS.   A class that is reused and possibly adapted from previous developments. Marked with underscore in BON static diagrams.

REVERSIBILITY.   The possibility of seamlessly translating changes made during a certain development phase back into earlier phases, so as to maintain consistency.

ROBUSTNESS.   The ability of a system to function reasonably also in situations that should never occur according to the system specifications. Robustness cannot be defined precisely, but includes things like restoring class invariants, guarding persistent data from corruption, stating the problem as clearly as possible to a system operator, saving traces for manual recovery, etc.

ROLE.   The purpose for which a certain class is used. Roles in combination with their corresponding types are crucial for understanding a system, since they reflect not only what abstractions are employed, but also how they are used in various contexts.

ROLE MULTIPLICITY.   The number of client relations from a client class to a supplier class. Each relation corresponds to the supplier being used by the client to fulfill a certain role. The number of instances involved in each relation may vary. *See also* INSTANCE MULTIPLICITY.

ROLE NAME.   The name of a role, usually captured as a symbol (entity) which is attached to an object. Sometimes the role name is the same as the class name, which means the class is just used in its general sense. In other cases the role name may reflect a typical specialization or a type of usage that was never anticipated.

ROOT CLASS.   A class of which one instance will be created when an object-oriented process is started, and whose initialization routine drives the execution.

ROOT OBJECT.   The root class instance created when an object-oriented execution starts.

SCALABILITY.   The ability of a method and notation to scale up from small textbook examples to sizable real applications without losing usability. For a notation, a "zooming" capability is essential so views can be presented at different levels without losing the overall system structure. BON uses compression and expansion to achieve this.

SCENARIO.   A script of a possible system execution showing the objects involved, which other objects they call, and the temporal order of these calls.

SEAMLESSNESS.   The quality of natural translation from problem domain specification, over system design, into executable code. To be really effective with respect to reuse and ease of maintenance, seamlessness needs to be combined with REVERSIBILITY.

SELF.   The Smalltalk term for the CURRENT OBJECT. Corresponds to *this* in C++ and *Current* in Eiffel.

SEMANTIC DATA MODEL.   A data model capturing the usage and meaning of information in a system that can be used as a basis for structuring the system data.

SEMANTIC LABEL.   In ER modeling, a label on a relationship between two entities stating its meaning. Sometimes used in BON as an attachment to an inheritance link to convey the designer's intent, or as a complement to the role name of a client link.

SERVER.   An object which provides a number of services to clients, often in parallel.

SERVICE.   One or a set of related operations that may be requested from a server.

SIDE EFFECT.   A system state change taking place as a result of calling a value returning function. Side effects are dangerous, because when they occur, there is no guarantee that a query will return the same result when called repeatedly. This makes logical reasoning about program correctness much more difficult. Maintaining a clear separation between state changing commands and side-effect-free queries may sometimes require a few extra instructions in an implementation, but the cost is negligible in view of the added clarity of the system.

SIGNATURE.   The type of the return value of a feature, if any, and the number

and types of all arguments, if any. The signature specifies the syntax of a feature call, while contracting elements in the form of assertions capture its semantics.

SINGLE CHOICE PRINCIPLE.   A principle stating that whenever there is a choice between a number of alternatives which the system needs to keep track of, the exact list should be known in only *one* module. The advantage is that updates to the list can be done in one place and will immediately take effect in all other parts of the system. With object-oriented techniques it is possible to come close to a strict application of this principle by relying heavily on dynamic binding.

SINGLE INHERITANCE.   The process of inheriting from at most one parent class.

SOFTWARE CONTRACTING.   *See* DESIGN BY CONTRACT.

SOFTWARE ENGINEERING.   A term which was invented by Douglas McIlroy in 1968 and presented at a NATO conference [McIlroy 1976]. It expressed a wish for the future rather than a description of the way software was produced at the time. McIlroy envisioned a software components industry, and the greatest potential of the object-oriented approach today lies in the eventual realization of this dream, which has proved much more difficult than expected.

SOFTWARE SYSTEM.   A set of executable components cooperating to fulfill a certain purpose.

SPECIALIZATION.   The act of adding more detail to a general pattern in order to solve a problem which fits the principles of the pattern. This is often done by introducing new descendant classes in the inheritance hierarchies of a system. *See also* GENERALIZATION.

STATE.   A summary of the current situation in some context (state of affairs). *See also* SYSTEM STATE and OBJECT STATE.

STATE TRANSITION DIAGRAM.   A graph depicting a number of states and possible transitions between them.

STATE VARIABLE.   A physical class attribute holding a value.

STATIC BINDING.   The act of deciding which version of a routine will be invoked as a result of a feature call based only on the static type of the reference used for calling the feature. Static binding contradicts one of the most important ideas in the object-oriented paradigm: to favor polymorphism and dynamic binding. If it is to be applied for efficiency, this should be done automatically behind the scenes by an optimizing

compiler, since only then can it be guaranteed that the statically bound version is also the correct one.

STATIC CHART. An informal BON chart recording static structure. There are currently three types of static chart: system chart, cluster chart, and class chart. *See also* DYNAMIC CHART.

STATIC MODEL. A model which shows the structure of a system: how modules and objects are related and depend on each other. A static model concentrates on the description of a system's behavior embodied in the specification given by the system classes, representing the *what* part. *See also* DYNAMIC MODEL.

STATIC TYPE. The declared type of an object reference. During system execution, only objects of this type or descendant types may be attached to the reference. *See also* DYNAMIC TYPE.

STATIC TYPING. A typing scheme (also called *strong typing*) where each object has a well-defined type, and where the type of each symbol used in a description is explicitly specified. In a statically typed language, a compiler can check before execution that there will always be an appropriate implementation to take care of every feature call. Eiffel and (to a lesser extent) C++ are examples of object-oriented languages with static typing.

STEPWISE REFINEMENT. A method of successively refining a high-level design until an executable level is reached.

STIMULUS. *See* SYSTEM EVENT.

STRONG TYPING. *See* STATIC TYPING.

SUBCLASS. A class which inherits from another class, directly or indirectly. Same as DESCENDANT CLASS.

SUBSYSTEM. A sizable part of a system, which is relatively independent of other parts and reasonably complete with regards to its function.

SUPERCLASS. The Smalltalk term for ANCESTOR CLASS.

SUPPLIER. Either a supplier object being called by another object (the client object), or a supplier class encapsulating a feature which is called by a feature of another class. *See also* CLIENT.

SYSTEM. *See* SOFTWARE SYSTEM.

SYSTEM BEHAVIOR. The collective behavior of the objects in a system.

SYSTEM EVENT. Something to which a system will respond with a certain

behavior. Typical events are keyboard input, data from sensory devices, and calls from other systems.

SYSTEM STATE. The sum of all information stored in a system. The system state is a representation of its history of events, although only those events that were actually recorded (explicitly or implicitly) may influence the future behavior of the system. Depending on system state and incoming events, the state may be changed by the commands in the system. Such a change is also called a transition from one state to another.

SYSTEM VIEW. In BON terminology, a system view is a hierarchical partitioning of the classes of a system into possibly nested clusters. The clustering structure is orthogonal to the classes and does not change the semantics or interfaces of these. The structure is merely a help for a human reader to better understand the system, albeit a very important one. Several system views are possible for the same set of classes, but in practice only one is elaborated.

TANGIBLE OBJECT. *See* PHYSICAL OBJECT.

THIS. The C++ term for CURRENT OBJECT. Corresponds to *self* in Smalltalk and *Current* in Eiffel.

TOP-DOWN DESIGN. A method of starting with the functions required at the highest level of a system and recursively decomposing these functions into smaller parts until an executable level is reached.

TOTAL FUNCTION. A function which is defined for all possible argument values, as opposed to a PARTIAL FUNCTION.

TRANSIENT OBJECT. The opposite of PERSISTENT OBJECT. Transient objects are destroyed when the execution of a system is over.

TRANSITION. A change from one state to another. *See* SYSTEM STATE.

TRADER. Roughly equivalent to object request broker. The term was introduced by the Advanced Network Systems Architecture (ANSA) project [Marshak 1991].

TUPLE. An ordered set of values, each from a specific domain. The term is used in the relational data model, and usually called *row* in commercial DBMS products and industry. A *relation* in this model (usually called *table* in industry) is a set of tuples drawn from the same cartesian product of domains.

TYPE. The pattern of behavior of a certain kind of object, specified as a

number of applicable operations and their semantics. A type is roughly equivalent to a class in this book, except that parameterized classes give rise to different types, depending on the type of the furnished parameters.

TYPE DERIVATION.   The act of deriving a specific type from a generic (parameterized) class.

TYPE INSTANTIATION.   *See* TYPE DERIVATION.

TYPING.   The policy with regard to types employed by a language. *See also* STATIC TYPING and DYNAMIC TYPING.

USE.   In this book, using a class means being a client of the class.

USE CASE.   A type of usage of a system. Roughly equivalent to a scenario in BON.

USER METAPHOR.   The mental model a system user has of the internal workings of a system.

VIEW.   *See* SYSTEM VIEW.

VIRTUAL FUNCTION.   In C++, a feature whose calls will be effected using dynamic binding.

VISIBILITY.   Specifies whether an operation is available to a client or not. Public features are always available, while restricted features may only be used by a certain group of classes and private features may only be called on the current object by features of the same class.

VOID REFERENCE.   A reference which is not attached to any object.

References

Adams 1994.

>Greg Adams and Jean-Pierre Corriveau. "Capturing Object Interactions." *Proc. Technology of Object-Oriented Languages and Systems* (TOOLS 13, Versailles, France, Mar. 1994), Prentice Hall, Hemel Hempstead, England, 1994.

Alexander 1977.

>Christopher Alexander, Sara Ishikawa, and Murray Silverstein. *A Pattern Language*. Oxford University Press, New York, 1977.

Alexander 1987.

>James H. Alexander. "Painless Panes for Smalltalk Windows." *Proc. Object-Oriented Programming Systems, Languages, and Applications (OOPSLA '87)* in *ACM SIGPLAN Notices* **22**(12), Orlando, FL, Oct. 1987, pp. 287–294.

Allworth 1990.

>R. T. Allworth and R. N. Zobel. *Introduction to Real Time Software Design*. 2nd edn, Macmillan, London, 1990.

Arango 1989.

>Guillermo Arango. "Domain Analysis: From Art to Engineering Discipline." *Proc. Fifth Int. Workshop on Software Specification and Design*, Pittsburgh, PA, May 1989, pp. 152–159.

Bailin 1989.

>Sidney C. Bailin. "An Object-Oriented Requirements Specification Method." *Commun. ACM* **32**(5), May 1989, pp. 608–623.

Beck 1989.

>Kent Beck and Ward Cunningham. "A Laboratory for Teaching Object-Oriented Thinking." *Proc. Object-Oriented Programming Systems, Languages, and Applications (OOPSLA '89)* in *ACM SIGPLAN Notices* **24**(10), New Orleans, LA, Oct. 1989, pp. 1–6.

Berard 1991.

>Ed Berard. "Object-Oriented Semantic Networks." Berard Software Engineering Inc., Gaithersburg, MA, 1991.

Blaha 1994.
  Michael Blaha, William Premerlani, and Hwa Shen. "Converting OO Models into RDBMS Schema." *IEEE Software* **11**(3), May 1994, pp. 28–39.

Boehm 1981.
  Barry W. Boehm. *Software Engineering Economics*. Prentice Hall, Englewood Cliffs, NJ, 1981.

Booch 1994.
  Grady Booch. *Object-Oriented Analysis and Design with Applications*. 2nd edn, Benjamin/Cummings, Redwood City, CA, 1994.

Booth 1989.
  P. Booth. *An Introduction to Human–Computer Interaction,* chapter 4. Lawrence Erlbaum Assoc., Hillsdale, NJ, 1989.

Bracha 1993.
  Gilad Bracha and David Griswold. "Strongtalk: Typechecking Smalltalk in a Production Environment." *Proc. Object-Oriented Programming Systems, Languages, and Applications (OOPSLA '93)* in *ACM SIGPLAN Notices* **28**(10), Washington, DC, Oct. 1993, pp. 215–230.

Brooks 1975.
  Frederick P. Brooks, Jr. *The Mythical Man-Month*. Addison-Wesley, Reading, MA, 1975.

Brooks 1987.
  Frederick P. Brooks, Jr. "No Silver Bullet: Essence and Accidents of Software Engineering." *IEEE Computer* **20**(4), Apr. 1987, pp. 10–19.

Carroll 1982.
  J. M. Carroll and J. Thomas. "Metaphor and the Cognitive Representation of Computing Systems." *IEEE Trans. Systems, Man, and Cybernetics* **SMC–12**(2), Mar./Apr. 1982.

Cattel 1991.
  R. G. G. Cattel. *Object Data Management: Object-Oriented and Extended Relational Database Systems*. Addison-Wesley, Reading, MA, 1991.

Charette 1989.
  Robert N. Charette. *Software Engineering Risk Analysis and Management*. McGraw-Hill, New York, 1989.

Chen 1976.
  Peter Pin-Shan Chen. "The Entity–Relationship Model—Toward a Unified View of Data." *ACM Trans. Database Systems* **1**(1), Mar. 1976, pp. 9–36.

Coad 1991a.
  Peter Coad and Edward Yourdon. *Object-Oriented Analysis*. 2nd edn, Prentice Hall, Englewood Cliffs, NJ, 1991.

Coad 1991b.

Peter Coad and Edward Yourdon. *Object-Oriented Design.* Prentice Hall, Englewood Cliffs, NJ, 1991.

Codd 1970.

E. F. Codd. "A Relational Model of Data for Large Shared Data Banks." *Commun. ACM* **13**(6), June 1970, pp. 377–387.

Codd 1985a.

E. F. Codd. "Is your DBMS really relational?" *Computer World*, Oct. 14, 1985, pp. ID/1–9.

Codd 1985b.

E. F. Codd. "Does your DBMS run by the rules?" *Computer World*, Oct. 21, 1985, pp. 49–60.

Codd 1990.

E. F. Codd. *The Relational Model for Database Management: Version 2.* Addison-Wesley, Reading, MA, 1990.

Colbert 1989.

E. Colbert. "The Object-Oriented Software Development Method: A practical approach to object-oriented development." *Proc. Tri-Ada*, New York, 1989.

Coleman 1994.

Derek Coleman, Patrick Arnold, Stephanie Bodoff, Chris Dollin, Helena Gilchrist, Fiona Hayes, and Paul Jeremes. *Object-Oriented Development: The Fusion Method.* Prentice Hall, Englewood Cliffs, NJ, 1994.

Constantine 1968.

Larry L. Constantine. "The Programming Profession, Programming Theory, and Programming Education." *Computers and Automation* **17**(2), 1968, pp. 14–19.

Cook 1994.

Steve Cook and John Daniels. *Designing Object Systems.* Prentice Hall, Hemel Hempstead, England, 1994.

Cook 1992.

William R. Cook. "Interfaces and Specifications for the Smalltalk-80 Collection Classes." *Proc. Object-Oriented Programming Systems, Languages, and Applications (OOPSLA '92)* in *ACM SIGPLAN Notices* **27**(10), Vancouver, Canada, Oct. 1992, pp. 1–15.

Cypher 1986.

A. Cypher. "The Structure of User Activities." In *User Centered System Design*, D. A. Norman and S. W. Draper (eds). Lawrence Erlbaum Assoc., Hillsdale, NJ, 1986.

Date 1983.

C. J. Date. *An Introduction to Database Systems,* Vol. II. Addison-Wesley, Reading, MA, 1983.

Date 1990.

C. J. Date. *An Introduction to Database Systems,* Vol. I. 5th edn, Addison-Wesley, Reading, MA, 1990 (6th edn to appear 1994).

Date 1993.

C. J. Date *with* Hugh Darwen. *A Guide to the SQL Standard.* Addison-Wesley, Reading, MA, 1993.

DeRemer 1976.

Frank DeRemer and Hans H. Kron. "Programming-in-the-Large versus Programming-in-the-Small." *IEEE Trans. Software Engineering* **SE-2**(2), June 1976, pp. 80–86.

Desfray 1992.

P. Desfray. *Ingénerie des Objets: Approche class-relation application à C++.* Editions Masson, Paris, 1992.

Dijkstra 1972.

Edsger W. Dijkstra. "Notes on Structured Programming (EWD 249, .Technical Univ. Eindhoven, 1969)." In *Structured Programming*, C. Anthony R. Hoare (ed.). Academic Press, London, 1972, pp. 1–82.

Dijkstra 1976.

Edsger W. Dijkstra. *A Discipline of Programming.* Prentice Hall, Englewood Cliffs, NJ, 1976.

Dijkstra 1982.

Edsger W. Dijkstra. "How to Tell Truths that Might Hurt?" In *Selective Writings on Computing: A Personal Perspective.* Springer-Verlag, New York, 1982, pp. 129–131.

Douglas 1983.

S. Douglas and Thomas P. Moran. "Learning text-editing semantics by analogy." *Proc. ACM Human Factors in Computing Systems (CHI '83),* Boston, MA, Dec. 1983.

Embley 1992.

David W. Embley, Barry D. Kurtz, and Scott N. Woodfield. *Object-Oriented Systems Analysis: A Model-Driven Approach.* Prentice Hall, Englewood Cliffs, NJ, 1992.

Farmer 1990.

William M. Farmer. "A Partial Functions Version of Church's Simple Theory of Types." *The Journal of Symbolic Logic* **55**(3), Sept. 1990, pp. 1269–1291.

Firesmith 1993.

Donald G. Firesmith. *Object-Oriented Requirements Analysis and Logical Design: A Software Engineering Approach.* John Wiley, New York, 1993.

Floyd 1967.

Robert W. Floyd. "Assigning Meanings to Programs." *Proc. Symposium in Applied Mathematics* **19**, J. T. Schwartz (ed), American Mathematical Society, 1967, pp. 19–31.

Gabriel 1991.

Richard P. Gabriel, Jon L. White, and Daniel G. Bobrow. "CLOS: Integrating Object-Oriented and Functional Programming." *Commun. ACM* **34**(9), Sept. 1991, pp. 28–38.

Gilb 1988.

Tom Gilb. *Principles of Software Engineering Management.* Addison-Wesley, Reading, MA, 1988.

Goldberg 1991.

Adele Goldberg. "Object-Oriented Project Management." *Technology of Object-Oriented Languages and Systems* (TOOLS 4, Paris, Mar. 1991), tutorial documentation, SOL, Paris, 1991.

Goldberg 1983.

Adele Goldberg and David Robson. *Smalltalk-80: The Language and its implementation.* Addison-Wesley, Reading, MA, 1983.

Gougen 1978.

Joseph A. Gougen, Jim W. Thatcher, and E. G. Wagner. "An Initial Algebra Approach to the Specification, Correctness, and Implementation of Abstract Data Types." In *Current Trends in Programming Methodology*, Raymond T. Yeh (ed.). Prentice Hall, Englewood Cliffs, NJ, 1978, pp. 80–149.

Gould 1988.

J. D. Gould. "How to Design Usable Systems." In *Handbook of Human Computer Interaction,* chapter 35, M. Helander (ed.). Elsevier Science Publisher, North-Holland, New York, 1988.

Graham 1994.

Ian Graham. *Object-Oriented Methods.* Addison-Wesley, Wokingham, England, 1994.

Grape 1992.

Per Grape and Kim Waldén. "Automating the Development of Syntax Tree Generators for an Evolving Language." *Proc. Technology of Object-Oriented Languages and Systems* (TOOLS 8, Santa Barbara, Aug. 1992), Prentice Hall, Englewood Cliffs, NJ, 1992, pp. 185–195.

Guttag 1977.

John V. Guttag. "Abstract Data Types and the Development of Data Structures." *Commun. ACM* **20**(6), June 1977, pp. 396–404.

Halbert 1987.

Daniel C. Halbert and Patrick D. O'Brien. "Using Types and Inheritance in Object-Oriented Programming." *IEEE Software* **4**(5), Sept. 1987, pp. 71–79.

Harel 1988.

David Harel. "On Visual Formalisms." *Commun. ACM* **31**(5), May 1988, pp. 514–530.

Hehner 1984.

Eric. C. R. Hehner. *The Logic of Programming.* Prentice Hall, Englewood Cliffs, NJ, 1984.

Henderson-Sellers 1994.

Brian Henderson-Sellers. *Book Two of Object-Oriented Knowledge: The Working Object.* Prentice Hall, Englewood Cliffs, NJ, 1994.

Hoare 1969.

C. Anthony R. Hoare. "An Axiomatic Basis for Computer Programming." *Commun. ACM* **12**(10), Oct. 1969, pp. 576–583.

Hoare 1978.

C. Anthony R. Hoare. "Communicating Sequential Processes." *Commun. ACM* **21**(8), Aug. 1978, pp. 666–677.

Hofstadter 1980.

Douglas R. Hofstadter. *Gödel, Escher, Bach: An Eternal Golden Braid.* Random House, Vintage Books, New York, 1980.

Hucklesby 1989.

Philip Hucklesby and Bertrand Meyer. "The Eiffel Object-Oriented Parsing Library." *Proc. Technology of Object-Oriented Languages and Systems* (TOOLS 1, Paris, Nov. 1989), SOL, Paris, 1989, pp. 501–507.

ISO 1990.

ISO WD 9241-11. *Ergonomic Requirements for Office Work with Visual Display Terminals (VDTs),* Part 11: Usability Statements, Version 2.5 Committee draft. International Organization for Standardization, 1990.

Jacobson 1992.

Ivar Jacobson, Magnus Christerson, Patrik Jonsson, and Gunnar Övergaard. *Object-Oriented Software Engineering: A Use Case Driven Approach.* Addison-Wesley, Wokingham, England, 1992.

Johnson 1992.

Ralph E. Johnson. "Documenting Frameworks using Patterns." *Proc. Object-Oriented Programming Systems, Languages, and Applications (OOPSLA '92)* in *ACM SIGPLAN Notices* **27**(10), Vancouver, Canada, Oct.

1992, pp. 63–76.

Johnson 1988.
Ralph E. Johnson and Brian Foote. "Designing Reusable Classes." *Journal of Object-Oriented Programming* **1**(2), June/July 1988, pp. 22–30, 35.

Kay 1977.
Alan C. Kay. "Microelectronics and the Personal Computer." *Scientific American*, Sept. 1977, pp. 231–244.

Kim 1990.
Won Kim. *Introduction to Object-Oriented Databases*. The MIT Press, Cambridge, MA, 1990.

Korson 1990.
Tim Korson and John D. McGregor. "Understanding Object-Oriented: A Unifying Paradigm." *Commun. ACM* **33**(9), Sept. 1990, pp. 40–60.

Krasner 1988.
Glenn E. Krasner and Stephen T. Pope. "A Cookbook for Using the Model-View-Controller User Interface Paradigm in Smalltalk-80." *Journal of Object-Oriented Programming* **1**(3), Aug./Sept. 1988, pp. 26–41, 48–49.

Kraut 1983.
R. Kraut, S. Hanson, and J. Farber. "Command Use and Interface Design." *Proc. ACM Human Factors in Computing Systems (CHI '83)*, Boston, MA, Dec. 1983.

Krol 1992.
Ed Krol. *The Whole Internet: User's Guide and Catalog*. O'Reilly and Associates, Inc., Sebastopol, CA, 1992.

Krueger 1992.
Charles W. Krueger. "Software Reuse." *Computing Surveys* **24**(2), June 1992, pp. 131–183.

Lakoff 1980.
George Lakoff and Mark Johnson. *Metaphors We Live By*. University of Chicago Press, Chicago, 1980.

Lano 1994.
Kevin Lano and Howard Haughton (eds). *Object-Oriented Specification Case Studies*. Prentice Hall, Hemel Hempstead, England, 1994.

LeJacq 1991.
Jean Pierre LeJacq. "Semantic-Based Design Guidelines for Object-Oriented Programs." In *Journal of Object-Oriented Programming: Focus on Analysis and Design*. SIGS Publications, New York, 1991, pp. 86–97.

Lieberherr 1989.
Karl L. Lieberherr and Ian M. Holland. "Assuring Good Style for Object-Oriented Programs." *IEEE Software* **6**(5), Sept. 1989, pp. 38–48.

Lieberman 1986.

Henry Lieberman. "Using Prototypical Objects to Implement Shared Behavior in Object-Oriented Systems." *Proc. Object-Oriented Programming Systems, Languages, and Applications (OOPSLA '86)* in *ACM SIGPLAN Notices* **21**(11), Portland, OR, Nov. 1986, pp. 214–223.

Linton 1989.

Mark A. Linton, John M. Vlissides, and Paul R. Calder. "Composing User Interfaces with InterViews." *IEEE Computer* **22**(2), Feb. 1989, pp. 8–22.

Loomis 1991.

Mary E. S. Loomis. "Objects and SQL." *Object Magazine* **1**(3), 1991, pp. 68–78.

Lovgren 1994.

John Lovgren. "How to Choose Good Metaphors." *IEEE Software* **11**(3), May 1994, pp. 86–88.

Marmolin 1993.

Hans Marmolin. *User Centered System Design.* UI Design AB (in Swedish), Linköping, Sweden, June 1993.

Marshak 1991.

David S. Marshak. "ANSA: A Model for Distributed Computing." *Network Monitor* **6**(11), Patricia B. Seybold, Boston, MA, Nov. 1991.

Martin 1992.

James Martin and James J. Odell. *Object-Oriented Analysis and Design.* Prentice Hall, Englewood Cliffs, NJ, 1992.

McIlroy 1976.

M. Douglas McIlroy. "Mass-produced Software Components." In *Software Engineering Concepts and Techniques (1968 NATO Conf. on Software Engineering)*, J. M. Buxton, Peter Naur, and Brian Randell (eds). Van Nostrand Reinhold, New York, 1976, pp. 88–98.

Mellor 1993.

Stephen J. Mellor, Sally Shlaer, Grady Booch, James Rumbaugh, Jim Salmons, Timlynn Babitsky, Sam Adams, and Rebecca J. Wirfs-Brock. "Open letter to the industry: Premature Methods Standardization Considered Harmful." *Journal of Object-Oriented Programming* **6**(4), July/Aug. 1993.

Meyer 1985.

Bertrand Meyer. "On Formalism in Specifications." *IEEE Software* **2**(1), Jan. 1985, pp. 6–26.

Meyer 1988a.

Bertrand Meyer. *Object-Oriented Software Construction.* Prentice Hall, Hemel Hempstead, England, 1988.

Meyer 1988b.
> Bertrand Meyer. "Cépage: Toward Computer-Aided Design of Software." *The Journal of Systems and Software* **8**(5), Dec. 1988, pp. 419–429.

Meyer 1990a.
> Bertrand Meyer. *Introduction to the Theory of Programming Languages.* Prentice Hall, Hemel Hempstead, England, 1990.

Meyer 1990b.
> Bertrand Meyer. "Tools for the New Culture: Lessons from the Design of the Eiffel Libraries." *Commun. ACM* **33**(9), Sept. 1990, pp. 69–88.

Meyer 1992a.
> Bertrand Meyer. *Eiffel: The Language.* Prentice Hall, Hemel Hempstead, England, 1992.

Meyer 1992b.
> Bertrand Meyer. "Design by Contract." In *Advances in Object-Oriented Software Engineering*, Dino Mandrioli and Bertrand Meyer (eds). Prentice Hall, Hemel Hempstead, England, 1992, pp. 1–50.

Meyer 1992c.
> Bertrand Meyer. "Applying 'Design by Contract'." *IEEE Computer* **25**(10), Oct. 1992, pp. 40–51.

Meyer 1993a.
> Bertrand Meyer. "What is an Object-Oriented Environment?" *Journal of Object-Oriented Programming* **6**(4), July/Aug. 1993, pp. 75–81.

Meyer 1993b.
> Bertrand Meyer. "Systematic Concurrent Object-Oriented Programming." *Commun. ACM* **36**(9), Sept. 1993, pp. 56–80.

Meyer 1994a.
> Bertrand Meyer. *Reusable Software: The Base Object-oriented Component Libraries.* Prentice Hall, Hemel Hempstead, England, 1994.

Meyer 1994b.
> Bertrand Meyer. *An Object-Oriented Environment: Principles and Application.* Prentice Hall, Hemel Hempstead, England, 1994.

Miller 1956.
> G. A. Miller. "The Magical Number Seven, Plus or Minus Two: Some Limits on Our Capacity for Processing Information." *The Psychological Review* **63**(2), Mar. 1956, pp. 81–97.

Miller 1975.
> G. A. Miller. "The Magical Number Seven after Fifteen Years." In *Studies in Long Term Memory*, A. Kennedy (ed.). John Wiley, New York, 1975.

Mills 1975.
> Harlan D. Mills. "How to Write Correct Programs and Know It." *Proc. Int. Conf. Reliable Software*, Los Angeles, CA, Apr. 1975, pp. 363–370.

Moran 1983.

T. Moran. "Getting into a System: External, Internal Task Mapping Analyses." *Proc. ACM Human Factors in Computing Systems (CHI '83)*, Boston, MA, Dec. 1983.

Nerson 1991.

Jean-Marc Nerson. "Extending Eiffel Toward O-O Analysis and Design." *Proc. Technology of Object-Oriented Languages and Systems* (TOOLS 5, Santa Barbara, July/Aug. 1991), assoc. paper, Prentice Hall, Englewood Cliffs, NJ, 1991, pp. 377–392.

Nerson 1992a.

Jean-Marc Nerson. "O-O development of a date and time management cluster." *Journal of Object-Oriented Programming* **5**(1), Mar./Apr. 1992, pp. 39–46.

Nerson 1992b.

Jean-Marc Nerson. "Applying Object-Oriented Analysis and Design." *Commun. ACM* **35**(9), Sept. 1992, pp. 63–74.

Nygaard 1970.

Kristen Nygaard, Ole-Johan Dahl, and Bjørn Myhrhaug. *The Simula 67 Common Base Language*. Norwegian Computing Center, Publ. No. S–22, Oslo, Oct. 1970.

Ogden 1923.

C. K. Ogden and I. A. Richards. *The meaning of meaning*. London, 1923.

OMG 1990.

OMG, Object Management Group and X/Open. "Object Management Architecture Guide 1.0." OMG TC Document 90.9.1, Nov. 1990.

OMG 1991.

OMG, Object Management Group and X/Open. "The Common Object Request Broker: Architecture and Specification." OMG Document Number 91.12.1, Dec. 1991.

Omohundro 1991.

Stephen M. Omohundro. "The Sather Language." Report: International Computer Science Institute, Berkeley, CA, 1991.

Page-Jones 1990.

Meilir Page-Jones, Larry L. Constantine, and Steven Weiss. "Modeling Object-Oriented Systems: The Uniform Object Notation." *Computer Language* **7**(10), Oct. 1990, pp. 69–87.

Parnas 1972.

David Lorge Parnas. "On the Criteria To Be Used in Decomposing Systems into Modules." *Commun. ACM* **15**(12), Dec. 1972, pp. 1053–1058.

Parnas 1979.

David Lorge Parnas. "Designing Software for Ease of Extension and Contraction." *IEEE Trans. Software Engineering* **SE-5**(2), Mar. 1979, pp. 128–137.

Parnas 1993.

David Lorge Parnas. "Predicate Logic for Software Engineering." *IEEE Trans. Software Engineering* **19**(9), Sept. 1993, pp. 856–862.

Parnas 1986.

David Lorge Parnas and Paul C. Clements. "A Rational Design Process: How and Why to Fake It." *IEEE Trans. Software Engineering* **SE-12**(2), Feb. 1986, pp. 251–257.

Penrose 1989.

Roger Penrose. *The Emperor's New Mind*. Oxford University Press, New York, 1989.

Premerlani 1994.

William J. Premerlani and Michael R. Blaha. "An Approach for Reverse Engineering of Relational Databases." *Commun. ACM* **37**(5), May 1994, pp. 42–49.

Prieto-Diaz 1987.

Ruben Prieto-Diaz. "Domain Analysis for Reusability." *Proc. IEEE Computer Software and Applications Conference (COMPSAC '87)*, Tokyo, Oct. 1987, pp. 23–29.

Quarterman 1990.

John S. Quarterman. *The Matrix: Computer Networks and Conferencing Systems Worldwide*. Digital Press, Digital Equipment Corporation, Maynard, MA, 1990.

Rahayo 1993.

Wenny J. Rahayo and Elizabeth Chang. "A Methodology for Transforming an Object-Oriented Data Model to a Relational Database." *Proc. Technology of Object-Oriented Languages and Systems* (TOOLS 12, Melbourne, Australia, Nov./Dec. 1993), Prentice Hall, Englewood Cliffs, NJ, 1993.

Reenskaug 1992.

Tryggve Reenskaug, Egil P. Andersen, Arne Jorgen Berre, Anne Hurlen, Anton Landmark, Odd Arild Lehne, Else Nordhagen, Eirik Nêss-Ulseth, Gro Oftedal, Anne Lise Skaar, and Pål Stenslet. "OORASS: Seamless support for the creation and maintenance of object oriented systems." *Journal of Object-Oriented Programming* **5**(6), Oct. 1992, pp. 27–41.

Robinson 1992.

Peter Robinson. *Hierarchical Object-Oriented Design*. Prentice Hall, Englewood Cliffs, NJ, 1992.

Rubin 1992.

Kenneth S. Rubin and Adele Goldberg. "Object Behavior Analysis." *Commun. ACM* **35**(9), Sept. 1992, pp. 48–62.

Rumbaugh 1991.

James Rumbaugh, Michael Blaha, William Premerlani, Frederick Eddy, and William Lorensen. *Object-Oriented Modeling and Design*. Prentice Hall, Englewood Cliffs, NJ, 1991.

Scott 1991.

A. C. Scott, J. E. Clayton, and E. L. Gibson. *A Practical Approach to Knowledge Acquisition*. Addison-Wesley, Reading, MA, 1991.

Seidewitz 1987.

E. Seidewitz and M. Stark. "Towards a General Object-Oriented Design Methodology." *Ada Letters* **7**(4), July/Aug. 1987.

Shlaer 1992.

Sally Shlaer and Stephen J. Mellor. *Object Lifecycles: Modeling the World in States*. Prentice Hall, Englewood Cliffs, NJ, 1992.

Shneiderman 1983.

Ben Shneiderman. "Direct Manipulation: A Step Beyond Programming Languages." *IEEE Computer* **16**(8), Aug. 1983, pp. 57–69.

Siemens 1993.

Siemens Nixdorf Informationssysteme AG. "MooD V1.0—Methodology for Object-Oriented Development: Introduction." Frankfurt/Main, Germany, 1993.

Stroustrup 1992.

Bjarne Stroustrup. *The C++ Programming Language*. 2nd edn, Addison-Wesley, Reading, MA, 1992.

Strunk 1979.

William Strunk, Jr. and E. B. White. *The Elements of Style*. Macmillan, New York, 1979.

Ungar 1987.

David Ungar and Randall B. Smith. "Self: The Power of Simplicity." *Proc. Object-Oriented Programming Systems, Languages, and Applications (OOPSLA '87)* in *ACM SIGPLAN Notices* **22**(12), Orlando, FL, Oct. 1987, pp. 227–242.

Velho 1992.

Amândio Vaz Velho and Rogerio Carapuça. "SOM—A Semantic Object Model: Towards an Abstract, Complete and Unifying Way to Model the Real World." *Proc. Third Int. Conference on Dynamic Modeling of Information Systems*, Noordwijkerhout, The Netherlands, 1992, pp. 65–93.

Velho 1994.

Amândio Vaz Velho and Rogerio Carapuça. "Attribute: A Semantic and Seamless Construct." *Proc. Technology of Object-Oriented Languages and Systems* (TOOLS 13, Versailles, France, Mar. 1994), Prentice Hall, Hemel Hempstead, England, 1994.

Wasserman 1990.

Anthony Wasserman, Peter A. Pircher, and Robert J. Muller. "The Object-Oriented Structured Design Notation for Software Design Representation." *IEEE Computer* **23**(3), Mar. 1990, pp. 50–63.

Wilkie 1993.

George Wilkie. *Object-Oriented Software Engineering: The Professional Developer's Guide.* Addison-Wesley, Wokingham, England, 1993.

Wirfs-Brock 1991.

Allen Wirfs-Brock. "Does Smalltalk need types?" *Journal of Object-Oriented Programming* **4**(6), Oct. 1991, pp. 62–67.

Wirfs-Brock 1989.

Rebecca J. Wirfs-Brock and Brian Wilkerson. "Object-Oriented Design: A Responsibility-Driven Approach." *Proc. Object-Oriented Programming Systems, Languages, and Applications (OOPSLA '89)* in *ACM SIGPLAN Notices* **24**(10), New Orleans, LA, Oct. 1989, pp. 71–75.

Wirfs-Brock 1990.

Rebecca J. Wirfs-Brock, Brian Wilkerson, and Lauren Wiener. *Designing Object-Oriented Software.* Prentice Hall, Englewood Cliffs, NJ, 1990.

Wirth 1971.

Niklaus Wirth. "Program Development by Stepwise Refinement." *Commun. ACM* **14**(4), Apr. 1971, pp. 221–227.

Zloof 1977.

M. M. Zloof. "Query-by-Example: A Data Base Language." *IBM Systems Journal* **16**(4), 1977, pp. 324–343.

Index

BON keywords are in boldface. Page numbers in boldface indicate places of definition or main discussions of the corresponding topic. Page numbers in italics refer to a corresponding entry in appendix E: "Glossary of terms."

A

Abstract class, *see* Class, deferred
Abstract data type, 179–180, 183, 186, 206, 242, *388*
Abstract feature, *see* Feature, deferred
Abstraction, *388*
    for reuse, 170–171
    layer of, 183, 217, 221
    premature, 220–221
    strong, 221, 222
    weak, 221, 222
Access control, *388*
Accidents, *see under* Software engineering
Acid test for object-orientedness, 225
Active object, *388*
Actor, *388*
Ada, 167
ADT, *see* Abstract data type
Agent, *389*
Aggregation, *see under* Client
Aggregation relation, *389*
Alexander, Christopher, 217
Algol, 5
Analysis, *389, 400*
    meaning of, 122–123, 151, 153, 172–173
    recursive, 123
    tasks, *see under* BON process
Analysis class, 9, 98, 122, 136, 143, 151, 172, 182, 184, 197, 252, 260, 275, 277
Ancestor, *see under* Class

ANSA (Advanced Network Systems Architecture), 408
Anthropomorphism, 185
Application, *389*
Architecture, *389*
Assertion, *see under* Software contracting
Assertion language, *see* BON assertion language
Association, *see under* Client
Attribute, *389*
    abstract, 50
    change, *see* **Delta**
    exported, 35
    of class, *see under* Class
Attribute (relational), 295

B

Barks, Carl, 94
Behavior, *389*
Bidirectional link, *see under* Client and Message
Binary association, *389*
Binding, *389*
Blind checking, *see* Defensive programming
BNF (Backus Naur Form), 350
BON acronym, 11
BON activities, 120
BON approach, 11–25
    general, 11–12
    position, 16–17